Vulnerabiliti[...]   Law

While in the past family life was characterised as a 'haven from the harsh realities of life', it is now recognised as a site of vulnerabilities and a place where care work can go unacknowledged and be a source of social and economic hardship. This book addresses the strong relationships that exist between vulnerability, care and dependency in particular contexts, where family law and social policy have a contribution to make.

A fundamental premise of this collection is that vulnerability needs to be analysed in a way that gets at the heart of the differential power relationships that exist in society, particularly in respect of access to family justice, including effective social policy and law targeted at the specific needs of families in mutually dependent caring relationships. It is therefore crucial to critically examine the various approaches taken by policy-makers and law reformers in order to understand the range of ways that some families, and some family members, may be rendered more vulnerable than others.

The first book of its kind to provide an intersectional approach to this subject, *Vulnerabilities, Care and Family Law* will be of interest to students and practitioners of social policy and family law.

Julie Wallbank is based at the University of Leeds; **Jonathan Herring** is at the University of Oxford.

Vulnerabilities, Care and Family Law

Edited by
Julie Wallbank
and Jonathan Herring

Routledge
Taylor & Francis Group

LONDON AND NEW YORK

First published 2014
by Routledge
2 Park Square, Milton Park, Abingdon, Oxfordshire OX14 4RN

Simultaneously published in the USA and Canada
by Routledge
711 Third Avenue, New York, NY 10017

First issued in paperback 2015

Routledge is an imprint of the Taylor & Francis Group, an informa business

British Library Cataloguing in Publication Data
A catalogue record for this book is available from the British Library

Library of Congress Cataloging-in-Publication Data
Vulnerabilities, care and family law / edited by Julie Wallbank, Jonathan Herring.
p. cm.
ISBN 978-0-415-85750-5 (hardback) -- ISBN 978-0-203-79782-2 (ebk)
1. Domestic relations--Social aspects--Great Britain.
I. Wallbank, Julie A., editor of compilation.
II. Herring, Jonathan, editor of compilation.
KD750.V85 2014
346.4101'5--dc23
2013023397

ISBN 13: 978-1-1389-2469-7 (pbk)
ISBN 13: 978-0-415-85750-5 (hbk)

Typeset in Baskerville by
Servis Filmsetting Ltd, Stockport, Cheshire

Contents

Notes on contributors

Nicola Barker is a Senior Lecturer in Law at the University of Kent, teaching family law and public law. She is the author of *Not the Marrying Kind: A Feminist Critique of Same-Sex Marriage* (Palgrave, 2012).

Alison Brammer is a Senior Lecturer in the Law School at Keele University and a solicitor. She is Director of two MA programmes (Child Care Law and Practice; Safeguarding Adults: Law, Policy and Practice). She is Legal Editor of the *Journal of Adult Protection*; Series Editor of the 'Focus on Social Work Law' series; and her textbook *Social Work Law* is in its third edition. Research interests focus on the law relating to social work practice and the developing law relating to safeguarding adults.

Jo Bridgeman is Professor of Healthcare Law and Feminist Ethics at the University of Sussex where she teaches healthcare law and ethics, family law and tort. Her research, at the intersection of these fields, adopts a critical feminist perspective informed by, and developing, the feminist ethic of care in the analysis of relational responsibilities. She has published work on the healthcare of babies, infants and young children; the care of disabled children; parental responsibilities; children and tort law; compassionate killings; teenagers and health.

Nicole Busby is Professor of Labour Law at the University of Strathclyde. Her research interests are in the areas of labour law and European social policy, specifically the relationship between paid work and unpaid care, the constitutionalisation of labour rights (with particular reference to the EU constitution post-Lisbon) and the experiences of claimants in the Employment Tribunal system. She is the author of *A Right to Care? Unpaid Care Work in European Employment Law* (Oxford University Press, 2011) and co-editor (with Grace James) of *Families, Care-giving and Paid Work: Challenging Labour Law in the 21st Century* (Edward Elgar, 2011).

Jennifer Collins is a Lecturer in Law at St Peter's College, Oxford. Her research focuses on theoretical issues in the criminal law, particularly the challenges posed by interpersonal exploitation. Her current DPhil work examines a type of exploitation which is primarily targeted at property interests, and considers its implications for criminal law theory.

Alison Diduck is Professor of Law at UCL. She is interested in jurisprudence, gender theory and legal history, and currently is particularly taken with the social and legal regulation of personal relationships. She has published her work in monograph form, in edited collections, academic and professional journals, and is co-author, with Felicity Kaganas, (3rd edn of *Family Law, Gender and the State*).

Michael Dunn is a Lecturer at the Ethox Centre, University of Oxford, and has additional appointments as a Research Associate at Green Templeton College, Oxford, and as an academic consultant at the Centre for Biomedical Ethics, National University of Singapore. His current research interests lie in the ethics of managing, organising and delivering community-based and long-term health and social care services. Another main area of focus in his current work is the relationship between philosophy and the social sciences in bioethical inquiry, and in providing sound theoretical and methodological justifications for empirical ethics research. Michael has published over twenty-five peer-reviewed papers and book chapters in the fields of bioethics, medical, social welfare and family law, and health/social services research. He is also an Associate Editor of the *Journal of Medical Ethics*, and sits on a number of working parties, committees and research advisory groups in the ethical and legal aspects of health and social care.

Jonathan Herring is a Fellow in Law at Exeter College, Oxford University and Professor of Law at the Law Faculty, Oxford University. He has written on family law, medical law, criminal law and legal issues surrounding caring. He has written over forty books including: *Caring and the Law* (Hart, 2013); *Older People in Law and Society* (Oxford University Press, 2009); *European Human Rights and Family Law* (Hart, 2010) (with Shazia Choudhry); *Medical Law and Ethics* (Oxford University Press, 2012); *Criminal Law* (4th edn, Oxford University Press, 2012); and *Family Law* (6th edn, Pearson, 2013).

Felicity Kaganas is a Reader in Law at Brunel Law School, Brunel University. Her research has included legal and socio-legal work as well as some examples of textual analysis. She specialises in family and child law and also feminist approaches to law. She is co-author, with Alison Diduck, of *Family Law, Gender and the State* (3rd edn, Hart, 2012).

Stephen McKay is Distinguished Professor in Social Research at the University of Lincoln. He is currently working on an ESRC project on applying quantitative methods, and a Nuffield Foundation project concerning how much child support should be paid by non-resident parents. He is part of the editorial boards of the *Journal of Poverty & Social Justice* and *Social Policy & Administration*. Most of his research concerns the causes and effects of inequality.

Christine Piper is a Professor in Brunel Law School, Brunel University. Her research and teaching interests are focused on family and child law and policy, sentencing and youth justice. She is a member of the Editorial Board of the *Child and Family Law Quarterly* and her books include *Investing in Children* (Routledge, 2008); (with Susan Easton) *Sentencing and Punishment: The Quest for Justice* (3rd edn, Oxford University Press, 2012); and (with Michael King) *How the Law Thinks about Children* (2nd edn, Ashgate, 1995).

Julie Wallbank is a Senior Lecturer at Leeds University. Her writing mainly concerns the legal regulation of family life. Her monograph *Challenging Motherhood(s)* (Pearson Education, 2001) provided a Foucauldian analysis of the social and legal construction of parenthood in the early to mid-1990s. She has also written on the law relating to reproductive technologies, focusing particularly on the parenthood provisions.

Chapter 1

Introduction: vulnerabilities, care and family law

Julie Wallbank and Jonathan Herring

Our law graduates are well versed in the law as it relates to the autonomous, independent, able-bodied man. They can advise on how to enter contracts, sue for injuries following bad advice from an accountant, and on the legal significance of owning a house. Most will not be well prepared to advise the mentally ill, the autistic child or the asylum seeker. In our law degrees mention is made of children, older people, those lacking capacity, caring and the like, but they are seen as providing troubling exceptions to the general rules. The vision of the world presented is a privileged, wealthy, healthy adult, male one.

This is all backed up by the jurisprudence used to underpin the traditional courses. These are commonly based on the importance of freedom, liberty and autonomy. Much weight is placed on our human rights: understood to be the rights to life, freedom from torture, the right to private life and freedom of speech. Again this is all far from the real world for most people, where identity is found in community with others, not in individualised rights. Dependence, mutuality and care-centred lives are the reality for most people.

In this book we explore, in the context of family law, two themes which highlight the inadequacies of the practical and theoretical reaches of the law: vulnerability and care. It is the experience of vulnerability and care which is at the heart of our lives and selves, yet is ignored in so much legal writing. This book seeks to emphasise their significance for lawyers generally, and family law in particular.

As will be seen throughout the book, the concepts of care and vulnerability are troublesome. State attempts to protect the vulnerable can simply exacerbate powerlessness. The description of the vulnerable can be used as a way of stigmatising individuals and groups. State attempts to support and enable care can in fact rob care of its value and involve the state in determining what care is good and what care is bad. These themes are explored throughout this book. In this introduction we seek primarily to explore the definitions of vulnerabilities and of care and in so doing bring out some of the themes of the book.

Defining vulnerabilities

Vulnerability is an emerging concept and a steadily burgeoning field of study. A range of disciplines see it as important. Attempts to define the term vary widely in scope with some authors taking a broad approach, conceptualising it as part of the human condition. A more restrictive and somewhat less encompassing approach to the definition of vulnerability sits at the other end of the spectrum where specific features are looked for in the conditions of particular subjects in order to make them worthy of specific considerations, accommodations and exceptions. These two approaches have been accused of being both 'too broad and too narrow'.[1] Much of the work in law has been influenced by Martha Fineman's seminal paper in which she notes its universality and constancy as part of the human condition.[2] Like Judith Butler before her she maintains that we are all vulnerable throughout our lives. According to Butler 'each of us is constituted politically in part by virtue of the social vulnerability of our bodies ... Loss and vulnerability seem to follow from our being socially constituted bodies, attached to others, at risk of losing those attachments, exposed to others, at risk of violence by virtue of that exposure.'[3]

It is clear that both theses do not suggest vulnerability as a purely inherent condition, experienced by all humans in the same way. Butler emphasises that humans experience vulnerability, and indeed are rendered vulnerable, due to the political construction of, for example, womanhood or conditions such as AIDS.[4] Fineman makes a similar point: 'vulnerability extends beyond the body with its interior weaknesses and fallibilities. Even fully realized and functioning adults remain vulnerable: to external "natural" forces, such as the environment or climate or to the machinations of human institutions.'[5] Others also stress the need to centralise vulnerability in respect of care provision and moreover to view dependency and vulnerability in a positive way, arguing that they are too often viewed as evidence of the failure to attain autonomy rather than as requisites for agency and autonomy.[6]

In Susan Dodds's view:

> Attention to *vulnerability* ... changes citizens' ethical relations from those of independent actors carving out realms of right against each other and the

1 Samia Hurst, 'Vulnerability in Research and Health Care; Describing the Elephant in the Room?' (2008) 22(4) *Bioethics* 191–202, 192.
2 Martha Fineman, 'The Vulnerable Subject: Anchoring Equality in the Human Condition' (2008) 20(1) *Yale Journal of Law & Feminism* 1–23.
3 Judith Butler, *Precarious Life: The Powers of Mourning and Violence* (Verso, 2004) 20.
4 Ibid.
5 Martha Alberta Fineman, 'Responsibility, Family, and the Limits of Equality: An American Perspective' in Jo Bridgeman, Craig Lind and Heather Keating (eds), *Taking Responsibility, Law and the Changing Family* (Ashgate, 2011) 37–49, 46.
6 Susan Dodds, 'Depending on Care: Recognition of Vulnerability and the Social Contribution of Care Provision (2007) 21(9) *Bioethics* 500–10.

state, to those of mutually-dependent and vulnerably-exposed beings whose capacities to develop as subjects are directly and indirectly mediated by the conditions around them.[7]

Much of the writing on vulnerability is a direct response to individual liberalism and the idea of the unencumbered legal subject who seeks to assert rights against others and the state. Some of the contributors to this volume embrace the universality and positive aspects of human vulnerability. Jonathan Herring's chapter notes how some of our vulnerability stems from our corporeality and the fact that our bodies are constantly in flux. He argues that much of society is geared towards masking our vulnerability to enable us to function in public life as if we were fully autonomous and independent of relational ties. For example, accommodations such as 24-hour cash points and the full range of available personal services are designed to allow the adult worker to participate on a full-time basis. Jonathan argues that these are overlooked while highlighting the facilities used to deal with the vulnerabilities of others. 'Further, we readily class those who need care from others as vulnerable, without seeing the vulnerability that caring creates for the carer.'[8] In others words, the person providing the care is constructed as without vulnerability and sets up a false dualism between the autonomous and the dependant. The carer may rely on help from others and also upon the person they are in a caring relationship with. Moreover, he argues that vulnerability and dependency are also constructed as lacking when in fact relationships of care are to be celebrated and valued going so far as to say that caring relationships should be centralised in family law rather than relationships based on the two-parent sexual family model. The argument is made that the two-parent norm may be usefully replaced by one which privileges caring relationships in all their particularities and diversities. However, it is not easy to come up with a meaningful and workable definition of vulnerability when certain people require enhanced protection. The task has been likened to the efforts of six blind men describing an elephant.[9] In an attempt to describe the animal in its entirety, the men cannot agree, having touched different parts of the elephant's anatomy. The moral of the tale, as explained by Schroeder and Gefenas, is that one may only be able to come up with part of the picture, depending on one's perspective and experience.[10] One of the problems with conceptualising vulnerability in a very broad way as part of the human condition is that if we are all equally vulnerable no one is entitled to special protection and in the healthcare context in particular it may be very important to offer special protection to vulnerable groups.[11] It may, therefore, be helpful to

7 Ibid, 501.
8 Bill Hughes, Linda McKie, Debra Hopkins and Nick Watson, 'Love's Labour's Lost? Feminism, the Disabled People's Movement and an Ethic of Care' (2005) 39 *Sociology* 259, 264.
9 Hurst, 'Vulnerability in Research' 192.
10 Doris Schroeder and Eugenijus Gefenas, 'Vulnerability: Too Vague and Too Broad?' (2009) 18(2) *Cambridge Quarterly of Healthcare Ethics* 113–21, 114.
11 Ibid, 118.

recognise a mutual inherent vulnerability, but also to emphasise ways in which particular individuals in some circumstances have extra vulnerability.

This last point is brought out in Jennifer Collins's chapter which urges us to recognise vulnerability as a 'real life' concept. We need, she argues, to focus on vulnerability as experienced by people, rather than abstract notions of universal vulnerability. This is not to say that the abstract concepts are not making valid points, but the lived-in experiences of vulnerability should be central to our thinking.

Using the research ethics context as an example, Schroeder and Gefenas argue that special protection should not be afforded to the population as a whole, based on their innate fragility. Rather, the focus should be on those at an identifiable risk of exploitation in medical research. They offer the following definition of vulnerability: 'To be vulnerable means to face a significant probability of incurring an identifiable harm while substantially lacking ability and/or means to protect oneself.'[12] This definition may be useful in the research ethics context, where for example the research subject may be at risk of exploitation. When thinking about the usefulness of a definition based upon objective harm, some harms are not readily imagined or identifiable, for example when thinking about what impact shifts in social policy and law reform might have on families. At the same time, the very means to protect oneself or to fend off vulnerability is inextricably linked to the social and the socio-economic climate and not necessarily attributable to the individual. The definition seems to suggest that problems and solutions may inhere in individuals and this gives a false impression. Some threats are posed externally by the state and families and indeed individuals working on the state's behalf can be rendered vulnerable as a result of novel approaches, as Felicity Kaganas illustrates when discussing child protection law reform. Additionally, others have argued that there are also problems with constructing the vulnerable by highlighting risk.

As Michael Dunn and others have argued in a previous paper the way that the 'vulnerable adult' is constructed in order to justify interventions into their lives is potentially disempowering because of the way that their subjective experience is sacrificed as a result of reducing that person's life to being the object of a series of risks, rather than placing that individual at the centre of the decision to intervene.[13] Charting the distinction between inherent and situational vulnerability, they outline that one of the problems with inherent vulnerability is that it is constructed around a set of fixed, intrinsic human characteristics which do not necessarily mean that the adult will be unable to lead a full and meaningful life.[14] They warn against the automatic judgement of being at increased risk

---

12 Schroeder and Gefenas, 'Vulnerability: Too Vague and Too Broad?' 116–17.
13 Michael Dunn, Isabel C. H. Clare and Anthony J. Holland, 'To Empower or to Protect? Constructing the "Vulnerable Adult" in English Law and Public Policy' (2008) 28(2) *Legal Studies* 234–53.
14 Ibid, 234–53. For a fuller discussion, see p 244.

relative to other adults, regardless of their circumstances because of the way it effaces the need for investigation into the lived life of the person. What might appear to an external observer to be a risk generating vulnerability may not be so perceived from the perspective of the individual themselves. Moreover, situational vulnerability, using an objective assessment of risk, can lead courts to outline the most pessimistic and negative predictions for the future, predictions which might also be based upon 'stereotyped or discriminatory attitudes towards certain decisions, or the different socio-cultural contexts within which these decisions are made'.[15]

The two examples the authors draw upon involve the arranged marriage context and they note that it is perhaps unlikely that the court would be persuaded of the need to intervene in a marriage decision where such arrangements were not common practice. It was also noted that the court feels it necessary to consider at length the distinction between arranged and forced marriage. Noting the difficulty of balancing the need to protect against the need to empower, what the authors do see as crucial is the inclusion of the voice of the adult right from the start of proceedings in order to justify intervention in the first instance.[16] They argue for a 'holistic account of human vulnerability, founded upon both objective and subjective perspectives, and requires that the court engages meaningfully with how "vulnerable adults" incorporate the issue at hand into the ways that they interpret, and ascribe meaning to, their lives'.[17] Indeed, this is a task which is invaluable to us all in seeking to live a good life. In many instances it may be necessary for the court to intervene to protect the vulnerable adult but the writers posit a convincing argument that the adult should be central to the decision right from the start, rather than treated as a subject for whom the court speaks and acts.

Writing within nursing theory has also noted the limitations of equating risk and vulnerability and two strands to vulnerability have emerged which are 'emic' and 'etic' approaches.[18] The etic approach refers to the externally evaluated risk which assigns particular individuals or groups of individuals at a higher probability of risk because of certain characteristics such as their socio-economic status, increased age or other characteristics. The etic approach is founded on sets of assumptions including 'normative social values' which will influence when and how vulnerability is perceived in the first place.[19] As some of the contributors to this volume suggest, Western society and its institutions values independence and autonomy as opposed to dependence and vulnerability, which are set up as in opposition rather than as relying on each other and as existing in partnership. A good example of this is Nicole Busby's chapter analysing the interaction

---

15 Dunn et al, 'To Empower or to Protect?' 244.
16 Ibid, 234–53.
17 Ibid, 252.
18 Judith Spiers, 'New Perspectives on Vulnerability Using Emic and Etic Approaches' (2000) 31(3) *Journal of Advanced Nursing* 715–21, 716.
19 Ibid, 717.

of employment law and caring. The government seeks to encourage carers to become financially independent and combine their employed work and care work obligations. This elevates the good of 'financial self-sufficiency' with little understanding of the huge practical problems facing those with caring responsibility entering the labour market.

A second assumption, akin to Dunn et al's argument, is that there must be an identifiable and objective harm or risk of harm which can be proven before intervention to promote the interests of the vulnerable person without paternalism. Definitions are based on the 'relative risk of harm of a particular group compared to the larger society'.[20] The emphasis on objective harm is not without its problems. An individual or group tends to be either vulnerable or not; it tends to be a dichotomous condition rather than gradated. Additionally, emotional vulnerability tends not to be viewed as a key determinant of vulnerability.[21] The implications of approaching vulnerability as if it attaches straightforwardly to one group over others is that it homogenises those who belong and those who do not belong and they are measured and judged against each other. For example, as Julie Wallbank points out in her chapter, classifying the vulnerable separating parent as one who has established the existence of domestic violence renders all other separating parents as fully functioning, able to resolve their disputes and without any vulnerability, when clearly this will not necessarily be the case at all. The primary assumption in respect of emic vulnerability is that it is, as viewed by other contributors, a universal part of the human condition. It exists as lived experience that individuals have a sense of themselves and it can only be determined by the person experiencing it. Therefore, vulnerability should only be described from the person's perspective.[22]

One of the issues that arose in our discussion about this edited collection was a concern to provide 'real life' understandings of vulnerability rather than come up with a 'one size fits all' definition. Kate Brown has recently noted that 'vulnerability means different things to different people' and that how it is defined is significant.[23] She notes its increased use by academics, policy-makers and practitioners, for example in the social care setting. Those who use it, she maintains, often do so without defining what they mean by it. However, she warns that it is 'so loaded with political, moral and practical implications that it is potentially damaging to the pursuit of social justice'.[24] Brown sets out two opposing views of vulnerability set out in social care, sociology and ethics literature. At one side of the debate vulnerability is viewed in a very negative way as patronising, paternalistic and oppressive. At the other, it is developed as a theoretical basis for the achievement of a more socially just society where vulnerability, dependency and

---

20 Ibid.
21 Spiers, 'New Perspectives on Vulnerability' 717.
22 Ibid, 719.
23 Kate Brown, '"Vulnerability": Handle with Care' (2011) 5(3) *Ethics and Social Welfare* 313–21, 313.
24 Ibid, 314.

relational autonomy are valorised.[25] She concludes that the tensions between these conceptualisations reveal the 'profound ethical implications of the concept'.[26]

The way that vulnerability is defined and the delineated boundaries between those rendered vulnerable and those not have the power to legitimise the giving and receiving of all too often increasingly scarce public resources. For those not construed as vulnerable, the withholding of these resources is justified as they are viewed as the opposite of vulnerable. A vulnerability label can protect against condemnation but it can also lead to some groups in society being patronised. On the other hand, as is highlighted in some of the chapters in this book, it has a transformative dimension used to reconceptualise traditional ideals of liberal autonomy to note the significance of relationships and the value of caring activities. What is very apparent, as Kate Brown points out, is that despite vulnerability being presented in a seemingly neutral or value-free way it is laden with value. It is also a highly malleable concept which can be used, for example, to excuse a failure to tackle structural vulnerabilities because of a presumption that the vulnerability inheres in an individual and is soluble by that individual rather or in addition to any external solutions.[27]

Some contributors to this collection have dedicated much more of their writing towards developing the definition of vulnerability and its meaning, whereas others rather take the definition for granted, i.e. that we know it when we see it, while pointing out the moral, political and practical implications at stake in defining vulnerability in certain ways. Jo Bridgemen, Jennifer Collins, Mikey Dunn, Alison Brammer Alison Diduck and Jonathan Herring provide very well-worked out definitions of vulnerability and contribute to the burgeoning literature on it as a theoretical and heuristic tool as well as providing concrete examples where it is useful. Chapters such as those by Nicola Barker, Felicity Kaganas, Steve McKay, Christine Piper and Julie Wallbank in their different case studies challenge the premise that the vulnerable and their vulnerabilities are readily identifiable. For example, Kaganas' chapter focuses on the reform of the child protection system. When the subject is public child law it is all too easy and understandable to read and write about the abused child as vulnerable without fully articulating the meaning given to the term. However, what is also gripping about Kaganas' chapter, for example, is the way that she develops the idea that the potential reforms may serve to render judges vulnerable, not a common reading and writing of the judiciary, but in light of her research very pertinent.

Vulnerability and the state

Although humans are all potentially vulnerable, whether one sees oneself or others as vulnerable will depend upon how vulnerability is characterised and

25 Brown, '"Vulnerability": Handle with Care'.
26 Ibid, 318.
27 Ibid, 313–21.

positioned in respect of other significant discourses such as autonomy. Whether or not one is characterised as vulnerable, for example, by the state and its institutions has a political dimension. Being identified as vulnerable justifies support and intervention in order to get the vulnerable subject back into the position of a fully autonomous actor. As Alison Diduck writes:

> [V]ulnerability becomes a property of the individual and like its other, autonomy, detaches individuals from their structural positions and conditions … The politics of meaning-making in this way include not only constructing or defining vulnerable and autonomous subjects in unrealistic and almost fetishised ways, but also reinforcing their opposition. Perhaps unsurprisingly, constructing autonomy and vulnerability in this way is also entirely consistent with the politics of neo-liberalism.
>
> (p. 102)

Her chapter is concerned with the way that family law's definition of the vulnerable subject is set up in opposition to the ideal 'autonomy'. Unless carers can show themselves as vulnerable through domestic violence (a position they have to adopt in order to receive legal aid) it is assumed that for all intents and purposes they are autonomous. Establishing the dichotomous relationship between vulnerability and autonomy 'violates both relational and recognitional ideas of autonomy' (p. 110). Alison notes the worth of Martha Fineman's vision of social justice but she has reservations because of the way that she seeks to substitute the vulnerable subject for the autonomous one rather than understanding that autonomy and vulnerability are inextricably linked and that autonomy needs vulnerability. In defining vulnerability in a narrow way as the domestic violence sufferer and denying the coexistence of vulnerability and autonomy, the state can legitimise its withdrawal from public support for private family disputes.

Whether a broad or narrow definition of vulnerability is adopted, as has already been hinted at, the boundaries which are drawn to delineate and describe vulnerabilities matter and the state may recognise or not that some vulnerabilities necessitate state intervention. Vulnerabilities are not distributed equally among human beings. Although we share the commonality of being born, living lives and dying, the ways we live a vulnerable life are likely to be highly differentiated and affected by factors such as ethnicity, sexuality, gender, age, health, social class, employment status and care responsibilities. Indeed the range of factors impacting upon vulnerability is limitless. Additionally, the condition or circumstances of vulnerability cannot always be predicted, for example becoming ill or caring for someone who is ill, being made financially insecure because of redundancy or being made worse off as a result of an economic recession or law and social policy changes.

Some may be fortunate to live their whole lives without succumbing to some of the most pernicious experiences of vulnerability so they may live their whole life, until death, free of any serious health conditions and may work, uninterrupted by periods of redundancy, retire with a rich pension pot and live a rich life until death. This is not to suggest they are without vulnerabilities (if the broad definition is accepted), nor is life without vulnerability necessarily a good one. Rather, that their need for NHS care or welfare benefit may be somewhat less than those who more desperately need care, provide care or those who require supplementary support, over and above what the state provides universally. Vulnerabilities therefore need to be looked at in their particularities and their iniquities, as well as in general. They provide a way to think about the distribution of power and resources and about the relationship between the state and its subjects.[28] In Carl Stychin's words:

> the concept of vulnerability has had significant impact in legal and political theory as a response to the primacy of the discourse of rights. Its explicit focus on the relationality of the subject, as well as its universal quality as an aspect of the human condition, makes it a potentially powerful rhetorical tool and heuristic device.[29]

There are clearly (at least) three strands to Stychin's argument about vulnerability. The issue of its universal quality has already been discussed above. At this point therefore, we will flag up the last two strands for discussion here as the challenge to rights discourse and its focus on relationality. As a heuristic device, Stychin's thesis on vulnerability gives rise to the centralisation of a discussion about the distribution of power and resources and the relationship between the state and its subjects.

Clearly, the state itself is comprised of a range of complex institutions, of which family law is but one, but it is 'Through the exercise of legitimate force in bringing societal institutions into legal existence and subsequently regulating them under its mandate of its public authority, the state also constitutes itself.'[30] There is often much at stake in bringing social institutions such as the family into existence as family is constructed according to dominant cultural norms that can mean social actors are denied full status in respect of distributive justice because they are not recognised as having parity with others embracing the desired norms.[31] In Nancy Fraser's view it is quite simply unjust that individuals or social groups are unable to participate equally because some categories of social actors are rendered normative and others lacking. To use Fraser's own words: 'When such patterns of disrespect and disesteem are institutionalized, they impede parity of participation, just as surely as do distributive inequities.'[32] Similar points can be made about care. If caring is taken as an essential good and norm from which the law should

---

28 See further, Carl Stychin, 'The Vulnerable Subject of Negligence Law' (2012) 8 *International Journal of Law in Context* 337–53.
29 Ibid, 337.
30 Fineman, 'The Vulnerable Subject' 6.
31 Nancy Fraser, 'Recognition without Ethics?' (2001) 18(2–3) *Theory, Culture & Society* 21–42.
32 Ibid.

build, our legal system becomes based on supporting and enabling caring relationships, rather than upholding individual rights. Ensuring the burdens of care are shared fairly and that people are enabled to exercise their right to care becomes a primary goal of the law.

Nicola Barker's chapter provides an illustration of the impact of the state's constitution of family along conservative lines in respect of the distributive inequities that can exist as a result, focusing particularly upon inheritance tax exemptions. Her chapter provides a valuable insight into the state's role in privileging a narrow range of conservative relationships in terms of wealth preservation. She examines the way that the inheritance tax system privileges the status-based relationships of marriage and civil partnership regardless of economic need because they have chosen to enter one of the two institutions. She convincingly challenges status-based economic privileges and argues instead for a radical reconceptualisation of the approach to inheritance tax, whereby the focus would be not be on recognising particular relationships but rather reflecting on the objective of the inheritance exemption and whether relationships fulfil objective-based functional criteria such as whether there is 'emotional and/or financial interdependence' (p. 71). Central to her new model is the avoidance of setting up legal rules that require intrusive examinations into the details of intimate relationships, unless necessary for the sake of protection from abuse. It is crucial, according to Barker, that in order to meet the principles of 'coherence and efficiency' (p. 71) 'laws have clear objectives, and that their legislative design corresponds with the achievement of these objectives'.[33] As she recognises, her proposals are radical for the way that they necessitate dismantling the package of rights and responsibilities associated with the status-based relationships and making them available (if they are deemed as necessary to meet an objectively assessed purpose) to anyone as determined by the same principled criteria. Her reworking of the way family law regulates relationships would require the state to systematically review its laws and their purpose. Furthermore, it would also necessitate the dismantling of the conservative status-based approach to rights and privileges. In respect of the inheritance tax system this would mean that exemptions would be based on the economic need of the surviving cohabitant rather than on the relationship status.

It is interesting to contrast Barker's chapter with the more positive role envisioned for family law by Jonathan Herring. His chapter imagines a new kind of family law which is focused on the promotion of caring relationships and protection from inequality within them. Barker's chapter highlights some of the concerns raised with such an approach. Could family law develop in the way Herring wishes, or will it always privilege certain kinds of caring relationship: those visible and acceptable to the law? Further, Barker raises the concern that if the law actively seeks to promote caring, this may lead to undesirable legal regulation of it.

33 Citing the Law Commission of Canada, see Nathalia Des Rosiers et al, *Beyond Conjugality: Recognizing and Supporting Close Personal Adult Relationships* (Law Commission of Canada, 2001) xii.

Barker's chapter challenges the basis upon which privileges are extended to narrow groups of people based upon legally established relationships rather than on interdependencies and economic need. If the state were to take on the challenge of critically reflecting upon the redistribution of its privileges and resources based upon need, a fairer and more just society would ensue, whereby the already wealthy in society would be required to pay due taxes, rather than having them ring-fenced through marriage. At the same time, established relationships of interdependence, regardless of status or sexual intimacy, would be able to achieve protection as and when necessary based upon establishing the requisite objective criteria. There might be less certainty as to when the criteria apply, but there is much more scope for the recognition of 'the realities and complexities of people's intimate (whether sexual or not) associations and parenting arrangements' (p. 72). Additionally, it is surely fairer to redistribute the resources of the economically stronger to those in rather more need or who are vulnerable through poverty. However, one of the clear stumbling blocks to redistributive justice is the way that 'the poor' (usually defined as workless) have been set up in opposition to workers and as the masters of their own destinies, capable of making the same choices as those in work. The Chancellor of the Exchequer George Osborne said on the reform of the benefits system limiting the maximum amount families will now be able to claim:

> We are simply asking people to make the same choices as working families traditionally do. These are the realities of life for working people and they should be the realities for everyone else too … For too long, we have had a system where people who do the right thing, get up in the morning and work hard, get penalised for it while others who do the wrong thing get rewarded. This time, nine out of 10 people will be better off as a result of the changes we are making … we are making work pay.[34]

The liberal subject as an independent, fully competent, autonomous individual informs Osborne's conception of both the worker (good) and the welfare recipient (bad). More generally it informs 'economic, legal, and political principles. It is indispensable to the prevailing ideologies of autonomy, self-sufficiency, and personal responsibility'.[35] A false dualism is established between those claiming benefits and those in work. Moreover, implicit (though not buried too far beneath) is the divide-and-rule tactic. There are good and bad choices – workers make the right choices and benefit recipients do not. The claiming of benefits is viewed quite simply as a decision made not to work, an irresponsible decision. Benefit recipients, so it goes for Osborne, need to take responsibility for their own

---

34 Paul Francis, 'Chancellor George Osborne defends welfare changes in speech at Morrisons depot in Kemsley', *KentOnline*, 3 April 2013 (www.kentonline.co.uk/kentonline/home/2013/april/2/george_osborne.aspx, accessed 31 May 2013).
35 Fineman, 'The Vulnerable Subject' 10.

plight and amend their choices. Workers (who are to be lauded) get penalised and benefit claimants (doing the wrong thing) are rewarded. This is further an implied stigma for those undertaking unpaid care work and who are thereby unable to be financially self-sufficient. Implicit within Osborne's comments are the promotion of the economically productive citizen as the only proper citizen, denigrating the contribution to society by those whose input cannot be measured in euros. This is a brief nod to the role of the state, which is represented as doing wrong by workers for making it too easy for welfare recipients not to work. The solution posited makes living on benefits harder. The realities for workers are harsh and so the realities for the targeted workless should be harsher still. The reasons that welfare recipients have been left behind is attributable to their own personal failures and making the wrong choices. There is clearly a strong political incentive to this view, as it avoids bringing the state to account for its own failures in respect of the socio-economic context and the financial deficit. The state can renounce any responsibility for the social conditions in which individuals and families are vulnerable due to poverty and unemployment. One of the cogent reasons for a book that explores the relationship between vulnerabilities, care, family law and the state is to explode the myth of the autonomous liberal subject, to examine the privileges and disadvantages offered to and withheld from certain individuals or groups. This is particularly true in relation to caring relationships and we now turn to explore those further.

Gender, care and family

Central to understanding the treatment of care is its gendered nature. Throughout history, care has been regarded as the work of 'slaves, servants, and women'.[36] The privileged position of men has been maintained through the lowly treatment of care.[37] Statistics indicate that women still undertake the majority of the care work.[38] The most accurate figures come from the 2001 census. Then 11 per cent of women were someone's main carer, while 7 per cent of men were. Of women, 5 per cent were engaged in more than 20 hours per week in caring tasks, as opposed to 3 per cent of men.[39] In the 50–59 age group 17 per cent of all men and 24 per cent of all women were carers.[40] In terms of the hours spent, women undertake a

---

36 Joan Tronto, *Moral Boundaries: A Political Argument for an Ethic of Care* (Routledge, 1993) 21.
37 Ibid.
38 Clare Ungerson, 'Thinking about the Production and Consumption of Long-term Care in Britain: Does Gender Still Matter?' (2000) 29(4) *Journal of Social Policy* 623; Francesca Bettio and Janneke Platenga, 'Comparing Gender Regimes in Europe' (2004) 10(1) *Feminist Economics* 85; Eva Feder Kittay, *Love's Labour: Essays on Women, Equality and Dependency* (Routledge, 1999); Jennifer Parks, *No Place Like Home? Feminist Ethics and Home Health Care* (Indiana University Press, 2003).
39 Lena Dahlberg, Sean Demack and Clare Bambra, 'Age and Gender of Informal Carers: A Population-based Study in the UK' (2007) 15(5) *Health and Social Care in the Community* 439.
40 House of Commons, Work and Pensions Committee, *Valuing and Supporting Carers* (Stationery Office, 2008) para 17.

higher number, supplying around 70 per cent of all care hours.[41] The impact of care affects women more harshly than men in economic terms. The likelihood of a male carer giving up paid employment as a result of caring responsibilities is 12.9 per cent; whereas for females it is 27 per cent.[42]

The gendered division of care labour in intimate relationships is marked. On marriage or cohabitation women's care work increases by 4.2 hours, while men's decreases 3.6 hours.[43] Even where both parents are working full-time, women do 75 per cent of the childcare.[44] This is so whether physical, moral or emotional care is considered.[45] Women are not just disproportionately represented among those giving care: 61 per cent of people receiving care are women too.[46]

Whether you look at care in the home, or care outside the home to relatives, friends, neighbour or strangers, the bulk is done by women.[47] Even where women are in paid employment, their care responsibilities constitute a 'second shift'[48] or even 'third shift' where they take on responsibilities not only for family members but also for friends.[49] It is true that in the past decade or so we have seen an increasing number of men have been involved.[50] The study which shows the highest proportion of men's care work is the European Panel Survey, which reported that women average 22 hours per week caring, as compared 18 hours for men.[51]

Care is strongly connected to society's expectations around womanhood. Hilary Graham argues:

> Caring is 'given' to women: it becomes the defining characteristic of their self-identity and their lifework. At the same time, caring is taken away from men: not caring becomes a defining characteristic of manhood.[52]

Of course the nature of some women's lives is changing. It has become easier for women to enter the professions and use hired staff to take on their care work. However, those hired staff are largely women. Ironically, increased used of paid

---

41 Ibid, para 344.
42 Fiona Carmichael and Susan Charles, 'The Opportunity Costs of Informal Care: Does Gender Matter?' (2003) 22(5) *Journal of Health Economics* 781.
43 Brid Featherstone, *Contemporary Fathering* (Policy Press, 2009) 26.
44 Ibid; Katharine Silbaugh, 'Turning Labor into Love: Housework and the Law' (1996) 91 *Northwestern University Law Review* 1, 82–3.
45 Whirlpool Corporation, *Report Card on the New Providers: Kids and Moms Speak* (Whirlpool, 1999).
46 Information Centre, NHS, *Survey of Carers in Households* 2009/2010 (Information Centre, NHS, 2011)
47 Naomi Gerstel, 'The Third Shift: Gender and Care Work Outside the Home' (2000) 23(4) *Qualitative Sociology* 467.
48 Arlie Hochschild, *The Second Shift* (Avon, 1989).
49 Gerstel, 'The Third Shift' 467.
50 Ungerson, 'Thinking about the Production' 623.
51 Sarah Harper, *Families in Ageing Societies* (Oxford University Press, 2004) ch 6.
52 Hilary Graham, 'Caring: A Labour of Love' in Janet Finch and Dulcie Groves (eds), *A Labour of Love: Women, Work and Caring* (Routledge & Kegan Paul, 1983) 13–30, 18.

care or labour furthers social inequality and is a real concern for feminism,[53] particularly as hired staff can suffer low wages, sexual harassment and lack legal protection – all of which adds to the general devaluing of care work. As Audrey Macklin bluntly states

> The grim truth is that some women's access to the high-paying, high-status professions is being facilitated through the revival of semi-indentured servitude. Put another way, one woman is exercising class and citizenship privilege to buy her way out of sex oppression.[54]

There is, therefore, no getting away from the gendered significance of care work. However, the nature of care and its impact on the lives of women varies depending on race, class and sexuality.

As Joan Tronto argues, the distribution of care is an exercise of power:

> Relatively more powerful people in society have a lot at stake in seeing that their caring needs are met under conditions that are beneficial to them, even if this means that the caring needs of those who provide them with services are neglected. More powerful people can fob caregiving work on to others: men to women, upper to lower class, free men to slaves. Care work itself is often demanding and inflexible, and not all of it is productive. People who do such work recognize its intrinsic value, but it does not fit well in a society that values innovation and accumulation of wealth.[55]

A definition of care

Producing a definition of care is far from straightforward. Interestingly, many of the official definitions seek to define a carer rather than care. This is significant, and will be criticised shortly. The government uses the following definition of a carer:

> A carer spends a significant proportion of their life providing unpaid support to family or potentially friends. This could be caring for a relative, partner or friend who is ill, frail, disabled or has mental health or substance misuse problems.[56]

---

53 Joan Tronto, 'The "Nanny" Question in Feminism' (2002)17(2) *Hypatia* 34.

54 Audrey Macklin, 'On the Outside Looking In: Foreign Domestic Workers in Canada' in Wenona Giles and Sedef Arat-Koç (eds), *Maid in the Market: Women's Paid Domestic Labor* (Fernwood Publishing, 1994) 34.

55 Joan Tronto, 'The Value of Care', *Boston Review*, February 2002 (http://bostonreview.net/ BR27.1/tronto.html, accessed 31 May 2013).

56 HM Government, *Carers at the Heart of 21st-Century Families and Communities* (Stationery Office, 2008) 18. The definition interpreted literally would include parents caring for children, but that is not how the government intended it to be understood.

This is a notably narrow definition. First, it is restricted to those who spend a significant portion of their life caring. Second, it only applies to those who are unpaid. Third, it is limited to family and only 'potentially friends'. This is surprising because the nature of a caring activity does not change simply because of the presence of absence of a blood tie between those involved. Fourth, it is restricted to those who need care due to one of the listed causes. Fifth, although not explicit, the definition was intended only to apply to people caring for adults and not children.

In social security legislation the definition of a carer is limited to a person caring for a 'disabled person'. Disabled people are those who are 'blind, deaf or dumb or who suffer from mental disorder of any description, and other persons aged eighteen or over who are substantially and permanently handicapped by illness, injury or congenital deformity'.[57] The very fact this language is archaic is revealing. It comes from a 1948 statute. The difficulty in definition is reflected in the fact no attempt has been made to update it. It is more restrictive than the government definition, as it only covers those who are caring in cases of a substantial and permanent 'handicap'.

Elsewhere, Jonathan Herring has sought to define care by setting out four key indicators of care.[58] This is not a 'bright line' definition of care, but where all four markers are clearly present there is undoubtedly care. As these markers are shown to lesser extent, the behaviour moves away from the core understanding of care.

Meeting needs

Caring relationships involve an activity which is essential to human survival: the meeting of people's needs.[59] We all have needs that must be met by others. Caring is an activity, rather than just a feeling. Here it is useful to draw on the distinction made by many care writers, that is, caring *about* and caring *for*.[60] Caring about something can be seen as essentially an attitude of mind, whereas caring for involves both cognitive and practical aspects. One can readily imagine a person who claims to care about all manner of things, but fails to put those feelings into practice.[61] In meeting the needs of others we need to recognise our moral commitment to them, to establish an appropriate care regime and to carry out the plan of action.

---

57 National Assistance Act 1948, s 29. Much of the language used in that definition would not be used by those working in the area.

58 This is taken from Jonathan Herring, *Caring and the Law* (Hart, 2013). For alternative analysis, see Tronto, *Moral Boundaries* 127–34.

59 Sarah Clark Miller, 'Need, Care and Obligation' (2005) 57 *Royal Institute of Philosophy Supplement* 157.

60 Tronto, *Moral Boundaries* 127–34.

61 Kathleen Lynch, 'Love Labour as a Distinct and Non-Commodifiable Form of Care Labour' (2008) 55(3) *Sociological Review* 550.

If care requires a successful application to needs, this still leaves the question of precisely what needs must be met to amount to care. We argue that care should be understood broadly to include the meeting of a full range of a person's needs. These include not only basic biological needs such as food and shelter, but also broader social interaction, emotional well-being and play.[62] Making practical arrangements, supervising professional care and working with bureaucracies can all be included.[63]

Daniel Engster takes a narrower view and suggests caring should be seen

> as helping individuals to meet their basic needs and to develop and sustain those *basic or innate capabilities* necessary for survival and basic functioning in society, including the ability to sense, feel, move about, speak, reason, imagine, affiliate with others, and in most societies today, read, write, and perform basic math.[64]

Engster's definition seems focused on bodily and rational activities, and excludes emotional well-being, although they possibly fitted within his reference to affiliation. Engster's approach is helpful if we are seeking to define the kinds of caring relationships that are particular worthy of state support. The closer they are to meeting what society regards as the basic needs of individuals, the stronger the case for state support. However, as a definition of care generally it seems somewhat narrow.

Respect

Respect is about recognising the other as a fellow human being with whom one is in a relationship, not as an object. It is about being alert to the other's needs and responding appropriately to them. Robin Dillon[65] argues:

> The term 'care' denotes here an epistemic attitude, understood as a moral ideal of attention: a commitment to attend, with intensely focused perception to all aspects of the irreducible particularity of individual human persons in their concrete contexts.[66]

The requirement of respect involves acknowledging the individuality of the other. They are not, for example, just 'a person with dementia', but a unique person.

---

62 This section is developed from Herring, *Caring and the Law*; see also M. Nussbaum, *Women and Human Development: The Capabilities Approach* (Cambridge University Press, 2000).

63 Ann Bookman and Mona Harrington, 'Family Caregivers: A Shadow Workforce in the Geriatric Health Care System?' (2007) 32(6) *Journal of Health, Politics, Policy and the Law* 1005.

64 Daniel Engster, 'Rethinking Care Theory: The Practice of Caring and the Obligation to Care' (2005) 20(3) *Hypatia* 50.

65 Robin Dillon, 'Respect and Care: Toward Moral Integration' (1992) 22(1) *Canadian Journal of Philosophy* 105.

66 Ibid, 105, 128.

This means that caring must involve a degree of empathy and anticipation.[67] It involves thoughtfulness and attention. Respect also involves listening to the other and ensuring there is consent. It requires treating a person in a dignified way and recognising their innate humanity. It also involves having an awareness of how the other person is experiencing the care. There must, therefore, be interaction and engagement with the individual.

This notion of respect shows why the emotional element is central to care. Imagine, for example, that there were available mechanical or robotic devices that could perform tasks that might otherwise be done by other humans. For example, apparently a human washing machine, known as an 'assisted-care bath', has been created. It is not at all clear that the level of care understood in the round would improve if provided in such a mechanical way. Social interaction and connectedness would be lost.[68] Car cleaning and human cleaning are different!

Responsibility

Caring involves an acceptance of responsibility. This is essential because people need a reliable provision of care to meet needs. In part this is because if one person enters a caring relationship with another, others may not then offer care to that person. They may assume that any needs are met by that relationship. This is particularly likely to happen because people's capacity to offer care is limited and inevitably can only be focused on a finite number of people. Without a sense of commitment, the need for security and emotional closeness will not be met.

Relationality

A central value in caring is that it should never be seen a unidirectional. Caring should be a relationship and therefore will require the person providing care to be open to receiving care.[69] Caring relationships require both (or all) parties to be open to receiving the support and help of the other.[70] Caring should be about a reciprocal relationship and not a one-way street.[71]

Too much of the academic writing and the public discourse divides up people into 'carers' and 'cared for'. Carers UK, an excellent charity, focuses on promoting the rights of carers. The government produces documents promoting policies

67 Lawrence Blum, *Moral Perception and Particularity* (Cambridge University Press, 1994) 30–61.
68 Jennifer Parks, 'Lifting the Burden of Women's Care Work: Should Robots Replace the "Human Touch"?' (2010) 25(1) *Hypatia* 100.
69 Vrinda Dalmiya, 'Why Should a Knower Care?' (2002) 17(1) *Hypatia* 34.
70 Mike Nolan, Gordon Grant and John Keady, *Understanding Family Care* (Open University Press, 1996) 39.
71 Thea Hassan, 'An ethic of care critique' (http://dspace.sunyconnect.suny.edu/bitstream/handle/1951/43954/An_Ethic_of_Care_Critique.pdf?sequence=1, accessed 31 May 2013); Sara Ruddick, 'Care as Labor and Relationship' in Joram Haber and Mark Halfon (eds), *Norms and Values: Essays on the Work of Virginia Held* (Rowman & Littlefield, 1998).

for carers. Even much of the academic writing on caring focuses on the work of care. This creates an artificial divide between those who are carers and those who receive care. It overlooks the powerful disability critique of care. Here the themes of care and vulnerability resonate powerfully.

Care and vulnerability

Peter Beresford has captured well the concerns over the idea of care:

> The reality seems to be that while care might be regarded by many of us as a good idea in principle and something that some people might need at some time, few of us identify with it for ourselves and actually want to be 'cared for' in this sense. There is a strong reluctance to see ourselves or to be in this position, because it implies dependence. Care is a concept that is primarily associated with children. Models for adult caring have tended to be borrowed from childcare and grow out of the unequal relationships associated with looking after children. This has been the basis for many people's assumptions and understanding of such care.[72]

Care can be experienced in a negative way. As one disabled person wrote:

> We are who we are as people with impairments, and might actually feel comfortable with our lives if it wasn't for all those interfering busybodies who feel that it is their responsibility to feel sorry for us, or to find cures for us, or to manage our lives for us, or to harry us in order to make us something we are not, i.e. 'normal'.[73]

Richard Wood contends

> Disabled people have never demanded or asked for care! We have sought independent living, which means being able to achieve maximum independence and control over our own lives. The concept of care seems to many disabled people a tool through which others are able to dominate and manage our lives.[74]

As this last quote indicates, many disability rights activists emphasise independence.[75] Rather than being the objects of care, they argue, disabled people need

---

72 Peter Beresford, *What Future for Care?* (Joseph Rowntree Foundation, 2008).
73 Colin, quoted in Sally French and John Swain, 'Whose Tragedy? Towards a Personal Non-Tragedy View of Disability' in John Swain, Sally French, Colin Barnes and Carol Thomas (eds), *Disabling Barriers – Enabling Environments* (Sage, 2004).
74 Quoted in Tom Shakespeare, *Help* (Venture Press, 2000) 63.
75 Nick Watson, Linda McKie, Bill Hughes, Debra Hopkins and Sue Gregory, '(Inter)Dependence, Needs and Care: The Potential for Disability and Feminist Theorists to Develop an Emancipatory Model' (2010) 38(2) *Sociology* 331.

to be able to exercise control over the help.[76] Care, therefore, should not be seen as something a 'carer' does to the other, but as a tool used by the disabled person to achieve independence.[77] The focus should be on empowerment, control and choice for those with disabilities, even if self-sufficiency is not possible.[78] Some disabilities activists have argued for the use of the term helper or personal assistant[79] rather than carer, in an attempt to remove any implication that the person needing care is suffering a particular misfortune, which needs attention, or is passive in the enterprise.[80]

Another way of analysing this issue is to recognise that power is a theme in caring relationships.[81] Zygmunt Bauman's warns that 'the impulse to care for the other, when taken to its extreme, leads to the annihilation of the autonomy of the other, to domination and oppression'.[82] Julia Twigg's recent qualitative research on older people's experiences of being bathed highlights this quite clearly:

> One person, strong and able, stands above and over another who is frail and physically vulnerable, forced to rely on their strength and goodwill. Being naked in the face of someone who is not, contains a powerful dynamic of domination and vulnerability, and it is often used in situations of interrogation and torture as a means of subjugating the individual.[83]

Whether care *necessarily* has these negative connotations may be questioned. There are certainly dangers it has, especially when the 'cared for' becomes reduced to no more than the object of receipt of care. This is why it is so important that we focus on caring relationships. When good care is seen as involving enabling and empowering both parties, some of the negative connotations fall away.

It may be helpful to contrast 'activity caring' and one based on 'relational caring'. The activity-based approach to care is likely to understand caring as involving 'doing something for someone else'.[84] The role of 'carer' and 'cared for' are clearly differentiated. However a relational model of care will challenge that separation. As Carol Gilligan writes: 'The ideal of care is thus an activity of relationships, of seeing and responding to need, taking care of the world by sustaining

---

76 Simon Brisenden, *A Charter for Personal Care* (Disablement Income Group, 1989) 9–10.

77 Jenny Morris, 'Impairment and Disability: Constructing an Ethics of Care that Promotes Human Rights' (2001) 16(4) *Hypatia* 1.

78 Ayesha Vernon and Hazel Qureshi, 'Community Care and Independence: Self-sufficiency or Empowerment?' (2000) 20(2) *Critical Social Policy* 255.

79 Christine Kelly, 'Making "Care" Accessible: Personal Assistance for Disabled People and the Politics of Language' (2011) 31 *Critical Social Policy* 562.

80 Hughes et al, 'Love's Labour's Lost?' 259.

81 Shakespeare, *Help*; Mary Daly, 'Care as a Good for Social Policy' (2002) 31(2) *Journal of Social Policy* 251.

82 Zygmunt Bauman, *Postmodern Ethics* (Blackwell, 1993) 11.

83 Jilia Twigg, 'Carework as a Form of Bodywork' (2000) 20(4) *Ageing and Society* 389.

84 Clare Ungerson (ed.), *Gender and Caring: Work and Welfare in Britain and Scandinavia* (Harvester Wheatsheaf, 1990).

the web of connection so that no one is left alone.'[85] The relational view of care would emphasise interdependence over dependency, and mutual vulnerability over the frailty of one person. The relational approach is likely to see care in the context of the relationship between two people in which each is contributing care to the other, be that in psychological, emotional or physical terms. Michael Fine and Caroline Glendinning capture this importance of the relational aspect of care in these words:

> Recent studies of care suggest that qualities of reciprocal dependence underlie much of what is termed 'care'. Rather than being a unidirectional activity in which an active care-giver does something to a passive and dependent recipient, these accounts suggest that care is best understood as the product or outcome of the relationship between two or more people.[86]

Activity caring regards the person needing care as being a problem, which the carer solves. This has the danger of glorifying the 'carer' role, while downgrading the 'cared for' role. It produces an unequal relationship in which the 'carer' has disproportionate power over the power-dependent cared for.[87]

This relational aspect is important because it puts the activities within their context, a context which provides those acts with meaning.[88] The provision of care only makes sense and can be properly understood when placed in the context of the parties' relationship.[89] That action of caring for the parties can have a meaning well beyond the here and now. It may reflect a long-standing commitment or a mutual responsibility. The act may have overtones recalling aspects of the relationship many years ago.

By seeing caring relationships, we can recognise that we are all givers and receivers of care. There are different ways of caring and the kinds of care involved differ. Importantly too the talk of caring relationships can capture the changing nature of relationship. Caregiving relationships change over time, so that pigeonholing the parties into categories of caregiver and care receiver become artificial.

There is another important point here and that is that the division of 'carer' and care receiver is not only false because it imagines that one party to the relationship is the provider of the care, but it also overlooks the point that the 'carer' may themselves be receiving care from others.[90] Notably, 378,000 carers are themselves registered as permanently sick or disabled according to official

85 Carol Gilligan, *In a Different Voice* (Harvard University Press, 1982) 73.
86 Michael Fine and Caroline Glendinning, 'Dependence, Independence or Inter-Dependence? Revisiting the Concepts of Care and Dependency' (2005) 25(4) *Ageing and Society* 601, 619.
87 Joan Orme, *Gender and Community Care* (Palgrave, 2001).
88 Mary Daly and Jane Lewis, 'The Concept of Social Care and the Analysis of Contemporary Welfare' (2000) 51(2) *British Journal of Sociology* 281.
89 Sibyl Schwarzenbach, 'On Civil Friendship' (1996) 107 *Ethics* 97, 102.
90 Watson et al, '(Inter)Dependence, Needs and Care' 221.

statistics.[91] Thus it is more accurate to acknowledge the networks of care that we live in than dividing us up into providers of and recipients of care.[92] All of us fall into both categories.

These points are very well illustrated in Jo Bridgeman's chapter. Taking the example of parenthood she demonstrates how, although it is easy to imagine the strong parent caring for the vulnerable child, the true picture is far more complex. The parents' caring role is dependent upon the support from others such as teachers and doctors. The parent becomes vulnerable through their care and need of support. The assumptions about who is caring for whom and who is the vulnerable party are made complex in her analysis.

Concluding remarks

When the contributors to this volume came together to discuss the collection and its ambit, one of the themes that emerged was how many gaps there were. Unfortunately, it is simply impossible to come up with a comprehensive account of the very different ways in which humans experience vulnerability. This is of course easily explainable by the very fact that vulnerability is ubiquitous. We therefore make no apologies for the gaps. Rather, we hope the collection provides a starting point for reflecting upon the relationship between vulnerabilities, care, family law and the state. The choice of the plural sense of the word is therefore no accident, as we wanted to draw out some of the many ways in which humans experience vulnerability.

---

91 Carers UK, *Facts about Carers* (Carers UK, 2009).
92 Clare Beckett, 'Women, Disability, Care: Good Neighbours or Uneasy Bedfellows?' (2007) 27(3) *Critical Social Policy* 360.

Chapter 2

The contours of 'vulnerability'

*Jennifer Collins**

Introduction

'Vulnerability' has emerged as a very important idea for those interested in family law. But it is an abstruse concept without further explanation. Given that we should require clarity in the ideas that we are using, this chapter aims to elicit some better ways of understanding vulnerability for family lawyers.

The context for discussion, and the reason for turning to this task now, is the recent broad claim that 'centralising' vulnerability in family law is key because everyone is vulnerable.[1] Whether or not this approach is viable, it assumes that we have a particular understanding of vulnerability in view. The point I want to emphasise in this chapter is that it would be more appropriate to begin to examine the complexity latent in 'vulnerability' as a concept, and the effect this might have on family lawyers' responses to it. For example, it is plausible to suggest that there may be different kinds and degrees of vulnerability. How should they be identified? And do family lawyers have reason(s) to be interested in the most serious kinds of vulnerability only? Certainly these key issues must be dealt with, and prior to placing vulnerability at the fore.

This chapter seeks to open up discussion by using moral theory to think about core and marginal examples of vulnerability.[2] It is a preliminary inquiry: the aim is to begin to consider whether any of these examples might shed light on 'vulnerability' for family lawyers, and to articulate questions which warrant exploration.

The chapter is divided into five sections. The first part begins by briefly examining some legal effects of vulnerability, and explains why a general claim to 'centralise' vulnerability can be challenged as incomplete. The focus of the second section is on vulnerability as a real-life concept. The third section enumerates four examples of vulnerability presented by Robert Goodin, and offers refinements

* I am grateful to the editors and participants in this volume for helpful discussion of an earlier draft, and to A. Ashworth and P. Billingham for written comments. The usual disclaimers apply.

1 For discussion, see Jonathan Herring, 'Vulnerability, Children and the Law', in Michael Freeman (ed.), *Law and Childhood Studies* (Oxford University Press, 2012) 258–60.

2 Robert Goodin, 'Exploiting a Situation and Exploiting a Person', in Andrew Reeve (ed.), *Modern Theories of Exploitation* (Sage, 1987).

to them. The fourth section is complementary to the third section in so far as it considers the implications of Goodin's account for family lawyers. It pinpoints questions about vulnerability which are important, and raises the issue that vulnerability should act as a pointer to the study of other cognate concepts. Finally, the chapter draws together the conclusions of the study.

The relevance of 'vulnerability'

It is compelling that family lawyers should want to have a clear idea of what is meant by 'vulnerability', since it performs several key functions in family law. Vulnerability acts as a justification for legal intervention to protect children's rights and the rights of other vulnerable persons. Also, the presence of vulnerability may determine whether legal effects may apply – on occasion it is a necessary factual element for intervention.

We can turn to family law and some closely connected provisions in the criminal law to see these functions illustrated.[3] The rights of children have been made prominent by international instruments, particularly the United Nations Convention on the Rights of the Child 1989.[4] In English law there are a number of child protection laws and criminal offences which use children's vulnerability as part of the justification for their existence.[5] Moreover, there are legal mechanisms which can be used to protect the welfare of vulnerable adults: the Mental Capacity Act 2005, the High Court's inherent jurisdiction, and the Mental Health Act 1983.[6] Some of these provisions require vulnerability for legal intervention.

It is well known that the system for the protection of children in English family law is premised on the welfare principle. Section 1(1)(a) of the Children Act 1989 states that 'when the court determines any question with respect to the upbringing of a child, the child's welfare shall be the court's paramount consideration'. The Act seeks to protect children by setting out a principle of parental responsibility in section 3(1). The drafters intended to present the parent–child relationship as a relationship in which a parent is responsible for nurturing a child, rather than a

---

3 Of course, vulnerability generates legal effects in other areas of the law, but they are not explored in this chapter.

4 Art. 3 of United Nations Convention on the Rights of the Child states that: 'In all actions concerning children, whether undertaken by public or private courts of law, administrative authorities or legislative bodies, the best interests of the child shall be a primary consideration.' The UNCRC is dependent on state implementation. Notably the European Convention of Human Rights has no specific provision on children. When the European Court of Human Rights had to decide the case of *T and V v United Kingdom* (2000) 30 EHRR 121, it borrowed from the UNCRC, and other international instruments. It has since been held in *SC v United Kingdom* [2005] Crim LR 130, that a child defendant must be given 'effective participation' (at [29]) in court proceedings.

5 For general discussion of issues relating to children's rights, see Laura Hoyano and Caroline Keenan, *Child Abuse: Law and Policy across Boundaries* (Oxford University Press, 2010).

6 Note the existence of defence of 'necessity'. For an analysis, see Jonathan Herring, 'Protecting Vulnerable Adults: A Critical Review of Recent Case Law' (2009) 21(4) CFLQ 498.

relationship of domination by one party over the other.[7] Such reasoning was also intended to inform the relationship between the state and individual family units, so that there is 'partnership between a child's family and the state in which the family feels able to ask for help and the local authority can give assistance which is relevant to the child and her family's needs'.[8] However, while the state is able to intervene to protect children by way of Part III of the 1989 Act, the duties on local authorities are fairly limited.[9]

Children are also protected by a number of criminal offences. An example of a homicide offence can be found in section 5 of the Domestic Violence, Crime and Victims Act 2004.[10] The offence extends to protect vulnerable adults, as well as children, and applies where there has been death or serious physical injury as a result of an unlawful act. Section 5 penalises those who commit an unlawful act, or those who (a) were or ought to have been aware of a risk of serious harm to the victim (V), and (b) failed to take reasonable steps to protect V from such harm, and (c) had foresight or ought to have had foresight that an act would be carried out in the circumstances. In all cases, it must be shown that the defendant (D) was a member of V's household who had frequent contact with V. It is clear that vulnerability is used as a justification for the offence. The government's concern was to target persons who inflict very serious injury where a vulnerable adult or child is involved, given the 'special responsibility that members of the same household bear for the vulnerable with whom they live'.[11] It is also clear that vulnerability is an essential component of the offence. The offence defines a vulnerable person as a child under 16, or an adult over 16 'whose ability to protect himself from violence, abuse or neglect is significantly impaired through physical or mental disability or illness, through old age or otherwise'.[12]

As well as the standard non-fatal non-sexual offences against the person (found in the Offences Against the Person Act 1861), there is a broad offence of child cruelty and neglect, found in section 1 of the Children and Young Persons Act 1933.

---

7 Hoyano and Keenan, *Child Abuse* 34.
8 Ibid, 35.
9 Michael Dunn and Jonathan Herring, 'Safeguarding Children and Adults: Much of a Muchness?' (2011) 23(4) *CFLQ* 528, 537.
10 As amended by the Domestic Violence, Crime and Victims (Amendment) Act 2012.
11 HC Deb 21 October 2011, vol 533, col 1184; for a critique of this offence, see Jonathan Herring, 'Familial Homicide, Failure to Protect and Domestic Violence: Who's the Victim?' [2007] *Crim LR* 923. For comment on the approach to be adopted regarding domestic violence under the amended 2004 Act, see HC Deb 21 October 2011, vol 544, col 1184: 'If one of the defendants has been the victim of, or a witness to, domestic violence, the steps that the defendant could reasonably have been expected to take may be more limited than the steps that someone not suffering or witnessing that violence could reasonably have been expected to take. Depending on the facts of the case, the court may find that it was not reasonable for the defendant to take some of the steps that might otherwise have been available to them. The same principles will apply to the extended offence. In other words, the offence will be sensitive to the circumstances in each case.'
12 Domestic Violence, Crime and Victims Act 2004, s 5(6).

The offence is applicable to persons over 16 years of age who have responsibility for a child or young person under 16, but who have not discharged that responsibility appropriately. Section 1 makes it an offence for such an individual to assault, ill-treat, neglect or abandon a child or young person, or to cause or procure these behaviours, where the likely effect is 'unnecessary suffering or injury to health' for the child. Section 1(2) states that neglect involves failing to provide a child with 'adequate food, clothing, medical aid or lodging'.

Moreover, it is clear that there are a number of sexual offences developed to protect children, some of which are found in the Sexual Offences Act 2003. It is impossible to go into detail regarding them here, save to note that they include: offences against children under 13,[13] offences against children under 16,[14] meeting a child following sexual grooming,[15] abuse of trust offences[16] and familial sexual offences.[17] Furthermore, the Protection of Children Act 1978 sets out offences relating to the creation and distribution of child pornography.[18]

Turning now to the protection of vulnerable adults, the Mental Capacity Act identifies when a person can be said to lack capacity. Section 2(1) states that a person lacks capacity to make a decision at a particular time if they are unable to make a decision about it 'because of an impairment of, or a disturbance in the functioning of, the mind or brain'. It follows that an individual may have capacity to make some decisions at a particular point in time, but lack capacity to make a decision about more serious matters.[19] The 2005 Act is structured so that the question of whether an individual lacks capacity is to be asked with a focus on enhancing an individual's decision-making autonomy, rather than denying them the possibility of exercising it. For example, the Act makes provision for practical steps to be taken to help an individual reach capacity.[20]

There is a concern that some vulnerable persons who fall outside of the Mental Capacity Act's definition of lack of capacity may require protective measures. The inherent jurisdiction of the High Court has been relied upon as a practical response to this problem. In *Re SA*, the court said that:

> A vulnerable adult who does not suffer from any kind of mental incapacity may nonetheless be entitled to the protection of the inherent jurisdiction if he or she is, or is reasonably believed to be, incapacitated from making the

13 Sexual Offences Act 2003, ss 5–8.
14 Ibid, ss 9–15.
15 Ibid, s15.
16 Ibid, ss 16–24.
17 Ibid, ss 25 and 26.
18 Protection of Children Act 1978, s 1(1). For a discussion of offences found in the Protection of Children Act 1979, see Suzanne Ost, *Child Pornography and Sexual Grooming: Legal and Societal Responses* (Cambridge University Press, 2009) 54–102. See also Sexual Offences Act 2003, ss 47–50.
19 It is a principle of the 2005 Act that practical steps are given to help an individual reach capacity, see Mental Capacity Act 2005, s 3(2). For further discussion, see Jonathan Herring, *Medical Law and Ethics* (Oxford University Press, 2011) 149–220.
20 Mental Capacity Act 2005, ss 3(2), 4 and 5.

relevant decision by reason of such things as constraint, coercion, undue influence or other vitiating factors.[21]

This would therefore include:

[S]omeone who, whether or not mentally incapacitated, and whether or not suffering from any mental illness, or mental disorder, is or may be unable to take care of him or herself, or unable to protect him or herself against significant harm or exploitation, or who is deaf, blind, or dumb, or who is substantially handicapped by illness, injury or congenital deformity.[22]

The jurisdiction exists to deal with serious vulnerability, but it is precariously open-ended. However, the Court of Appeal recently defended its existence in *A Local Authority v DL*, and affirmed the authority of *Re SA*.[23] Consideration was given to the wording of the 2005 Act – which does not exclude the inherent jurisdiction – and the pressing need to protect the personal autonomy of vulnerable adults against abuse where they have been constrained, coerced, subject to undue influence, or unable to express real and genuine consent.[24]

Vulnerable adults are also protected by the Mental Health Act 1983.[25] This is a compulsory jurisdiction used in connection with competent patients who have a mental disorder and withhold their consent to medical treatment.[26] It should be noted that the criminal law also protects those with mental disorders against unwanted sexual activity. The Sexual Offences Act 2003 contains a number of offences, such as: sexual activity involving a person with a mental disorder who is unable to consent to the sexual activity; sexual activity with a person with a mental disorder where agreement to the activity has been obtained by an inducement, threat or deception; and sexual activity of care workers with a person with a mental disorder.[27] It is controversial whether the 2003 Act has appropriately protected the sexual autonomy of those who come within the category of 'mental disorder'.[28]

Several points can be discerned from this brief discussion. The first function of vulnerability highlighted – the idea of vulnerability being used as a justification

---

21 *Re SA (Vulnerable Adult with Capacity: Marriage)* [2006] 1 *FLR* 867, Munby J [79].
22 Ibid [82]; Michael Dunn, Isabel Clare and Anthony Holland, 'To Empower or to Protect? Constructing the "Vulnerable Adult" in English Law and Public Policy' (2008) 28(2) *Legal Studies* 234, 239, point out that this definition is based upon the Law Commission's Report, see Law Commission, *Mental Incapacity* (Law Com No 231, 1995) 163.
23 [2012] EWCA Civ 253.
24 Ibid [54].
25 As amended by the Mental Health Act 2007.
26 Mental Health Act 1983, ss 2–3; see Herring, *Medical Law and Ethics* 565.
27 Sexual Offences Act 2003, ss 30–33, 34–37, and 38–41.
28 For discussion, see John Stanton-Ife, 'Mental Disorder and Sexual Consent: Williams and After', in Dennis J. Baker and Jeremy Horder (eds), *The Sanctity of Life and the Criminal Law: The Legacy of Glanville Williams* (Cambridge University Press, 2013).

for legal intervention – is used to justify different types and levels of legal intervention. These include: restrictions on a child's contact with their parents, the loss of individual opportunities to make decisions, and criminal censure.[29] In so far as it is used as a justification, we ought to know the doctrine's legitimate limits. This is particularly important, given the large number of offences in the United States which impose positive legal duties on professionals and certain other individuals to report abuse of vulnerable persons.[30] The second function noted was that of using vulnerability as a necessary requirement for intervention. But there is a large amount of diversity in legal approaches to 'vulnerability': the criminal law has drawn some category-based ways of defining vulnerability on the basis that certain groups of people are vulnerable, but the approach drawn in family law with regard to the inherent jurisdiction leaves the meaning of vulnerability open-ended. It must be possible to know with a degree of certainty when an individual will be judged to be vulnerable.

Now all of this must be put against the context for discussion, which is the claim that centralising 'vulnerability' in family law should be key. Jonathan Herring has recently argued that rather than viewing certain groups of individuals as vulnerable, we should be attentive to the fact that everyone is vulnerable.[31] This argument is a response to Martha Fineman's call to 'richly theorize' a concept of vulnerability, which 'can be used to redefine and expand current ideas about state responsibility towards individuals and institutions'.[32] Fineman argues that because vulnerability is 'universal and constant, inherent in the human condition',[33] the '"vulnerable subject" must replace the autonomous and independent subject asserted in the liberal tradition'.[34] Building on this argument, Herring suggests that 'children's "vulnerability" is in essence no different to that faced by adults'.[35] This leads to the further argument that vulnerability should be centralised as an appropriate legal response.

It makes sense to say that family law should be concerned with vulnerability (and perhaps, as Herring argues, other branches of the law should be more concerned with vulnerability).[36] However, by attributing significance to Fineman's understanding of the concept, Herring sets a low standard for vulnerability. The

---

29 See Hoyano and Keenan, *Child Abuse* 45–54, for an overview of the structure of English family law legislation relating to child protection.

30 See Sandra G. Thompson, 'The White-Collar Police Force: "Duty to Report" Statutes in Criminal Law Theory' (2002) 11(1) *William and Mary Bill of Rights Journal* 3.

31 Herring, 'Vulnerability, Children and the Law'.

32 Martha Fineman, 'The Vulnerable Subject: Anchoring Equality in the Human Condition' (2008) 20(1) *Yale Journal of Law & Feminism* 1–23, 1–2.

33 Ibid, 1.

34 Ibid, 2.

35 This is to move beyond the point made by Fineman, 'The Vulnerable Subject' 8 that: 'In discussions of public responsibility, the concept of vulnerability is sometimes used to define groups of fledgling or stigmatized subjects, designated as "populations" ... Children or the elderly are prototypical examples of more sympathetic vulnerable populations.'

36 Herring, 'Vulnerability, Children and the Law' 262.

worry is that this is not an illuminating argument because everyone is vulnerable to some extent simply by virtue of being human. To argue that the appropriate response is to centralise vulnerability is to overlook the further assumption that we are often independent in other respects too (the Mental Capacity Act 2005, for example, seeks to protect individuals' capacity to make decisions for themselves if possible).[37] We do not tend to single out vulnerability for attention unless it is serious or unusual or pronounced: an assessment if you like of the ways in which an individual is more vulnerable than independent, in order to see if the balance is tipped in favour of vulnerability. To be meaningful, we must ask whether some types of vulnerability are significant. And this involves identifying and scrutinising various types of vulnerability before thinking about the specific functions they should play in family law.

However, Dunn and Herring's 2011 argument observes that the state's obligation to protect children, vulnerable adults and those lacking capacity does not present uniform issues. They say that 'the source of the "vulnerability" may differ between these groups, and the grounds for justifying intervention may differ'.[38] But, if this argument is accepted, Herring's latest contribution encourages an unrealistic view of vulnerability on two fronts: first, by assuming that there is common understanding around vulnerability; and, second, by excessively relying on vulnerability, assuming that it is robust to answer the legal intervention question, too. And so a key theme of this chapter is that the proposition 'everyone is vulnerable' is the beginning of an argument, rather than a conclusion.

To be analytically useful, an idea of vulnerability must be differentiated, and then understood in relation to reasons for legal intervention. It follows that there are two logically distinct questions to consider. The preliminary question is whether there could be different kinds or levels of vulnerability: for example, might there be kinds of vulnerability which are brought about by dependency on others, and some which are not? Of course, an account of vulnerability makes no reference to what family lawyers should take vulnerability to mean. Presuming that it is possible to isolate examples, the second question must be to ask whether family lawyers should be interested in only some kinds of vulnerability. To return to Herring's most recent argument, the claim that there is vulnerability which is to be celebrated, and vulnerability which requires protection, is overly broad.[39] It is crucial to be more precise about the matter. For example, might we want to say that only certain kinds of serious vulnerability merit legal intervention? And should that amount to a positive legal duty on a person to act in a certain way in relation to a vulnerable person?[40] This is to begin to build a more substantial account of the concept for family law. There is a great deal of work to be done, and this chapter is primarily concerned to bring into focus the first question, and

---

37 Mental Capacity Act 2005.
38 Dunn and Herring, 'Safeguarding Children and Adults' 538.
39 Herring, 'Vulnerability, Children and the Law' 261.
40 John M. Eekelaar, *Family Law and Personal Life* (Oxford University Press, 2006) ch 2.

to identify some normative issues which should be evaluated in answering the second.

How to study 'vulnerability': vulnerability as a real-life concept

To understand what vulnerability might be taken to mean – the first question set out above – it must be studied as a real-life concept. To describe a concept in this way is to say that it has a reasonably firm intuitive core, but has scope for uncertainty at its margins.[41] H. L. A. Hart exposed the point in the following way:

> Sometimes the difference between the clear, standard case or paradigm for the use of an expression and the questionable cases is only a matter of degree. A man with a shining smooth pate is clearly bald; another with a luxuriant mop clearly is not; but the question whether a third man, with a fringe of hair here and there, is bald might be indefinitely disputed, if it were thought worthwhile or any practical issue turned on it.[42]

This is surely a coherent approach: few would say that a single exhaustive definition of vulnerability is desirable – it would overlook the fact that vulnerability represents all the rich complexity that we might expect of a real-life concept, and we should want this to be reflected in analysis of it. Thus, we should reasonably expect to identify marginal examples of the concept. How, then, should we hope to achieve this real-life understanding of vulnerability?

The starting point is to emphasise that identifying vulnerability requires an evaluative judgement. It is submitted that this evaluation may be more apparent on some occasions than others. Sometimes a discrete group of individuals may be described as vulnerable. This is a familiar approach in family law and the criminal law: minors, those with cognitive or physical impairment, vulnerable workers (particularly those who have been trafficked) have all been said to be vulnerable persons in certain statutes or case law.[43] However, this approach should not obscure the fact that there has been evaluation to decide which groups of individuals should be regarded as vulnerable in the first place. Nor can we overlook the limitations of this approach. Defining all elderly persons or children as vulnerable, for example, is unfavourable to both groups as it reduces their claim to make valuable and realistic life choices for themselves.[44] Also, on occasion it may be necessary to look to an individual's circumstances to determine if their vulnerability

---

41 For a different interpretation of a real-life concept, see Fineman, 'The Vulnerable Subject' 10. Fineman argues that: 'Understanding the significance, universality, and constancy of vulnerability mandates that politics, ethics, and law be fashioned around a complete, comprehensive vision of the human experience if they are to meet the needs of real-life subjects'.

42 H. L. A. Hart, *The Concept of Law* (Clarendon, 1997) 4.

43 For discussion, see the first section of this chapter.

44 For good discussion of some of the critical tensions which arise in viewing children as inherently vulnerable, see Ost, *Child Pornography* 6–20.

is increased or aggravated. The Sentencing Council's recent Sexual Offences Guideline Consultation has stated the importance of referring to vulnerability factors in assessing the severity of offences involving children or victims of trafficking for the purposes of criminal law sentencing.[45] The consultation proposes that evidence of a child being in care or subject to sexual abuse is an aggravating factor for the offences found in section 48, 49 and 50 of the Sexual Offences Act 2003.[46] Moreover, individuals who have been trafficked might be especially vulnerable to sexual exploitation if they are from dysfunctional backgrounds.[47]

References to context are key when considering marginal examples of vulnerability. Exploring why some cases are marginal can be confronted using the following example. It has been reported that numbers of elderly persons are being charged by their adult children for delivery of their weekly groceries or pensions.[48] In some cases this is for a relatively small sum, such as £10 given for the delivery of groceries. But there are also examples of it being much more than this. While we know that adult children have no legal duty to look after elderly parents who do not live in their household, this does not mean that we cannot be interested in whether these elderly parents might be vulnerable.[49] I do not seek to claim that this example is intuitively complete, but it is a way of probing the margins of vulnerability.

There are reasons to say that the elderly parents are vulnerable in the example. One significant feature is a high degree of dependency. The first claim therefore is that dependency may sometimes point to the presence of vulnerability. Of course, the reason for dependency is unlikely to be uniform. For example, elderly persons who are frail and infirm are more likely to be dependent on others to meet their basic needs. They may also be dependent on others for access to up-to-date information or knowledge, such as the current price of basic groceries. Furthermore, the need for emotional support or friendship can mean that an individual is dependent on others. Arguably many elderly persons are isolated and fear exclusion from social contact and significant relationships. If a person is dependent in this sense then they may seek to preserve existing relationships, even where they have gone bad (for example, where there is an implicit expectation that elderly parents should remunerate their adult children for basic tasks). Moreover, it could be said that the parents in the example are vulnerable because elderly persons may be perceived as having greater means, and are therefore susceptible to being a target for exploitative practices.

---

45 Sentencing Council, 'Sexual Offences Guideline Consultation', *Sentencing Council*, 6 December 2012 (http://sentencingcouncil.judiciary.gov.uk/docs/sexual_offences_consultation_guideline_ (web).pdf, accessed 26 May 2013).

46 Ibid, 99.

47 Ibid, 109.

48 For example, see Bergen-Passaic, 'Children Abusing Elderly Parents: A Growing Concern in New Jersey', *FindLawKnowledgeBase*, 2 August 2010 (http://knowledgebase.findlaw.com/kb/2010/ Jul/141546.html, accessed 7 May 2013).

49 See Jonathan Herring, *Older People in Law and Society* (Oxford University Press, 2009).

However, some other features may cast doubt on the presence or resilience of vulnerability in the example, and require careful analysis. It would be artificial to gloss over the fact that the elderly parents benefit from their dealings with their adult children. It may be the case that they do not have to pay an external party to do the task in question, and this would seem to trump any vulnerability present (perhaps especially where payment to an external party would be for a greater amount). But there is a concern with this analysis. Why should all benefit to an individual have to be gone before they can be viewed as being vulnerable in relation to another? If we should still want to say that the elderly parent is vulnerable, we could introduce the idea of someone being more or less vulnerable.

Another issue relates to the fact that in most cases the parents will have consented (in some sense) to paying their adult children for delivery of the groceries or pension. Might this negate vulnerability arising in the first place, or override any recognised vulnerability? The consent issue is not straightforward, and there are at least two ways in which it can be understood. First, we could say that the consent is not fully valid in these kinds of cases: elderly parents have not given valid consent if they can be shown to have been vulnerable (though perhaps only if they are vulnerable to a serious or substantial degree). Of course, there will be all sorts of difficulties in saying that we should find consent to be invalid because one party is understood to be vulnerable, particularly those relating to personal autonomy. The second is to say that although the elderly parents are able to consent to their adult children charging for delivery of groceries and pensions, the consent may be rendered invalid where the elderly parents can be shown to be vulnerable (again, perhaps to a more serious extent).[50] The reason for this is because vulnerability does something to taint the consent. This position operates in a similar manner to vitiating factors, which are a feature of the civil law. Both models are plausible, but require serious scrutiny of the idea of 'consent' if they are to have any sort of mileage for family law.

Another possibility is to ask whether the existence of vulnerability should depend on how family members characterise the interaction. For example, should it matter if an elderly parent says that they do not feel vulnerable when their adult child charges them for delivering their groceries because they want 'to help them out', 'tide them over', 'give them something for petrol', or something similar? Should vulnerability depend on an individual's own subjective sense that they feel vulnerable? Or should it be assessed objectively? If an objective approach is preferable, communication of willingness to help out an adult child might exclude vulnerability. I return to this discussion in the fourth section.

The example serves to show that pressure can be put on a real-life concept of vulnerability, but also that it is possible to present 'thick' and 'thin' accounts of the concept. A 'thin' account may be to say that everyone is vulnerable. A 'thicker' account would require careful consideration of some of the marginal issues highlighted above.

---

50 For example, should we regard consent as valid if the elderly parent knows that he or she is being overcharged, but decides to go along with the arrangement for prudential reasons?

Using moral theory to probe the limits of vulnerability

Now that we have seen that the margins of a real-life concept of vulnerability might reasonably be disputed, we can begin to contribute to the debate raised by the question: what does it mean to be vulnerable? In order to explore this question I propose to take my lead from moral theory, and specifically an interesting piece of work by Robert Goodin.

How does 'vulnerability' feature in Goodin's account? The setting for the argument is a positive thesis about exploitation. Goodin suggests that every case of interpersonal exploitation involves an individual (D) breaching two sorts of moral duties, which he holds in relation to another individual (V). Crucially, both duties arise if V is considered vulnerable in relation to D, because D has 'a heavy moral responsibility to protect the weaker'.[51] The proposed definition of breach is that D has violated those norms which govern his social interaction with V, and this is to be judged objectively.[52] Specifically, D must be appraised on the basis of whether he has engaged in 'fair play'. The fair–unfair play distinction is drawn as follows:

> 'Fair play' is play according to the formal rules and informal ethos of the game. 'Unfair play' is play at variance with those standards. 'Taking unfair advantage', seen in this light, would consist in availing oneself of strategic opportunities which are denied to one under the rules and ethos of the game at hand.[53]

It should now be clear just how central 'vulnerability' is to Goodin's thesis. This is because, absent V's vulnerability, neither moral duty will attach to D. Goodin's assertion is that a person is vulnerable in relation to D if their interests are strongly affected by D's 'actions and choices, regardless of the particular source of their vulnerability'.[54] This is a fairly loose notion of vulnerability.

> Some people are vulnerable to other people quite generally a large proportion of the time and with respect to a broad range of threats to their well-being. Other people are vulnerable only to particular other people, or only

51 Goodin, 'Exploiting a Situation and Exploiting a Person' 167. What of the nature of these two moral duties? The first is a negative duty on D to restrict or curtail his behaviour in circumstances where V is particularly vulnerable to him. This is the case even though it may be perfectly acceptable for D to engage in these behaviours in other interpersonal relationships. The salient fact, which triggers the duty, is V's known vulnerability in relation to D. The second form of moral duty also attaches to D where V is taken to be vulnerable in relation to him. By contrast with the first, the second duty is framed in positive terms: D is under a duty to take positive measures to come to V's aid in circumstances where V is vulnerable.

52 Ibid, 184. If indeed it is possible to settle on community norms of behaviour. Consider the difficulties determining the meaning of 'dishonesty' in the law of theft (see Theft Act 1968, s 2 and *R v Ghosh* [1982] 2 All ER 689).

53 Ibid, 183.

54 Goodin, 'Exploiting a Situation and Exploiting a Person' 187.

in certain passing circumstances, or only with respect to a narrow range of threats. The more vulnerable people are to you, and you alone, in any given situation, the stronger your duty to protect them in that circumstance.[55]

Leaving aside the issue of exploitation, the pertinent question is this: if V is vulnerable when his interests (broadly construed) are 'strongly affected' by D's actions and choices (and we might want to argue that 'affected' should suffice at this stage), in what circumstances will this be the case?[56] Goodin identifies four circumstances where V is vulnerable, and there is potential for D to breach his duties to V. Each circumstance will now be examined.

V is unfit or otherwise unable to play in games of advantage

The first suggestion is that 'it is thought wrong to play for advantage against other players who are unfit or otherwise unable to play in games of advantage'.[57] I am most interested in the idea of 'unfitness'. How should we assess unfitness? Consider the two specific examples given by Goodin. The first is that it is unfair for dieters to be offered chocolates at low prices at supermarkets checkout counters, because it plays on their weakness of will – they are to be regarded as vulnerable. The second is that 'unfitness' might (partially) explain 'why we think that drug pushers exploit addicts, and snake-oil salesmen exploit cancer patients: those people are "in no position to bargain"'.[58] However, it is doubtful whether Goodin identifies 'unfitness' in the first example.

It seems clear that dieters are not unfit (no pun intended) to play in games of advantage. The problem is that Goodin infers from their intention to diet that they have a weakened will to resist cheap sugary hits. But this point rests on faulty logic. It makes no conceptual space for the individual who might persistently be on a diet but who is not overweight at all, nor very frequently disposed to give into their will. If anything, the dieter might have greater strength of will than the general population. The point is that Goodin has not actually shown that V's will has been weakened – for that would require him to give into an offer which he finds tempting, and the example conceals this fact. It is possible that the second example does not utilise the same logic, and so fares better. The argument is that V is unfit, and is vulnerable because he is caught up in a position of extremity and/or addiction. Using the ordinary meaning of the word 'addict' would mean that V has repeatedly given in to the urge to take drugs in the past, and would therefore qualify as 'unfit'.

---

55 Ibid, 196; see also Fineman, 'The Vulnerable Subject'.
56 For a different view on what interests must be affected, see Ruth Sample, *Exploitation: What Is It and Why Is It Wrong* (Rowman & Littlefield, 2003) 74. Sample argues that relevant interests should be taken to mean 'an extreme dependency with respect to something that one needs – not merely something that one wants'.
57 Goodin, 'Exploiting a Situation and Exploiting a Person' 185.
58 Ibid.

Can an idea of unfitness shed light on vulnerability? One point is that vulnerability can derive from a person's characteristics, traits or predispositions. So a person might be vulnerable because they always assume the best in others, therefore automatically trusting them, for example: this is consistent with their character traits. Moreover, a person's characteristics may mean that they are susceptible to being vulnerable. This is consistent with the law's position of describing children and those who lack mental capacity as vulnerable. The idea is that different persons will be susceptible to being vulnerable to different extents.

The word 'unfitness' further prompts questions about V's choice in bringing about their own vulnerability. Should we say that an individual is unfit, and therefore vulnerable, because of their choices? A proper analysis would be to question the extent to which an individual has freedom to choose, especially in cases of addiction. For example, the addiction inherent in taking drugs is generally regarded as being more serious than addiction to sugar and fattening foods (though this point may be contested). Moreover, the temptation to give in to these urges may be greater, too. Thus the issue of lack of choice comes to the fore. Finally, it may be more convincing to argue that those susceptible to drug addiction have greater proximity to harm, or the risk of it, which is lacking in the dieter's example. That might support a reading of heightened vulnerability. It is surely impossible to assess vulnerability without reference to both the characteristics and choices of a person. More will be said about this example in the fourth section.

V has renounced playing for advantage themselves

Goodin's second suggestion is that a person may be vulnerable because he has renounced playing for advantage.[59] It seems plausible that this might be a way of identifying vulnerability. The reasoning is trust based: in paradigmatic close interpersonal relationships, such as that of friends and lovers, trust is at a premium. It is therefore 'deemed inappropriate (unfair, exploitative) to strive for … advantage over friends and lovers, who have renounced any such pursuit of advantage over you'.[60] V may have renounced his pursuit of advantage by agreeing to forbear for mutual benefits, or (outside of the close trust paradigm) where V has 'let down his guard' to D.[61]

If the trust-rationale is correct, we might ask why V need do anything at all to convey that he has 'renounced playing for advantage' in close intimate relationships. We might read into this set of relationships an implicit agreement to mutually forbear *because* individuals are vulnerable, morally speaking. Conversely, I assume that Goodin accepts the following key proposition: in those relationships farthest away from the intimate trust relationship paradigm, D has no reason not

59 Ibid.
60 Ibid.
61 Ibid.

to play for advantage, morally speaking. While relational norms might inform the social institutions of promise and friendship to a great(er) degree, we must not assume that two individuals have a moral obligation not to play for advantage against one another in a business context. Provided neither party breaks the criminal law, or commits a civil law wrong, it seems unproblematic to assume that both parties can play for advantage against the other. In principle, there is no reason to say that a crafty business operator should not be able to seek to drive his much weaker competitor out of business. Therefore, Goodin's point that this holds true unless one party displays 'vulnerability' by 'letting down his guard' is surprising, for reference to vulnerability is not frequently made in this context.

Probably this analysis takes too many steps. Even if we have certain moral intuitions about these cases, it is unlikely that we should want to read into intimate trust relationships that V is necessarily vulnerable because he has 'renounced playing for advantage', nor that in non-intimate trust relationships that V cannot be found to be morally vulnerable if he has 'let down his guard'. In order to refine it, we could look at Goodin's distinction between V 'renouncing playing for advantage', and V 'letting down his guard' to D. In the latter, Goodin concedes that V's 'letting down his guard' need not be completely at loggerheads with his own 'quest for egoistic advantage'.[62] I read this to mean that V need not have completely given up all claim to his own personal advancement outside of the intimate trust paradigm before he could be considered vulnerable. This seems like a necessary concession from Goodin. However, there are perhaps few examples of individuals completely giving up claim to their own advancement in life, even where they have let down their guard in an intimate trust relationship to some extent. It follows that the concession should be extended to the intimate trust relationship paradigm, too.

Suppose this modified account of identifying 'vulnerability' is plausible. Much will depend on what V needs to do in order to renounce playing for advantage. It is a shortcoming in Goodin's account that he uses difficult terminology without explaining what he means by it. What should it mean for V to 'renounce playing for advantage' in the intimate relationship paradigm, or to 'let down his guard' outside of it?

Goodin suggests that it is a question of V doing something to convey vulnerability, and this is to be taken as an objective fact judged by prevailing community norms. Of course, this means that V's own sense that he has been strongly affected by D's behaviours might not necessarily correlate with an objective view that this is the case. It is V's vulnerability in this context, judged as an objective fact, which is salient. In the fourth section I will consider what questions this poses for family lawyers. Also puzzling is the idea of V 'letting down' his guard. It does not seem to be perspicuous, at least without further explanation. What amounts to letting down one's guard? For example, would it suffice that V is in a precarious financial position? Need V make this clear to D, or to anyone else for that matter? Or will

62 Ibid.

it suffice that D has otherwise heard about it: for example, someone else hears of it and passes the information on to D?

One important point of principle should emerge: it is that V's 'letting down his guard' will need to be stronger to displace the prevailing norms as it moves farther from the intimate trust relationship paradigm. To put it differently, V must do something more to relay or manifest that he has 'let down his guard'. This is because vulnerability appears to be a more difficult concept (or perhaps does not seem as relevant) in interactions between persons in a commercial context.[63]

V is no match for D

A third example of 'vulnerability' is where D plays for advantage 'against other players who are no match for [him] in games of advantage'.[64] The argument is summarised in the following statement:

> Even in games of sport, you play only those who are a fair match for you in size or skill. This, perhaps, is the central objection to all forms of economic exploitation. In cases involving vastly disproportionate bargaining power, we think it inappropriate (unfair, exploitative) for the strong to press their advantage against a hopelessly outmatched opponent.[65]

The working assumption is that interpersonal relationships are a reason for vulnerability. So far we have seen that vulnerability may have a number of causes: V's own characteristics, traits and predispositions may be one source. We might propose that vulnerability might also come about because of the circumstances in which V finds himself. But D's involvement with V may also affect V's vulnerability. On the one hand, it is possible for D to perpetuate vulnerability that is already present. On the other hand, D might bring about V's vulnerability. The idea of D bringing about vulnerability can be with or without fault. For example, D may bring about vulnerability for V without fault in the context of a caring relationship. In fact, the caring relationship might bring about vulnerability for D, too. By contrast, bringing about vulnerability with fault is seen to be problematic, and there is provision for dealing with it in the criminal law. For example, trafficking another person into or out of the United Kingdom makes a person vulnerable to sexual or labour exploitation, and in this example the criminal law censures the trafficking itself.[66] Of course it is a logically distinct matter whether D goes on to unfairly use V's vulnerability.

The idea of 'vastly disproportionate bargaining power' draws a limit on

---

63 Vulnerability is explored here as an interpersonal concept, but there may be exceptions to this. For example, vulnerability may be relevant within a commercial setting between commercial entities.

64 Goodin, 'Exploiting a Situation and Exploiting a Person' 185.

65 Ibid.

66 See Sexual Offences Act 2003, ss 57–59; Immigration and Asylum (Treatment of Claimants, etc) Act 2004, s 4; and Coroners and Justice Act 2009, s 71.

vulnerability: since we do not often require parties to transactions to have exactly the same level of bargaining power, it might be argued that vulnerability could be understood too loosely if any level of bargaining imbalance will suffice.[67] Of course, it is possible to conceive of many different variations of interpersonal relationships, with 'vastly disproportionate bargaining power' typical of only a few.

V is in a position of grave misfortune

The final example is that an individual is vulnerable where they are in a situation of grave misfortune. In other words, it is the circumstances themselves which make a person vulnerable. This analysis would seem familiar, since we have reasonably clear ideas about what it means to be in a situation of 'grave misfortune'. But we must bear in mind that there will be more subtle factors too: an individual could be vulnerable because of institutional or societal factors. It may be the case that D has created the situation of misfortune, which leads to vulnerability (consider trafficking), and this may carry legal consequences. Alternatively we could say that circumstances of grave misfortune could aggravate V's pre-existing vulnerability. So vulnerability can derive from, or be aggravated by, an individual's circumstances.

Some implications

The idea of vulnerability must be made intelligible, and moral theory is one way to bring into focus important questions about the concept. In this section I highlight some questions, which should be examined in a more thorough way by family lawyers.

Should family law synthesise any of these moral understandings of vulnerability?

The idea of unfitness would seem to calibrate with the paradigmatic legal example of vulnerability: that is, V is vulnerable because he lacks capacity. But the practical argument is that unfitness does not explicate what it means to lack capacity – it is too vague an idea. The approach outlined in the Mental Capacity Act 2005 is a more principled tool, especially since, as we saw in the first section, the Act seeks to support an individual's capacity to make decisions where possible.

While the usefulness of unfitness should not be overstated, it does act as a prompt to other evaluative questions which are outstanding. Perhaps the most

---

67 And there may be a legal analogue to this point. In contract law, while it is generally accepted that both duress and misrepresentation are independently valid routes to set aside a contract, it is controversial whether (in the absence of illegitimate pressure or a relationship of influence) a contract can be set aside on the basis of unconscionability alone. No doubt this is partly attributable to concerns regarding maintaining the security of bargains for third parties.

important practical issue is to know when an individual will count as a 'vulnerable adult' for the purpose of the High Court's inherent jurisdiction. The assumption underlying the jurisdiction is that an individual can be vulnerable even if he has capacity for the purposes of the Mental Capacity Act. The Court of Appeal said in *A Local Authority v DL* that the inherent jurisdiction can be invoked where a person with capacity is:

> (a) under constraint; or (b) subject to coercion or undue influence; or (c) for some other reason deprived of the capacity to make the relevant decision or disabled from making a free choice, or incapacitated or disabled from giving or expressing a real and genuine consent.[68]

The argument is that the jurisdiction is required to enhance or liberate 'the autonomy of a vulnerable adult whose autonomy has been compromised by a reason other than mental incapacity'.[69] But what exactly constitutes enhancing an individual's personal autonomy when it comes to interfering in their ability to make decisions for themselves – in *A Local Authority v DL*, the decision of an elderly couple to determine their parental and financial relationship with their son? A key concern must be to develop principled jurisprudence in scenarios where V has capacity but the court is found to have inherent jurisdiction.

There are a range of possible issues here, but an idea of unfitness points to important questions about the Court of Appeal's third criterion. Do certain characteristics, traits or predispositions increase susceptibility to vulnerability? And should an idea of vulnerability be subject to exclusions in the way in which we saw that an idea of unfitness might need to be? For example, might an individual's addiction or dependency be said to cause vulnerability? There is the further question of whether the source of the addiction or dependency should matter: should only the more obvious dangers associated with alcohol and/or drugs cross a relevant threshold, or should socially accepted addictions, such as addiction to food by habitual comfort eating, suffice? Even if it is possible to isolate core examples it may be difficult to be confident about the degree or level of addiction which may be appropriate. Logically the inherent jurisdiction should operate not only where an individual is vulnerable, but in order to protect or enhance the personal autonomy of the vulnerable. But there is greater uncertainty regarding whether intervention might be justified in order to protect an addict's personal autonomy. One reason why the issue is not easily resolved is that there must be legitimate concerns surrounding personal responsibility. We might well want to say that addicts should still be held to a standard of responsibility for their actions. It remains to be answered whether there are some overarching principles which might be relevant in drawing the limits with regard to addiction and/or dependency and elucidating vulnerability. It is important to think through which ideas are core to unfitness

68 *A Local Authority v DL* [54].
69 Ibid.

The contours of 'vulnerability' 39

and which ones are marginal, because this may help to draw principled limits to the inherent jurisdiction in a way that respects personal autonomy.

Another idea is whether V – let us assume he has capacity – may be considered vulnerable because he has 'renounced playing for advantage'. I suggested that a higher threshold should be set outside of close interpersonal relationships because the idea of 'letting down one's guard' seems less relevant in commercial contexts. However, if this is accepted, focusing on close interpersonal relationships seems immediately problematic. Recall that Goodin's account requires V's renouncing playing for advantage to be objectively ascertained: that is, judged by prevailing community norms. There must be serious analysis of a number of questions: are there core instances of these norms? How should we recognise them? And who should judge whether V has renounced playing for advantage?

Moreover, ideas of 'renouncing playing for advantage' or 'letting down one's guard' jar with Dunn et al's argument in the context of health and social care practice. Dunn et al propose a distinction between an individual who is 'at risk' in the context of an objective and external reality, and an individual who is vulnerable as a subjective and experiential state.[70] The latter focuses 'on the subjective reality of a person's everyday life': vulnerability as a 'lived experience'.[71] The rationale for this approach is to avoid the 'voice' of the vulnerable adult being excluded, which would lead to their disempowerment. It appears that this supplement of subjective experience is lacking in Goodin's account. If subjective feelings of vulnerability are considered sufficiently stable to inform policy, what should it mean to place an individual 'at the heart of the decision to intervene'?[72]

It is argued here that an idea of vulnerability rests on both a contextual view of the situation V finds himself in, as well as upon V's subjective experience of vulnerability. On the one hand, V's 'renouncing playing for advantage' could provide evidence of vulnerability. Since vulnerability is often explicable in the context of a relationship, the concern is to establish whether an individual has clearly signalled that they are vulnerable. But the right approach must be to avoid reading too much into the context to decide whether an individual is vulnerable. This is because an individual's subjective experience of vulnerability may also be important, particularly where V has given consent to D but has felt pressured to do so. However, the subjective approach acts as a supplement to the contextual inquiry, since an individual could quite irrationally feel vulnerable, and another person might be unaware of their vulnerability. Further study is needed to explore the relevance of consent to ideas of vulnerability. Might an individual who has given consent at the same time renounce playing for advantage? Can a person be vulnerable where consent is given? And must this rest on an objective consideration of the facts, or an individual's feeling of vulnerability?

A third idea is that 'grossly unequal bargaining power' may be a means of

70 Dunn et al, 'To Empower or to Protect?' 245.
71 Ibid.
72 Ibid, 234.

identifying vulnerability. More precisely, it may act as evidence of V's vulnerability. If it is true that vulnerability may be discerned from an interpersonal relationship, we need to ask how far we can read into a power imbalance that V is vulnerable. Need the imbalance of bargaining power be gross, or merely present? To this end, it is important to highlight that there may be degrees of vulnerability, since imbalances in bargaining power can be subtle. On this approach, degrees can be ranged along a spectrum, and different adverbs and adjectives used to represent the different degrees. So there is a need for family lawyers to elucidate this range.

A fourth idea is that V is vulnerable when he is in a position of grave misfortune. One possible reading is that this is similar to an idea of 'situational' vulnerability already known to family lawyers. Dunn and Herring have argued that one reason why the distinction between 'external' (i.e. situational) and 'internal' (i.e. inherent) vulnerability is important is because: 'in the case of an external source of the adult's "vulnerability", the obligation to act may be stronger precisely because of the practicability of interventions that can remove the external harmful influence'.[73] However, there is a concern that judging vulnerability on the basis of circumstances alone risks extrapolating to the worst-case scenario:

> Vulnerability becomes a concept tied to the personal, social, economic and cultural circumstances within which individuals find themselves at different points of their lives, and an endemic feature of humanity. Accordingly, justifying substitute decision-making on the basis of situational vulnerability could lead to interventions that are potentially infinite in scope and application.[74]

To be rigorous, we require a better understanding not only of what it means to be vulnerable, but also of what it means to be used by another person when vulnerable. Only then can the intervention question be appropriately answered. The aims or objectives for intervention must be identified, of which one aim may be to protect the personal autonomy of persons who are vulnerable.

To that end, it would be fitting to think more thoroughly about the following two issues rather than tying them down within ideas of inherent and situational liability. First, we might separate out the issue of whether V is vulnerable only in those circumstances where D does something to gain advantage over V. This issue was apparent in Goodin's third and fourth examples. Surely the point is that V will not often be considered vulnerable in the abstract, but in relation to another individual in a particular context. More must be done to decide what relevant conduct D may need to engage in, or refrain from engaging in, and whether this might come within an account of 'vulnerability'.

A second issue is whether D should be under a legal duty to do anything about V's vulnerability. The considerations highlighted by Dunn and Herring are likely

---

73 Dunn and Herring, 'Safeguarding Children and Adults' 538.
74 Dunn et al, 'To Empower or to Protect?' 241.

to be right: the clearest case for a positive duty on D must be where V is in danger of imminent harm, and a positive duty can reasonably be expected of D. In other words, the kind of vulnerability identified may influence the type and level of legal intervention deemed appropriate. But it is difficult to understand why the two should be inextricably bound up. The better approach must be to ask what duties may attach to D in the light of V's vulnerability, however that vulnerability is construed.

To this end, applying Goodin's position on moral duties may be interesting. Recall that there are two such duties: a negative duty not to prey on V's vulnerability, and a positive duty to assist V, who is vulnerable in relation to him. Goodin advances the following thesis: if D breaches the positive duty he is less morally culpable than if he breached the negative duty.[75] Presumably this is because a duty to take positive measures to aid V is a deeper incursion on D's personal autonomy – one of its demands, if you like, is that D must make choices in favour of V. But transposing moral duties into legal duties is (probably) not so straightforward. We may expect the legal answer to vary depending on whether it is a strong duty on D to protect V, or something considerably less. Accordingly, most liberals would seem to agree with Goodin's conclusion that a positive duty to discharge responsibility should weigh less heavily upon D in the legal sphere, too. Further work should be done, however, since it seems possible to question whether this characterisation is sound.

Does a study of vulnerability point us towards the study of other cognate concepts?

The fourth section identified some evaluative questions which family lawyers need to support with analysis. In this brief section, the question is whether vulnerability points towards the study of other cognate concepts. It is argued that even if it is possible to come up with a complete explanation of vulnerability, only so much rests on it. It is a further question whether there are other concepts which may need to be given close attention, and we might tentatively add that they may provide the justificatory basis for legal intervention. On this view, vulnerability may only be part of what we must make moves to understand. If correct, this may set up an interesting new direction for future discussion.

This is not a particularly far-fetched hypothesis. As a matter of ordinary language, it seems to be the case that when we ask whether an individual is vulnerable, we expect to know what they are vulnerable to, be it sexual or financial exploitation, coercion or manipulation. A further point is that there seems to be strong reason to suggest that 'vulnerability' is considered a necessary but not sufficient condition for legal intervention in the context of the care of 'vulnerable adults'. Commentators have highlighted that the Law Commission conceptualised 'vulnerability' as a threshold criterion in their report on mental capacity: 'the

---

75 Goodin, 'Exploiting a Situation and Exploiting a Person' 167.

fact that a person is vulnerable … only means that he or she *may* need services and has a *potential* for suffering harm or serious exploitation'.[76]

The argument then is that there is a danger of overestimating just how much 'vulnerability' can achieve for family law. In principle there may be other forms of problematic behaviour which vulnerability may act as a pointer to. This may be part of the value of using Goodin's account of exploitation to elucidate vulnerability, since it explores the concept within an analysis of other cognate concepts.

Needless to say, the outstanding question is: what other concepts may vulnerability act as a pointer to? For example, in the light of the Law Commission's report on mental incapacity, it seems possible to forge new connections between vulnerability and exploitation. We may want to be concerned to understand conduct which exploitatively preys on vulnerable individuals. However, exploitation presents a difficult subset of issues. It is impossible to understand exploitation without considering the relevance of consent and harm, and these factors require careful exposition.[77] The point of this brief discussion is to argue that vulnerability may have an 'opening-up' function in family law. In order to make progress, we should seek increased exposure to cognate concepts to 'vulnerability'.

Conclusion

The fact that 'vulnerability' is an important idea in family law does not mean that the normative argument that it be 'centralised' succeeds. Since vulnerability is not a unitary idea there may be all sorts of reasons for, and ways of, paying attention to the concept. But we should seek first to elicit a better understanding of vulnerability, and to pay sufficient regard to the complexities presented by the concept, some of which are highlighted in this chapter. Viewing vulnerability as a real-life concept emphasises that there will be core features which are identifiable, but also difficult marginal issues for family lawyers to consider.

What if an adequate explanation of vulnerability as a real-life concept can be found? I have argued that there is another reason to resist the centralising tendency in relation to 'vulnerability'. It is unlikely that vulnerability will always suffice to operate as an organising principle or justification for legal intervention. It seems plausible to assume that the task of elucidating vulnerability is tied to other problems. If this is correct, close attention must be given to highlighting them, namely by bringing to the surface cognate concepts which are ripe for analysis.

---

76 Dunn et al, 'To Empower or to Protect?' 249; see also Law Commission, *Mental Incapacity* 163.
77 For an argument that vulnerability and/or exploitation may have effects on the validity of consent where V has suffered physical harm, see J. Tolmie, 'Consent to Harmful Assaults: The Case for Moving Away from Category Based Decision Making' [2012] *Crim LR* 656, 660.

Chapter 3

Making family law more careful

Jonathan Herring

Introduction

Traditionally sexual relationships between adults have been the focus of family law textbooks and legal analysis. Marriage, Civil Partnership and Cohabitation are foundational subjects in any family law course. While it is true that in recent times parenthood has come to play a more prominent role for family lawyers, legal understandings of parenthood are classically seen to flow from sexual relationships between parents. Family law is still shackled by the heteronormative ideals of parenthood.[1] We need to break away from the narrow focus on sex and biological parenthood and appreciate that what in fact we ought to be promoting, protecting and regulating are caring relationships. Family law needs to be less sexy and more careful.

This chapter will start with a brief analysis of caring and its place in family life and society. It will then progress to outline the key elements in an ethic of care, which will be relied upon to provide an ethical foundation for family law. The chapter will then turn to consider what a family law focused on an ethic of care would look like.

Family and care

As explained in the Introduction, care and particularly care within the home has been a major part of many women's lives throughout history. That includes providing care work in their own home and providing care work for wealthier people. Pregnancy, nursing, cleaning, washing, food preparation and 'domestic economy' were the mainstays of life. As a substantial literature on care shows these practices have been ignored and devalued in law generally. By regarding such care work as 'family work' the law generally has been able to sideline care as not a subject of the public law's focus. Perhaps surprisingly it has also been sidelined within family law. Of course, it would be wrong to assume that care only takes place within a

---

1 Julie McCandless and Sally Sheldon, 'The Human Fertilisation and Embryology Act 2008 and the Tenacity of the Sexual Family Form' (2010) 73(2) *MLR* 175.

family. Indeed care outside a traditional family model is rendered utterly invisible by assumptions that care is a private family matter.

The argument will be developed later, but the emphasis on the sexual relationship being at the heart of family life has reinforced the need for privacy. The equation of family life with sexual relationships naturally leads to concerns that the law should not pry too deeply into the intimate life of the couple. The mysteries and subtleties of family relationships cannot be subject to too close an inspection. The equation of family life and sexual life also reinforces the idea that family life is not particularly important for the public good. All of this leads to a prioritising of the values of privacy and autonomy within the family. This chapter advocates a rather different approach, one based on an ethics of care.

Ethics of care

Many commentators reflecting on the ethical and legal responses to caring relationships have been drawn to an ethic of care.[2] This approach provides a challenge to the way legal rights and responsibilities are commonly understood. The standard approach to rights is based on the assumption that we are competent, detached, independent people who are entitled to have our rights of self-determination and autonomy fiercely protected.[3] This sees the role of legal rights and rules as being to draw boundaries around ourselves and protect us from interference from others. However, this image of us is false. The reality is that we are ignorant, vulnerable, interdependent individuals. Our strength and reality is not in our autonomy, but our relationships with others.[4] An approach based on an ethic of care seeks to use these facts as a starting point to the law's response. It starts with a norm of interlocking mutually interdependent relationships, rather than an individualised vision of rights.[5] The role of rights and interests is not to protect individuals per se,

2 Leading works on ethics of care include: Carol Gilligan, 'Moral Orientation and Moral Development' in Eva Kittay and Diana Meyers (eds) *Women and Moral Theory* (Rowman & Littlefield, 1987); Milton Mayeroff, *On Caring* (William Morrow, 1990) 19–33; Marilyn Friedman, 'Liberating Care' in Marilyn Friedman, *What Are Friends For? Feminist Perspectives on Personal Relationships and Moral Theory* (Cornell University Press, 1993) 142–83; Joan Tronto, *Moral Boundaries: A Political Argument for an Ethic of Care* (Routledge, 1993); Selma Sevenhuijsen, *Citizenship and the Ethics of Care: Feminist Considerations on Justice, Morality, and Politics* (trans. Liz Savage, Routledge, 1998); Nel Noddings, *Educating Moral People: A Caring Alternative to Character Education* (Teachers College Press 2002); Nel Noddings, *Starting at Home: Caring and Social Policy* (University of California Press 2002); Eva Feder Kittay, *Love's Labour: Essays on Women, Equality and Dependency* (Routledge, 1998); Ruth Groenhout, *Connected Lives: Human Nature and an Ethics of Care* (Rowman & Littlefield, 2004); Virginia Held, *The Ethics of Care* (Oxford University Press, 2006); Daniel Engster, *The Heart of Justice: Care Ethics and Political Theory* (Oxford University Press, 2007); Jo Bridgeman, *Parental Responsibility, Young Children and Healthcare Law* (Cambridge University Press, 2007); Jonathan Herring, *Caring and the Law* (Hart, 2013).
3 Liz Lloyd, 'Mortality and Morality: Ageing and the Ethics of Care' (2004) 24(2) *Ageing and Society* 235.
4 Christopher Meyer, 'Cruel Choices: Autonomy and Critical Care Decision-Making' (2004) 18(2) *Bioethics* 104.
5 Robin West, *Caring for Justice* (New York University Press, 1997) 356.

but to uphold and maintain networks of relationships. This is not downgrading the value of people, because it is in their relationships that people will find value and meaning in their lives.

Much has been written on an ethic of care. I will, here, just summarise some of the main themes, before returning to the significance for family law.

Care is part of being human

We all have needs, and caring for others in meeting these needs is a universal experience.[6] Dependency and care are an inevitable part of being human.[7] Caring relationships are the very stuff of life.[8] Wendy Hollway argues that 'care is the psychological equivalent to our need to breathe unpolluted air'.[9]

Martha Fineman has argued that looking at a typical lifespan there will be times of different capacity and strengths. The typical 'adult liberal subject' focuses on just one part of that lifespan, one where there are typically fewest needs and fewest caring responsibilities, and essentialises that as the norm for all people. We could take other sections of the typical lifespan as the norm and have a very different ideal around which to base a legal system. As Martha Fineman argues:

> The vulnerability approach recognizes that individuals are anchored at each end of their lives by dependency and the absence of capacity. Of course, between these ends, loss of capacity and dependence may also occur, temporarily for many and permanently for some as a result of disability or illness. Constant and variable throughout life, individual vulnerability encompasses not only damage that has been done in the past and speculative harms of the distant future, but also the possibility of immediate harm. We are beings who live with the ever-present possibility that our needs and circumstances will change. On an individual level, the concept of vulnerability (unlike that of liberal autonomy) captures this present potential for each of us to become dependent based upon our persistent susceptibility to misfortune and catastrophe.[10]

I would go further and question whether even in our 'prime' we do have the kind of autonomy and capacity traditional liberalism claims for adults. My point

---

6 Held, *The Ethics of Care* ch 1.

7 Martha Fineman, *The Autonomy Myth: A Theory of Dependency* (The New Press, 2004) xvii; Traci Levy, 'The Relational Self and the Right to Give Care' (2006) 28(4) *New Political Science* 547.

8 Fiona Williams, 'The Presence of Feminism in the Future of Welfare' (2002) 31(4) *Economy and Society* 502.

9 Wendy Hollway, 'Introducing the Capacity to Care' in Wendy Hollway (ed.), *The Capacity to Care: Gender and Ethical Subjectivity* (Routledge, 2006) 1–22.

10 Martha Fineman, 'The Vulnerable Subject: Anchoring Equality in the Human Condition' in Martha Fineman (ed.), *Transcending the Boundaries of Law: Generations of Feminism and Legal Theory* (Routledge, 2011) 168.

is that we are *all* vulnerable.[11] We are all profoundly dependent on others for our physical and psychological well-being.[12] Our society has built up a wide range of structures and forms of assistance which disguise our vulnerability. Indeed we are forced by a wide range of societal pressures to disguise or mitigate our vulnerability so that we can behave in an acceptable way in the public realm. In a powerful article Kate Lindemann contrasts the emphasis that is paid to the accommodations for disabled people so as to minimise the impact of their disability, with the lack of appreciation of the similar accommodations for the able bodied:

> Colleagues, professional staff members, and other adults are unconscious of the numerous accommodations that society provides to make their work and life style possible. ATMs, extended hours in banks, shopping centres and medical offices, EZpass, newspaper kiosks, and elevators are all accommodations that make contemporary working life possible. There are entire industries devoted to accommodating the needs of adult working people. Fast food, office lunch delivery, day time child care, respite care, car washing, personal care attendants, interpreters, house cleaning, and yard and lawn services are all occupations that provide services that make it possible for adults to hold full time jobs.[13]

We thus highlight the facilities used to deal with the vulnerabilities of others, while overlooking the accommodations 'we' need to deal with our vulnerabilities. Further, we readily class those who need care from others as vulnerable, without seeing the vulnerability that caring creates for 'us'.[14]

Care is a good part of life

Not only is care an inevitable part of life, it is a good part of life. Care should be treasured and valued. Care is the manifestation of that most basic moral value: love. It involves meeting the needs of others, which is a primary good.[15]

There is, however, a danger here, because if we see care as a good because it meets needs, it might be assumed that having needs is bad. There is no doubt that

---

11 Martha Fineman, 'Responsibility, Family and the Limits of Equality: An American Perspective' in Craig Lind, Heather Keating and Jo Bridgeman (eds), *Taking Responsibility, Law and the Changing Family* (Ashgate, 2011).

12 Groenhout, *Connected Lives*.

13 Kate Lindemann, 'The Ethics of Receiving' (2003) 24(6) *Theoretical Medicine and Bioethics* 501, 502.

14 Bill Hughes, Linda McKie, Debra Hopkins and Nick Watson, 'Love's Labour's Lost? Feminism, the Disabled People's Movement and an Ethic of Care' (2005) 39 *Sociology* 259.

15 Sarah Clark Miller, 'Need, Care and Obligation' (2005) 80(57) *Royal Institute of Philosophy Supplement* 137.

dependency and vulnerability are commonly assumed to be bad things. David Archard, writing on childhood, has stated:

> There may be features of childhood but not of adulthood which are valuable, such as innocence, wonder and trust. There may, correspondingly be features of adulthood but not childhood which are valuable, such as experience and independence. It is also evident that there may be features of childhood but not of adulthood which are not valuable, such as dependence and vulnerability.[16]

Such a view is profoundly mistaken. Vulnerability and dependence are not only inevitable parts of humanity, they are greatly to be welcomed. They are often virtues, not vices.

Self-reliance has become a dominant theme in social policy.[17] Be it lone parents or care in the community, autonomy and independence have become key policy goals. But this ignores the fact that as humans we are interdependent.[18] Any personal achievements are typically the product of many people's efforts.[19] No one can be truly independent.

Emotions are ethically significant

Much of the law emphasises the importance of rationality and intellect. The concepts of mental capacity, informed consent, compliance with standards expected by a responsible body of opinion – all privilege in legal discourse logical thought and sound judgement. There is nothing wrong in that, but the emotional side of humanity is lost. The love which goes on caring and caring, the grief, disappointment, frustration, anger and despair, which are all part of life, find no place.[20] The exclusion of emotion means the voice of carers talking about how their cared-for one should be looked after finds no ready legal mouthpiece. The law struggles often to respond to issues which are not readily reducible to an economic value nor expressed in terms of individualised rights. That can be seen, for example, in the law of tort where damages for an economic loss are readily recoverable, whereas loss for distress, unwanted pregnancy or bereavement find the courts

16 David Archard, 'Philosophical Perspectives on Childhood' in Julia Fionda (ed.), *Legal Concepts of Childhood* (Hart, 2001) 43, 52.

17 Knut Halvorsen, 'Symbolic Purposes and Factual Consequences of the Concepts "Self-Reliance" and "Dependency" in Contemporary Discourses on Welfare' (1998) 7(1) *International Journal of Social Welfare* 56.

18 Susan Dodds, 'Gender, Ageing, and Injustice: Social and Political Contexts of Bioethics' (2005) 31(5) *Journal of Medical Ethics* 295.

19 Michael Fine and Caroline Glendinning, 'Dependence, Independence or Interdependence? Revisiting the Concepts of "Care" and "Dependency"' (2005) 25(4) *Ageing and Society* 601.

20 Occasionally it peeps through (see the refusal of the medical team who had done so much work to care for the patient in *Re B (Adult: Refusal of Medical Treatment)* [2002] All ER 449 that they felt unable to switch off her life support machine as the court ultimately ordered).

struggling to produce a coherent response. An ethic of care seeks to acknowledge the role that emotion and rationality plays in relationships. We do not live by rational thoughts alone.[21]

Intermingled interests

An ethic of care is based on the belief that persons see themselves as relational. They do not seek to promote their own interests, not because they are 'selfless' but because their interests are tied up with the interests of others. They cannot seek to promote their own interests with no attention paid to others. It is the improvement of the relationship they seek. If good things happen to those they are in a positive relationship with, then that is good for them. And if bad things happen that is bad for them.

An ethic of care, therefore, takes a particular view of the nature of the self.[22] One that is constructed through and finds its meanings in relation to others.[23] Supporters of an ethic of care do not need entirely to reject the notion of an individual self; simply recognise that its identity and nature can only be appreciated through relation to others.[24] As Catriona Mackenzie writes: 'To be a person is to be a temporally extended embodied subject whose identity is constituted in and through one's lived bodily engagement with the world and others.'[25] This can produce complex psychological tensions, as explained by Polona Curk:

> Intimacy constitutes the self as a dynamic entity, constructing its meanings (including the meaning of oneself) in close relationships with others. This immediately evokes vulnerability at the foundation of such meaning-making, based in the dynamics that includes both dependency and power relationship with the intimate other. These are held in mind in a shaky balance, with a constant defensive tendency to repudiate and hide one's own needy and vulnerable parts. Yet the desire to relate to another continually re-opens issues of attachments and mutual dependencies.[26]

21　Allan Gibbard, *Wise Choices, Apt Feelings: A Theory of Normative Judgement* (Harvard University Press, 1990); and Simon Blackburn, *Ruling Passions: A Theory of Practical Reasoning* (Clarendon Press, 1998).

22　Susan Sherwin, 'A Relational Approach to Autonomy in Health Care' in Susan Sherwin (ed.), *Politics of Women's Health: Exploring Agency and Autonomy* (Temple University Press, 1998) 19.

23　Chris Crittenden, 'The Principles of Care' (2001) 22(2) *Journal of Women, Politics & Policy* 81; Susan Andersen and Serena Chen, 'The Relational Self: An Interpersonal Social–Cognitive Theory' (2002) 109(4) *Psychological Review* 619–45; Jonathon Brown, *The Self* (McGraw-Hill, 1998).

24　Jocelyn Downie and Jennifer Llewellyn, *Being Relational* (University of British Columbia Press, 2011).

25　Catriona Mackenzie, 'Personal Identity, Narrative Integration and Embodiment' in Sue Campbell, Letitia Meynell and Susan Sherwin (eds), *Embodiment and Agency* (Pennsylvania State University Press, 2009); Polona Curk, 'Passions, Dependencies, Selves: A Theoretical Psychoanalytic Account of Relational Responsibility' in Lind et al (eds), *Taking Responsibility*.

26　Polona Curk, 'Passions, Dependencies, Selves: A Theoretical Psychoanalytic Account of Relational Responsibility' in Lind et al (eds), *Taking Responsibility*; Marilyn Friedman, 'Feminist and Modern Friendship' in Carl Sustein (ed.), *Feminism and Political Theory* (University of Chicago Press, 1990).

In relationships of caring and dependency interests become intermingled.[27] We do not break down into 'me' and 'you'. To harm one person in a caring relationship is to harm the other. There should be no talk of balancing the interests of 'the carer' and the person 'cared for'. A better approach is to emphasise the responsibilities they owe to each other in the context of a mutually supporting relationship.[28] Indeed in a caring relationship each party is caring for each other and we should move away from the language of 'carer' and 'cared for'.

The importance of responsibilities

Ethics of care emphasise the importance of responsibilities within caring relationships. While not necessarily opposed to the idea of legal rights, they are wary of the dominance in the legal discourse that they have obtained, and the dangers that rights are used in an individualistic way. Supporters of ethic of care argue that rather than the primary focus of the legal or ethical enquiry being whether it is my right to do X, the question should be: what is my proper obligation within the context of this relationship?[29] Rights primarily exist to enable people to carry out their responsibilities.[30]

The classic liberal perspective is that one is 'born free' and that any responsibilities one takes must be in some sense voluntarily assumed.[31] However, for an ethic of care approach, with its starting point being that people are relational, then the supposition is there will be responsibilities for others. We are born into relationships which then carry responsibilities.

Therefore, the question is not: is there a good reason to restrict my freedom? But, rather: is it possible to have some freedom, given the responsibilities of those I am connected to? This might to some seem shocking. Surely, they say, we should start with a presumption of freedom, rather than responsibility. However, I suggest two reasons why we should not. First, this reflects the reality of life for most people. Our lives are not marked by freedom, but by our responsibilities to others. There is no one who has not benefited from a relationship with another, in gestation, birth and being raised as a child at the very least. Second, it is in our responsibilities that relationships flourish and in our relationships that we flourish. As Polona Curk puts it: 'We take responsibility for each other because we continue to need each other and because we establish meaningful relationships through taking responsibility for each other.'[32]

---

27 Tom Shakespeare, *Help: Imagining Welfare* (Venture Press, 2000).
28 Grace Clement, *Care, Autonomy and Justice: Feminism and the Ethic of Care* (Westview Press, 1996) 11.
29 Held, *The Ethics of Care* 15.
30 Fiona Williams, 'The Presence of Feminism in the Future of Welfare' (2002) 31(4) *Economy and Society* 502.
31 Victoria Davion, 'Autonomy, Integrity, and Care' (1993) 19(2) *Social Theory and Practice* 161.
32 Polona Curk, 'Passions, Dependencies, Selves'.

The sexiness of family law

Traditionally family law has focused on sexual relationships. Marriage and cohabitation are still major themes in family law. Typically textbooks on family law open with an explanation of the law of marriage, with an overly detailed analysis of the law on consummation. The authors explain that other relationships which are marriage-like (by which is meant sexual relationships) are protected in varying degrees. Moving on to parenthood, students are taught that parenthood is paradigmatically established by marriage or the biological link. While textbooks on family law have extensive chapters on marriage, cohabitation and parenthood little is written on, for example, the relationships between an adult child and her parent; a parent and an adult disabled child; a friend and someone with a disability; or the position of older people in families. Sex and blood ties are the meat and bones of family law.

The centrality of sex to current understandings of marriage are laid bare by the Marriage (Same Sex Couples) Act 2013. While the Bill is designed to ensure that equal marriage is available to same-sex and opposite sex couples, Part 3 of Schedule 4 of the Act means that differences will remain. Non-consummation will not be a ground of annulment between a same-sex couple, but it will for opposite sex couples. Further, the definition of adultery will be restricted to opposite-sex couples. Conservative commentators have been quick to pick up on this as revealing that same-sex marriage cannot be the same as opposite-sex marriage.[33]

The case against same-sex marriage has rested on the significance of sex. Leading commentators Roger Scruton and Phillip Blond argue:

> Put simply, there are two competing ideas of marriage at play in the current debate. The first is traditional and conjugal and extends beyond the individuals who marry to the children they hope to create and the society they wish to shape. The second is more privative and is to do with a relationship abstracted from the wider concern that marriage originally was designed to speak to. Some call this pure partnership or mere cohabitation …
>
> Conjugal marriage has several strengths which partnership marriage does not. It is inherently normative, which is fundamentally good, for it stabilises and secures people in their most profound relationships. Conjugal marriage cannot celebrate an infinite array of sexual or intimate choices as equally desirable or valid. Instead, its very purpose lies in channelling the erotic and interpersonal impulses between men and women in a particular direction: one in which men and women commit to each other

---

33 See eg Anglican Mainstream, 'Consummation, adultery, and the physical impossibility of sex outside of marriage' (www.anglican-mainstream.net/2013/02/04/consummation-adultery-and-the-physical-impossibility-of-sex-outside-of-marriage/, accessed 27 April 2013).

and to the children that their sexual unions commonly (and even at times unexpectedly) produce.[34]

Much could be said about these comments, but it is notable how what they describe as the traditional and conjugal model focuses on the sexual relationship as central to the definition of marriage.

Gillian Douglas notes that over the last fifty years parenthood has gradually replaced marriage as 'the organizing principle and cornerstone of family law in England and Wales'.[35] That, however, may be an exaggeration. Marriage still plays a major role in proof of parenthood. For example, a husband of a mother is automatically presumed to be the father, while an unmarried partner would need to establish his paternity through a parental agreement, court order or being registered as the father on the birth certificate.[36] As a result of the allocation of parenthood, married and unmarried fathers are treated differently for the purposes of allocation of parental responsibility. In the financial consequences of separation for parents, marriage still plays a major role. Carol Smart notes that the

> thinking behind the Children Act presumed that a distinction could be made between adult/adult relationships and adult/child relationships within a marriage (or cohabitation). Thus part of the argument resided in the idea that while divorce would foreclose on the spousal relationship, it need not affect the parents' relationship with the child. Thus two sets of relationships are envisaged which appear to be autonomous of one another and which can operate independently of one another.[37]

As Smart goes on to argue, we cannot treat the parents' relationship with their children as separate from their relationship with each other.

Writing in 2008 Lisa Glennon comments that:

> Marriage remains the central adult relationship to which obligations legitimately attach notwithstanding that these find expression, not during the relationship, but on divorce where strict property entitlements can be overridden, and maintenance obligations imposed at the court's discretion. Thus it is the ancillary relief system, which allocates capital and income on divorce, that is most expressive of the legal obligations created by marriage.[38]

34 Roger Scruton and Phillip Blond, 'Marriage equality or the destruction of difference?', ABC, *Religion and Ethics*, 4 February 2013 (http:www.abc.net.au/religion/articles/2013/02/04/3682721. htm, accessed 27 April 2013).

35 Gillian Douglas, 'Marriage, Cohabitation, and Parenthood – From Contract to Status?' in Sanford Katz, John Eekelaar and Mavis Maclean (eds), *Cross Currents: Family Law and Policy in the US and England* (Oxford University Press, 2005) 211.

36 See Jonathan Herring, *Family Law* (Pearson, 2011) ch 7, for the detail.

37 Carol Smart, 'The "New" Parenthood: Fathers and Mothers after Divorce' in Carol Smart and Elizabeth Silva (eds), *The New Family?* (Sage, 1999) 100.

38 Lisa Glennon, 'Obligations between Adult Partners: Moving from Form to Function?' (2008) 22 *International Journal of Law, Policy and the Family* 22.

More than this we see even in the law on parenthood an emphasis on the genetic connection to the child, typically through the sexual act, as determining parenthood. The current approach of the law is based on the heterosexual married model, with its presumption that a husband is the father of his wife's child and that a child have one father and one mother.[39] That a moment's ejaculation makes a father, but months of care does not, speaks volumes about the emphasis in family law on sex over care.

The function of family law

A popular starting point in deciding the nature of family law is to focus on what would be regarded as the functions of family law.[40] This is a dangerous approach to take. It is easy to assume what functions family law has and from that form a particular image of the family. Nevertheless, it is helpful to identify what family law is trying to do. I would respectfully adopt John Eekelaar's[41] suggestion of three primary functions of family law:

(1) Protective: to guard members of a family from physical, emotional or economic harm.
(2) Adjustive: to help families which have broken down to adjust to new lives apart.
(3) Supportive: to encourage and support family life.[42]

My claim will be that for each of these roles the existence of a sexual relationship between the parties is irrelevant. Rather, a caring relationship should be key.

Protective

One crucial role of family law is to tackle domestic abuse. For now it is sufficient to emphasise a sexual element is not a prerequisite for domestic abuse. The violence, structural inequality or coercive control which can mark domestic abuse can occur in non-sexual as well as sexual relationships[43] as the writing on abuse

---

39 Julie Wallbank, 'Channelling the Messiness of Diverse Family Lives: Resisting the Calls to Order and De-centring the Hetero-Normative Family' (2010) 32 *Journal of Social Welfare and Family Law* 353.
40 See N. Polikoff, *Beyond (Straight and Gay) Marriage* (Beacon Press, 2008).
41 John Eekelaar, *Family Law and Social Policy* (Weidenfeld & Nicolson, 1984) 24–6. For the difficulties and dangers of using a functionalist approach, see John Dewar, 'The Normal Chaos of Family Law' (1998) 61 *Modern Law Review* 467.
42 The extent to which family law should facilitate, rather than support, family law is open to considerable debate.
43 Although, of course, sexual relations might be one part of structural inequality in a particular relationship. Occasionally in England the courts have been willing to grant parents non-molestation orders against their violent teenage children: *Re H* [2001] 1 *FLR* 641.

of the elderly shows.[44] It is the intimacy of the relationship, not its sexual nature, which is key to the wrong in domestic violence. Therefore this function of family law is correctly focused not on sexual relationships, but on intimate ones, typically marked by care.

Some have questioned whether an ethic of care can provide an effective protection against abuse within a close relationship. I argue it can. Indeed it is uniquely well placed to do so.[45] Because an ethic of care places such weight on the importance of the quality of the relationship it is able to recognise the severity of the wrong that takes place in intimate abuse. The wrongs of breach of trust and coercive control which are central to an understanding of domestic abuse can only be fully appreciated by a deeply relational approach.[46] Further, if caring relationships are to be nurtured and promoted, then it is essential that they are safe places to be and that those entering intimate relationships can be confident they will be protected. The failure to respond effectively to domestic abuse is a central part of the way the law has failed to value caring relationships adequately.

The other area of protection which is central to family is protection from financial exploitation. In particular, the law on financial orders on divorce ensures that one party does not leave the relationship with an unfair share of the economic benefits or disadvantages of the relationship. Care work is closely tied to financial inequality. In a relationship in which neither party has to dedicate significant amounts of time to care for others, it is unlikely there is any financial unfairness that requires a remedy. Sexual relationships do not themselves cause financial loss! Caring relationships typically do.[47]

The extent of disadvantage for women on divorce[48] is closely related to their employment history during marriage.[49] There is convincing evidence that following divorce those who have undertaken primary care of the child (normally the wife) suffer significantly.[50] Childcare responsibilities mean that women are far more likely to have given up employment than men; and where they are employed, mothers are more often in part-time, low-status, poorly paid jobs.[51]

44 See eg Jonathan Herring, *Older People in Law and Society* (Oxford University Press, 2010).

45 Virginia Held, 'Can the Ethics of Care Handle Violence?' (2010) 4(2) *Ethics and Social Welfare* 115.

46 Jonathan Herring, 'The Serious Wrong of Domestic Abuse and the Loss of Control Defence' in Alan Reed and Michael Bohlander (eds), *Loss of Control and Diminished Responsibility: Domestic, Comparative and International Perspectives* (Ashgate, 2011) 65–78.

47 See further, eg Lisa Glennon, 'Obligations between Adult Partners: Moving from Form to Function?' (2008) 22(1) *International Journal of Law, Policy and the Family* 22.

48 Karen Funder, 'Women, Work and Post-Divorce Economic Self-Sufficiency: An Australian Perspective' in Marie Thérèse Meulders-Klein and John Eekelaar (eds), *Family, State and Individual Economic Security* (Kluwer, 1988).

49 For a useful discussion of compensation claims, see Ashley Murray, 'Guidelines on Compensation' (2008) 38 *Fam Law* 756.

50 Shirely Dex, Kelly Ward and Heather Joshi, 'Changes in Women's Occupations and Occupational Mobility over 25 Years' (Centre for Longitudinal Studies, CLS Working Paper 2006/1).

51 Jacqueline Scott and Shirely Dex, 'Paid and Unpaid Work' in Joanna Miles and Rebecca Probert (eds), *Sharing Lives, Dividing Assets* (Hart, 2009).

Even where they have returned to full-time employment, the time taken out to care for children will have set back their earning potential.[52] The conclusions of a recent study of the impact of divorce on women was blunt:

> The stark conclusion is that men's household income increases by about 23 per cent on divorce once we control for household size, whereas women's household income falls by about 31 per cent. There is partial recovery for women, but this recovery is driven by repartnering: the average effect of repartnering is to restore income to pre-divorce levels after nine years. Those who do not repartner ... the long term economic consequences of divorce are serious.[53]

The need for the protection function of family law is, therefore, not in respect of sexual relationships, but rather relationships of care.

Adjustive

As to the adjustive role, a primary function of family law is to ensure that at the end of a relationship, suitable arrangements are made for any child who has been living with the parties and to ensure a suitable distribution of the assets of the marriage. Again both of these are required whether there is a sexual relationship between the parties or not. While there may be some debate over whether there is an appropriate difference in the way property is distributed between those who have formalised their relationships in marriage or civil partnerships and those who have not, the sexual nature of their relationships seems particularly irrelevant to the discussion, as we have seen.

A caring perspective is crucial to determine the legal response to couples who have a dispute over their children. Children, as we all do, live in the context of relationships. We cannot separate either the welfare or the rights of children from their parents. Their interests and rights are so intertwined and the parties so interdependent that to consider what order will promote the welfare of the child, as an isolated individual, and without consideration of the interests of the parents, is simply an impossibility.[54]

A care-centred approach would require us to consider the child in the network of relationships within which they live. Relationship-based welfare[55] argues that children should be brought up in relationships which overall promote their

---

52 Ibid.
53 Hayley Fisher and Hamish Low, 'Who Wins, Who Loses and Who Recovers from Divorce?' in Jo Miles and Rebecca Probert (eds) *Sharing Lives* 254.
54 Jonathan Herring, 'The Human Rights Act and the Welfare Principle in Family Law – Conflicting or Complementary?'(1999) 11 *CFLQ* 223.
55 Ibid; see also Jo Bridgeman, 'Children with Exceptional Needs: Welfare, Rights and Caring Responsibilities' in Julie Wallbank, Shazia Choudhry and Jonathan Herring (eds), *Rights, Gender and Family Law* (Routledge 2010) 239–56.

welfare.[56] Relationships are central to the lives of children and so should be at the centre of decisions about their lives.[57] It is beneficial for a child to be brought up in a family that is based on relationships which are fair and just. A relationship based on unacceptable demands on a parent is not furthering a child's welfare. Indeed, it is impossible to construct an approach to looking at a child's welfare which ignores the web of relationships within which the child is brought up. Supporting the child means supporting the caregiver and supporting the caregiver means supporting the child.[58] In making decisions about children the court should look back at the relationships within which the child lived and look forward to the burdens and benefits the future may bring.

Supportive

It is in the supportive function of family law where there is likely to be most dispute. Are sexual relations between adults, or even particular kinds of sexual relationship, of such significance that they deserve promotion through the law?[59] I would argue that what might make a relationship worthy of promotion by the state is care and mutual support, rather than sex. To be blunt, society does not really gain much from a couple having sex, however pleasurable it may be for the participants! However, the state does benefit from care, particularly where that is of a person whose needs would otherwise fall on the state. It is such relationships that should receive the support of the state. Whether the relationship has a sexual side is a red herring.

It might be argued that given the fluid nature of care, we can use sex as a proxy for care. However, that is a very weak argument. Nowadays sexual relationships often take place in the context of casual relationships. Any assumption that sex is a sign of commitment looks terribly old-fashioned. Certainly care can take place outside a sexual relationship.

And, if sex is not a good marker of commitment or intimacy, why should it be of any legal significance?[60] The only answer seems to be that society has an interest in ensuring that sex takes place in order to produce a sufficient number of children. However, the vast majority of sexual encounters do not produce children. Further, at least currently in Western Europe it is the care of children that poses far greater challenges than their production.[61] If the law or state is to

---

56 Selma Sevenhuijsen, 'A Third Way? Moralities, Ethics and Families: An Approach through the Ethic of Care' in Alan Carling, Simon Duncan and Rosalind Edwards (eds), *Analysing Families* (Routledge, 2002) 129.

57 Matthew Kavanagh, 'Rewriting the Legal Family: Beyond Exclusivity to a Care-based Standard' (2004) 16 *Yale Journal of Law and Feminism* 83.

58 Ibid.

59 Linda McClain, 'Love, Marriage, and the Baby Carriage: Revisiting the Channelling Function of Family Law' (2007) 28(101) *Cardozo L Rev* 2133.

60 This is not to say I think the Burdens should not pay inheritance tax. That is an issue which raises broader issues about inheritance taxation policy (see Herring, *Older People* ch 9).

61 Laura Kessler, 'Community Parenting' (2007) 24 *Wash U JL & Pol'y* 47.

promote certain kinds of relationship through family law, it should do so for caring relationships, rather than sexual ones.[62]

An alternative vision for family law might focus on relationships of care for dependants, rather than sexual relationships.[63] This would make the carer–dependant the paradigm relationship for family law, rather than marriage.[64] That would produce a very different kind of family law. The focus of state support and legal confirmation would not be marriage-like sexual relationships, but rather be those in which care is provided and received. This would make the primary focus of family law in some ways narrower (there might be some marriages in which there was insufficient caring of dependency to justify legal support) while there would be other relationships of care not currently covered (eg an adult caring for an older dependent relative) which would be covered. It would move closer to adopting Iris Marion Young's[65] definition of a family:

> as people who live together and/or share resources necessary to the means for life and comfort; who are committed to caring for one another's physical and emotional needs to the best of their ability.

There are signs of this happening.[66] England has shifted its support in the tax system away from marriage and towards those who raise children, by replacing married couples' tax allowance with child tax credits, but is still behind in failing to adequately support those who care for dependent adults.[67]

This last comment highlights two difficulties with my approach. First, how can we determine when the degree of care and commitment in a relationship is sufficient to justify state protection and legal recognition? I accept that the current family law legal system with its focus on marriage and civil partnership has an ease of use which would be lost by a focus on care and commitment. Nevertheless I believe that there are many relationships of care where there is a need for the adjustive, protective and supportive functions of family law to be used, but which fall outside the scope of the law. The plight of those whose care goes unrecognised and unrewarded justifies any increased bureaucratic difficulties.

The second is that if we are to centre care we should abandon the terminology 'family law'. This claim is likely to be made by those who think that there

---

62 Jonathan Herring, 'Caregivers in Medical Law and Ethics' (2008) 25 *J Contemp Health L & Pol'y* 1.

63 Fineman, *The Autonomy Myth*.

64 Leslie Murray and Marian Barnes, 'Have Families Been Rethought? Ethic of Care, Family and "Whole Family" Approaches' (2010) 9(4) *Social Policy and Society* 533.

65 Iris Young, *Intersecting Voices* (Princeton University Press, 1997) 106.

66 But for a strong view in favour of marriage promotion, see the Conservative Party, *The Conservative Manifesto 2010: An Invitation to Join the Government of Britain* 2010 (www.conservatives.com/~/media/Files/Activist%20Centre/Press%20and%20Policy/Manifestos/Manifesto2010, accessed 28 April 2013).

67 Jonathan Herring, 'Where Are the Carers in Healthcare Law and Ethics?' (2007) 27(1) *LS* 51.

is something 'fundamentally natural'[68] about what a family is. It is difficult to respond to such an argument. I can only note that family forms have varied enormously over the ages and that the notion of what a family is or what family life involves changes between generations and societies. Even if there is such a thing as a natural family form that does not tell us what the state should do about that. In any event the label is of little importance – if we need to abandon the label of family law and replace it with relationship or caring law, we should do that.

There is a deeper concern that may be raised at this point. John Eekelaar notes that if we attach legal obligations to selfless relationships, then there is a danger that these relationships will become polluted with people using friendship for personal or material advantage. One of the joys of intimate relationships is that they are 'law free'. It is not the values of legal obligations which govern them but love, trust and care. We should be wary of losing these virtues. Craig Lind, however, argues:

> If the intimate and caring relationships that people now form resemble friendship more closely than they do marriage, but fulfil functions – both at the social and personal level – which marriage traditionally fulfilled (or was, in an idealized way, meant to fulfil), it has become necessary, it is submitted, to bring friendship (or at least some attributes of friendship) into the realms of the regulation which we offer families and their members.[69]

He goes on to explain why legal intervention is important:

> Voluntarily assumed responsibility creates vulnerabilities and (inter) dependencies. These benefit our society while the relationships in which they are discovered continue. When those relationships end, the law's tendency to refuse recognition to those responsibilities – its refusal to acknowledge the vulnerabilities and dependencies that are their result – places the onus on the side of the powerful and against the powerless.[70]

While, therefore, as Eekelaar points out, there are dangers in legal intervention in relationships of care, there are also dangers in not doing so. Given that the legal interventions primarily operate at the end of the relationship, doing so is likely to protect those disadvantaged by relationships and is unlikely to pollute ongoing relationships.

Concerns about the care-based family law

Nicola Barker (Chapter 4, this volume) expresses concern at extending marriage to cover caring relationships. She sees the benefit of removing care from the

68 Rick Santorum, *It Takes a Family: Conservatism and the Common Good* (ISI Books, 2005) 28.
69 Craig Lind, 'Power and the taking of responsibility: shifting the legal family from marriage to friendship' in Lind et al (eds), *Taking Responsibility* 76.
70 Ibid.

family, 'Without the family unit to shoulder the burden of privatised care the relationship between providing care and derivative dependency would be impossible to ignore.'

Her concerns are justified. Historically, marriage has been used to disguise the costs of care and the unequal sharing of its burdens. If it were thought that the remedies of financial orders on divorce were the sole response of the law to the financial inequalities produced by care, that would clearly be inadequate. It would mean that only those married to wealthy spouses could expect an effective recognition of their care work. However, I still support the use of family law to extend to carers for the following reasons.

First, through family law important remedies are available in relation to the protection from violence and abusive behaviour. As argued above, these remedies are needed for all within intimate caring relationships.

Second, the concepts of family and marriage are so embedded in our society that they are unlikely to fall away. Those concepts bring social recognition and support and so should emphasise the central aspects which deserve that recognition and support, namely the care within that relationship, rather than the sexual elements.

Third, if we were to remove the protections of family law from care work, while it would become true as Nicola Barker argues that dependency and care would become 'impossible to ignore', it does not follow that any state protection or support would ensue. Or if it did follow it would be very different from that which applies to married couples. The ideal is a combination of both family law and public law support. Support for the extension of family law to caring relationship does not entail assuming care should become privatised.

Conclusion

This chapter has explored how care is a central human activity. To date it has largely been ignored and undervalued, in the law generally and in family law. That has been to the great detriment of women. Family law needs to be refocused away from the promotion of marriage and the heteronormative family, to emphasise care. It is caring relationships that need the promotion, the protection from abuse and the power to adjust offered by family law.

Chapter 4

Why care? 'Deserving family members' and the conservative movement for broader family recognition

Nicola Barker

Introduction: idle sexual partners and deserving family members

Over the last decade, with the introduction of civil partnerships for same-sex couples and now a Conservative-led coalition government introducing same-sex marriage, the debate about family recognition appears to be changing. It was notable that those campaigning against civil partnerships in 2004 generally did so by pointing to those excluded from the legislation (particularly biological family members) rather than by making the type of overtly homophobic statements that were common just a few years earlier. This is not to suggest that homophobia was absent but it is perhaps small progress that many felt compelled to try to hide it by claiming to be concerned with the continued exclusion of siblings and other close family members. Out of this conservative focus on broadening the definition of civil partner to include close family members springs an unlikely and no doubt unintended common ground with those of us within the feminist and queer communities who critique the privileging of the sexual nuclear family. In this chapter I explore the conservative arguments for recognising care in the context of civil partnerships and suggest that these should sound a warning to those of us who might be tempted to see the legal recognition of caring relationships as a means to protect against or mitigate the (economic) vulnerability of both the carer and the cared for.

In her analysis of the legal recognition of siblings and grandparents, as compared to that of civil partners, Baroness Deech concludes by identifying the 'preference' of English law for the 'idle sexual partner' as opposed to the 'deserving family member'.[1] The Civil Partnership Act triggered a number of such comparisons, as did similar provisions designed to recognise same-sex relationships in other jurisdictions.[2] The so-called 'spinster sisters' were invoked to highlight the

---

1 Baroness Ruth Deech, 'Sisters Sisters – And Other Family Members' [2010] 40(Apr) *Fam Law* 375, 380.

2 In New South Wales, where the provision had been proposed by the LGBT community, the discourse of the (gendered) 'deserving' family member also emerged during the parliamentary debates

privileged position of the (same-sex) sexual partner as against the more deserving but discriminated against biological kin.[3] These sisters were later embodied in the form of Joyce and Sybil Burden, who complained to the European Court of Human Rights that they, as sisters who had taken care of each other and cohabited all their lives, were discriminated against as they could not benefit from the inheritance tax break available to civil partners. These claims attract limited sympathy from feminists, partly due to their anti-tax discourse, and they are rooted in a form of homophobia. However, I would suggest that the underlying claim should not be dismissed too easily: it is difficult to justify recognising in the tax system (and for other purposes) a marriage/civil partnership that has lasted a brief time while refusing to recognise a long-term caring, non-sexual relationship, whether this is a sibling relationship or a caring relationship between those who are not legally recognised family members. The conservative approach is to expand recognition only as far as those in extended family relationships and only for purposes of tax avoidance. This is not an approach I would endorse but it does open an interesting debate about what types of relationship should be recognised and for which purposes. I begin by outlining the conservative proposals and the Burden litigation. I then examine some more progressive proposals for shifting legal recognition from sex to care, before considering how even these might be used by a conservative state to further privatise care and its resulting vulnerability within the expanded family.

The parliamentary debates on civil partnerships

As noted above, there were few expressions of overt homophobia during the parliamentary debates on the Civil Partnership Bill 2004 (the Bill). Instead, objections to the provision were framed, like Baroness Deech's critique, in a way that emphasised the unfair exclusions of the Bill. In response to the government's claims that the Bill was about equality, justice and legal protections (especially inheritance tax exemptions) rather than same-sex marriage, some of the more conservative peers attempted to attach an amendment to the Bill in the House of Lords.[4] This amendment to clause 4 would have provided that two people can become civil

in the form of a 'woman caring for her elderly father', as did the undeserving, seducing, wealthy homosexual, luring men away from their families only to take the family wealth: Jenni Millbank and Kathy Sant, 'A Bride in Her Every-Day Clothes: Same Sex Relationship Recognition in NSW' (2000) 22(2) *Syd LR* 181, 203–4; see also Lisa Glennon, 'Displacing the "Conjugal Family" in Legal Policy – A Progressive Move?' (2005) 17(2) *CFLQ* 141, describing the purported reasons for including non-conjugal relationships in Alberta's Adult Interdependent Relationships Act 2002 as 'little more than disingenuous flannel unsubstantiated by a sound analytical base ... [and] introduced as a smokescreen to avoid the express recognition of same-sex couples'.

3 For example, the Christian Institute placed a full-page advert in *The Times* to that effect on 30 November 2004. See also in the Australian context, Reg Graycar and Jenni Millbank, 'From Functional Family to Spinster Sisters: Australia's Distinctive Path to Relationship Recognition' (2007) 24 *Wash U J L & Pol'y* 121, 154.

4 This was not an initiative of the Conservative Party, which allowed a free vote on the Bill.

partners if they are within the specified degrees of relationship (including parent/ child and siblings),[5] have lived together for at least twelve years as adults, and are over the age of 30. The argument made by several peers and MPs was that, as a matter of justice, inheritance tax exemptions should also be extended to family members who cohabit and some who supported the amendment also expressed their support for the Bill itself. However, Baroness O'Cathain's statement in tabling the amendment reveals her underlying aim to restrict the recognition function of the Bill:

> The government insist that a civil partnership is not gay marriage. The name is clearly different, but anyone with any nous can see that the legal rights are the same. If the amendments are accepted, the House will be making it much clearer that the Bill is not a gay marriage Bill. If civil partnership were to become an arrangement open to close relations, the Government could have greater confidence in their assertion that the Bill was not a gay marriage Bill but only one to remove injustice.[6]

This amendment was described as both a tax avoidance tool and a wreck-ing amendment, intended to make the Bill unworkable.[7] Baroness O'Cathain's intentions are clear from the above statement and the civil partnership of family members would certainly have resulted in a number of absurdities. For example, according to the divorce-like dissolution process, a parent and child who entered into a civil partnership together would have to demonstrate the 'irretrievable breakdown' of their relationship if they wanted to dissolve the civil partnership. This amendment was removed during the House of Commons Committee Stage.

In the House of Commons, further amendments were proposed. Edward Leigh MP moved a separate set of rules for 'civil partners other than same-sex couples', which included restricting eligible family members to siblings only but the result-ing legal consequences would remain the same.[8] In response to the criticisms that were made of the requirement for family members in civil partnerships to demon-strate irretrievable breakdown under Baroness O'Cathain's amendment, the dis-solution process was revised so that siblings would only need to demonstrate to the court that the other partner has been served notice of the application to dissolve.[9] This amendment, like that in the House of Lords, is an opportunistic attempt to attach an inheritance tax avoidance measure to a Bill that they opposed but did

---

5 These are the same as the prohibited degrees of relationship for marriage: parent/child; siblings; grandparent/grandchild; aunt or uncle/niece or nephew.
6 HL Deb 24 June 2004, vol 662, col 1363.
7 See for example, HL Deb 10 May 2004, vol 661, col 15GC (Lord Goodhart); HL Deb 1 July 2004, vol 663, col 392 (Lord Lester).
8 HC Deb 9 November 2004, vol 426, col 724.
9 Ibid.

not have enough votes to defeat.[10] Again, the underlying hostility to recognising same-sex relationships becomes evident during the debate:

> We did not ask for the Bill; in fact, we oppose the principle of the Bill. [Hon. Members: 'Oh!'] So what? We have never made any secret of that, and we will vote against the Bill. We have a perfect right to do that in a free House of Commons. All we are saying is that although we did not ask for the Bill, the completely novel idea has been introduced that a particular group of people should be helped outside of marriage. If we are establishing the principle that one group of people should be helped outside marriage, we say that others should be helped as well.[11]

The rationale of the amendments appeared to be that while there was justification for privileging marriage over sibling relationships, once privilege was extended to same-sex relationships there was no longer any justification for excluding siblings.[12] There is, then, a clear undercurrent of homophobia in the implication that same-sex relationships are not as worthy of legal protections as heterosexual married couples or 'deserving' family members. There also remained questions about why the amendment was not concerned with all home-sharers and why, as was noted in the debate, it was restricted to two siblings.[13]

The stated intention behind the amendments was to distinguish civil partnerships from marriage, or alternatively to make the government 'more honest' about the fact that the Bill was essentially a 'gay marriage' Bill. For example:

> I will withdraw the motion if the Minister says that the new clause is totally inappropriate because the Bill will create gay marriages and it would be quite wrong to add such provisions to a marriage Bill.[14]

It is possible that through these amendments another alternative form of recognition may have developed. However, it would have been an alternative that was based on the normative nuclear family structure, a structure to which conjugality is central. The restriction of the amendments, first to family members, then to siblings, along with the focus on tax avoidance and valorisation of the nuclear family represent traditional, conservative values. Any deviation from the sexual family in

10 See for example the speech of Gerald Howarth MP supporting this proposed amendment: 'I have made it absolutely clear that I wholly oppose the Bill. It is a profound mistake. Its consequences have been as yet unfathomed by many of those who support it, but fathomed only too clearly by some of those who support it very enthusiastically, and great damage will be done to our country in consequence … Would that we could by the new clause wreck the Bill. Sadly, we will not be able to do so' (HC Deb 9 November 2004, vol 426, col 767).

11 HC Deb, 9 November 2004, vol 426, col 731 (Edward Leigh MP).

12 See for example ibid, col 727 (Edward Leigh MP). See also the rhetoric used by the Burden sisters in arguing that the Civil Partnership Act 2004 discriminates against them because they are not lesbians (discussed below).

13 Ibid, col 729 (Alistair Carmichael MP).

14 Ibid, col 734 (Edward Leigh MP).

these proposed amendments would have been restricted to the inclusion of those already privileged by normative and conservative family discourse and, indeed, by legal recognition as family members.

A separate and wider-ranging amendment was proposed by Christopher Chope, MP and would have made civil partnership available to a much broader range of people than either of the previous amendments: parents and children; siblings; and unmarried cohabiting couples in a sexual relationship.[15] The Chope amendment was analogised to the French *pacte civil de solidarité* (PaCS). However, this analogy appeared to be based only on its status as a more easily dissolvable alternative to marriage because there are a number of differences between the PaCS and these proposals; not least that it, unlike PaCS, would be open to those within the prohibited degrees of relationship and the legal consequences would be much more extensive. Christopher Chope describes his proposed amendment as creating, 'a completely different and distinct legal relationship that is more like a contract and therefore totally unrelated to marriage'.[16] Both its broader range of relationships and the ease with which it could be dissolved move the Chope amendment further away from the marriage model: 'People would be able to enter that system of registration, knowing that it would commit them not to a lifetime, permanent relationship, but to a relationship for the time being.'[17] This amendment was not widely supported but did pressure the government into undertaking a Law Commission review of cohabitation.[18] The terms of reference for the Law Commission consultation were, however, as I have noted elsewhere, restricted to (hetero)normative cohabitation by sexual partners.[19] Unsurprisingly, the resulting consultation paper and report concerned only conjugal relationships, whether different or same sex.[20] There was no consideration of siblings or other non-sexual home-sharers.

The Burden sisters

Following the passage of the CPA, two elderly sisters took this suggestion that siblings were discriminated against through their exclusion from the Act to the European Court of Human Rights, claiming that their inheritance tax liability constituted a breach of Article 14 of the Convention (in conjunction with Article 1 of Protocol 1).[21] Joyce Burden was quoted as saying:

15 Ibid, col 745.
16 Ibid, col 746.
17 Ibid, col 748 (Christopher Chope MP).
18 Ibid, col 780 (Jacqui Smith MP).
19 See Nicola Barker, 'Sex and the Civil Partnership Act: The Future of (Non) Conjugality' (2006) 14(2) *Fem LS* 241.
20 See Law Commission, *Cohabitation: The Financial Consequences of Relationship Breakdown: A Consultation* (Law Com No 179, 2006); and Law Commission, *Cohabitation: The Financial Consequences of Relationship Breakdown* (Law Com No 307, 2007).
21 *Burden v United Kingdom* (2007) 44 *EHRR* 51; *Burden and Burden v United Kingdom* (2008) 47 *EHRR* 38. The sisters were not claiming that Article 1 of Protocol 1 had been breached but rather that the government were using their powers under Article 1 in a discriminatory manner.

This government is always going out of its way to give rights to people who have done nothing to deserve them. If we were lesbians we would have all the rights in the world. But we are sisters and it seems we have no rights at all.[22]

The Burden sisters lived together in a house that was built on land they inherited from their parents. The house had significantly increased in value over the thirty-one years that they had lived there.[23] In addition they jointly owned adjoining land, two further properties and other assets worth up to £475,000.[24] The surviving sister would be liable for inheritance tax of 40 per cent of that part of the estate that exceeds the inheritance tax threshold of £300,000.[25] This tax liability was estimated to be £100,000–£200,000 based on the value of their assets at the time of the case.[26] The sisters' complaint was that when the first sister dies the survivor faces an inheritance tax liability that a surviving spouse or civil partner would not.

The CPA played a prominent role in the sisters' submission to the court for two reasons: first, because the absence of a sexual relationship does not preclude them from the analogy to civil partnership as it might to marriage;[27] and second because of the unsuccessful amendments tabled during the parliamentary debates that would have included them. Their submission quotes at length from the speech of Baroness O'Cathain,[28] who emphasises the caretaking that takes place between sisters, or a daughter looking after an elderly mother, for example, to

22 James Slack, Luke Salkeld and Nick McDermott, 'Euro-court denies sisters the same tax breaks as gay couples' *Mail Online*, 12 December 2006 (www.dailymail.co.uk/news/article-422225/Euro-court-denies-sisters-tax-breaks-gay-couples.html, accessed 6 May 2013); see also Frances Gibb, 'Sisters Joyce and Sybil Burden lose legal appeal over death duties', *The Times*, London, 30 April 2008 (www.thetimes.co.uk/tto/news/uk/article1918370.ece, accessed 7 May 2013).

23 The Chamber cites the expert valuation of the house to be £875,000, while the Grand Chamber cites the valuation as £425,000 or £550,000 if sold together with adjoining land. It is not clear why the valuation is cited differently in each judgment, although the Grand Chamber refers to two additional properties worth £325,000 in total, which may have been bundled with the valuation of the sisters' home in the Chamber.

24 This is according to the Grand Chamber's assessment, *Burden and Burden v United Kingdom* (2008) 47 *EHRR* 38, para 11. The Chamber's estimate is that the additional land and assets total £300,000, see *Burden and Burden v United Kingdom* (2007) 44 *EHRR* 51, para 10.

25 This was the threshold at the time of the case. It has since increased.

26 Brian Dempsey, 'Burden v UK: "Dissin" Lesbians or Decentring Marriage?' (2009) (February) SCOLAG 35, estimates this at £115,000, whilst Rosemary Auchmuty, 'Beyond Couples: Burden v United Kingdom (2008)' (2009) 17(2) *Fem LS* 205, 212 calculates it at £191,000. Either way, sale of the other assets owned by the sisters would comfortably meet the tax bill without it being necessary to sell their home, contrary to the media reports of the case.

27 See further Barker, 'Sex and the Civil Partnership Act' 241; as Auchmuty notes, it would have been inconceivable for the sisters to argue for inclusion within marriage ('Beyond Couples' 211).

28 Sam Grodzinski (Counsel for the Applicants) 'Observations of the Applicants on the Merits and Admissibility of Application No 13378/05 made by (1) Miss Joyce Mary Burden and (2) Miss Sybil Dorothy Burden; Responding to the Observations of the United Kingdom Government' (on file with the author). I would like to thank Nancy Polikoff for providing me with this document.

argue that the hardship caused to same-sex couples through exclusion from the legal protections of marriage also applies to these cases.

At the first hearing the Chamber of the European Court of Human Rights (Fourth Section) found, by a majority of 4:3, no violation of the Convention. The majority left aside whether sibling relationships could be analogous to marriage, ruling that any difference in treatment could be objectively justified and pursued the legitimate aim of promoting stable, committed (sexual) relationships. Excluding siblings was held to be within the state's margin of appreciation. However, in their joint dissent, Judges Bonello and Garlicki disagreed that the difference in treatment could be justified. They suggest that once the government extended the exemption past married couples, they must 'satisfy general standards of reasonableness and non-arbitrariness resulting from Art. 14'.[29] In other words, the government must be able to justify why the exemption has been extended to some unions (same-sex civil partners) while being withheld from others (sisters). The majority's reference to the margin of appreciation was insufficient justification:

> The situation of permanently cohabiting siblings is in many respects – emotional as well as economical – not entirely different from the situation of other unions, particularly as regards old or very old people. The bonds of mutual affection form the ethical basis for such unions and the bond of mutual dependency form the social basis for them. It is very important to protect such unions, like any other union of two persons, from financial disaster resulting from the death of one of the partners. The national legislature may establish a very high threshold for such unions to be recognised under tax exemption laws; it may also provide for particular requirements to avoid fraud and abuse. But unless some compelling reasons can be shown, the legislature cannot simply ignore that such unions also exist.[30]

Like the dissenting judgments in the Chamber, the Grand Chamber also considered whether the sisters were analogous to a married couple. The 15:2 majority held that 'the relationship between siblings is qualitatively of a different nature to that between [spouses or civil partners]':

> The very essence of the relationship between siblings is consanguinity, whereas one of the defining characteristics of a marriage or Civil Partnership Act union is that it is forbidden to close family members … The fact that the applicants have chosen to live together all their adult lives … does not alter this essential difference between the two types of relationship.[31]

29 *Burden v United Kingdom* (2007) (n 21) para O-I2.
30 Ibid, para O-I3. The third dissenting judge, Judge Pavlovschi, also rejected the reference to the margin of appreciation as a justification and suggests that the judgment of the Chamber is 'legal, but unfair' (at para 0-II4). This conclusion appears to be based on the sisters' assertion that the inheritance tax bill would force the surviving sister to sell her home (see para O-II7-10), an assertion that has been disputed (see Dempsey, 'Burden v UK'; Auchmuty, 'Beyond Couples').
31 *Burden and Burden v United Kingdom* (2008) (n 21) para 62.

There was no discrimination because siblings were not comparable to marriage/civil partnership.

In dissent, Judge Zupancic takes the approach that a tax exemption restricted to married couples would be justifiable, but once it is extended to civil partners

> [T]his black and white distinction is broken and the door is open for reconsideration of the question whether the denial of the tax advantage to other modes of association is rationally related to a legitimate government interest.[32]

In her commentary on the case Baroness Deech agrees, arguing that the reasoning of the majority, in holding that the state was justified in distinguishing between marriage and non-conjugal relationships, was weak on the basis that 'the clear blue line that used to exist between marriage and single-hood was blurred once the exemption was extended to gay couples'.[33] I have argued elsewhere that, on the contrary, civil partnership reinforces both the institution of marriage and the boundaries between normative spousal relationships and alternative family forms, including those that are not based on sexual relationships, such as chosen families.[34] I would also not wish to change the conclusion that the court reached on the facts of this particular case: these sisters have significant assets and on that basis should pay inheritance tax. Nevertheless, I find the reasoning of the majority judgments in *Burden* to be flawed, as I outline next, and I would agree in principle with arguments that sexual partners should not be legally privileged over other 'deserving' family members, including members of chosen families.[35]

The reasoning of the majority judgment in the Grand Chamber is circular: the sisters are unlike spouses because they are forbidden from marrying by virtue of being sisters.[36] This is reminiscent of the reasoning from those who

32 Ibid, para O-III12-13.
33 Deech, 'Sisters Sisters' 376.
34 Nicola Barker, *Not the Marrying Kind: A Feminist Critique of Same-Sex Marriage* (Palgrave, 2012) ch 2.
35 The term 'chosen families' originates from sociological studies of friendship networks in the lesbian and gay communities. See: Kath Weston, *Families We Choose: Lesbians, Gays, Kinship* (Columbia University Press, 1991); Jeffrey Weeks, Brian Heaphy and Catherine Donovan, *Same-Sex Intimacies: Families of Choice and Other Life Experiments* (Routledge, 2001). However, subsequent research has demonstrated that complex networks of friends (as well as partner(s), children and other family) play a vital role in everyday care and support for people of all sexual identities (see: Sasha Roseneil, 'Why We Should Care about Friends: An Argument for Queering the Care Imaginary in Social Policy' (2004) 3(4) *Social Policy and Society* 409; Sasha Roseneil and Shelley Budgeon, 'Cultures of Intimacy and Care beyond "the Family": Personal Life and Social Change in the Early 21st Century' (2004) 52(2) *Current Sociology* 135–59; Shelley Budgeon, 'Friendship and Formations of Sociality in Late Modernity: The Challenge of "Post Traditional Intimacy"' (2006) 11(3) *Sociological Research Online* (www.socresonline.org.uk/11/3/budgeon.html, accessed 6 May 2013).
36 Judge Borrego Borrego, dissenting, also considered the majority's reasoning to be circular as the facts that they rested their judgment on (the relationship of consanguinity between the sisters and the legal status of civil partnerships) were undisputed facts (at para O-IV8), which the judgment then simply restated without giving a reply to the actual issues raised by the Burden sisters ((n 21) para O-IV11).

oppose same-sex marriage on the grounds that marriage is by definition hetero-sexual.[37] The special status of marriage, according to the court, is a result not of the length or supportive nature of the relationship but instead 'the existence of a public undertaking, carrying with it a body of rights and obligations of a contractual nature'.[38] However, the sisters were prevented from such a public undertaking through the prohibited degrees of relationship exclusions in the Matrimonial Causes Act 1973, s 11(a)(i), and the Civil Partnership Act 2004, s 3(1)(d). Furthermore, the conclusion that the sisters are not in a similar situation to a married couple is contestable for the reasons that the joint dissenting opinion of Judges Bonello and Garlicki, cited above, outline. In their submission to the court the sisters argued that there was no significant difference between their relationship and a marriage with the exception that they are legally prohibited from having a sexual relationship with each other: 'Put simply, they have lived together in a loving, committed and stable relationship for several decades; they have and continue to share their only home; and they have had no other partners.'[39] This description, focusing on love, commitment and stability, is remarkably similar to the description of marriage in *Ghaidan v Godin-Mendoza*, where Lord Nicholls described spouses as those who 'share each other's life and make a home together'.[40]

The facts of this case highlight a problem with extending spousal recognition to non-sexual relationships through the tax system but I would go further to argue that this case highlights one of the existing problems with privileging sexual rela-tionships through the tax system: rich spouses, just by virtue of being spouses, are exempted from inheritance tax regardless of need.[41] To extend this further than spouses and civil partners would have significant implications for tax revenue and would continue to include people who do not need tax exemption for financial reasons. However, rather than reject the idea that siblings, or other non-sexual relationships, should be eligible for inheritance tax exemptions as though they were spouses, I would suggest instead that it would be more appropriate to reform the tax system so that inheritance tax exemptions are targeted on the basis of

---

37 See, for example: Robert H. Knight, 'How Domestic Partnerships and "Gay Marriage" Threaten the Family' in Robert M. Baird and Stuart E. Rosenbaum (eds), *Same-Sex Marriage: The Moral and Legal Debate* (Prometheus Books, 1997); Cardinal Keith O'Brien, 'We cannot afford to indulge this madness' *The Telegraph*, 3 March 2012 (www.telegraph.co.uk/comment/9121424/We-cannot-afford-to-indulge-this-madness.html, accessed 6 May 2013).

38 (n 21) para 65.

39 Grodzinski (n 28) para 8.

40 *Ghaidan v Godin-Mendoza* [2004] 2 AC 557, 568. It is, however, worth noting that several judges have, in same-sex marriage cases, taken the view that marriage is simply 'a formal relationship between a man and a woman' (per Sir Mark Potter in *Wilkinson v Kitzinger* [2006] EWHC 2022); see also Lord Millett (dissenting) in *Ghaidan v Godin-Mendoza* [2004] 2 AC 557, 588.

41 As noted above, the inheritance tax liability of the surviving sister would not, as reported, require the surviving sister to sell their house to pay the tax bill. On the contrary, the surviving sister would be left with assets in excess of £1 million and in any event would have the option of paying the tax in instalments over ten years; see Dempsey, 'Burden v UK'.

economic need (of the surviving cohabitant) rather than relationship status.[42] More generally, the Burden case highlights the need for a principled re-evaluation of the legal benefits associated with marriage: is there a good reason why legal protections of various kinds must be sexually transmitted, or could they be disaggregated from the institution of marriage and distributed in a different way, or could they be abolished? This questioning was central to the analysis of the Law Commission of Canada, which I turn to below. First, I consider the reasons why care ought to be recognised in the legal system at all and the extent to which this overcomes the criticisms of the sexual family.

Why recognise care? The spectre of privatisation

There are a number of strong arguments for switching the focus of legal recognition from sexual to caring relationships. Of course, many relationships are both sexual and caring but it is for those for whom sex and care exist in separate relationships that this distinction becomes crucial (for example, a single parent who has a casual sexual partner or partners) as well as for those for whom a non-sexual caring relationship is the most important in their life (for example, close friends who have been cohabiting for many years or the 'spinster sisters' discussed above). However, there is also a broader argument to be made. Those who advocate for care, rather than sex, to be the signifier of a legally privileged relationship point to the important societal benefits of care as well as to the economic vulnerability of the carer. Martha Fineman's work is seminal in this regard. She notes that dependency is both inevitable (everyone is dependent at some point in our life) and creates derivate dependency (the caretaker is in turn themselves dependent on resources necessary to carry out care work, whether state aid or private resources within the family). As such, Fineman argues that:

> The universal nature of inevitable dependency is central to the argument for the imposition of societal or collective responsibility. The realization that this form of dependency is inherent in the human condition is the conceptual foundation upon which can be built a claim to societal resources on the part of the caretakers of inevitable dependents, in order to facilitate their care. Justice demands that society recognize that caretaking labor produces a good for the larger society. Equality demands that this labor must not only be counted, but also valued, compensated, and accommodated by society and its institutions.[43]

---

42 See also Auchmuty, 'Beyond Couples' 216, recommending that the UK's spousal inheritance tax exemption be removed and replaced by a substantial increase in the nil rate band to match house price inflation, meaning that those who were wealthy would pay regardless of relationship status, while those who are less well off would not lose their homes to an unaffordable tax bill. In the Canadian context, see Claire F. L. Young, *What's Sex Got to Do with It? Tax and the Family* (Law Commission of Canada, 2000), recommending that in many instances spousal and family relationships should not be recognised by the tax system.

43 Martha A. Fineman, *The Autonomy Myth: A Theory of Dependency* (The New Press, 2004) 38.

The sexual family structure means that derivative dependency is hidden within the family, 'its public and inevitable nature concealed'.[44] It is not merely, as for example is assumed in provisions relating to the division of marital assets on divorce, that the individual receiving or benefiting from care work ought to provide compensation to the carer. Society as a whole owes a *collective* debt to carers, who produce and reproduce society.[45] Fineman argues that one way to recognise this 'dependency deficit' is to redraw the boundaries of familial relationships from the sexual unit to caretaking or dependency units, such as parent and child.[46]

In the UK context, Jonathan Herring also argues that caring and interdependent relationships are 'of greater importance to society and need promotion' as well as being the type of relationship that is 'most likely to cause the greatest disadvantage, especially in economic terms and, therefore need the protective and adjustive work of family law'. He adds that:

> Family law should seek to protect those abused within relationships; structure decision-making on relationship breakdown; promote and protect those relationships which are important to the state. The relationships where these are needed are not those marked by sex, but rather by care and commitment.[47]

Unlike the conservative proposals and the Burden case, discussed above, which would have merely expanded the protections afforded to those within the legally recognised family who cohabit (providing certain conditions were met), Fineman and Herring seek to abolish the marriage model and move away from the sexual family entirely.[48] This is a goal that I fully support but I am less convinced that care is a suitable alternative framework, particularly if our concern is with the economic vulnerability of the carer (and the cared for).

My critique of the sexual family is centred around the issue of the privatisation of care and dependency. This refers to the burdens and costs of social reproduction (for example raising a child) being borne almost exclusively by the family unit as the state retracts welfare provision and support services. For example, an expectation that childcare will be done in the home for free by mothers, despite government policy being that mothers claiming state benefits must be available

44 Ibid.
45 Ibid, 48.
46 Ibid, 293; see also Martha A. Fineman, *The Neutered Mother, the Sexual Family and other Twentieth Century Tragedies* (Routledge, 1994).
47 Jonathan Herring, 'Sexless Family Law' (2009) 11 *Lex Familiae, Revista Portuguesa de Direito da Familia* 3
48 There are also other proposals that would occupy a middle ground between these propositions. For example, Maxine Eichner and Nancy Polikoff have argued in favour of more subtly decentring the marriage model by expanding the range of forms of relationship recognition available in addition to marriage or civil partnership (Nancy Polikoff, *Beyond (Straight and Gay) Marriage: Valuing All Families under the Law* (Beacon Press, 2008); Maxine Eichner, 'Principles of the Law of Relationships among Adults' (2007) 41(3) *Fam L Q* 433).

for paid work,[49] is linked to both childcare work being underpaid and the absence of publicly funded childcare.[50] The privatisation of care and dependency can also refer to an expectation of mutual support between partners, which results in the reduction or withdrawal of state support such as unemployment benefits based on a partner's income. If caring relationships were to be recognised, it is very likely that this expectation would also be extended to non-sexual caring relationships. In other words, it is well established that proposals for the recognition of care and dependency through family law can be made in a very conservative way to *demand* that care and dependency be taken care of within the private family, only providing recognition for it from the resources of the family itself rather than providing additional state resources.[51] I would suggest that in this circumstance, recognition and support for care and dependency would be likely to operate as another form of welfare retrenchment by encouraging broader categories of people to take on these roles privately. When the argument for familial recognition relies on establishing, among other things, mutual support and the examples used are those relating to carers, it is easy to imagine how an extension of the privatising impulse might be a result. Therefore, it is necessary to consider the extent to which the recognition of caring relationships might create the opportunity for co-option into an expanded private, 'self-sufficient' sphere, entrenching the notion that care is private and letting society 'off the hook' for the consequential dependency of the caretaker while failing to acknowledge the societal benefits of women's caretaking labour.[52] There is no doubt that while the sexual family remains at the heart of family law, there is little incentive for reforms such as fully paid maternity leave and universal childcare that would recognise care as a collective responsibility as well as a responsibility that ought to be shared equally within the family. However, replacing the sexual family model with a caring family model is also likely to only improve the situation of carers through the family's individual resources rather than provide incentive for a broader collective contribution. In addition to neglecting collective responsibility for care, privatised 'rewards' also render the carer vulnerable to changing family circumstances.

It is in the interests of the neo-liberal state to expand legal recognition to caring relationships not only in order to make the distinction between (heterosexual)

---

49 Mothers claiming state benefits must now be available for paid work once their youngest child reaches the age of 5. The policy of compelling single mothers to work was introduced in 2008, when Income Support was removed from mothers whose youngest child was aged 12 or older and instead they were required to claim Jobseeker's Allowance. In 2009, the age was reduced to 10. In 2010, it was reduced to 7. In 2012 it was reduced again to age 5.

50 Susan B. Boyd, *Challenging the Public/Private Divide: Feminism, Law and Public Policy* (University of Toronto Press, 1997) 14.

51 See Susan B. Boyd, 'Family, Law and Sexuality: Feminist Engagements' (1999) 8(3) *S & LS* 369, 377.

52 Ibid; I am using the term 'women' here to highlight the undisputed fact that most carers are female. However, to the extent that a man occupies the feminine gendered caretaking role, he would also be included in this analysis.

marriage and (asexual) civil partnership clear, as conservatives proposing the failed amendments to the Civil Partnership Act wanted, but also in order to further expand the privatisation of care and dependency. The latter is also served by the progressive goal of reorienting family law away from the sexual family and towards relationships of care. This raises the question of what the solution might be. There must be a way for the state and society to recognise the significant relationships in one's life and any state that is determined to privatise care and dependency will surely find a way, however legal relationships are organised. I would suggest, then, that the answer might lie in the Law Commission of Canada's proposal, which moves away from recognising particular relationships for all purposes and instead advocates 'a fundamental rethinking of the way in which governments regulate relationships'.[53]

Beyond conjugality: a new approach

The Law Commission of Canada (LCC) rejected a relationship-based approach so far as is possible and focused instead on the objective of the individual provision. In other words, in the case of the Burden sisters' complaint, the question would not be about how 'deserving' the sisters are of recognition but rather about what the objective of the inheritance tax exemption is and whether the sisters' relationship fulfils an objective-based criterion.

This approach was based on a number of principles, central to which were values of equality and autonomy.[54] This involves a focus on the functional characteristics of the relationship rather than its status, especially whether there is emotional and/or financial interdependence. It also involves paying attention to equality within relationships, with particular mention made of inequality between men and women and the need for the state to ensure the personal security (physical, psychological and economic) of those in relationships. The principles of autonomy, privacy and religious freedom mean that the state should 'remain neutral with regard to the form or status of relationships and not accord one form of relationship more benefits or legal support than others' and should 'avoid establishing legal rules that require intrusive examinations … [into] the intimate details of … relationships, unless the relationship involves violence or exploitation'. Finally, the principles of coherence and efficiency require that 'laws have clear objectives, and that their legislative design corresponds with the achievement of these objectives'.[55]

The LCC proposed a methodology for determining whether a law or proposed law meets these principles. This involves asking four questions:

---

53 Law Commission of Canada, *Beyond Conjugality: Recognizing and Supporting Close Personal Adult Relationships* (2001) ix.
54 Ibid, xi.
55 Ibid, xii.

First, are the objectives of the law still legitimate? If the objectives of a law are no longer appropriate, the response may be to repeal or fundamentally revise a law rather than to adjust its use of relational terms. Second, if a law is pursuing a legitimate objective, are relationships relevant to the objective at hand? If relationships are not important, then the legislation should be redesigned to allocate the rights and responsibilities on an individual basis. Third, assuming that relationships are relevant, could the law allow individuals to decide which of their close personal relationships should be subject to the law? Fourth, if relationships do matter, and self-definition of relevant relationships is not a feasible option, is there a better way for the government to include relationships?[56]

This is a radical set of proposals because it involves dismantling and fundamentally redistributing the 'package' of rights and responsibilities that are associated with marriage. This proposal also rejects any other 'one size fits all' framework, including those based on care rather than sex. For example, the Burden sisters might be eligible for a provision such as a tax exemption not by virtue of either being sisters or having a caring relationship but according to the same principled criteria as anyone else. Determining these criteria would involve looking at the purpose of the inheritance tax exemption and considering whether it should be revised to attach to the individual rather than a relationship status or to apply to a broader range of relationships. This would be an advantage in considering cases such as the Burden sisters, who have a reasonable claim that there is not really a good justification for treating them differently than if they were a lesbian couple, by avoiding a conclusion either where sisters are excluded based on circular and unprincipled reasoning or where rich sisters (and others) would gain a method of tax avoidance.

This methodology provides a principled way in which it is possible to begin to think about family differently, to move away from the sexual family, and to include non-sexual relationships and broader 'families of choice'. This inclusion is not on a wholesale 'one size fits all' basis, but rather in situations where there is a good reason why relationships should be central to a legal provision and that provision can be either designated by the relevant individual, or expanded to include a range of relationships that have some familial function or other relevant significance to the legal provision concerned. The absence of a single comprehensive provision along the lines of either marriage or a caring relationship model means that there is less certainty but there is also more scope for nuanced recognition of the realities and complexities of people's intimate (whether sexual or not) associations and parenting arrangements. It would not be possible under this type of reform to assume that maternity leave, for example, can be self-funded from within the family resources because 'the family' would have little legal meaning or recognition by virtue of status alone. Instead, there would be a series of 'relational

56 Ibid, 29–30.

definitions' that vary according to the objective and nature of the particular policy. Without the family unit to shoulder the burden of privatised care the relationship between providing care and derivative dependency would be impossible to ignore.

Conclusion

The conservative support for broader family recognition in the context of the amendments to the Civil Partnership Bill and, more generally, tax avoidance schemes is in some respects unremarkable. It does, however, share some principled arguments with those writing from a more progressive standpoint; though the facts of the Burden case and the arguments made by Baroness O'Cathain and others attract limited sympathy, it is difficult to ignore the injustices caused in some circumstances by the absence of spousal recognition for caring, non-sexual, relationships. Recognising such relationships holds clear appeal to those of us who seek to move beyond the much-critiqued and legally privileged sexual family but I suggest that recognition could increase, rather than decrease, the economic vulnerability of carer, cared for and those who are interdependent as care and dependency are increasingly privatised within a newly expanded family unit. It may well be that this privatisation is inevitable in a neo-liberal state but for those who seek to go beyond a conservative family framework, the Law Commission of Canada provides an alternative that is well worth further exploration in the UK context.

Chapter 5

Universal norms, individualisation and the need for recognition: the failure(s) of the self-managed post-separation family

Julie Wallbank

Introduction

> In the vast majority of cases mediation is a much more sensible way for couples to conduct their separation – it is quicker, cheaper, less confrontational and it encourages people to resolve their issues rather than turning to judges and lawyers.[1]

> Based on the insights generated through the primary research, a suite of interventions were proposed to address negative child maintenance behaviours. These interventions were grouped into four broad categories: [including] Support such as mentoring, counselling and mediation.[2]

> We believe that families themselves are best placed to determine what arrangements work best for them.[3]

> For many families court proceedings are not the best way to settle disputes about their children's future. Unless there are serious concerns about the welfare of children, it may be preferable for parents who are separating to reach their own agreements about the care of their children and their finances without going to court.[4]

There can be no doubt in any family lawyer's mind that one of the recurring themes of the current government's approach to family law and social policy on separating parents is firm encouragement towards self-management, albeit

1 Rt Hon Kenneth Clarke QC MP, 'Clarke: Mediation the Future for Separating Families', Ministry of Justice, Press Release, 23 January 2012 (www.gov.uk/government/news/clarke-mediation-the-future-for-separating-families, accessed 5 May 2013).
2 Child Maintenance and Enforcement Commission, *Report Summary Promotion of Child Maintenance: Research on Instigating Behaviour Change* (Child Maintenance and Enforcement Commission 1(I), 2011) 3.
3 Department for Work and Pensions, *Strengthening Families, Promoting Parental Responsibility: The Future of Child Maintenance* (Cm 7990, 2011) 6.
4 Ministry of Justice and Department for Education, *The Government Response to the Family Justice Review: A System with Children and Families at Its Heart* (Centre for Social Justice Cm 8273, 2012) 19.

with varying degrees of assistance from support services. There can also be no doubt that the agenda is driven to a large extent by the economic climate and the government's need to use the most economically efficient means to deal with the consequences of family breakdown. Parents are to be encouraged to embrace the norm of self-reliant separation rather than use the law and the courts. Issues that separating families will need to deal with may include residence and contact and child maintenance. Accompanying the civilising norms of self-management are potential legal reforms which stand to detrimentally impact on those among the most vulnerable families in society, for example, the abolition of legal aid for private family law disputes, compulsory mediation, the presumption or norm of shared parenting and charging resident parents for child support services.[5]

One of the aims of the government is to reduce the significant burden of cost upon 'the taxpayer' from 'funding unnecessary litigation' in the age of financial austerity.[6] In the foreword of the proposal for legal aid reform, Kenneth Clarke states that the legal aid scheme has been continuously expanded across a wide range of areas of litigation, and 'has encouraged people to bring their problems before the courts too readily, even sometimes when the courts are not well placed to provide the best solutions'.[7] This chapter is concerned with examining the increasing emphasis being placed upon the norm of self-management by reference to the two relevant theoretical concepts of individualisation and recognition. Its focus is on outlining and critically reflecting on two of the interventionist techniques that the government has selected to help parents help themselves. It will look in some detail at the use of compulsory mediation and the introduction of the shared parenting presumption. However, these mechanisms of intervention will also be examined in light of the cuts to legal aid for private family disputes in order to get a greater sense of the potential effects.

The chapter will suggest that the concept of 'support' has been defined in a way that fails to address the needs of the most vulnerable post-separation families. The argument will be made that the government's focus on the potential of all individuals to develop the requisite characteristics and skills to come to their own agreements draws normative boundaries around those who are seen as functioning in the appropriate manner and those who are not. By drawing upon the concept of individualisation it will be shown that there is a class dimension to the government's approach to the post-separation family which fails to respond to the needs of particularly vulnerable families at a time which is already stressful. It will be concluded, by drawing on some of the available evidence, that the pursuit of

---

5 Ministry of Justice, *Proposals for the Reform of Legal Aid in England and Wales* (Cm 7967, 2010); Legal Aid, Sentencing and Punishment of Offenders Act 2012; on child maintenance, Child Maintenance and Enforcement Commission (n 2); on the principle of shared parenting on separation, see further the Ministry of Justice and Department for Education (n 4).

6 Ministry of Justice and Department for Education, *The Government Response to the Family Justice Review* (n 4) 3.

7 Ibid, 6.

intervention strategies such as mediation and the inculcation of universal norms such as shared parenting is dangerous for these families. It is therefore imperative that the already vulnerable are not rendered even more insecure as a result of the increased use of the elected 'support' interventions tailored specifically towards the norms of self-resolution and shared parenting. By drawing on Nancy Fraser's concept of recognition it will be suggested that the current government's approach to law and social policy means that significant factors impacting upon the post-separation family's well-being are overlooked. The norms that are developed are inappropriate and fail to recognise and respond to individual needs. The norms are offensive and exclusionary and the abolition of legal aid for vulnerable groups means that when combined, they are rendered unable to participate fully and equitably in social interaction. The chapter serves as a warning that these families may well experience a huge sense of social exclusion as a result of the current trajectory of social policy and law.

Social class and individualisation

The government's conceptualisation of private family disputes as best resolved through individualised negotiation processes demarcates those who can self-manage post-separation family life from those who cannot. It also distinguishes families from the rest of society, seeing family issues as a private matter of interest or significance just for family members.[8] Those deemed unsuccessful will need to resort to one or other or a combination of several interventions to achieve the outcomes which are laid down by the relevant government departments. The available interventions such as parenting plans, parenting classes, counselling, mentoring and mediation are regarded as capable of addressing through 'support' the specific 'shortcomings' of individual families experiencing difficulties with post separation life.[9] It will be suggested, however, that the overarching norm of parents reaching private agreements will risk important factors being missed such as poverty, gendered power imbalances, violence and control.

Poorer families will be rendered rather more disadvantaged by the self-management project than those with the capacity to fund their dispute through the use of solicitors or the courts. A stark division also ensues therefore between those who have and those who have not. In other words, if an intractable dispute occurs between a couple financially well-off in their own capacity, each person will have a choice about access to legal fora. There will be a great number of others, many of them women, not in this fortunate position and for them the insidious

---

8 I am grateful to Jonathan Herring for this point and on this see Jonathan Herring, 'Why Financial Orders on Divorce Should Be Unfair' (2005) 19(2) *Int J Law Policy Family* 218–28.

9 For compelling discussions of some of the problems with the therapeutic response to family problems, see further Helen Reece, 'Parental Responsibility as Therapy' (2009) 39 *Fam Law* 1167; Felicity Kaganas, 'Regulating Emotion: Judging Contact Disputes' (2011) 23(1) *CFLQ* 63–93.

creep towards individualised methods designed to achieve self-resolution of disputes may have bleak personal consequences and wider social consequences in respect of fairness and access to justice.[10]

As a concept, individualisation is now commonly used as a way of making sense of the shifting nature of the boundaries between family law, the state and family life.[11] It is used in different ways, which depend in part on the discipline and in part on the author's interpretation of it as a concept.[12] Furthermore, it also depends on what the subject under investigation is and what the researcher is seeking to reveal. This chapter is concerned with highlighting the significance and impact of individualistic norms and techniques for resolving private family disputes and the way that the emphasis on individual responsibility defines those unable to resolve their post-separation difficulties as social failures. It is therefore necessary to explain how this chapter defines individualisation and its use as a means for investigating recent trends in family policy and law.[13]

My concept of individualisation is heavily influenced by contemporary sociological class theorists. Anthony Giddens has suggested that social distinctions are now explicable at the level of the individual, raising questions about the need to focus on sociological analyses with class, ethnicity or gender at its heart.[14] According to Giddens, personal advancement is achieved by way of individualised self-governance by embracing dominant norms and a failure to do so becomes a failure attributable to the self rather than to socio-economic and cultural factors such as social class. Giddens's work has prompted much debate about the extent to which the persistence of social inequalities is explicable at the level of the individual and that individual's personal qualities or psychology rather than in terms of their status as a member of a particular social group. Bev Skeggs argues that within Giddens's highly theoretical work on individualisation 'the self becomes a project on which to be worked … it requires a self that reflects upon itself'. However, the self that is revealed in Giddens's work is without class, race or gender and as such appears as a:

---

10 However, as illustrated by J. Eekelaar, M. Maclean and S. Beinart, *Family Lawyers: The Divorce Work of Solicitors* (Hart, 2000), having a legal advocate to assist in the process can alleviate some of the difficulties.

11 See, for example, Alison Diduck and Felicity Kaganas, *Family Law, Gender and the State* (Hart, 2012) ch 5; Anthony Giddens, *The Transformation of Intimacy: Sexuality, Love & Eroticism in Modern Societies* (Polity Press, 1992); Mary Daly and Kirsten Scheiwe, 'Individualisation and Personal Obligations – Social Policy, Family Policy, and Law Reform in Germany and the UK' (2010) 24(2) *IJLPF* 177–197; Val Gillies 'Raising the "Meritocracy": Parenting and the Individualization of Social Class' (2005) 39(5) *Sociology* 835–53.

12 See further Daly and Scheiwe (n 11) 179.

13 I do not intend to trace the history of the concept of individualisation, as this has been covered by much more eminently qualified commentators. See, for example, Daly and Scheiwe, 'Individualisation and Personal Obligations'; Gillies, 'Raising the "Meritocracy"'.

14 See, for example, Ulrich Beck, *Risk Society: Towards a New Modernity* (Sage, 1992); Giddens, *Transformation of Intimacy*; Anthony Giddens, *The Third Way: The Renewal of Social Democracy* (Polity Press, 1998).

[N]eutral concept available to all, rather than an inscription, a position of personhood produced to retain the interests of a privileged few, requiring for its constitution the exclusion of others.[15]

Skeggs notes 'the division between those who theorise the social and cannot see class within their perspective and those who study it empirically and note its ubiquity and increased inequality'.[16] Mike Savage also provides a response by arguing that although there may have been a decline in class cultures as traditionally conceived, a shift has occurred 'from working-class to middle-class modes of individualization, but classed, nonetheless'.[17] Skeggs and others are clearly sceptical of Giddens's reading of the rise of individualisation. She pithily notes that the self, as produced by their account of individualisation, is devoid of cultural markers and influences such as class, gender, sexuality, ethnicity, etc. The 'failures' of the self-management project are marginalised, treated as wilfully rejecting the entrenched norms and as irresponsible citizens. They are seen as not belonging to the civilised and civilising society. As she states:

> [M]oral divisions … Self-responsibility and self-management … become the mechanisms by which class inequality is reproduced and refigured, individualized as a marker of personal volition and inclusion, excluding groups from belonging and participation.[18]

The expulsion of class from discussions about social inequalities means that those who are regarded as without the desired characteristics and as unable to self-manage according to the lauded norms are blamed. They are marked out as responsible for their own failure. As Stephanie Lawler argues: 'Explanations for inequality come to inhere within the subjectivities of persons who are then marked as "wrong" or "right", "deficient" or "acceptable".'[19] As such, they are open to public vilification and to being viewed as outside the parameters of the good society. The rhetorical device of 'the taxpayer' only serves to strengthen that positioning. It works by oversimplifying the relationship between 'the taxpayer' and 'the non-taxpayer' in respect of legal aid and child maintenance claims. It wrongly suggests that claimants are inevitably non-taxpayers and it also situates the taxpayer on the side of the angels with the non-taxpayer vilified as the scourge of the good taxpayer and society more generally. Furthermore, and perhaps more importantly, the 'non-taxpayer' is rendered a caricature rather than viewed as a three-dimensional citizen without a stake in society because of the lack of available opportunities due to the socio-economic climate.

---

15 Beverley Skeggs, *Class, Self, Culture* (Routledge, 2004) 53.
16 Ibid.
17 Referring though not directly citing Beck, *Risk Society*; Giddens, *The Third Way*; Michael Savage, *Class Analysis and Social Transformation* (Open University Press, 2000) 52.
18 See Skeggs, *Class, Self, Culture* 60.
19 Stephanie Lawler, 'Introduction: Class, Culture and Identity' (2005) 39(5) *Sociology* 797, 798.

Additionally, new forms of language are developed to encourage individuals to embrace the self-reflexive and self-actualising progressive project according to widely disseminated and much heralded norms.[20] In respect of the post-separation family these norms are concerned with conciliation and mediation. Adults in the process of negotiating post-separation family life are supposed to be giving and forgiving, mediatory, self-sacrificing, cooperative and forward-looking.[21] As highlighted at the start of the chapter, those families who reach agreements between themselves are held up as more successful than those who do not. These discourses are central to the current socio-political agenda and the government are putting in place a network of apparatuses in order to encourage self-management and divert families away from the court system as will be highlighted later. Along with the creation of new sets of discourses and norms about the benefits of self-reflection there has also been 'the formation of new categories of "inclusion" and "exclusion" … with the term social exclusion replacing a more general concept of working-class disadvantage'.[22] The effect is to treat socio-economic factors and significant cultural categories such as class and gender as irrelevant. The focus on self-management and individual responsibility effaces the need for a discussion about socio-economic and cultural factors, which is of course a convenient strategy for political parties to avoid putting their policies under the microscope. It is far easier for governments to see the problem and solution of social exclusion as residing in the individual. Giddens's reflections on individualisation have, as Skeggs and others have identified, influenced the former Blair government and the New Labour project more widely and they continue to shape neo-liberal politics as demonstrated in the next section.

The policy initiatives on shared parenting and contact

Policy-makers are increasingly focusing on the parenting deficit and they are concerned to institutionalise 'good' parenting through individualised behaviour modification programmes. This section looks broadly at the recent policy initiatives which evidence the influence of the individualisation thesis. It will also look in detail at two of the suggested interventions in order to question their appropriateness and to suggest that the proposed initiatives do violence to some of the most vulnerable members of society by setting down social policy and strategies that stigmatise them as deficient or inferior because of their perceived failure to achieve the much lauded values of self-management, cooperation and agreement. It will then be argued, by drawing upon the work of Nancy Fraser on social status recognition, that social policy needs to be directed towards accommodating the

---

20 See further Helen Reece, *Divorcing Responsibly* (Hart, 2003).
21 See further Julie Wallbank, '"Bodies in the Shadows": Joint Birth Registration, Parental Responsibility and Social Class' (2009) 21(3) *CFLQ* 267–82.
22 Gillies, 'Raising the "Meritocracy"' 837.

varied needs of vulnerable parties in resolving the difficulties of post-separation family life.[23]

The government reports that the vast majority of parental separations, about 90 per cent, result in the couple working out arrangements for the children without reference to the courts.[24] What is immediately suggested by the government, in highlighting the 10 per cent, is that the norms of cooperation, collaboration and agreement are very firmly inculcated within the majority who resolve their own post-separation matters. Although the government conceives private family disputes as best resolved through individualised negotiation processes, the norms to be embraced are promoted as universally applicable. The use of statistics on the 90/10 per cent division consolidates the universality and the desirability of the virtues of cooperation and collaboration. The 10 per cent are singled out as being very much in the minority but more importantly as lacking in respect of their abilities to reflect upon and operationalise the accepted norms as conventions.[25] They therefore are also perceived as failing to embrace the values which are heavily promoted by the government.

The remaining 10 per cent rely on the court. The Centre for Social Justice is of the view that the adversarial system does nothing to aid relationships and that many couples are seen to enter the system unaware of alternatives.[26] It is believed that there are many benefits of diverting such couples away from the court system to other available resources such as mediation. These services are designed to 'support' parents to resolve issues through discussion and negotiation and at lower cost than going to court. Early intervention strategies such as mediation are designed not only to divert post-separation parents from expensive court proceedings; they are also intended as educative devices to provide parents with the skills needed to successfully negotiate arrangements for children. The shared parenting presumption is developed as an overarching concept that will guide the negotiation process despite the fact that shared parenting presumption is at the time of writing not yet statutory law.[27]

There are existing techniques such as parenting plans and parenting programmes that target those deemed without the skills to come up with their own agreements and the government has suggested a more extensive regime. The range of regulatory techniques will inevitably expand through the increased use of mentoring, counselling and mediation.[28] The government has also increased the

23 Nancy Fraser, 'Recognition without Ethics?' (2001) 18(2–3) *Theory Culture & Society* 21–42.
24 Ministry of Justice and Department for Education (n 4) 5–6; there is an interesting discussion of this often-cited statistic by Rob George's 'Legal Liberal' blog – see Rob George, 'Right thinking, wrong result? Commentary on Re F (Child: International Relocation)', *Legal Liberal*, 24 October 2012 (http://legalliberal.blogspot.co.uk, accessed 6 May 2013).
25 See further Andrew Sayer, 'Class, Moral Worth and Recognition' (2005) 39(5) *Sociology* 947–63.
26 Reece, *Divorcing Responsibly*.
27 Ministry of Justice and Department for Education (n 4) 19, para 64.
28 See for example the Child Maintenance and Enforcement Commission (2011) Report Summary Promotion of Child Maintenance: Research on Instigating Behaviour Change.

budget for mediation by £10 million to £25 million per annum as part of its early intervention approach to post-separation family life.[29] The increase in available funds for mediation needs to be appreciated against the backcloth of extensive cuts to legal aid for private family disputes. However, what is clear is that the government is placing much confidence in behaviour modification programmes to address post-separation conflicts with the emphasis firmly on getting parents to embrace private dispute resolution rather than resorting to the courts. The inclusion of the legislative presumption of shared parenting means it is imperative to critically reflect upon the potential role of mediation in light of the new statutory presumption as this will clearly have an impact on the aims of mediation as it is likely to be treated as the desired end.

Early intervention strategies are available for universal use but specifically target post-separation parents who are identified as failing to embrace the lauded values of post-separation life and needing 'support'. The 90 per cent of separating parents may or may not choose to use the available regulatory mechanisms and as long as agreements have been reached, it is assumed (rather than established) that parents have acted in ways that will benefit child welfare in the short and long term. The majority of parents who manage post-separation privately are to a large extent left alone. The government intends to remove the requirement for the court to consider arrangements for children in divorce proceedings 'since the very large majority of divorces are not contested'.[30] This will mark a drawing back of the state monitoring (albeit of negligible degree) of the vast majority of divorcing parents, with a stark line drawn between those who are seen as capable of successfully managing post-separation life and those who are not.[31] Any agreement between parents, whatever it constitutes, is thus rendered the main objective rather than there being any focus at all on the quality of the arrangements and the child's best interests. Effectively, it is assumed that any dispute that parents take to court results from their own personal failures to cooperate and negotiate about their children's needs rather than from legitimate concerns about child welfare. Moreover, the growth of regulatory techniques to 'support' post-separation parents also fails to account for the potential gendered implications of such strategies. I will take this up in the next section but it has been noted by social policy commentators that the increasing emphasis and universality of discourses on responsibility disproportionately impacts upon mothers (particularly lone mothers).[32]

Evidence of the expansion of the use of 'informal' regulatory techniques can be found in several sources. The Ministry of Justice and Department for Education's

29 Ministry of Justice and Department for Education (n 4) 19.
30 Ibid, 23.
31 For a discussion of the redrawing of state boundaries in respect of wider social policy, see further Kate Morris and Brid Featherstone, 'Investing in Children, Regulating Parents, Thinking Family: A Decade of Tensions and Contradictions' (2010) 9(4) *Social Policy and Society* 557–66.
32 See, for example, Brid Featherstone, 'Writing Fathers in But Mothers out!!!' (2010) 30(2) *Critical Social Policy* 208–24, 210.

response to the Family Justice Review outlines its suggested reforms to private family law:

> We strongly believe that in most circumstances, *mother and fathers, working together, are the best people to make arrangements about their children's lives* … We therefore want parents to be *supported in developing flexible and co-operative agreements, which focus clearly on their children's needs.*[33]

Compulsory mediation

Mediation, where necessary and appropriate, will be aimed at securing parental agreements although sufferers of domestic violence are supposedly to be exempted and will still have access to legal aid if certain criteria are met.[34] Making concessions to commentators concerned about the government's original intention to use both a narrower definition of domestic violence and a more restricted range of evidence, it has opted to use the Association for Chief Police Officers' (ACPO) definition:

> [A]ny incident of threatening behaviour, violence or abuse (psychological, physical, sexual, financial or emotional) between adults, aged 18 and over, who are or have been intimate partners or family members, regardless of gender and sexuality.[35]

It is encouraging to see that the government has been responsive to some of the concerns that have been flagged up during the Act's controversial passage by using the ACPO definition and extending the list of evidence. However, there remain some significant issues about the exemptions for the domestic violence sufferer. In the Interim Report of the Family Justice Review, reassurance was given that mediators would 'assess whether there are risks of domestic violence, imbalance between the parties or child protection issues that require immediate diversion to the court process'.[36] However, in 2000, Christine Piper's study of divorce mediation found that 57 per cent of parents who 'indicated a fear of violence' were still

---

33 Ministry of Justice and Department for Education (n 4) 18 (emphasis added).
34 Justice Secretary Kenneth Clarke has widened the list of evidence that will be accepted as proof of domestic violence to entitle victims to legal aid for private family disputes. The government has suggested evidence from GPs or other medical professionals, social workers and domestic violence refuges, a police caution for domestic violence and an undertaking given to a court by the other party in lieu of a protective order or injunction in addition to other official legal channels. Clarke also agreed to double the time limit from 12 months to 24 months to allow a party to bring forward evidence to establish domestic violence. Catherine Baksi, 'Domestic violence concession as MPs back legal aid cuts', *Law Society Gazette*, 18 April 2012 (www.lawgazette.co.uk/news/domestic-violence-concession-mps-back-government-s-legal-aid-stance, accessed 6 May 2013).
35 Association of Chief Police Officers (ACPO) and the National Policing Improvement Agency (NPIA) (2008) *Guidance on Investigating Abuse* ACPO and NPIA: Bedfordshire at 7.
36 Interim Report of the Family Justice Review at 172.

found to be suitable for mediation at their first meeting.[37] Furthermore, more recent evidence from the AIFS's (Australian Institute of Family Studies) extensive research into their similar reforms suggests that for a substantial proportion of separated parents, issues relating to violence, safety concerns, mental health, and alcohol and drug misuse are relevant to parents' concerns about contact. The evaluation suggests that up to one-fifth of separating parents had safety concerns that were linked to parenting arrangements. Moreover, it was concluded that 'shared care time in cases where there are safety concerns correlates with poorer outcomes for children'.[38]

Although the study accepted that the reformed system has some way to go in being able to respond effectively to these issues, particularly in respect of identifying violence and abuse, it is extremely concerning that families where violence had occurred were no less likely to have shared care-time arrangements than those where violence had not occurred. Not unsurprisingly, parents who reported safety concerns tended to provide less favourable evaluations of their child's well-being compared with other parents. But the poorer reported outcomes for children whose mothers expressed safety concerns were considerably more marked for those children who were in shared care-time arrangements.[39] As warned by Helen Rhoades, for the benefits to be found from mediation to come to fruition in practice, 'much will depend on the culture of collaboration and the training of practitioners'.[40] However, some are dubious as to the likelihood of such referrals to court being workable in conjunction with the legal aid cuts – parties will lack the funding to be represented in court, and this 'will leave the parties in limbo'.[41] They will therefore be rendered much more vulnerable as a result.

There may also be a range of significant forms of behaviour that the parent with primary care has identified as placing children at risk such as substance abuse or mental health problems, yet they do not necessarily constitute domestic violence. That point has not been missed by family law practitioners and other interested parties. In the Solicitors Family Law Association response to the White Paper 'Looking to the Future' it was stated that 'Mediation will be unsuitable where there are complex finances, domestic violence, a power imbalance in the marriage, or where one or other party is obstructive or dishonest.'[42] The House of Commons Justice Committee concluded that 'We are not convinced that using

37 Christine Piper, *The Responsible Parent: A Study in Divorce Mediation* (Harvester Wheatsheaf, 1993).
38 Rae Kaspiew, Matthew Gray, Ruth Weston, Lawrie Moloney, Kelly Hand, Lixia Qu and the Family Law Evaluation Team, *Evaluation of the 2006 Family Law Reforms* (Australian Institute of Family Studies, Report for the Attorney General's Department and Department of Families, Housing, Community Services and Indigenous Affairs, 2009) 366.
39 Ibid, 364.
40 Helen Rhoades, 'Mandatory Mediation of Family Disputes: Reflections from Australia' (2010) 32(2) *J Soc Wel & Fam L* 183–94.
41 Rosemary Hunter, 'Doing Violence to Family Law' (2011) 33(4) *J Soc Wel & Fam L* 343–59.
42 Solicitors Family Law Association, 'Looking to the Future: Mediation and the Ground for Divorce' (Lord Chancellor's Department, White Paper, CM2799, 1995) (www.official-documents.gov.uk/document/cm27/2799/2799.pdf , accessed 6 May 2013).

domestic violence as a proxy for the most serious cases is advisable and we call on the Government to look at other ways Legal Aid can be focused on the most serious family law cases.'[43] It has been argued that litigants who have drug and alcohol addictions, suffer from mental ill-health, brain injury or learning impairment, are illiterate, have limited English language ability and/or are recent immigrants from a minority culture[44] should not be disregarded as cases which pose significant risks.

There are several important issues here. The first is that the definition of a vulnerable family is set at an unreasonably and inappropriate high level. In all 'other' circumstances mediation is deemed more appropriate than formal legal measures and legal aid is withdrawn for these 'other' cases. Mediation is founded on the idea that both parents are of equal standing, with equal bargaining power. The fear is that parties who are already vulnerable could be 'supported' into 'agreeing' to decisions they would object to if they had that freedom. Additionally there will be other factors that might bear on one party being in a stronger position than another. As Jonathan Herring noted, there are various reasons for one party being in a disadvantaged position to another during mediation other than as a result of domestic violence, such as through a lack of verifiable information, a lack of negotiation skills or a psychological disadvantage.[45] One party may have had experience of negotiation in his or her career, to the detriment of the other party's bargaining position. Additionally, one party may be psychologically disadvantaged because of poor upbringing and/or under developed social skills. If one party has a weaker bargaining position than the other, the principle of equality upon which mediation relies is discarded, and the weaker party is at risk of being manipulated.[46]

In cases where domestic violence or abuse are not evidenced, responsibility for resolving private disputes falls to couples themselves, outside law but 'supported' by potent norms and frameworks for assistance such as mediation; the aim of securing agreement over residence and contact will dominate, especially in light of the inclusion of a presumption of shared parenting. This will leave many families extremely vulnerable. As John Eekelaar has suggested:

> it seems that the very presence of the law, and the idea of legal entitlements, in the context of serious family breakdown is being questioned by some policy-makers. They concede that law has a role to play to protect the vulnerable, but vulnerability is ill-defined, and the attempts to identify vulnerable people are clumsy, and could generate more cost.[47]

---

43   Ministry of Justice and Department for Education (n 4) 3.
44   Piper, *The Responsible Parent* 344.
45   Jonathan Herring, *Family Law* (4th edn, Pearson Longman, 2009) 142–3.
46   Ministry of Justice and Department for Education (n 4).
47   John Eekelaar, '"Not of the Highest Importance": Family Justice under Threat' (2011) 33(4) *J Soc Wel & Fam L* 311–17, 317.

Anxieties about child welfare may stem from a variety of factors which are allowed to disappear due to the high standard set for the exemption from mediation. Vulnerability is narrowly and poorly defined. Additionally, the support offered by mediators is likely to be directed at achieving a particular end because of the legal entrenchment of the presumption of shared parenting.

It is very apparent that the government has given a particular meaning to 'support' in the context of post-separating parents. Support does not refer to any material benefit to help with the transition from intact to separated family. Indeed, the cuts to the legal aid budget means that rather more women will be left vulnerable and unable to qualify for assistance due to new evidential burdens to prove that domestic violence has taken place. 'Support' refers exclusively to the attainment of the goal of self-dependency with parents being able to see that children's needs are best met by highly collaborative, reflexive and flexible parents with all the requisite skills to ensure child welfare. Frank Furedi has identified this as the increasing professionalisation of childrearing.[48] There is a scarcity of discussion in the government documents of the existence of circumstances which might militate against the possibility and indeed wisdom of securing cooperation between parents such as domestic violence, drug misuse or alcoholism where other forms of support may be much more appropriate. Neither is there any discussion of socio-economic factors which potentially impact on post-separation life. As Val Gillies states: '"support" initiatives are promoted as being relevant to all parents regardless of their circumstances, but this concern to regulate childrearing practices is for the most part directed at those families defined as socially excluded'.[49] Thus, the factors which may be out of the individual's control are not deemed as significant as personal responsibility. Support, is therefore, rather more concerned with educating parents about the extent and range of their responsibilities towards children post-separation whatever their personal circumstances. The effacement of wider socio-economic factors and structural constraints from the discussion about reform of the family justice system suggests that there is an expectation that all post-separating parents should have the abilities to self-manage regardless of their social position. They are expected to embrace the universally accepted norms of post-separation life and the perceived failure to do so is attributed to personal shortcomings rather than to other obstacles. As Gillies cogently states:

> Articulated through the language of inclusion and exclusion, this approach promotes a highly moralistic and ultimately authoritarian stance, isolating parenting practices from their situated, interpersonal context ... Class is thus obscured by its re-framing in terms of an included majority of reasonable, rational, moral citizens who seek the best for their children, and an excluded minority who are disconnected from mainstream values and aspirations.[50]

48 Frank Furedi, *Paranoid Parenting: Abandon Your Anxieties and Be a Good Parent* (Allen Lane, 2001).
49 Gillies, 'Raising the "Meritocracy"' 839.
50 Ibid, 840.

Of course not all the 10 per cent of separating parents resorting to the family courts will be socio-economically disadvantaged. The point is, however, that individualisation when combined with discourses of inclusion and exclusion conveys the sense that social class and disadvantage can be readily transcended and as such no longer matter in respect of social policy and family law. All parents *ought* to be able to successfully negotiate the vagaries of life to come to agreements about their respective responsibilities regardless of their situation. The normative aspect is extremely important. Self-regulation is represented as a thing which is desirable in its own right, something for which all other obstacles should be overcome. It is also seen as being achievable by all separating parents and gender is not a significant factor. The small minority of parents who turn to the courts are therefore represented as disengaged from the much lauded values of the majority. They are at the same time seen as incapable of achieving the desired ends. 'Poor' parents are thus defined as those who cannot achieve the requisite levels of cooperation, self-sacrifice and conciliation in managing their transition from intact to post-separation family. They are therefore also demarcated as culturally rather than economically poor. After April 2013 when the government brings in its changes to legal aid for private family disputes those socio-economic factors which have been expelled from governmental debates will become extremely significant.[51] The parents among the 10 per cent without the economic ability to fund a private dispute will have no access to the courts and will be forced into resolving their dispute by any means available outside the family courts. It will therefore become imperative that the early intervention strategies and new regulatory techniques are appropriate to the individual interpersonal and socio-economic context. Otherwise there may be extreme risks for some of the most vulnerable families. However, the inculcation of universal legal norms such as the shared parenting presumption is designed to augment the government agenda.

The shared parenting presumption

The shared parenting presumption is to be consolidated by getting rid of residence and contact orders in favour of the child arrangements order designed to eradicate the notion that there are winners and losers of residence in family disputes.[52] Additionally, in order to ensure that solutions are found outside the court process the government will introduce a 'coherent pathway' with the starting point of ensuring that *parents understand what is expected of them in respect of their obligations and responsibilities*.[53] The extent to which the government has elected to progress its individualisation agenda is strongly in evidence with this proposal. Although the ultimate goal is to get parents to assume full responsibility for post-separation family life, it is ironic that the expansion of state control in this matter is insidious.

51 Legal Aid, Sentencing and Punishment of Offenders Act 2012.
52 Ministry of Justice and Department for Education (n 4) 23.
53 Ibid, 19–20.

The inclusion of a statutory presumption is a relatively cost-effective way of reaching all separating parents, as whether they go down the informal or formal law route they will be forced to work with it.[54] As Mary Daly and Kirsten Scheiwe have argued, individualisation means that 'external control of family functioning and behaviour of individual members is even strengthened and reinforced (often in the name of the child's best interest)'.[55] Parents will be expected to follow the same path, to exhibit the same kinds of behaviour and to reach identical outcomes, i.e. parental agreement about their respective roles and responsibilities in meeting the best interests of the child. It is a one-size-fits-all approach. One of the problems with this approach is that the social science literature on how to accommodate children's interests after separation is complex and contested.[56] Additionally, the emphasis on training parents to manage themselves also allows for other modes of response, such as improved social conditions and material resources to fade into the background.[57]

The Family Justice Review, which preceded the Ministry of Justice's recommendations, recommended against the presumption on the advice of family law academics, children's groups and evidence from Australia.[58] In 2006 Australia introduced a rebuttable presumption that it is in the child's best interests for parents to have equal shared parental responsibility which, if applied, requires courts to consider making an order for equal time-sharing or for 'substantial and significant' time for the child to have a 'meaningful relationship' with both parents after separation.[59] The presumption is rebuttable on the basis of family violence and abuse. The 2006 Act has been the subject of much critical debate. It is notoriously complex and has caused a huge amount of confusion and problems, particularly for mothers who are expected to manage post-separation parenting. Significantly for this chapter, Zoe Rathus has written:

> it is at the point of separation – when the *Family Law Act* is triggered – that mothers risk exclusion from membership of community of 'good' mother citizens. In an intact heterosexual nuclear family, 'good' mother citizens are expected to maximise their time with their children … and risk criticism if they do not. But the mother who has separated from the father will face a different set of expectations … Although she is still the same woman, and mother, she

54 It is ironic however that the renewed attempt to affect the way parents bring up their children 'lies in fears that "a small minority" of parents have lost control over their children, and that this threatens social order' (John Eekelaar, 'Self-Restraint: Social Norms, Individualism and the Family'(2012) 13(1) *Theo Inq L* 75–95, 87).

55 Daly and Scheiwe, 'Individualisation and Personal Obligations' 182.

56 For a comprehensive discussion of the literature and its complexities, see Stephen Gilmore, 'Contact/Shared Residence and Child Well-Being: Research Evidence and Its Implications for Legal Decision-Making' (2006) 20(3) *IJLPF* 344.

57 Val Gillies, 'Meeting Parents' Needs? Discourses of "Support" and "Inclusion" in Family Policy' (2005) 25(1) *Critical Social Policy* 70–90, 87.

58 Centre for Social Justice (n 24).

59 Family Law Act 2006.

is now expected to behave differently to be a 'good' post-separation mother citizen … she is expected to willingly and graciously relinquish time with them in favour of the father.[60]

Rathus's work is important for flagging up the way that gender is eradicated from the neutral framing of the relevant issues as involving 'parents'. She also shows how the mother, in particular, is expected to be able to renegotiate and be responsive to the new set of demands placed on her as a result of the separation. She may have assumed primary care for the child while the relationship was intact, but post-separation the expectation will be that she is reflexive, flexible and facilitative to sustain the father–child relationship. Although undoubtedly there will be stresses for the separated father, it will often be the mother who is charged with managing post-separation family relationships. Furthermore, where poverty is an added feature of family life, insufficient attention is paid by the government to the:

> (gendered) relationship between financial deprivation and the ability of parents to fulfil the parenting responsibilities expected of them. It is a gendered relationship because … women still carry the main day-to-day responsibility for the care and upbringing of children; this is obscured by the gender-neutral language of parenting.[61]

Women are more likely to experience financial deprivation at the end of a relationship but the individualisation of post-separation family life expunges any discussion of the mother's socio-economic needs, instead requiring her to overcome any factors which might impact negatively on her facilitative abilities.[62] Legal aid cuts are likely to be catastrophic for poor women and children who are suffering domestic violence, abuse or other problems such as substance misuse.[63] The emphasis on shared parenting and securing parental agreements requires concerned mothers to sideline their own feelings, doubts and disagreements about the competence of the non-resident parent in meeting the children's needs. It relies on the premise that what are very real concerns about child welfare can be sidelined to facilitate ongoing relationships. However, it may be the case that resistance to contact has arisen as 'an almost inevitable result of trying to do the

---

60 Zoe Rathus, 'Of "Hoods" and "Ships" and Citizens: The Contradictions Confronting Mothers in the New Post-Separation Family' (2010) 19(3) *GLR* 438–71, 453.

61 R. Lister, 'Children (But Not Women) First: New Labour, Child Welfare and Gender' (2006) 26(2) *Critical Social Policy* 315–35, 327.

62 Indeed, an important role for solicitor advocates is to provide women with legal advice as to their rights of protection as highlighted in the research of Eekelaar et al, *Family Lawyers*.

63 The 2009/10 BCS estimated 'that in total there were approximately 9.6 million crimes against adults resident in households in England and Wales' (John Flatley et al (eds), *Crime in England and Wales 2009/10: Findings from the British Crime Survey and Police Recorded Crime* (Home Office Statistical Bulletin 12/10 No 9, 2010) ch 2, p 13).

right thing'.[64] In her empirical study of twenty-seven separated unmarried parents Karen Laing noted that mothers who had primary responsibility for childcare during the relationship 'continued and reinforced this role after the separation'.[65] Mothers' concerns over the safety of their children may have provided a source of anxiety during the relationship and remained after relationship breakdown.

The range of behaviours that mothers believe place children at risk is wider than domestic violence and child abuse, yet they may not be regarded as sufficient to exempt them from mediation let alone negate the presumption of shared parenting. Anxieties about child welfare may stem from a variety of factors which are allowed to disappear due to the ultimate goal of securing private agreements and ongoing shared parenting. Perry and Rainey's research shows that the legal system tends to:

> [D]ownplay genuine concerns ... of a potentially serious nature – there is nothing trivial or unwarranted about concerns that a child may be driven by a drunk parent, or that a parent refuses to use a car-seat ... parents ... who raised such concerns were made to feel ... that they were making ... contact unnecessarily difficult.[66]

There is evidence to suggest that concerned parents would fare no better in the mediation process. Helen Rhoades's contribution to the Family Justice Review included data from the AIFS study, and a Family Violence Review conducted by Professor Richard Chisholm, a former Family Court Judge (the Chisholm Review). Although the AIFS study suggested a degree of success it also, rather worryingly, indicated that shared care-time arrangements had frequently been made in situations where there were ongoing safety concerns. The Chisholm Review suggested that the operation of the 'meaningful relationship' provision had played a role in this problem. In particular, it suggested that the conjunction of this factor with 'a provision requiring the courts to have regard to the need to protect the children from harm had contributed to an assumption that there are, rather over-simplistically, "two basic types of case", namely "the ordinary case", in which the courts endeavour to ensure that children spend time with both parents, and 'the case involving violence or abuse'. The AIFS report suggested that rather than functioning as an exception to the provision focusing judicial officers on the need to maintain a relationship with both parents, the tension between these factors had seen the development of advisory practices in which parental involvement with children was often emphasised 'at the expense of protection for family members'. Although the Chisholm review focused on how the 'meaningful

---

64 Karen Laing, 'Doing the Right Thing: Cohabiting Parents, Separation and Child Contact' (2006) 20(2) *IJLPF* 169–80, 174.

65 Ibid, 175.

66 Alison Perry and Bernadette Rainey, 'Supervised, Supported and Indirect Contact Orders: Research Findings' (2007) 21(1) *IJLPF* 21–47, 39.

relationship' provision had been interpreted in the courts, it is all too apparent that the inclusion of a statutory presumption is designed to have an impact at all stages of negotiation, including the mediation process, and will inevitably colour all work done to resolve disputes.

Additional evidence provided to the domestic Family Justice Review about the Australian legislation showed that people place different interpretations on time-sharing and on the requirement that judicial officers should have regard to 'the benefit to the child of having a meaningful relationship' with both parents, and that it is interpreted in practice by counting hours spent with each parent, disregarding the quality of the time and the damaging consequences for children. The reluctance to include presumptions in family law is most certainly influenced by the view that they can militate against the application of the paramountcy principle in individual cases. By drawing on the convincing evidence against the presumption of shared parenting from the Australian experience of a similar provision, the Family Justice Review concluded that legislation risks creating the impression of a parental 'right' to a particular amount of time with a child which potentially undermines the central principle of the Children Act 1989 that the welfare of the child is paramount. It seems that the government has elected to ignore the stark evidence and has decided to press ahead and put the presumption onto a statutory footing. It will be argued in the next section that the suggested proposals for reform risk doing violence to already vulnerable families, which involves them not being able to participate in civil society in ways that their better-off peers can. Additionally, Fraser's work will be used to signal the way forward for social policy to do justice to those unable to participate in society on a more equitable footing. First, it is useful to briefly summarise the significant points thus far.

The policy approach to separating parents is one of 'support' to encourage parents to embrace the norm of private dispute resolution with 'support' referring exclusively to the attainment of the goal of self-dependency. Moral and normative divisions are forged between parents that can be seen to agree and those constructed as unable to. As part of a network of discourses of inclusion and exclusion the government-created schism between 'the taxpayer' and 'the non-taxpayer' adds rhetorical force to the marginalisation of parents unable (often for very good reasons) to reach agreements about children post-separation. Although the government has been responsive to some of the concerns about domestic violence, significant issues remain which is clear from research into mediation and the use of a shared parenting presumption in Australia. Negotiation under the shadow of potent norms will leave many families extremely vulnerable. Ignoring significant categories of analysis such as social class and gender means that those who are regarded as failing to attain the lauded norms are blamed. In real terms, those without the economic means will also not have the option to take their dispute to the family court. The next section draws on Nancy Fraser's work on recognition in order to argue that the government's approach to social policy and law fails the most vulnerable in society by failing to recognise and attend to their specific needs. Moreover, the promulgation of the dominant norms of private dispute resolution and shared parenting impede parity of participation in social life, especially when considered in light of the abolition of legal aid for private family disputes.

Recognition

Nancy Fraser's work attempts to reconcile two philosophical concepts, which, prior to her influential contribution, had been regarded as polarised and incompatible.[67] Her thesis treats 'recognition' as a matter of *'social status'*, which requires an examination of institutionalised 'patterns of cultural value for their effects on the relative standing of social actors'.[68] Only when group members can participate fully and equitably in social interaction can it be said that we can speak of *'reciprocal recognition* and *status equality'*.[69] Its concomitant 'misrecognition', therefore, does not simply refer to the undervaluing of a social group's identity; it means, instead, *'social subordination'*, which prevents full participation in social life.[70] Importantly, 'misrecognition arises when institutions structure interaction according to cultural norms that impede parity of participation' and social actors are denied full status in respect of distributive justice because they are not recognised as having parity with others embracing the desired norms.[71] Examples that she uses include marriage laws that exclude same-sex partnerships as illegitimate and social-welfare policies that stigmatise single mothers as irresponsible scroungers.[72] The usefulness of Fraser's thesis in the context of this chapter is that it aids the understanding of how institutionalised norms may detrimentally impact on the social participation of those who are seen as failing to embrace the lauded values of post-separation. It also assists in flagging up the dangers of the proposed law reforms which use universal norms to target individual 'problem' families in order to re-educate them to resolve their disagreements without taking account of significant factors such as gender, power, and wider social and economic factors. Fraser's thesis is complementary to the work of the social-class theorists discussed above because of the potency of her writing on misrecognition.

In her view it is quite simply unjust that individuals or social groups are unable to participate equally because some categories of social actors are rendered normative and others lacking. As well as being complementary to the work on individualisation it is also supplementary as it develops the convincing argument that rather than focus on 'individual' or 'interpersonal' psychological explanations for

---

67 Fraser, 'Recognition without Ethics?' 21–42. Rather than rehearse her full discussion about the distinction between the theories of 'recognition' and 'redistribution' and the need for the integration of the two approaches, I will move straight to elaborating the aspects of her thesis which are relevant for examining the current approach to the law and social policy on post-separation families.

68 Ibid, 24 (italics in original).

69 Ibid.

70 Ibid.

71 Ibid.

72 Ibid, 25.

social exclusion and disadvantage, misrecognition, construed as status subordination, 'locates the wrong in social relations' rather than with the individual.[73]
Misrecognition is therefore exclusionary and oppressive and fully justifies a claim
for recognition in the name of justice. To use Fraser's words: 'When such patterns
of disrespect and disesteem are institutionalized, they impede parity of participation, just as surely as do distributive inequities.'[74] There are two aspects to 'parity
of participation'. First, what Fraser calls the 'objective condition' which refers to
the fair distribution of material resources to ensure independence and 'voice' and,
second, the 'intersubjective condition' which requires the eradication of institutionalised norms that demean and exclude groups of people and the 'qualities
associated with them' by overemphasising ascribed differences or by refusing to
acknowledge more significant distinctiveness.[75]

It is hoped that this chapter has gone a significant distance towards highlighting
how the proposed reforms will fail to ensure both senses of parity of participation. The cuts to the legal aid budget in respect of private family disputes will
quite simply deny the socially and economically disadvantaged a legal voice. In
respect of the intersubjective condition the proposed reforms do violence to the
most vulnerable separating parents, the 10 per cent, by highlighting their ascribed
distinctiveness from the majority. The fact that they are singled out as failing to
achieve the desired norm of agreement demeans them. This is consolidated by
the strength of the norms that parents *should* assume responsibility for coming to
agreements for themselves and that both parents continue to be involved after
the adults' relationship breaks down. The dominance of these norms means that
other, more significant differences are ignored. It is therefore crucial that the techniques which are used to facilitate agreement can take account of the important
differences between separating parents which may result from lack of access to
social and economic support structures. Currently, exemption from mediation
is set at a very high level. Additionally, as a practice it presupposes equality of
participation. The fear is that already vulnerable parties will be rendered more
at risk by agreeing to arrangements which, on the basis of their past experiences,
they believe will not benefit their children. This is particularly significant for
those parents without financial resources as that group will be disproportionately
disadvantaged by the reforms.

Moreover, the gender dimension cannot be ignored. Women are more likely to
experience financial deprivation at the end of a relationship and they are expected
to be facilitative of the post-separation family relationships. Research has shown
that women's concerns about contact frequently (though of course not always)
stem from concerns about the pre-existing quality of the father–child relationship. Women's concerns about contact may include a wide range of behaviours
falling outside domestic violence. These may be effaced for the sake of achieving

73 Ibid, 27.
74 Ibid.
75 Ibid, 29.

agreement on shared parenting. The extensive research base from Australia suggests that there has been an oversimplification of the range of post-separation scenarios, there being a view that there are only two types of case where either the parents agree or there is violence or abuse. Fraser's position on recognition is that it is a means of remedying social injustice and as such needs to be pragmatic and flexible to respond to the various forms of misrecognition. It is therefore contingent on the form and context of misrecognition, requiring those who make social policy and law to be able to see and appreciate the needs of subjugated groups and how those needs differ from those of dominant groups. However, a significant aspect to this is the need to put justice at the centre of the pragmatic exercise so that '*only those claims that promote parity of participation are morally justified*'.[76] Responses to subordinated groups therefore need to focus on what should be provided to enable full participation in social life. It is submitted that the individualised nature of the reforms do nothing to promote parity of participation. It has been shown in this chapter that quite the reverse is the case.

Conclusion

It is beyond doubt that the regulation of post-separation families has proved an extremely difficult problem for consecutive governments in a minority though significant constituency of parents. To a great extent this is probably due to the strength of feelings and hostilities at a very difficult period in the lifespan of the family. Where parents have been unable to come to agreements between themselves they have been forced to rely on specifically tailored legal advice and the courts for help. For many, it is likely to be a last resort rather than the first port of call as suggested by Kenneth Clarke. With the abolition of legal aid for private disputes, excepting where domestic violence is established, many already vulnerable parents will be left without legal recourse. This will leave the poorest parents unable to fully participate in public life on a par with the better-off in society. In practice, compulsory mediation will only ever be compulsory for those who cannot afford legal advice, thus creating a two-tier society of the 'haves and have-nots'. Additionally, the promulgation of the individualistic but dominant universal norms of self-management and shared parenting do very real violence to vulnerable families. The prominence of norms that some families simply cannot embrace (often for very serious reasons) renders them outside the boundaries of acceptable moral behaviour and, as such, on the periphery of social life. There is also a distinction made between those that can (the majority) and those that cannot (the 10 per cent). That placing of the minority outside civilised society is assisted by the discourses of inclusion and exclusion.

However, it is not simply a case of language and symbolism. The use of individualistic universal norms directed towards the whole population of separating parents is what renders important aspects of human life inconsequential in respect

76 Ibid, 30–1.

of the development of social policy and law. All parents, regardless of social class, gender, social and economic position are seen as capable of resolving their own problems. It is therefore also rendered legitimate for governments to evade more costly forms of support interventions to assist parents in the transition to separated and functioning family. Universal norms and individualisation serve the state, and the most powerful and secure in society stand to lose little as a result of the individualistic trajectory of the suggested reforms. In respect of the two support mechanisms discussed herein, the chapter seeks to flag up some warnings about the need to be fully vigilant of the specific needs of prospective mediation users. There is a need for the reintroduction of important categories such as class, gender and wider socio-economic factors. The exemption for domestic violence is unacceptably high and there may well be a wide range of other forms of behaviour that militate against its use. However, the presumption of shared residence is designed to augment the government's reform trajectory towards getting parents to help themselves and its very existence is likely to have an impact upon the very nature of the mediation process. Mediation is not a neutral event; it occurs against the background of the state cutting costs, of diverting disputes from the court, of getting parents to resolve disputes for themselves and of trying to enforce ongoing parental responsibility. It could of course be argued that these are laudable aims but, as extensive research, particularly from Australia, has shown, the use of compulsory mediation and the shared parenting presumption have not been without problems in respect of child welfare and the more vulnerable separating families in society.

Chapter 6

Autonomy and vulnerability in family law: the missing link

Alison Diduck

Introduction

The landscape of family justice is changing at a more rapid rate than even the speedy pace it achieved over the last decade. In the last five years alone we've seen the Law Commission review both financial relief for cohabitants and prenuptial agreements, areas that many thought were fixed in the policy consciousness as unchangeable. We now have the Law Commission engaging also with the principles of financial relief on divorce and dissolution of civil partnerships, the Supreme Court telling us that prenuptial agreements are deserving of protection, and the government telling us not only that most private family law matters are not worthy of legal support by the state, but that access to the child support agency is yet another commodity that must be purchased by the consumer.

Unsurprisingly, as was begun years ago under New Labour, most of these policy and legal shifts have at their heart a promotion of individual responsibility,[1] whose 'other', or opposite, is dependency. Then, like now, families and family members were to take responsibility for themselves; dependence on the state was deplored and stigmatised. This remoralising of responsible behaviour[2] has continued; incapacity benefit and housing benefit for those under the age of 25 are characterised as 'something for nothing',[3] and most forms of dependence continue to be stigmatised.[4] It seems to me, however, that the responsibility rhetoric has now shifted; there is a new strand entwined with it. In previous work I explored a similar shift in the discourse of ancillary relief on divorce, from

---

1 Fiona Williams, *Rethinking Families* (Calouste Gulbenkian Foundation, 2004).
2 See for example, Shelley Day Sclater and Christine Piper, 'Re-moralising the Family? Family Policy, Family Law and Youth Justice' (2000) 12 *CFLQ* 135; Martha Fineman, *The Autonomy Myth: A Theory of Dependency* (The New Press, 2004); Williams, *Rethinking Families*.
3 The Rt Hon David Cameron MP, 'Welfare Speech', Cabinet Office and Prime Minister's Office, Bluewater, Kent, 25 June 2012 (www.number10.gov.uk/news/welfare-speech, accessed 24 May 2013).
4 N. Fraser and L. Gordon, 'A Genealogy of Dependency: Tracing a Keyword of the US Welfare State' (1994) 19(2) *Signs* 309.

traditional patriarchy to equality to individual responsibility.[5] Here, I see a similar process at work; the language has again shifted. It is now that of autonomy. As Herring wrote in 2010, 'autonomy has achieved a "sacred status" not only among lawyers, but within the wider society'.[6] 'The presumption is', he reminds us, 'that citizens should be free to make their own choices in the light of their own values.'[7] Emphasis on autonomy, even in family law matters, was beginning to become evident in government policy documents in the mid 2000s[8] but it now displays a new explicitness in family law and the language is deployed proudly. Autonomy has become both the principle underpinning and the goal of new legislation and judicial decisions in family matters. While there is a link between responsibility and autonomy, however, that link is nuanced.

Autonomy is in many ways the friendly face of individual responsibility. Autonomy in the liberal polity and in liberal law is like motherhood – it is hard to argue against it, even while interrogating its content, consequences and import means those arguments are sometimes necessary. The value autonomy adds to individual responsibility rhetoric is that it is easier to defend politically and philosophically. Individual responsibility can smack of individualism and meanness and in times of austerity and the 'Big Society' can become associated with 'selfishness'[9] and the withdrawal of historic and cherished public services. In these times, it may be a more difficult 'sell' politically. Autonomy, on the other hand, achieves the same goals as individual responsibility, but when framed in this new way, in a discourse of freedom[10] or equality, dignity, choice and respect,[11] becomes easier to protect and promote in law and policy. On the one hand, it is a curious principle to privilege in family justice because autonomy is not something that fits easily into ideas of 'family', the relations of which are normally thought to remain in the realm of altruism, connection, love, (inter)dependency and the greater good. But deployed for post-separation families as a contrast with paternalism or dependency, autonomy makes political sense. The problem is of course that the interdependencies and connections that are simultaneously encouraged and rendered invisible in pre-separation families too often are forgotten or become irrelevant in the rush to promote the parties' autonomy post separation.

Remoralising family living has not stopped now that responsibility has shifted to autonomy. In an autonomy discourse, 'the state's role is limited to assisting

5 Alison Diduck, 'What Is Family Law for?' (2011) 64(1) *CLP* 287.
6 Jonathan Herring, 'Relational Autonomy and Family Law' in Julie Wallbank, Shazia Choudhry and Jonathan Herring (eds), *Rights, Gender and Family Law* (Routledge, 2010) ch 12, 257.
7 Ibid, 258, quoting A. Alghrani and J. Harris, 'Reproductive Liberty: Should the Foundation of Families Be Regulated? (2006) 18 *CFLQ* 191, 192.
8 Herring, 'Relational Autonomy' 259.
9 See David Utting (ed.), *Contemporary Social Evils* (Joseph Rowntree Foundation, 2009) in which respondents to a consultation on modern social evils included selfish individualism as an undesirable element shaping contemporary society.
10 As in the US, see Fineman, *Autonomy Myth*.
11 As in Canada, see *Quebec (Attorney General) v A* [2013] SCC 5.

parties to reach an agreement'[12] when they are no longer able, or said to *choose*,[13] to live together. In this way choices about family living, family living itself and its consequences are returned firmly to the private sphere in which the state has no duty or legitimate authority to intervene,[14] except to promote individual choices and enforce their consequences. Indeed, to do otherwise, would be seen to be 'patronising' or 'paternalistic'.[15] In these cases, the state's role is simply to educate the parties to make their own best decisions. Indeed, one of the terms of reference for and 'guiding principles' of the then newly announced Family Justice Review was that 'individuals should have the right information and support to enable them to take responsibility for the consequences of their relationship breakdown'.[16]

But like individual responsibility, autonomy cannot exist without *its* 'other', which in current rhetoric has become vulnerability. In the same way that autonomy may be the 'friendly face' of individual responsibility, vulnerability may be the friendly face of dependency. Vulnerability connotes a state for which the individual is not so obviously to blame. '"[T]he vulnerable" tend to be constructed in policy and social welfare practice as those who are less accountable for their circumstances or actions.'[17] There may, therefore, be less moral culpability attached to vulnerability than was attached to dependency; vulnerability implies disability, lack of capacity, incompetence or victimhood, rather than the irresponsibility which tended to pervade dependency discourse. The vulnerable may be 'those who have less "agency" in the development of perceived difficulties in their lives',[18] but this means also that they are usually adjudged to have less agency in developing perceived accomplishments. As I will suggest, this view is problematic for many reasons, not least because in family law matters the label 'vulnerable' is restricted primarily to the incompetent (children, the elderly) or to victims (usually of domestic violence). In family law discourse the vulnerable need the assistance or intervention of the state, either to protect them if they are vulnerable children or the incompetent elderly (although the definitions of vulnerable even for these categories of people is changeable),[19] and for which 'gift' of protection they must

---

12 Herring, 'Relational Autonomy' 259.

13 See Ministry of Justice, for example, Ministry of Justice, *Proposals for the Reform of Legal Aid in England and Wales* (Consultation Paper 12/10, 2010) para 4.19); Diduck, 'What Is Family Law For?'

14 Eekelaar describes a system in which the state allows families themselves to define the obligations members owe to each other and then recognise that authority with the force of law as an 'authorisation' model of the state–family relationship (John Eekelaar, 'Self-Restraint: Social Norms, Individualism and the Family' (2012) 13(1) *Theoretical Inquiries in Law* 75, 84.

15 *Radmacher v Granatino* [2010] UKSC 42 [78], [2011] 1 AC 534.

16 House of Commons, *Financial Provision Orders on the Breakdown of a Relationship* (Commons Library Standard Note, SN/HA/5655 22 July 2010) para 4; see also Catherine Fairburn, House of Commons, *Financial Provision Orders on the Breakdown of a Relationship* (Commons Library Standard Note, SN/HA/5655 12 September 2013); Eekelaar ('Self-Restraint') would describe this as a version of the 'purposive abstention' model of the state–family relationship.

17 Kate Brown, 'Re-moralising Vulnerability' (2012) 6(1) *People, Place & Policy Online* 41, 42.

18 Ibid.

19 Ibid.

be appropriately grateful. If they were once competent adults, the purpose of legal intervention is to help them to attain or regain their autonomy. For this group, law's role is limited to incentivising and educating. As Brown notes, this idea of the vulnerable ties in with a particular idea of the autonomous: 'Notions of "vulnerable groups" serve to underline the particular construction of individuals which is central to economic liberal models of citizenship: the citizen as capable adult, unbound by structural constraints, who needs "activating".'[20] Indeed, introducing the Welfare Reform Bill in 2010 the prime minister said, 'we will look after the most vulnerable and needy. We will make the system simple. We'll make work pay. We'll help those who want to work, find work. But in return we expect people to take their responsibilities seriously too.'[21]

Just as dependence excluded one from the class of the responsible, vulnerability seems in the new rhetoric to preclude one from being classed as autonomous.

> Despite gesturing towards notions of mutuality, the idea of the 'Big Society' seems to be premised on these notions of the 'otherness' of 'the vulnerable' … According to the moral undertones in 'the Big Society', the vulnerable citizen tends not [to be] seen as potential or actual contributors to shared public life.[22]

It is as though the vulnerable (family law) subject embodies a different subjectivity from the autonomous subject. The autonomous are not perceived as victims or as otherwise incompetent or dependent on others. They have the capacity and the freedom and consequently both the right and the responsibility to make their own choices and to contribute to society and law's role must be to protect this freedom. Law must permit, even encourage, autonomy to flourish by enabling and attributing moral and social value to 'choice'. To my mind these conceptions of family law's subjects and the state's role in respect of them are potentially problematic for a number of reasons, not least because they raise issues of gender justice.

Autonomy and vulnerability: defining and moralising

It is important to state at this point that autonomy is an important and fundamental concern for all citizens and all legal subjects and for women, children and other previously disenfranchised groups it is has particular significance. I in no way wish to be understood as downplaying that importance. But the particular understanding of autonomy that constructs an 'other' in vulnerability and is promoted in the recent policy and legal statements is in my view an impoverished

20 Ibid, 48.
21 Speech delivered by the Prime Minister David Cameron on the Welfare Reform Bill. See The Rt Hon David Cameron MP, 'PM's Speech on Welfare Reform Bill', Cabinet Office and Prime Minister's Office, London, 17 February 2011 (www.number10.gov.uk/news/pms-speech-on-welfare-reform-bill/, accessed 24 May 2013).
22 Brown, 'Re-moralising Vulnerability' 48.

one that fails those who for many reasons are unable or unwilling to idealise and express it. Before I pursue this critique, however, let me illustrate what I mean by the particular type of autonomy expressed in recent family law. In 2010 Herring saw an emphasis on autonomy in calls for no-fault divorce, greater use of mediation, pressuring parties to resolve contact disputes themselves, enforcement of pre-marriage contracts and the privatisation of child support.[23] Indeed, it seems clear that an idea or norm of autonomy runs through these examples. Since then, the legal and policy discourse has become further and more deliberately suffused with autonomy. Mr Justice Ryder who in 2011 was appointed to oversee the 'modernisation' of the family justice system (and reported in 2012)[24] took as a given in a speech in 2008 entitled 'The Autonomy of the Citizen in the Context of Family Law Disputes' that autonomy was one of the commonly held and shared principles underpinning family justice and that

> [T]he time is ripe for an increasing emphasis on autonomy, social responsibility and flexibility of service delivery … The state must be prepared to listen to individuals and be seen to do so. That will include allowing them to come to their own agreements more often than we do.[25]

Such overt linking of the old – personal responsibility, with the new – autonomy, in family relationships is not limited to policy statements, however. The courts have taken up the autonomy banner as well. The first example, of course, is the majority of the Supreme Court in *Radmacher v Granatino*, which endorsed autonomy as a fundamental principle governing the enforceability of pre- and post-marital contracts.[26] And, importantly, the Supreme Court's view, similar to Ryder J's, is of a particular kind of autonomy: 'The husband's decision to abandon his lucrative career in the city for the fields of academia' said the majority in *Radmacher*, 'was not motivated by the demands of the family, but reflected his own preference.'[27] The majority here clearly saw these kinds of decisions to be made by a free, self-interested, autonomous agent. That that agent's choices must be 'respected' was also clear to them:

> The reason why the court should give weight to a nuptial agreement is that there should be respect for individual autonomy. The court should accord

23 Herring, 'Relational Autonomy' 259.
24 Mr Justice Ryder, 'Judicial proposals for the modernisation of family justice' (Judiciary of England and Wales 2012) (www.judiciary.gov.uk/publications-and-reports/reports/family/the-family-justice-modernisation-programme/fjmp-final-report/family-modernisation-final-report, accessed 24 May 2013).
25 Mr Justice Ryder, 'The autonomy of the citizen in the context of family law disputes', Conkerton Memorial Lecture, 30 October 2008 (www.judiciary.gov.uk/media/speeches/2008/speech-ryder-j-30102008, accessed 24 May 2013).
26 *Radmacher* (n 15) [78].
27 Ibid [121].

respect to the decision of a married couple as to the manner in which their financial affairs should be regulated. It would be paternalistic and patronising to override their agreement simply on the basis that the court knows best.[28]

The majority's view of autonomy is not universal, however. Compare it with Lady Hale's view in dissent:

> Most spouses want their partners to be happy – partly, of course, because they love them and partly because it is not much fun living with a miserable person. So, choices are often made for the overall happiness of the family [...] These sorts of things happen all the time in a relationship. The couple will support one another while they are together.[29]

As we shall see, Lady Hale is advocating here a different kind of autonomy; one that recognises that competent adults make decisions all the time that are not exclusively about their own preferences. They are made in the context of and in the interest of relationships with others; they are, in effect, vulnerable to and in those contexts and relationships. *Radmacher* was not the first case in which she did so. In *Miller v Miller; McFarlane v McFarlane* in explaining how financial 'need' could arise even in the most modern of marriages, in effect how the vulnerability generated by intimate relationships may, in turn, generate further vulnerability in the form of dependency or need when those relationships end, she observed:

> A further source of need may be the way in which the parties chose to run their life together. Even dual career families are difficult to manage with completely equal opportunity for both. Compromises often have to be made by one so that the other can get ahead. All couples throughout their lives together have to make choices about who will do what, sometimes forced upon them by circumstances such as redundancy or low pay, sometimes freely made in the interests of them both.[30]

Those who are 'in need' at the end of their marriage as a result of the decisions they took with their partner about 'who will do what' may feel it is important and not patronising at all for the law to recognise the context of those decisions. Indeed, as Lady Hale continued, they may want and need the court to do so:

> Some may regard people who are about to marry as in all respects fully autonomous beings; others may wonder whether people who are typically (although not invariably) in love can be expected to make rational choices in the same way that businessmen can. Some may regard the recognition of

28 Ibid [78].
29 Ibid [188].
30 *Miller v Miller: McFarlane v McFarlane* [2006] UKHL 24 [2006] 2 FCR 213 [138].

these factual differences as patronising or paternalistic; others may regard them as sensible and realistic.[31]

The types of 'compromises' and decisions about who will do what that were recognised in *Miller/McFarlane* in 2006 as a realistic part of family living were recast in *Radmacher* in 2010 as an expression of Mr Granatino's 'own preference', or expression of his autonomy. It is probably not surprising that autonomy finds its clearest expression in the jurisprudence around nuptial agreements; contract is the perfect expression of legal autonomy. But the autonomy discourse has not remained confined to agreements. In the area of family finances and property on divorce/dissolution, one court has gone so far as to say autonomy has become an element of fairness, alongside sharing, need and compensation when the court is conducting its s 25 discretionary review of a claim for financial provision. According to Charles J:

> To my mind, [the *Radmacher* decision] necessitates a significant change to the approach to be adopted, on proper application of the discretion conferred by the MCA, to the impact of agreements between the parties in respect of their finances. At the heart of that significant change, is the need to recognise that weight should now be given to autonomy, and thus to the choices made by the parties to a marriage.[32]

The autonomy in all these statements is an abstract or 'theoretical'[33] autonomy; it is the autonomy of liberalism premised on the myth of a pre-existing equal playing field on which each individual has equal freedom, power and capacity to express it. Law's presumed objectivity and a contextual point-of-viewless-ness means that it is 'conceived of in its application'[34] to this abstract individual. This autonomy is not necessarily impervious to dependency or structural and social conditions but when these are not rendered irrelevant in its mythical ideal expression they are taken to revoke, or at least to damage, the subject's autonomy. They reconstruct the subject as vulnerable, afflicting the subject with almost a kind of disability that requires repair so that he or she can become autonomous again.

Autonomy's other, vulnerability, is therefore also constructed in a particular way. Again, consider Mr Justice Ryder's view from 2008. To him, the vulnerable in family law are the legally incompetent: children and those assessed as incompetent under the Mental Capacity Act 2005 and the role of the law is to provide whatever means are necessary to enable the vulnerable to participate 'on a level playing field';[35] to be 'provided with an effective means of exercising their

---

31 *Radmacher* (n 15) [135].
32 *V v V* [2011] EWHC 3230 (Fam) para 38; see for comment on this case Ashley Murray, 'The Principle of Autonomy and Guidance for Appeals: *V v V* [2012] *Fam Law* 417.
33 *Quebec v A* (n 11) (McLaughlin CJ).
34 Herring, 'Relational Autonomy' 261.
35 Ryder, 'Autonomy of the citizen' 4.

autonomy'.[36] Again it is not surprising that the Family Justice Review included as a 'guiding principle': 'the court's role should be focused on protecting the vulnerable from abuse, victimisation and exploitation and should avoid intervening in family life except where there is a clear benefit to children or vulnerable adults in doing so'.[37] It is as if the autonomous are not also vulnerable to abuse, victimisation and exploitation. This non-interventionist theme continues in the Legal Aid, Sentencing and Punishment of Offenders Act 2012 (LASPO) which was designed to 'protect the most vulnerable in society'.[38] For its purpose, the 'vulnerable' in family justice means being either a child or a victim of domestic violence. As Eekelaar notes, 'potential loss of legal entitlements is not sufficient'.[39] Family law, therefore, seems to be reserved for the vulnerable. For the autonomous, there is freedom *from* law, or as McLaughlin, Chief Justice of Canada called it, 'a state-free zone'.[40]

Vulnerability in this discourse is therefore not quite like dependence in the old, but it is linked. While dependence can render one vulnerable (as in the Mental Capacity Act 2005) unlike the former dependence discourse, vulnerability is not to be deplored as a moral failing. Rather it is understood as an unfortunate status that attaches to an individual by his or her membership in a class. It becomes almost akin to a protected characteristic in equality law, albeit an under-defined one.[41] But, also like in equality law, vulnerability is something that can be remedied. With the appropriate assistance, the vulnerable can achieve autonomy. In the LASPO 2012 it is assumed that access to courts with the protection, rules and oversight, not to mention principles (such as equality and non-discrimination?), they offer will provide this remedy. And indeed they may. But, understood in this way, vulnerability, like autonomy, becomes a property of the individual. This understanding is important, when we see also that it tells us that autonomy is to be respected and promoted while vulnerability is to be pitied, remedied or alleviated.

Once more, this understanding of vulnerability and of the importance of law to assist and protect the vulnerable may be true in many situations, but it is the universality of the assumptions and categorisations that is striking. The politics of meaning-making in this way include not only constructing or defining vulnerable and autonomous subjects in unrealistic and almost fetishised ways, but also reinforcing their opposition. Perhaps unsurprisingly, constructing autonomy and vulnerability in this way is also entirely consistent with the politics of neo-liberalism:

---

36 Ibid, 8.
37 Ministry of Justice, *Family Justice Review* (Final Report, November 2011) annex A, 182.
38 Ministry of Justice, *Reform of the Legal Aid in England and Wales: The Government Response* (Cm 8072, 2011) para 45.
39 John Eekelaar, '"Not of the Highest Importance": Family Justice under Threat' (2011) 33 *Journal of Social Welfare and Family Law* 311, 312.
40 *Quebec v A* (n 11) [443].
41 See Jennifer Collins (Chapter 2 in this volume).

As spending cuts are made, drawing on notions of vulnerability offers a rhetorical means of reassuring the public that those who need and deserve services the most will not be affected, thereby bolstering the moral and economic credentials of the government.[42]

And:

These politics of vulnerability focus attention on the individual and distract attention from the structural forces which expose the different vulnerabilities people experience at different times and in different ways that exacerbate disadvantage. They implicitly emphasise [...] self-regulation and individual 'responsibilisation'.[43]

It may not be surprising that this 'responsibilisation' is so keenly associated with their other – autonomy.

In the next section, I will look at situations in which autonomy and vulnerability seem to exclude each other in family law, focusing particularly on financial matters on separation/divorce/dissolution. In these situations the adult subject is by default characterised as an autonomous subject unless she can claim vulnerable status by reason of her domestic violence victimhood or other inability to express her autonomy properly. Financial dependencies or disadvantage arising from (inter)dependence, relationships and care are difficult to establish as vulnerability in law, but the perverse end result is that if a claim to financial or other victim-based vulnerability succeeds, the subject relinquishes her autonomous status. She is seen at this point as requiring the paternalism or protection of the court, usually to the extent of 'fixing' her or making her whole again by helping her to become autonomous.

Autonomy and vulnerability in family finances

And so we have autonomy and vulnerability as the twin focuses in family law. The law acknowledges both statuses and that a person may inhabit each at different moments in their lives, but not that they can coexist. Policy is to encourage individual autonomy and avoid law's 'interference' with it. Only if a family law subject is classified as vulnerable is law justified in intervening in her post-separation financial affairs, but that intervention is usually limited to assisting her to become autonomous. It will therefore provide legal assistance so that the court can exercise its discretion to do fairness, of which autonomy may now be an element, but certainly has autonomy as its goal: 'to give each party an equal start on the road to independent living'.[44]

42 Brown, 'Re-moralising Vulnerability' 45.
43 Ibid, 48.
44 *Miller/McFarlane* (n 30) [144] (Baroness Hale).

Let me review three specific examples of what I mean. First, and hovering over the entire landscape, is the LASPO 2012. Legal aid for litigation over financial orders will be approved only to protect the vulnerable, categorised as victims of domestic violence and children. The financial disadvantage of other claimants is assumed to arise from their own choices and is therefore not suited to juridical intervention. As the government said: 'Where the issue is one which arises from the litigant's own personal choices, we are less likely to consider that these cases concern issues of the highest importance.'[45] But, if the parties have not anticipated these issues in advance and concluded a prenuptial or marital agreement to deal with them, legal aid will be provided for mediation in order to assist them to reach an agreement, in effect, to prove their autonomy, after separation. And contained within the 'shadow of the law' under which their negotiations/mediations take place is that autonomy may now be a part of the fairness of any agreement that they reach.[46]

This approach fits into broader social policy focused upon protecting the vulnerable, but ignores the contextualised person in favour of the abstract one. Why, for example, are domestic violence victims presumed to be vulnerable? Many, if not most, are, but equally many may not see themselves in this way. Why are primary caretakers of children or other adults *not* presumed to be vulnerable? Care responsibilities can have a significant impact upon one's financial security and prospects, one's bargaining power and freedom to make choices about how to arrange one's life. And apart from these crude classifications, neither the domestic violence victim nor the carer is either exclusively autonomous or vulnerable. It is more likely each is both, as is the person cared for, the non-primary carer and the non-'victim'. The real questions then become, why, in order to be entitled to state-supported access to a court of law, must one first be classified within a pre-identified group of potential vulnerable subjects? And, second, why should one have to claim this problematic status at all?

The second example I wish to draw attention to is the development of child support. The autonomous contractor has replaced the dependent carer in child support discourse. Lone parents might just as easily have been categorised as vulnerable (remember they are dependent) but unless they are victims of abuse, they are not. While remoralisation is a part of the autonomy–vulnerability discourse generally, child support is an interesting example of its shifting meaning for lone parents. Their 'responsible behaviour' ten years ago included applying to the Child Support Agency to remedy their dependency on the state, but now, that behaviour is not good enough. Their claim for access to a legal and public service is recast as irresponsible. In autonomy discourse, they must both demonstrate and achieve their autonomy either by entering into a contract with the other parent or, if that is unsuccessful, a consumer transaction with the state.

45 Ministry of Justice, *Proposals for the Reform of Legal Aid in England and Wales* (Consultation Paper CP12/10, 2010) para 4.19; Eekelaar, '"Not of the Highest Importance"'.
46 See *V v V* (n 32); Murray, 'Principle of Autonomy'.

Finally, cohabitants left disadvantaged or in hardship on the breakdown of their relationships are not constructed as vulnerable, but rather as autonomous. Despite the recommendations of the Law Commission,[47] and the results of recent research[48] separating cohabitants are deemed to have chosen not to marry/ register their partnership and must therefore live with the consequences of that choice, regardless of the disadvantage it may confer upon them. This position is justified by the claim that it would be a violation of their autonomy and therefore unfair to subject them to a regime which they had chosen to avoid. Again, however, the autonomy presumed by this position is a theoretical one. As Lady Hale stated in *Gow v Grant*,[49] 'This case [under the Scottish legislation providing for support when cohabitants separate] also illustrates the fact, well-established by research, that many, even most, cohabiting couples have not deliberately rejected marriage.' In this case, like in many, only one of the parties made a choice not to marry. The other partner's only choice was between staying in the relationship and ending it. Ms Gow only agreed to move in with Mr Grant if they became engaged; it was Mr Grant who refused to marry.

The autonomy of cohabitants, protecting their freedom from law, has been discussed recently by the Supreme Court of Canada. In *AG Quebec v A*[50] the court considered the constitutionality of a Quebec scheme which denied the same rights of property division and support to de facto spouses as it offered to married spouses. Five of nine members of the Supreme Court found that the scheme violated the equality provision of section 15 of the Charter of Rights and Freedoms, but one of them, the Chief Justice, found that the violation was justified under section 1 in a free and democratic society. In the result, her conclusion, when read together with the minority of four judges who found no violation of equality, meant that the Quebec scheme was upheld. The judicial language of both the majority and minority was steeped in the language of autonomy. All were concerned to protect autonomy even as they disagreed about the point in their constitutional analysis at which it became relevant. While the court by necessity engaged in an analysis of Charter jurisprudence and Canadian constitutional law, its comments about the nature and place of autonomy in a liberal society are relevant beyond that context.

Four members of the court found that autonomy was a fundamental value underlying equality itself and therefore by assuming that cohabitants exercised an autonomous choice not to marry, the Quebec scheme did not violate their Charter guarantee of equality.

> The principle of personal autonomy or self-determination, to which self-worth, self-confidence and self-respect are tied, is an integral part of the values

---

47 Law Commission, *Cohabitation: The Financial Consequences of Relationship Breakdown* Law (Law Com No 307, 2007).

48 Anne Barlow, Simon Duncan, Grace James and Alison Park, *Cohabitation, Marriage and the Law* (Hart, 2005).

49 [2012] UKSC 29, [51].

50 (n 11).

of dignity and freedom that underlie the equality guarantee. Safeguarding personal autonomy implies the recognition of each individual's right to make decisions regarding his or her own person, to control his or her bodily integrity and to pursue his or her own conception of a full and rewarding life free from government interference with fundamental personal choices.[51]

On the other hand, the Chief Justice, with whom four other members of the court agreed in part, found that while the value of autonomy was indeed of primary importance in a free and democratic society, it ought not to be understood as an element of equality, but rather as an important element of public interest and therefore is more properly considered in the second stage of legal analysis, when the court asks whether the discriminatory provision is justifiable. In finding, therefore, that Quebec's scheme violated the Charter's equality protection, she then went on to consider whether that violation was justifiable:

> Freedom of choice and autonomy are public interest considerations. They are relied on by Quebec to justify the obvious fact that its law may disadvantage some *de facto* spouses by denying claims to property division and support in circumstances where they may not have truly chosen to forego the protections of the mandatory regime, but rather have been unable to access them due to their partner's refusal to marry.[52]

She found that in the attempt to 'strike a balance between claims of legitimate but competing social values',[53] the value of autonomy was more pressing than the value of non-discrimination in this case: 'The objective of the law is sufficiently important to justify an infringement of the right to equality.'[54]

> The impugned provisions enhance the freedom of choice and autonomy of many spouses as well as their ability to give personal meaning to their relationship. Against this must be weighed the cost of infringing the equality right of people like A, who have not been able to make a meaningful choice. Critics can say and have said that the situation of women like A suggests that the legislation achieves only a formalistic autonomy and an illusory freedom. However, the question for this Court is whether the unfortunate dilemma faced by women such as A is disproportionate to the overall benefits of the legislation, so as to make it unconstitutional. Having regard to the need to allow legislatures a margin of appreciation on difficult social issues and the need to be sensitive to the constitutional responsibility of each province to legislate for its population, the answer to this question is no.[55]

---

51 Ibid [139] (LeBel), journal references omitted.
52 (n 11) [422] (McLaughlin CJ).
53 Ibid [439].
54 Ibid [437].
55 Ibid [449].

Even the minority, which would have found that (at least parts of) the scheme violated substantive equality and were not justified under and therefore, saved by section 1, framed their decision in the discourse of autonomy. But Abella J, with whom three justices agreed, preferred to see autonomy in a more relational, realistic way:

> The choice to formally marry is a mutual decision. One member of a couple can decide to refuse to marry or enter a civil union and thereby deprive the other of the benefit of needed spousal support when the relationship ends. In her dissenting reasons in *Walsh*, L'Heureux-Dubé J. observed that '[t]his results in a situation where one of the parties to the cohabitation relationship preserves his or her autonomy at the expense of the other: "The flip side of one person's autonomy is often another's exploitation"'. The case before us resonates with this observation: Ms. A consistently wanted to marry, but Mr. B refused, depriving Ms. A of access to the possibility of spousal support at the end of the relationship.[56]

In Abella J's minority view, the important value of autonomy expressed as 'choice' must 'defer to the more important social goal of remedying a legal and social barrier to equality'.[57] Abella J's words here resonate with those of Lady Hale in *Radmacher*:

> Perhaps above all, some may think it permissible to contract out of the guiding principles of equality and non-discrimination within marriage; others may think this a retrograde step likely only to benefit the strong at the expense of the weak.[58]

The theme in all these family law examples is the social value placed upon autonomy and the role of law in upholding it either as an element of the social 'good' (if not constitutional principle) of equality, or as its own inherent social good. In England and Wales, both options are discernible in *Radmacher*, the first in Lady Hale's words, the second in the words of the majority.

> On the one hand, the sharing principle reflects the egalitarian and non-discriminatory view of marriage, expressly adopted in Scottish law [...] and adopted in English law at least since *White v White*. On the other hand, respecting their individual autonomy reflects a different kind of equality.

> The reason why the court should give weight to a nuptial agreement is that there should be respect for individual autonomy.[59]

56 Ibid [375] (Justice Abella), journal references omitted.
57 Ibid [308].
58 *Radmacher* (n 15) [135].
59 Ibid [178] (Lady Hale), and [78] (Lord Phillips) (references omitted).

In both views, however, autonomy must be weighed in the balance against other social goods.

In these family law examples, we see also the way in which autonomy/responsibility is constructed in opposition to dependency/need/vulnerability and that family law recognises neither the vulnerability inherent in relational living, nor in the financial, situational or social disadvantages or constraints that may result from it. Where vulnerability is recognised in family law, as resulting from domestic violence, it is as something that happened to the autonomous individual as a harm or injury to her autonomy.

In one sense, acknowledging at least that all have the potential to become vulnerable as a result of situations not always within our control is realistic. At least it acknowledges that context affects our ability to express our autonomy. But in another sense this view does nothing to disrupt the autonomy–vulnerability dichotomy; it still sees vulnerability as an injury to autonomy, as a condition that can be remedied. But these need not be the only alternatives.

Autonomy and vulnerability: retheorising

Both autonomy and vulnerability have been theorised differently. Consider, first, autonomy. There is, of course, a vast literature theorising autonomy. For my purposes, I wish to draw attention only to a few examples that have particular resonance for family law subjects. One example is those who adopt a feminist critique of liberalism's abstract autonomy that is rooted in the social.[60] Whether this view of autonomy becomes a part of substantive equality because it 'looks not only at the choices that are available to individuals, but at "the social and economic environments in which [they] pla[y] out"',[61] or simply provides an element of material and bodily reality to the politics of social policy, it acknowledges the abstracted and therefore purely theoretical nature of liberal autonomy.

Others take the contextual nature of autonomy further. These scholars suggest that law should not be based on the assumption that people are competent, detached and independent, and thus entitled to have this form of autonomy protected, but that the law should actively acknowledge our interdependence with others. This idea of autonomy, often called 'relational autonomy', takes the individual to be 'first and foremost a social being with an important network of people with whom she/he has a close relationship, forming part of his/her identity'.[62] It

---

60 See for example, Jennifer Nedelsky, 'Reconceiving Autonomy: Sources, Thoughts and Possibilities' (1989) 1 *Yale Journal of Law & Feminism* 7; Herring, 'Relational Autonomy'; Catriona Mackenzie and Natalie Stoljar, *Relational Autonomy: Feminist Perspectives on Autonomy, Agency and the Social Self* (Oxford University Press, 2000).

61 *Quebec v A* (n 11) [342] (Justice Abella), quoting Margot Young, 'Unequal to the Task: "Kapp'ing" the Substantive Potential of Section 15' in Sanda Rodgers and Sheila McIntyre (eds), *The Supreme Court of Canada and Social Justice: Commitment, Retrenchment or Retreat* (LexisNexis Canada, 2010) 183.

62 Roy Gilbar, 'Family Involvement, Independence and Patient Autonomy in Practice' (2011) 19(2) *Med L Rev* 192, 198.

is this relationship with others and not the individual's separation from them that enables the individual to make autonomous decisions.

> This conception of autonomy takes into account the relationships that affect the individual's efforts to be a self-determining and responsible person. Relational autonomy is thus a reciprocal process because it places the individual in the context of a dynamic balance between people who are closely involved in each others' lives. Relational autonomy is also collaborative in that the individual recognises his/her dependence on close intimates when trying to achieve a goal.[63]

As Herring says, 'a relational life is inevitable'; 'Our decisions are not just "ours", they usually affect those we are in relationship with and their decisions will affect others'.[64] Lady Hale's statements regarding Mr Granatino's choices in the *Radmacher* case resonate with this relational idea of autonomy.

Anderson and Honneth's[65] critique of liberal autonomy prefers a Hegelian perspective of mutual recognition that criticises the individualistic bias in liberal accounts of autonomy that they say underestimate 'our dependence on relationships of respect, care and esteem'[66] which have 'crept in to modern theories of social justice'.[67] They set out a theory of autonomy that highlights vulnerabilities that are overlooked by even the conceptions of social justice and relational autonomy that 'accommodate the material and institutional circumstances of autonomy'.[68]

> In a nutshell, the central idea is that the agentic competencies that comprise autonomy require that one be able to sustain certain attitudes toward oneself (in particular self-trust, self-respect, and self-esteem) and that these affectively laden self-conceptions – or to use Hegelian language, 'practical relations-to-self' – are dependent, in turn, on the sustaining attitudes of others … One's relationship to oneself, then, is not a matter of a solitary ego reflecting on itself, but is the result of an on-going intersubjective process, in which one's attitude toward oneself emerges in one's encounter with another's attitude toward oneself.[69]

63 Ibid; Ann Donchin, 'Autonomy and Interdependence: Quandaries in Genetic Decision Making' in Mackenzie and Stoljar, *Relational Autonomy*; Herring, 'Relational Autonomy'.

64 Herring, 'Relational Autonomy' 267; of course, this recognition of the reality of interdependent living does not detract from the idea that our decisions are still in some sense 'ours' and must be 'owned' by the individual. It simply acknowledges that others, context and situation play a part in how we, as agents, experience that process and its outcomes. I am grateful to Julie Wallbank for discussion on this.

65 Joel Anderson and Axel Honneth, 'Autonomy, Vulnerability, Recognition, and Justice' in John Christman and Joel Anderson (eds), *Autonomy and the Challenges to Liberalism New Essays* (Cambridge University Press, 2005) ch 6.

66 Ibid, 127.

67 Ibid, 128.

68 Ibid, 130.

69 Ibid, 131.

But because self-esteem, self-trust and self-respect are fragile and vulnerable to various forms of injury, violation and denigration,[70] they must be protected in a just world. To be protected, they, together our intersubjective vulnerability, must be acknowledged as part of what makes us human.[71] Central to this idea of autonomy is our ability to establish ways of relating to *oneself* practically and therefore to require as a condition of its possibility, a supportive recognitional infrastructure.[72]

For Anderson and Honneth, such a supportive recognitional infrastructure as a condition for social justice would include a shift 'away from exclusively distributive issues'.[73] For them, symbolic–semantic resources and the way cultural patterns limit the range of available options are important factors that must be considered[74] for humans to be able to develop the metaphysical, psychological and moral capabilities to achieve self-esteem, self-respect and self-trust. This is important. In our examples of family finances, a supportive recognitional infrastructure might include a revaluation of care such that both carers and the cared for, those whose identities are linked in this way are not understood to be less than autonomous. The provision and receipt of care would be understood as a fundamental part of humanness, and thus would be accorded social value. Further, and crucially, the actual work of caregiving would not be associated with gender so as to limit the range of available life options for men and women.

Theorising vulnerability is coterminous with theorising autonomy. It also has generated a vast literature.[75] Again, for my family law purposes, for relational autonomy theorists, vulnerability is the individual interest's ever present susceptibility to the interests and influence of others.[76] Along with Anderson and Honneth, they would see vulnerability as an integral part of autonomy that to varying degrees could connote strength or weakness or something in between.

Fine and Glendinning's[77] work on carers and dependants also demonstrates that both dependency (or vulnerability in the new language), and autonomy are contested and constructed concepts. They draw upon a feminist discourse of care which calls attention both to the active doing of care work and to its universal-ness in the ethical realm and therefore as a precondition for justice. They argue that instead of viewing care as the product or outcome of a relationship between two

---

70 Ibid, 137.

71 Ibid, 140.

72 Ibid, 144.

73 Ibid, 142.

74 Ibid, 143.

75 Much of this literature regarding vulnerable adults is situated in the context of mental incompetence, ageing, incapacity, childhood or other so-called 'unusual' susceptibility to harm or risk. See, for example, Jonathan Herring, 'Vulnerability, Children, and the Law' in Michael Freeman (ed), *Law and Childhood Studies, Current Legal Issues Volume 14* (Oxford University Press, 2012) ch 16; and sources cited in Jennifer Collins (Chapter 2 in this volume), who draws particularly on the moral philosophy of Robert Goodin.

76 Herring, 'Vulnerability, Children, and the Law'.

77 Michael Fine and Caroline Glendinning, 'Dependence, Independence or Interdependence? Revisiting the Concepts of "Care" and "Dependency"' (2005) 25(4) *Ageing and Society* 601.

or more people, which is always relational and often mutual, policy on carers and dependents (dependent/vulnerable adults or children) casts the cared for and the carers into distinct and dichotomised fields[78] which assumes 'those who depend on care have interests, needs and perspectives that are radically different from the people who see themselves as responsible for providing it'.[79] This is because, they say, 'research and theory on dependency and care-giving have emerged from different theoretical paradigms and proceeded along largely separate lines';[80] 'so while concepts of autonomy and independence have received critical attention, they are promoted as the antithesis of dependency and as unproblematic and universally desirable goals'.[81] They argue, like the previous authors on autonomy, that these dichotomous fields are socially constructed, have an ideological dimension, are products of social relations rather than individual attributes, and finally that vulnerability is not, as it is perceived in law/policy, a negative state that must be alleviated.

Fineman[82] theorises vulnerability slightly differently. While she agrees that it is universal, constant and significant, she sees vulnerability as 'arising from our embodiment, which carries the ever-present possibility of harm and injury from mildly unfortunate to catastrophically devastating events'.[83] Because these events and everyone's risk of them are beyond human control they can be avoided by no one, even though we are positioned differently within a web of economic and institutional relationships so that our vulnerabilities vary. She therefore suggests that the 'vulnerable subject' rather than the liberal autonomous subject ought to rest at the heart of law and social policy. In this way, she therefore wishes to 'free "vulnerability" from its limited and negative associations' with victimhood, deprivation, dependency or pathology';[84] 'I wish to claim the term "vulnerable" for its potential in describing a universal, inevitable enduring aspect of the human condition that must be at the heart of our concept of social and state responsibility'.[85] While this is a laudable goal, and has much in common with the view of those judges who take a more expansive view of vulnerability than does, for example, the LASPO, Fineman still seems to understand vulnerability as a weakness that must be remedied, as a risk of danger, albeit one that all individuals constantly face on some level and to some degree. I suppose she aims to destigmatise it by highlighting its universality, but to me she still posits it as a condition that is opposed to

---

78 Ibid, 608.
79 Ibid, 602.
80 Ibid.
81 Ibid.
82 Martha Fineman, 'The Vulnerable Subject: Anchoring Equality in the Human Condition' in Martha Fineman (ed.), *Transcending the Boundaries of Law: Generations of Feminism and Legal Theory* (Routledge, 2011) 168; this chapter was originally published in (2008) 20 *Yale L J & Feminism* 1. All page references are to the 2011 publication.
83 Ibid, 166.
84 Ibid.
85 Ibid.

autonomy, rather than as a part of what makes us autonomous. Vulnerability for Fineman seems to be empowering exclusively because of the fact that all actors are at risk of suffering it. Her vision of social justice would be to minimise, equally for all, that risk and/or its consequent suffering. The autonomous subject would be replaced in law and policy by the vulnerable subject, rather than by a subject with a differently understood autonomy that contained, indeed needed, vulnerability.

Despite their differences, however, each of these re-theorsiations sees the independence that comes with autonomy and the vulnerability that comes with connection as fundamental to us all at all times. To a greater or lesser extent, they see the legal subject as characterised by both autonomy and vulnerability. Each also sees that positions, situations and relations affect or influence or determine what these mean to us and to the law/state. These views are different from the autonomy and vulnerability expressed in law. The question then becomes what they can contribute to analysis of disputes about financial issues in families, which are fundamentally gendered issues. In other words, not only do the current dominant meanings of autonomy and vulnerability offer an impoverished view of family living in both its private and public expressions, they have particular and direct impact upon women.

Autonomy and vulnerability as a gender issue

My first example of the gendered impact of current autonomy–vulnerability rhetoric is to claim that the dejuridification of financial issues on divorce, in the name of party autonomy, reinforces the view that any financial disadvantage that may result from familial (inter)dependence and/or care responsibilities is the result of a private, freely made choice rather than of those very relationships and other social structural factors and influences. This assumption is problematic because when justice has *come to mean* the freedom to express your choices, there is little law can do about disadvantage that results from them other than either reinforce it or to encourage its remedy also by choice, in the private sphere of contract. The public gaze that comes with the courts and the justice of other values, like equality or relationality are properly relevant only to the non-autonomous: the vulnerable. This means that because care work remains the primary function of families,[86] this view of justice simply reinforces the idea that both the value and the work of care lie inside the private concept of justice characterised by autonomy and choice, and outside the public, unless one successfully can claim 'vulnerable' status.

But the court, the public gaze of the law, must be able to influence what justice means in intimate relationships. By permitting courts to review disputes about the financial consequences of relationship decisions we bring into the public eye the relational nature and context of choices to care and not to care, not to mention their social and financial consequences. Care thus becomes a public issue. Its value is made visible which could have both distributional and recognitional

86 Diduck, 'What Is Family Law For?'

consequences. As Herring reminds us, '[w]e already live in a society in which care work goes largely unrecognised and unvalued. The making of financial orders on divorce is one of the few areas in which care work is recognised.'[87] By breaking down the autonomy–vulnerability (private–public) boundary the court can reinforce social values that the parties (or the stronger party) may ignore. Recall Lady Hale's observation in *Radmacher*, 'some may think it permissible to contract out of the guiding principles of equality and non-discrimination within marriage; others may think this a retrograde step likely only to benefit the strong at the expense of the weak'.[88] While women continue to perform the majority of care work in society and while care work itself is linked to gender no matter who does it, this is a real concern, both for the women involved and for society generally.

Finally, acknowledging that care work can render an autonomous person financially vulnerable and not merely be an expression of her autonomy begins to see vulnerability differently from LASPO's circumscribed vision of it and would be an improvement on the rigidity of the category boundaries in the current rhetoric. But even this view would still require carers to claim vulnerable status and thereby relinquish their autonomy before the court became involved with them rather than seeing care work as an expression of simultaneous vulnerability and autonomy. While autonomy is promoted as the ideal legal and moral state to which all should aspire, being forced to claim the unfortunate 'condition' of vulnerability undermines carers and the work that they do. It violates both relational and recognitional ideas of autonomy.

The second reason why autonomy and vulnerability are gender issues relates specifically to the LASPO. Legal aid in family matters is used disproportionately by women compared to men, and the LASPO provisions will thus be felt more keenly by women[89] who will be forced to claim domestic violence victimhood in order to gain access to the courts. As mentioned above, the effect this has upon their recognitional autonomy is significant. Further, when the vulnerable do get to court, the court's role is seen to be to promote their autonomy by remedying their vulnerability. But like the feminist questions asked of formal equality, why should this vision of the legal subject, and what justice means for him, be the standard all are meant to achieve?

The question above links to a further and broader gender aspect of this discussion. Note also that like other dichotomies in liberalism, the autonomy–vulnerability dichotomy is gendered. While the actual autonomous or vulnerable person is not always sexed male and female, the vulnerable side of the dichotomy is feminised and the autonomous side is masculinised. Each needs the other to give

---

87 Herring, 'Relational Autonomy' 270; Alison Diduck, 'Relationship Fairness' in Anne Bottomley and Simone Wong (eds), *Changing Contours of Domestic Life, Family and Law: Caring and Sharing* (Hart, 2009) ch 5.

88 *Radmacher* (n 15) [135].

89 Ministry of Justice, *Reform of Legal Aid in England and Wales: Equalities Impact Assessment* (Ministry of Justice 2011) (webarchive.nationalarchives.gov.uk/20111121205348/http://www.justice.gov.uk/downloads/consultations/eia-scope-changes.pdf, accessed 24 May 2013).

it meaning. And while autonomy is linked to independence and freedom, its other will always be linked to connection and dependence. Combined with the reality that actual care work is linked to gender, vulnerability and autonomy are continually reinforced as gendered concepts. In this light, the state's active pursuit and promotion of autonomy, one side of the dichotomy it itself has created, the masculine side, leaves it open to meaningful feminist critique. This feminist critique would reveal the way in which in a 'male' state, an impoverished, 'male' idea of autonomy would be the default subject status and the default 'neutral' standard of justice. In this state, an equally impoverished, 'female' idea of vulnerability would define autonomy's 'other' or deficit that required a remedy, usually in the form of protection or beneficence. Further, in this state, fairness in financial arrangements on separation would mean less non-discrimination, equality, meeting of need, and recognition of inherent vulnerability in all, and would mean instead not only the assumption of, but the active promotion of the abstract, 'male' autonomy which then *comes to define* fairness and objectivity. In this state, we would see an example of the power of the powerful to create reality and truth (here of 'fairness') from one point of view only; '[f]rom a feminist perspective, male supremacist jurisprudence erects qualities valued from the male point of view as standards for the proper and actual relations between life and law'.[90] In this state, therefore, when there is a balance to be struck between the 'competing values' of non-discrimination and substantive equality on one side and freedom and autonomy on the other, perhaps it is not surprising that autonomy wins.

Catharine MacKinnon claims that feminist method does not seek to revitalise the subjugated part of a dichotomy, or to create equality between them, but to reject and overthrow the distinctions themselves.[91] To the extent that relational or recognitional autonomy and vulnerability do this, they are profoundly feminist. Most clearly, however, to the extent that family law reinforces the dichotomy between the vulnerable and the autonomous at the same time as it seeks to protect both, it remains blind to the reality of family living and to the gendered justice it endorses for family subjects. The consequences for family carers, overwhelmingly women, and family care may be serious.

90 Catherine MacKinnon, *Toward a Feminist Theory of the State* (Harvard University Press, 1989) 238.
91 Ibid, 120–1.

Chapter 7

Mediation and vulnerable parents

Christine Piper

Future oriented – a new start?

> We believe that mediation is all about story telling. It opens with each client presenting a story. It continues as the mediator helps the clients develop a mutual story about their problem. While doing this, the story moves from a blaming past-focus, to a cooperating, future-focus that leads to an agreement embodying a future with a difference for all involved.[1]

Family mediation is predicated on the future. John Haynes, a pioneer in the USA and then worldwide of mediation development and training in the 1980s and 1990s,[2] stated that a mediator can mediate only in the future tense.[3] In the UK the Consultation and the White Papers on divorce reform issued by the then Lord Chancellor's Department in 1993 and 1995 were entitled *Looking to the Future: Mediation and the Ground for Divorce*. Their focus was a period of 'reflection and consideration' in which arrangements would be made for the future and their contention was that '[a] divorce process based on a requirement to reflect rather than recriminate will help to reduce conflict and encourage cooperation, which will in turn minimise the distress caused to children'.[4] The current divorce law with its focus on fault in the past or on pre-divorce separation would have gone. Nevertheless, the procedure for divorce and for decisions about the children of separating parents – as well as the thinking about what is 'best' – has been influenced greatly by the explosion of interest in mediation in those decades. Changes in legal aid funding, together with the use – or non-use – of the family courts for

---

1 John M. Haynes, Gretchen L. Haynes and Larry Sun Fong, *Mediation: Positive Conflict Management* (State University of New York Press, 2004) 9.
2 See Thelma Fisher, 'John Haynes' *Guardian* (Obituaries, 9 March 2000) (www.guard ian.co.uk/news/2000/mar/09/guardianobituaries1, accessed 25 May 2013), for a summary of his achievements.
3 Haynes et al, *Mediation* 7.
4 Lord Chancellor's Department, *Looking to the Future: Mediation and the Ground for Divorce: The Government's Proposals* (Cm 2799, 1995) para 4.37.

such decision-making,[5] have further consolidated and enhanced this focus on the future and on the ability of parents to mediate an acceptable outcome.

This chapter stems from a concern that this future focus might downgrade or make invisible in mediation the nature of the parents' relationship and parenting before separation and that this might produce or exacerbate vulnerability. Of particular concern is the management by mediators of issues around the parenting contributions and decision-making of the parents pre-separation, and around the possibility that the relationship between the parents may have involved abuse, violence or other forms of control. This chapter will discuss both of these issues. It would be problematic – in terms of the safety of family members and also of the abused parent's ability to negotiate – if domestic abuse was not dealt with appropriately. [6] However, the downgrading of past parenting might also be problematic, notably if it left a parent with unhelpful feelings of injustice or if the sidelining of information about a child's care led to child welfare concerns in the future. While these issues have been part of long-standing concerns about gender differentials in mediation[7] and child-focused disputes,[8] current developments in law and policy may well intensify the creation of vulnerability in mediation.

Reconfiguring parenting

The concern that those who do most or all of the caregiving – still usually the mothers[9] – might find that the expertise, experience and years of hard parenting work are not given full weight by lawyers and mediators is certainly not new. Researchers in the late 1980s and early 1990s were becoming aware of this.

> The problem, then, that faces mothers is how to be heard, because, although the repertoire of maternal instinct is alive and well in everyday life, it is increasingly an exhausted script in the divorce courts and solicitors' offices.[10]

5 See, for example, Julie Doughty and Mervyn Murch, 'Judicial Independence and the Restructuring of Family Courts and Their Support Services' (2012) 24(3) *CFLQ* 333–54; Mavis Maclean and John Eekelaar, 'Legal Representation in Family Matters and the Reform of Legal Aid: A Research Note on Current Practice' (2012) 24(2) *CFLQ* 223–33.

6 For a review of the early literature, see Felicity Kaganas and Christine Piper, 'Domestic Violence and Divorce Mediation' (1994) 3 *J of Social Welfare and Family Law* 265–78.

7 See, for example, Joan B. Kelly and Mary A. Duryee 'Women's and Men's Views of Mediation in Voluntary and Mandatory Mediation Settings' (1992) 30(1) *Family and Conciliation Courts Review* 34–49, and see other articles on gender in that issue; Robert Dingwall, David Greatbatch and Lucia Ruggerone, 'Gender and Interaction in Divorce Mediation' (1998) 15(4) *Conflict Resolution Quarterly* 277–87.

8 Carol Smart, 'The Legal and Moral Ordering of Child Custody' (1991) 18(4) *Journal of Law and Society* 485–500.

9 See, for example, Jo Bridgeman, Heather Keating and Craig Lind (eds), *Regulating Family Responsibilities* (Ashgate, 2011) chs in Part 1.

10 Smart, 'Legal and Moral Ordering' 486; Carol Bruch, 'And How Are the Children? The Effects of Ideology and Mediation on Child Custody Law and Children's Well-Being in the United States' (1988) 2(1) *Int J Law Policy Family* 106–26.

My personal experience ... had led to a feeling of unease that the past lives of parents attending mediation were being treated ... in a somewhat cavalier fashion and, in particular, that their parenting 'histories' were being made irrelevant by the concentration on present disputes and future new beginnings.[11]

Research then and since has revealed three sets of developments which have facilitated a sidelining of past experience of caring for children and a consequent change in the balance of arguments and ideas feeding into a mediated solution. First, mediators have developed strategies to reconstruct the contributions of parents so that they can present them as more 'equal' and 'joint'. Second, ideas about 'the welfare of the child' have in practice narrowed: particular wider aspects of a child's well-being have been given priority – and others downgraded – in a development linked to reconstructions of what counts as parental responsibility. Third, an increasingly important focus of policy and practice on information and advice for separating parents supports the idea that post-separation parenting is a new start in which both parents equally need to learn what to do: again the past is not relevant.

Mediator techniques[12]

Parents, notably mothers, who still do more care work with the children of a family, may raise issues in mediation about pre-separation parenting differentials and may wish to base arguments on that experience. Mediators may then 'neutralise' past responsibilities[13] such that inputs into parenting in the past are either constructed as more equal or are treated as not relevant. One tactic is to balance caring about with caring for, so equating the weight of 'emotional' and practical care.[14] This can be contextualised within the long-standing feminist concern that the (low) 'worth' of 'caring for' is determined by those who are able to avoid doing it[15] and also within feminist analysis which contrasts an ethic of care – whereby morality centres 'around the understanding of responsibility and relationships'[16] – with an ethic of justice.

11 Christine Piper, *The Responsible Parent: A Study of Divorce Mediation* (Harvester Wheatsheaf, 1993) 160; Dingwall et al, 'Gender and Interaction' 277–87.
12 For a recent theoretical article on mediator techniques generally, with reference to research, see J. A. Wall, Suzanne Chan-Serafin and Timothy Dunne, 'Mediator Pressing Techniques: A Theoretical Model of their Determinants' (2012) 21(5) *Group Decision and Negotiation* 601–19.
13 Piper, *Responsible Parent* 91.
14 Smart, 'Legal and Moral Ordering' 491.
15 See, for example, Joan Tronto, *Moral Boundaries : A Political Argument for an Ethic of Care* (Routledge, 1993); Selma Sevenhuijsen, *Citizenship and the Ethics of Care: Feminist Considerations on Justice, Morality, and Politics* (trans, Liz Savage) (Routledge, 1998); Chapters 3 and 11 in this volume by Jonathan Herring and Jo Bridgeman.
16 See, Carol Gilligan, *In a Different Voice: Psychological Theory and Women's Development* (Harvard University Press, 1982) 19.

Another technique is simply to ignore, in effect, a parent's comment about the past as Dingwall and colleagues found in the 1990s. They noted that mediators did not respond to comments such as 'men don't do their fair share of the housework' and argued that the lack of challenge 'is bound into the structural realities of neutrality within mediation'.[17] The researchers admit that not challenging stereotypes could be seen as unethical but do not address the fact that the lack of challenge might give a particular message. Nor do they address the issue as to whether a parent's comments about parenting (in)abilities might need to be addressed. However, on the basis of more recent research, Trinder and colleagues refer to similar mediator techniques – in relation to allegations of abuse – as 'passing up opportunities' and 'closing down and changing topics': the issue is not followed up or the response is such that the mother decides not to pursue it.[18] They also found another set of techniques which they refer to as 'historicising' the critical comment of a parent, 'characterising the allegation as relating only to the past and with no on-going or current relevance'[19] and emphasising new starts. This corresponds with a comment in a much earlier study where, for example, a mother who complained that the father in the past did not want to look after children on a Saturday was told, 'I think you have got to remember that when you do split up life is exceedingly different for both of you'.[20]

Another tactic is to suggest that the less experienced parent is learning. What a father aspires to do if given the opportunity to see or look after the child – his 'aspirational' investment – may, therefore, be given considerable weight.[21] However this rests on what Wallbank refers to as 'an optimistic view of fathering'[22] whereby a father can be constructed as being worthy to engage with contact and caregiving to the future benefit of the child.[23] However, Smart's research led her to conclude: 'Fathers in this situation are regarded much like the prodigal son and mothers feel a serious sense of injustice when the work and loyalty they have demonstrated over many years is treated so lightly by comparison.'[24] As one mother interviewed after mediation said, 'They [the mediators] kept pointing out what he was trying to do and I felt my hard work looking after the children wasn't acknowledged'.[25]

---

17 Dingwall et al, 'Gender and Interaction' 281, 283.
18 Liz Trinder, Alan Firth and Christopher Jenks, '"So Presumably Things Have Moved on Since Then?" The Management of Risk Allegations in Child Contact Dispute Resolution' (2010) 24(1) Int J Law Policy Family 29–53, 34–8.
19 Ibid, 41.
20 Piper, *Responsible Parent* 92.
21 Julie Wallbank, '(En)Gendering the Fusion of Rights and Responsibilities in the Law of Contact' in Julie Wallbank, Shazia Choudhry and Jonathan Herring (eds), *Rights, Gender and Family Law* (Routledge, 2010) 107.
22 Ibid, 104.
23 Wallbank consequently argues for more account to be taken of patterns of investment in caregiving before separation (ibid, 114).
24 Smart, 'Legal and Moral Ordering' 485–500, fn 19.
25 Piper, *Responsible Parent* 162; see also, for discussion of another mediator technique to control the process, Robert Dingwall and David Greatbatch, 'Selective Facilitation: Some Preliminary

Parenting also involves decision-making – indeed it is the essence of the legal concept of parental responsibility[26] and a mediator technique is simply to make clear that the mediator is assuming that parents both have relevant experience and can make joint decisions: an assumption it would be difficult for a parent to refute. Although Joan Kelly, a clinical psychologist and early supporter of divorce mediation, explicitly argued that 'most parents that seek a divorce were not in major conflict regarding child rearing issues during marriage' so that such parents 'are likely candidates for co-operation concerning child rearing after divorce',[27] decision-making can also have been problematic pre-separation. A lack of major conflict does not mean that there was active cooperation and joint decision-making, or that separate spheres of decision making had been mutually negotiated: there are, then, several possible models of pre-separation decision-making.[28] Empirical research science on marital/couple decision-making is, however, sparse and rarely focuses on decisions about the upbringing of the children. Certainly in the 1970s and 1980s, when the new ideas about joint parenting and the benefits of mediation were emerging, the evidence as to how decisions were made in practice most often centred on choice of residence, job, friends and large consumer purchases.[29] Further the results often depended on exact definitions of 'joint' and 'shared' and by no means always implied 'equal', in much the same way as 'shared parenting' now covers a wide range of 'sharing' in the context of residence and contact. More recent good research is sparse. The research by Butler and colleagues sheds light on family decision-making but concentrates on parent–child decision-making.[30]

Much of the literature also assumes that the exercise of decision-making establishes the power of the decision-maker but it might, I have argued, indicate 'a wife to whom the power of making trivial decisions about soap powders, socks and sausages had been delegated against her will'.[31] That conclusion was based on interviewing a sample of 16 fathers and 14 mothers who were interviewed after mediation in the mid-1980s. They were asked separately about their parenting and decision-making prior to separation and they gave the highest percentage of 'jointly decided' answers for the following two decisions: where the children were to be born (79 per cent) and whether the children should be involved in any religious instruction or activity (78 per cent). Several other decisions, such as

Observations on a Strategy Used by Divorce Mediators' (1989) 23(4) *Law and Society Review* 613–41.

26 Children Act 1989, s 3.

27 Joan Kelly, 'Further Observations on Joint Custody' (1983) 16 *U C Davis L Rev* 762–70, 762.

28 For a categorisation into five models, see Piper, *Responsible Parent* 37.

29 Ibid, 38–9 for references to research by Blood, Edgell, Feree, Godwin, le Masters, Platt, Scanzoni, Weiss and Wolfe.

30 Ian Butler, Margaret Robinson and Lesley Scanlan, *Children and Decision Making* (National Children's Bureau, 2005).

31 Piper, *Responsible Parent* 39; see also Constantina Safilios-Rothschild, 'Family Sociology or Wives' Sociology?' (1969) 31(2) *Journal of Marriage and the Family* 290–301.

which should be the child's first school or when the child could first walk to school without adult supervision, were decided jointly in just over half the families. The areas with the fewest joint answers and the most 'mother-only' answers concerned potty training (12 per cent joint) and whether friends of the children could come to the house (22 per cent). Overall these parents felt that four out of ten child-related decisions had been decided jointly but that the mother had been responsible for making nearly all the remaining decisions.[32] Although the data is difficult to interpret, the latter would seem to be the result of the greater caring load born by mothers – a differential which Herring's chapter in this volume shows has continued.

The prevailing view of the child's best interests

The other development which has facilitated the downplaying of the past is the change in the way in which children and their best interests are conceptualised. In practice an examination of the best interests of the child has been narrowed in scope by the emergence and consolidation of three particular ideas: that the best outcome is one agreed by the parents (not professionals, and certainly not courts); that contact with both parents is so crucial a benefit for children that it can outweigh other, possibly detrimental, factors; and that the future well-being of the children can override current issues.

These ideas about the welfare of the child are influential in mediation at least in part because it is usually an 'abstract' image of the child which is the focus of mediation. There is rarely a clear idea of the 'real' child in question to underpin the discussions in mediation. Analysis of audiotaped in-court conciliation sessions found that mediators referred to constructs of children and concluded that 'conciliators rely on applying universal child welfare principles to individual children whom they have never met'.[33] Dingwall et al also noted in relation to their analysis of mediation sessions in the early 1990s that 'Fathers were more likely than mothers to refer to abstract as opposed to experiential knowledge about children and their needs' and so 'fathers were more likely to discuss children's needs in terms of what children in general require than to their specific children'.[34] They go on to state, 'Both male and female mediators tended to refer mainly to abstract knowledge about children and their needs' and that, as children were not present, 'mediators could only legitimate comments about the needs and feelings of particular children by references to children in general. This could lead to both male and female mediators formulating issues concerning the children in ways more similar to those of fathers than of mothers.'[35] The researchers commented that in

---

32 Ibid, 42–3.
33 Liz Trinder, Christopher Jenks and Alan Firth, 'Talking Children into Being *in absentia*? Children as a Strategic and Contingent Resource in Family Court Dispute Resolution' (2010) 22(2) *CFLQ* 234–57, 256.
34 Dingwall et al, 'Gender and Interaction' 281.
35 Ibid.

this sample, this was 'balanced by the active solicitation of experiential knowledge from both parents' and that 'it was noticeable that if fathers did not produce such knowledge, this might undermine their position'.[36] Yet as we noted above, the disregarding or discounting of the caregiving parent's comments could undermine their position too.

Responsible parents agreeing

Nearly thirty years ago, in an article for *Family Law* entitled 'Research on Divorce and Children: Implications for Reform in Divorce Proceedings', the Child Care and Development Group at Cambridge referred to 'what is maybe the new norm in society about divorce when children are involved that two adults may be free to decide they want to end their marital relationship but they are not relieved of their joint responsibilities towards their children'. [37] This points up an increasingly important issue at that time – the development and use by law of what might be termed child welfare science. The title of a book by Clulow and Vincent in 1987 – about the involvement of divorce court welfare officers in mediation – also had an instructive title: *In the Child's Best Interests*.[38] Alongside the 'truth' that good parents do not use courts was an idea rapidly becoming established as a truth about mediation – that mediated outcomes are best for children. A few years later Judge Pearce asked a rhetorical question which is now very familiar: 'The prime objective is, and always has been, the best interest of the child. The rest follows on because what could be better for the child than to have parents and other carers sharing parental responsibility and ordering their family affairs by agreement?'[39]

More recently, the same ideas about the benefits and feasibility of parentally mediated outcomes can be found in the Consultation Paper on Legal Aid[40] and the Norgrove review of the family justice system in England and Wales.[41] The guiding principles of the latter[42] and the thrust of the former make clear the aim is to ensure as far as possible that separating parents use mediation and do not use the courts and that, if necessary, parents would have to be 'educated' into accepting such ideas as to what is responsible parenting. So, for example, the Legal Aid Green Paper stated:

36 Ibid.
37 Mary Lund, 'Research on Divorce and Children: Implications for Reform in Divorce Proceedings' (1984) 14 *Fam Law* 198–201, 200.
38 Christopher Clulow and C. Vincent, *In the Child's Best Interests* (Sweet & Maxwell/Tavistock, 1987).
39 N. Pearce, 'First Impressions of the Children Act: A Judge's Assessment' (1992) 2(1) *Family Conciliation* 10–13, 10.
40 Ministry of Justice, *Proposals for the Reform of Legal Aid in England and Wales* (Cm 7967, 2010). The government consequently issued the Legal Aid, Sentencing and Punishment of Offenders Bill in June 2011.
41 David Norgrove, *Family Justice Review. Interim Report* (Ministry of Justice, 2011)
42 The 'Terms of Reference' were announced on 20 January 2010; they are reproduced at Annexe A of the *Final Report* (www.gov.uk/government/uploads/system/uploads/attachment_data/file/162302/family-justice-review-final-report.pdf.pdf, accessed 27 May 2013).

These proposals support wider plans to move towards a simpler justice system; one which is more accessible to the public, which limits the scope for inappropriate litigation and the involvement of lawyers in issues which do not need legal input; and which supports people in resolving their issues out of Court, using simpler, more informal remedies.[43]

The Interim Review, in setting out what it considered to be the way forward, also focused on parental responsibility for coming to agreement:

There is a great need for parental education across the board – from parental responsibility, to how the law is applied, to likely outcomes of parental disputes. The focus of conflict resolution should be clear: children have *rights* – to be cared for, to have meaningful relationships with both their parents and to be financially supported; parents have *responsibilities* to provide this.[44]

The Consultation Paper on child maintenance in the same year, explicitly aiming 'to reflect the general direction of the on-going Family Justice Review,'[45] also emphasised parental responsibility: 'We want to enable and empower parents to have more responsibility in making their own informed choices to establish enduring post-separation arrangements'.[46] As the Paper explained:

Underlying our approach is the assumption that government should use mechanisms to encourage and support parents to … make *family-based arrangements* concerning these issues wherever possible, which is better for children, rather than relying on government services to step in and administer these arrangements on parents' behalf.[47]

The Legal Aid Green Paper clarified what was considered to be 'inappropriate litigation':

We do not consider that it will generally be in the best interest of the children involved for these essentially personal matters to be resolved in the adversarial forum of a court. The Government's view is that people should take responsibility for resolving such issues themselves, and that this is best for both the parents and the children involved.[48]

43 Ministry of Justice, *Proposals for the Reform of Legal Aid* para 2.5.
44 Norgrove, *Interim Report* para 5.59.
45 Department for Work and Pensions, *Strengthening Families, Promoting Parental Responsibility* (Cm 7990, 2011) 'Ministerial Foreword', 5.
46 Ibid.
47 Department for Work and Pensions, *Strengthening Families* 6, emphasis in original; but see Gillian Douglas and Members of the Network on Family, Regulation and Society, 'Contact Is Not a Commodity to Be Bartered for Money' (2011) 41 *Fam Law* 491–6 for a robust critique of the suggestion that contact and payment of maintenance might be linked.
48 Ministry of Justice, *Proposals for the Reform of Legal Aid* para 4.20.

Consequently, the Legal Aid, Sentencing and Punishment of Offenders Act 2012 legislated to remove the possibility of obtaining funded legal advice and representation in relation to family matters: Schedule 1 lists the types of case which can receive civil legal aid but disputes over contact and residence are not included there unless they come within the exceptional cases listed in s 9 and defined in the Schedule. Funding remains available for mediation.[49]

So we have a concept of welfare which requires a certain kind of parent: one who is able – and must – make joint decisions about the children as part of their personal family matters. This is, of course, very different from the ideas which underpinned the lack of confidence of the Royal Commission on Marriage and Divorce, reporting in 1956, that parents could safely be left to make arrangements when emotionally affected by their divorce.[50] Their concern led to the requirement that the court should oversee arrangements for all children of divorcing parents (now section 41 of the Matrimonial Causes Act 1973). In her chapter Wallbank notes that the government intends to remove what has become an anomaly in the new discourse of parental competence and empowerment.

This reconstruction of what counts as good parenting has taken place over the last thirty to forty years: research on the process of mediation[51] in the 1980s and early 1990s led to convincing empirical data suggesting that crucial concepts such as parenting and responsibility were being constructed with particular meanings[52] and that those constructions of the 'responsible parent' were an immensely important tool in achieving agreement in mediation.[53] Mediation was then being presented as an ideal medium for both allowing and encouraging parental responsibility. The Booth Committee set up in 1982 stated, for example, that '(i)t is the essence of conciliation that responsibility remains at all times with the parties themselves'.[54] Such ideas are now taken for granted[55] in policy discussion but they had to be established as such – and might not have been. They were not the dominant 'truths' of any system of communication prior to the 1970s.

---

49 The Children and Families Bill 2013 clause 10 would give a statutory basis for the compulsory Family Mediation Information and Assessment Meeting for anyone wishing to make a family application to the court.

50 Cmd 9678 (the 'Morton Commission').

51 Usually referred to as conciliation until the end of the 1980s: in December 1991 the National Family Conciliation Council changed its name to the National Association of Family Mediation and Conciliation Services. For a review see Brenda Hale, '30 years of National Family Mediation: Past, Present and Future' (2012) 42(11) *Fam Law* 1336–43.

52 Robert Dingwall and David Greatbatch, 'Behind Closed Doors: A Preliminary Report on Mediator/Client Interaction in England' (1991) 29 *Family and Conciliation Courts Review* 291; Christine Piper 'Divorce Conciliation in the UK: How Responsible are Parents?' (1988) 16 *International Journal of the Sociology of Law* 477–94.

53 Piper, *Responsible Parent* 84–106.

54 Dame Margaret Booth, *Report of the Matrimonial Causes Procedure Committee* (HMSO 1985) para 3.10.

55 That knowledge is taken for granted as being true is the third stage in the social process of constructing reality as identified by Peter Berger and Thomas Luckmann in *The Social Construction of Reality* (Doubleday, 1966).

The resulting entrenched and controlling ideas about parental responsibility[56] have led to a range of binary moral judgments as to what is considered good or bad in relation to separating parents. A good divorce 'is harmonious and is characterised by behaviour which plans properly for the future'[57] and 'divorce has been reinterpreted as a moral lesson': the divide is 'now between good and bad divorce'.[58] By the end of the 1990s there were also clear distinctions being assumed by policy-makers and lawyers between 'good' and 'bad' family solicitors.[59] So the 'good parent' aspiring to a 'good divorce' is one who uses good solicitors or, preferably, mediation, and agrees to arrangements for the children. Within family policy, and also in wider social policies, parental responsibility has come to be used in such a way that culpability is often implied[60] and a normative message is always given.[61] Those messages are clear and consistent: mediation is 'simpler', parents must exercise their responsibility to make 'family-based' decisions, litigation is 'inappropriate' and, if necessary, parents will be 'taught' how to be responsible. And what is best for the child is to have this sort of parent.

This valorising of mediation and mutually agreed plans in relation to the child's welfare is significant for a concern with vulnerability because of the psychological (and, increasingly, financial) pressure it puts on parents to try to achieve a mediated agreement, a pressure which might not be felt equally by the parents and which might silence concerns. It is true not all parents will internalise this[62] but differential internalisation becomes even more of an issue when the message is so

---

56 Jo Bridgeman, 'Parental Responsibility, Responsible Parenting and Legal Regulation' in Jo Bridgeman, Craig Lind and Heather Keating (eds), *Responsibility, Law and the Family* (Ashgate, 2008); Kathryn Hollingsworth, 'Responsibility and Rights: Children and Their Parents in the Youth Justice System' (2007) 21(2) *IJLPF* 190–219; Rebecca Probert, Stephen Gilmore and Jonathan Herring (eds), *Responsible Parents and Parental Responsibility* (Hart, 2009); Helen Reece, *Divorcing Responsibly* (Hart, 2003); Helen Reece, 'From Parental Responsibility to Parenting Responsibly' in Michael Freeman (ed), *Law and Sociology: Current Legal Issues* (Oxford University Press, 2006) 459–83.

57 Shelley Day Sclater, *Divorce: A Psychosocial Study* (Ashgate, 1999) 178.

58 Reece, *Divorcing Responsibly* 158.

59 Bren Neale and Carol Smart, '"Good" and "Bad" Lawyers? Struggling in the Shadow of the New Law' (1997) 19(4) *Journal of Social Welfare and Family Law* 377–402; Michael King, '"Being Sensible": Images and Practices of the New Family Lawyers' (1999) 28(02) *Journal of Social Policy* 249–73.

60 Shelley Day Sclater and Christine Piper, 'Remoralising the Family: Family Policy, Family Law and Youth Justice' (2000) 12(2) *CFLQ* 135–51; S. Edwards and A. Halpern, 'Parental Responsibility: An Instrument of Social Policy' (1992) 22 *Fam Law* 113–18; Kathryn Hollingsworth, 'Responsibility and Rights: Children and Their Parents in the Youth Justice System' (2007) 21(2) *IJLPF* 190–219; Christine Piper, 'Divorce Reform and the Image of the Child' (1996) 23(3) *Journal of Law and Society* 364–82.

61 The explicitness of the normative messages issuing from Lord Chancellor's Department in the Consultation and White Paper documents leading up to the Family Law Act 1996 (LCD 1993, 1995) pointed out the novelty of using family law in such a clear way to give 'messages': see John Eekelaar, 'Family law: Keeping Us "on Message"' (1999) 11(4) *CFLQ* 387–96; Christine Piper, 'How Do You Define a Family Lawyer?' (1999) 19(1) *LS* 93–111.

62 See, for example, Karen Laing, 'Doing the Right Thing: Cohabiting Parents, Separation and Child Contact' (2006) 20(2) *IJLPF* 169–80. This article reports a study of couples who had attended a pilot information meeting in 1998–9.

strong and specific and, as Kaganas and Day Sclater concluded, parents internalise the messages of the welfare discourse in different and often unexpected ways.[63] One of those clear messages concerns the involvement in the child's life of both parents after separation.

The benefits of contact outweigh other factors

Maidment wrote in 1984 in her book on divorce and child custody that 'The child's right to be protected against damage caused by losing one parent should thus be seen as creating a correlative duty or responsibility on each parent to continue his role as parent to a child.'[64] This somewhat spurious discourse of the child's right to contact and the parents' duty to continue to share parenting has, of course, become more influential since then. The narrowing of the concept of the welfare of the child to one which upholds above all else the 'good' of contact – and increasingly now of shared residence – is clearly problematic given that academics have regularly explained that the 'science' underpinning such a narrowing is very complex and does not unequivocally uphold contact as always beneficial.[65] To make matters worse, the science is now used to prove that short-term pain leads to considerable long-term gain and so the nature and quality of present contact is downgraded.[66]

Such assumptions mean that concerns about contact – including concerns relating to physical caring for the child during contact – and about other aspects of the child's life are themselves downgraded. The Children and Families Bill 2013 would introduce an even stronger assumption about the benefit of parental involvement after separation by inserting a new sub-section 2A into the welfare test in s 1 of the Children Act 1989:

> A court, in the circumstances mentioned in subsection (4)(a) or (7), is as respects each parent within subsection (6)(a) to presume, unless the contrary

---

63 Felicity Kaganas and Shelley Day Sclater, 'Contact Disputes: Narrative Constructions of "Good" Parents' (2004) 12 *Feminist Legal Studies* 1–27.

64 Susan Maidment, *Child Custody and Divorce* (Croom Helm, 1984) 167.

65 R. Bailey-Harris, G. Davis, J. Barron and J. Pearce, *Monitoring Private Law Applications under the Children Act: A Research Report to the Nuffield Foundation* (University of Bristol, 1998); Judith Wallerstein and Julia Lewis, 'The Long-Term Impact of Divorce on Children: A First Report from a 25-Year Study' (1998) 34(3) *Family and Conciliation Courts Review* 368–83; Christine Piper, 'Assumptions about Children's Best Interests' (2000) 22(3) *Journal of Social Welfare and Family Law* 261–76; Stephen Gilmore, 'Contact/Shared Residence and Child Well-being: Research Evidence and Its Implications for Legal Decision-Making' (2006) 20(3) *Int J Law Policy Family* 344; Stephen Gilmore, 'The Assumption that Contact Is Beneficial: Challenging the "Secure Foundation"' (2008) 38 *Fam Law* 1226; Adrienne Barnett, 'The Welfare of the Child Re-visited: In Whose Best Interests? Part 1' (2009) 39 *Fam Law* 50; Belinda Fehlberg, Bruce Smyth, Mavis Maclean and Ceridwen Roberts, 'Caring for Children after Parental Separation: Would Legislation for Shared Parenting Time Help Children?' (Department of Social Policy and Intervention, Family Policy Briefing Paper No 7, 2011).

66 Christine Piper, 'Investing in a Child's Future: Too Risky?' (2010) 22(1) *CFLQ* 1–20.

is shown, that involvement of that parent in the life of the child concerned will further the child's welfare.[67]

On the basis of Australian experience after the implementation of the 'friendly parent' addition to the Australian welfare checklist by the Shared Parental Responsibility Act 2006, Rhoades urges caution about using statutory principles.[68] Until removed by the recent Family Violence Act 2011 the Australian provision required the courts to have regard to each parent's willingness to 'facilitate, and encourage, a close and continuing relationship between the child and the other parent' when deciding what orders to make.[69] The changes in 2006 also introduced a presumption of 'equal shared parental responsibility for children' which, if it applied, directed the court to consider orders for the child to spend equal time with each parent.[70] That presumption could be displaced by evidence of abuse within the family.[71] Research has suggested, however, that a focus on encouraging a 'meaningful relationship' between non-resident parent and child was sometimes at the expense of protection for family members; further, that a focus on violence diverted from an assessment of other potential or actual harms to the child.[72] Where the presumption applies, therefore, a full discussion of 'best interests' is precluded.

What the assumptions in English law and the presumptions in Australian law have produced is an implicit acceptable range of outcomes – the 'parameters of the permissible' as Davis and colleagues phrased it in relation to mediated agreements:[73] 'Within these parameters, mediators generally hold back and allow clients to work out their own deals … However, the residential parent who declares that "s/he will not agree to contact at all has breached these parameters and may come under direct pressure to yield".'[74] Nevertheless, there is mediator concern that the shadow of the law is becoming detrimental to children: 'I will argue that in a societal context legislation can "set the tone" but that, with regard to the management of disputes in the family law arena, there are real dangers of unintended consequences.'[75] In particular, Stevenson argues, 'There is a real

---

67 Clause 11 in the original Bill; there would also be a new sub-section 6 which would note that the presumption applied only if the child was not at risk of harm from the involvement. Section 1(4)(a) of the Children Act 1989 refers to s 8 applications and the new s 1(7) refers to s 4 applications.

68 Helen Rhoades 'Legislating to Promote Children's Welfare and the Quest for Certainty' (2012) 24(2) CFLQ 158–75, 167.

69 Family Law Act 1975, s 60 CC(3)(c), as inserted by the Family Law Amendment (Shared Parental Responsibility) Act 2006.

70 Ibid, s 61DA, s 65DAA(1).

71 Ibid, s 61DA(2).

72 See Rhoades 'Legislating to Promote Children's Welfare' 158–75, 164–6 and the references therein.

73 G. Davis et al, *Monitoring Publicly Funded Family Mediation: Final Report to the Legal Services Commission* (Legal Services Commission, 2000) 242.

74 Ibid; see also Alison Diduck, *Law's Families* (Butterworths, 2003) 119–22.

75 Marion Stevenson, 'Cooperative parenting following family separation' (2012) 42(11) *Fam Law* 1396–98, 1396.

danger that a strong expectation of parental involvement may overshadow a child's actual unique needs at the time in question.'[76]

Educating parents

Pressure to conform to expected parenting norms post-separation is increasingly applied via the third means by which the past is downgraded and the post-separation period is marketed as a new start, that of parental education.[77] Parental education programmes are not new: they were prevalent in the USA by the 1990s at a time when the Department of Health was also funding initiatives in the UK.[78] Further, the titles of early programmes, for example the *SMILE* (Start Making It Liveable for Everyone),[79] *GRASP* (General Responsibilities as Separating Parents) and *Sensible Approach to Divorce*[80] programmes in Michigan and Kansas pointed up the normative function of such courses to feed into and reinforce the current political ideology of the family.[81] In the UK the previous New Labour governments evidenced 'a preoccupation with the governance of parenting'[82] and developed policies that Lubcock referred to as 'performance managed parenting'.[83] However, the pressure to access and internalise such 'education' is now arguably of a quite different order. As Gillies has argued, policy-makers, for reasons of policy wider than family disputes, 'have sought to establish parenting as a complex skill which must be learnt': '"Knowledge" about childrearing is now portrayed as a necessary resource which parents must have access to in order to fulfil their moral duty as good parents.'[84] Within the context of family breakdown, policy 'has focused on ensuring family breakdowns are better managed' and couples are to be encouraged to use mediation[85] and access knowledge 'in order to fulfil their moral duty as good parents'.[86]

There has consequently developed 'a new ideology of family competence'[87] which now finds its site of learning in the information hub (referred to as

---

76 Ibid, 1397.
77 See, for example, Susan Pollet and Melissa Lombreglia, 'A Nationwide Survey of Mandatory Parent Education' (2008) 46(2) *Family Court Review* 375.
78 See Piper, 'Divorce Reform' 371.
79 See Margie Geasler and Karen Blaisure, 'Court Connected Programs for Divorcing Parents in Michigan' (1995) 33(4) *Family and Conciliation Courts Review* 484–94, 486.
80 P. Salem, 'The Emergence of Parent Education Programs in the United States' (1995) 5(1) *Family Mediation* 5.
81 Piper, 'Divorce Reform' 364–82.
82 C. Henricson, 'Governing Parenting: is there a Case for A Policy of Review and Statement of Parenting Rights and Responsibilities?' (2008) 35(1) *Journal of Law and Society* 150–165, 150.
83 B. Lubcock, 'Adoption Support and the Negotiation of Ambivalence in Family Policy and Children's Services' (2008) 35(1) *Journal of Law and Society* 3–27, 15.
84 Val Gillies, 'From Function to Competence: Engaging with the New Politics of Family' (2011) 16(4) *Sociological Research Online* 11, para 6.1 (www.socresonline.org.uk/16/4/11.html, accessed 26 May 2013).
85 Ibid, para 8.3.
86 Ibid, para 6.1.
87 Ibid, para 4.3.

FISH – Family Information Services Hub or Family Information and Support Hub – in some areas, the Parenting Hub in others),[88] the Child Maintenance Options site,[89] and the new government 'Sorting out Separation' site set up in November 2012.[90] The message implicitly given is that all parents need to learn at the point of separation, difficulty, or dispute: past experience is neither sufficient nor necessary. An evaluation of PIP (the Separated Parent Information Programme), the first nationally available court-ordered education programme for use in the UK in private law cases, has raised questions about its limited impact.[91] Smith and Trinder argue that underpinning the programme materials and approach there is a 'normative presumption that contact should take place' and that 'There is no question here that contact might not be in the children's best interests', notwithstanding the ever-increasing body of research showing that contact is not a given good.[92] Consequently, 'The effects of the intensity and management of parental conflict on the value of contact are sidelined'[93] as are the consequences for the children and a vulnerable parent.

Domestic violence

> The only time I lay down the law and I'm heavy handed is if I've got a mother who's not allowing contact … I try to beat everybody into submission … I've got a particularly difficult case at the moment where the mother [the client] has … been subject to what seems to be some nasty incidences of violence and fled the area specifically to get away … Now persuading her to get contact up and running again is very, very difficult. And in fact we [the two lawyers] were able to arrange that … It's a question of building up mutual trust again.
>
> (Male solicitor)[94]

The second main concern of this chapter is whether 'past' domestic abuse is dealt with appropriately to ensure vulnerability is neither created nor exacerbated. As the above quotation from a lawyer in the 1990s shows, even if a professional knows that abuse has occurred the concern to ensure that contact occurs may lead

---

88 See, for example, Jonathan Herring, 'Divorce, Internet Hubs and Stephen Cretney' in Rebecca Probert and Chris Barton (eds), *Fifty Years in Family Law, Essays for Stephen Cretney* (Intersentia, 2012).

89 Child Maintenance Options (www.cmoptions.org, accessed 26 May 2013).

90 Sorting Out Separation (www.sortingoutseparation.org.uk/en/hub.aspx, accessed 26 May 2013).

91 Liz Trinder, Caroline Bryson, Lester Coleman et al, *Building Bridges: An Evaluation of the Costs and Effectiveness of Separated Parents Information Programme (PIP)*, Research Report DFERR 1140 (Department for Education, 2011).

92 Leanne Smith and Liz Trinder, 'Mind the Gap: Parent Education Programmes and the Family Justice System' (2012) 24(4) *CFLQ* 428–52, 438–9.

93 Ibid, 440.

94 Quoted in Bren Neale and Carol Smart, '"Good" and "Bad" Lawyers? Struggling in the Shadow of the New Law' (1997) 19(4) *Journal of Social Welfare and Family Law* 377–402, 392.

to the downgrading of the abuse of one partner by the other. Such a concern led Hester, Radford and colleagues to focus on the danger of contact arrangements for abused mothers[95] and also on the approach of the, then, divorce court welfare service in providing mediation in relation to clients who had experienced, or who were experiencing, domestic violence.[96] Other commentators pointed out that the assumption that contact is beneficial was leading courts to describe parental opposition to contact as implacable (unreasonable) hostility and to believe a child's opposition was the result of deliberate alienation by the mother.[97]

One result of early research and the work of pressure groups was that National Family Mediation and the Divorce Court Welfare Service introduced screening and good practice in relation to domestic violence, and the NFM Code of Practice, for example, now includes the following clear statement:

> In all cases, mediators must try to ensure that participants take part in the mediation willingly and without fear of violence or harm. They must seek to discover through a screening procedure whether or not there is fear of abuse or any other harm and whether or not it is alleged that any participant has been or is likely to be abusive towards another. Where abuse is alleged or suspected mediators must discuss whether a participant wishes to take part in mediation, and information about available support services should be provided.[98]

The government's endorsement of the argument that domestic abuse should not be overlooked was also made clear in the Family Law Act 1996 which introduced the following as one of its general principles:

> The court and any person, in exercising functions under or in consequence of Parts II and III, shall have regard to the following general principles – (d) that any risk to one of the parties to a marriage, and to any children, of violence from the other party should, so far as reasonably practicable, be removed or diminished.
>
> (Section 1(d))[99]

95 Marianne Hester and Lorraine Radford, *Domestic Violence and Child Contact Arrangements in England and Denmark* (Policy Press, 1996).

96 Marianne Hester, Chris Pearson and Lorraine Radford, *Domestic Violence: A National Survey of Court Welfare and Voluntary Sector Mediation Practice* (Policy Press, 1997).

97 G. Davis and J. Pearce, 'The Welfare Principle in Action' (1999) 29 *Fam Law* 144–8; Christine Piper, 'Assumptions about Children's Best Interests' (2000) 22(3) *Journal of Social Welfare and Family Law* 261–76; Julie Wallbank, 'Castigating Mothers: The Judicial Response to Wilful Women in Cases Concerning Contact' (1998) 20(4) *Journal of Social Welfare and Family Law* 357–77.

98 National Family Mediation Policy Manual (NFM, 2010) D 7: NFM Code of Practice (approved by Family Mediation Council) para 5.8.2.

99 This principle applies to Parts 2 and 3 of the Act. Only s 22 of Part 2 has been implemented (funding for marriage support services) and the Children and Families Bill 2013 proposes to repeal the rest of Part 2: see Catherine Fairbairn, 'Divorce: Repeal of Family Law Act 1996 Part 2' (Standard

Further, in relation to cases coming before the courts, so including those where mediation has been screened out, the Children Act Sub-Committee of the Advisory Board on Family Law produced an influential report in 2000[100] which fed into the case of *Re L (Contact: Domestic Violence)* in that year.[101] That case set up a procedure for fact-finding hearings and for making decisions in regard to contact in the context of domestic violence and best practice guidance was issued in 2002.[102] In 2010 the then President of the Family Division evidenced appreciation of the issues: 'The current position is that we are now much more acutely aware of the significance of domestic abuse in contact cases. Gone, I think, are the days when a man could be violent to the mother of his children and yet still be considered a good father.'[103] There has, therefore, been general acceptance that domestic violence necessitates that exceptions be made to processes and legal requirements.

Consequently, the 2010 Legal Aid Consultation Paper stated: 'For this reason we are proposing that legal aid be retained for family mediation in private law family cases ... This will generally apply to cases where domestic violence is not present.'[104] So domestic abuse is to be one of the few exceptions to the non-availability of legal aid in family law cases and the paper proposed that cases with the following elements stay within the scope of legal aid in private law children and family proceedings:

- where there are ongoing domestic violence (or forced marriage) proceedings brought by the applicant for legal aid, or proceedings in the last 12 months and an order was made, arising from the same relationship;

Note, SN/HA/1409, Home Affairs Section, House of Commons Library, 13 February 2013). Part 3 was repealed by the Access to Justice Act 1999. The Practice Directions in relation allegations of abuse in relation to s 8 applications have, in effect, introduced that principle but the 2010 Guidance on the necessary split hearing to establish whether there has been abuse noted that there should be a hearing only if that would affect the outcome.

100 Advisory Board on Family Law Children Act Sub-Committee, *A Report to the Lord Chancellor on Contact between Children and Violent Parents* (Stationery Office, 2000).

101 *Re L (Contact: Domestic Violence)*; *Re V (Contact: Domestic Violence)*; *Re M (Contact: Domestic Violence)*; *Re H (Contact: Domestic Violence)* [2000] 2 *FLR* 334.

102 See, for example, Advisory Board on Family Law Children Act Sub-Committee, *Report to the Lord Chancellor on the Question of Parental Contact in Cases where there is Domestic Violence* (HMSO, 2002) section 5: 'Guidelines for Good Practice on Parental Contact in Cases where there is Domestic Violence'.

103 Speech given at a Resolution conference by Sir Nicholas Wall, 'Seeking Safety: The Whole Picture', Keynote Address' (National Resolution Domestic Abuse Conference, London, 15 October 2010) (www.judiciary.gov.uk/Resources/JCO/Documents/Speeches/pfd-resolution-conf-speech-15102010.pdf, accessed 25 May 2013); reported in Newsline Extra, 'Seeking Safety: The Whole Picture' (2010) *Fam Law* 1335–37, 1335.

104 Although this passage continued: 'but even in those cases where domestic violence is present, we intend to offer support through family mediation, as some couples may still be able to obtain value from the mediation process' (Ministry of Justice, *Proposals for the Reform of Legal Aid* para 4.70).

- where there is a non-molestation order, occupation order, forced marriage protection order or other protective injunction in place against the applicant's ex-partner ...
- where the applicant's partner has been convicted of a criminal offence concerning violence or abuse towards their family (unless the conviction is spent).[105]

Essentially that scheme was incorporated in the Legal Aid, Sentencing and Punishment of Offenders Act 2012, with the only significant concession around the definition of domestic violence. There have been strong critiques of the 'exceptional funding' provision in relation to human rights[106] and the evidential standard required to fit a case into the domestic abuse exception, and warnings of the problems for courts and vulnerable parties resulting from the inevitable increase in litigants in person.[107] In a recent case McFarlane LJ noted, 'We do know that the mother did not choose to give oral evidence before the judge. We are told that is because she did not wish to face cross-examination from the father as a litigant in person.'[108]

Screening for domestic abuse

There are also other sources of concern that this policy of protection of the vulnerable abused parent or child is not deliverable. Crucially the same question might be asked as that posed in the wake of the passage of the Family Law Act 1996: 'How will they know there is a risk?'[109] That question was prompted by research about the ways in which specialist family solicitors 'picked up' domestic abuse and suggested a misplaced optimism by professionals that they could 'smell' abuse or clients would tell them.[110] Certainly if parents who have made 'unsuccessful' allegations of abuse end up in mediation the fact of the allegations will probably be known. It is also the case, as we have seen, that screening for abuse – at least in theory – is now a routine part of the initial interview with clients. However, research would suggest that not all good practices are routinely followed by all individual mediators even after the necessity for risk assessment and screening has been established.[111] Trinder and colleagues,

---

105 Ibid, para 4.67.
106 Jo Miles, 'Legal Aid, Article 6 and "Exceptional funding" under the Legal Aid (etc) Bill 2011' (2011) *Fam Law* 1003; Jo Miles, Nigel Balmer and Marisol Smith, 'When exceptional is the rule: mental health, family problems and the reform of legal aid in England and Wales' (2012) 24(3) CFLQ 333-354.
107 Maclean and Eekelaar, 'Legal Representation in Family Matters' 223–33.
108 *Re F (children) (residence order: appeal against change in residence)* [2012] EWCA Civ 1793, [2].
109 Christine Piper and Felicity Kaganas, 'The Family Law Act 1996 s 1(d): How Will "They" Know There Is a Risk of Violence?' (1997) 9(3) CFLQ 279–89.
110 See also Felicity Kaganas and Christine Piper 'Divorce and Domestic Violence' in Shelley Day Sclater and Christine Piper (eds), *Undercurrents of Divorce* (Ashgate, 1999) 195–9.
111 For example, the Research by HM Magistrates' Court Service Inspectorate in 2003 found unacceptable, unsafe and confused policy and practice in regards to risk assessment and that such

when collecting in-court mediation data in 2004–5, found that 'the screening tools used in the four courts remained limited despite national-level efforts to introduce more rigorous initial risk assessments' and that CAFCASS officers 'relied heavily on a very brief conversation with each of the parties in the court corridors'.[112] More recent research suggests that financial and managerial considerations have led to the situation where screening may no longer be a major part of the already limited time for funded initial meetings for voluntary sector mediation.[113] Whether abuse – which may affect a parent's ability to engage fully in mediation – is 'diagnosed' and whether the mediator response is appropriate cannot be taken as read.

Recent research which found that, of a sample of people divorced or separated post-1996, 17 per cent said the reason they had rejected using mediation was because of fear the ex-partner (with a further 19 per cent giving as the reason 'feeling unable to talk to an ex-partner')[114] would suggest a lack of confidence in protection in and after mediation. Furthermore, the researchers add, 'one theme emerging from our preliminary analysis of the semi-structured interviews with parties who have used mediation shows, worryingly, that even in quite recent cases screening for domestic violence is far from foolproof and parties may not be seen or telephoned individually at or prior to the initial intake session or MIAM'.[115]

If screening does lead to allegations of abuse, then the discussions between mediator and client could lead to mediation or to the parent considering an application to court. A premium is put on mediator skills in ensuring protection and fairness within the mediation process in the former case and research suggests allegations are still sometimes marginalised and downgraded in mediation.[116] However, it would be wrong to assume that abuse will always be taken into account by a court.

The shadow of the law

The *Re L* case did not introduce the presumption against contact when domestic violence has occurred as recommended by the Sturge and Glaser report but left an assumption that needs to be rebutted by proven evidence of violence and by an 'amount' of violence which weighs the welfare balance against contact.[117] The change of nomenclature to 'assumption' has not proved adequate, however, to

---

assessment, which includes screening, was 'somewhat hit and miss' (MCSI, *Seeking Agreement: A Thematic Review of CAFCASS Schemes in Private Law Proceedings* (MCSI, 2003) 48–9)).

112 Trinder et al, '"So Presumably Things Have Moved on Since Then?"' 33.

113 See P. Morris, 'Screening for Domestic Violence in Family Mediation Practice' (2011) 41 *Fam Law* 649–51.

114 Anne Barlow, Rosemary Hunter, et al, 'Mapping Paths to Family Justice – A National Picture of Findings on Out of Court Family Dispute Resolution' (2013) *Fam Law* 306-9, 308.

115 Ibid.

116 Trinder et al, '"So Presumably Things Have Moved on Since Then?"' 38–44.

117 Christine Piper, 'Commentary' and Felicity Kaganas 'Judgment' on *Re L (A Child) (Contact: Domestic Violence)* in Rosemary Hunter, Clare McGlynn and Erika Rackley (eds), *Feminist Judgments: From Theory to Practice* (Hart, 2010); Piper, 'Investing in a Child's Future' 1–20.

ensure consideration of the full welfare checklist in all cases and *Re L* did not make sufficiently clear that references to the 'hostility' of and 'alienation' by the mother should be used with extreme care. The case did not, therefore, make courts any less reluctant to focus on the mother as 'the problem' in relation to contact, so precluding a discussion of vulnerability.[118]

More crucially, the 2009 practice direction considerably altered the likelihood of a fact-finding hearing. *Practice Direction: Residence and Contact Order: Domestic Violence and Harm* 14 January 2009[119] in effect advises against a fact-finding hearing if the court believes that a finding of domestic violence would not impact on the decision as to contact. Then *Guidance* by the then President in relation to split hearings states that hearings are '(1) taking place when they need not do so; and (2) are taking up a disproportionate amount of the courts' time and resources'.[120] Further, 'a fact-finding hearing should only be ordered if the court takes the view that the case cannot properly be decided without such a hearing'[121] and that 'it will be a rare case in which a separate fact-finding hearing is necessary'.[122] The Guidance also drew attention[123] to *Re C (Child) (Contact Order: Fact Finding Hearing)* which included a reminder that insufficient attention was being given to the burdens that domestic violence allegations were placing on the courts[124] – despite that having been a reason for the 2008 Direction.[125] Recent research on fact-finding hearings reveals the result of such thinking:

> The majority of respondents said that fact-finding hearings are held in only 0–25% of cases in which domestic violence is raised as an issue, with the largest group (42%) estimating that fact-finding hearings are held in fewer than 10% of such cases. Responses suggest that the decision not to hold a fact-finding hearing is very often based on a view that disputed allegations may be disregarded. Where allegations are considered relevant, they may instead be dealt with as part of the substantive hearing.[126]

---

118 See for example, Alison Diduck and Felicity Kaganas, *Family Law, State and Gender* (3rd edn, Hart, 2012) 451–9 and 481–90 for relevant cases and analysis.

119 [2009] 2 FLR 1400.

120 *President's Guidance in relation to Split Hearings* [2010] 2 FCR 271, [1] (Sir Nicholas Wall).

121 Ibid [6].

122 *President's Guidance* (n 121) [7].

123 Ibid [12].

124 [2009] EWCA Civ 994, [14].

125 Gillian Douglas in her comment on the case report for *Family Law* notes that 'It would be highly unfortunate, to say the least, if the present judgment were taken as a green light to revert to the previous down-playing of violence as a factor which might affect the decision as to what is in the child's best interest in residence and contact proceedings' ([2010] 586, [587]).

126 Rosemary Hunter and Adrienne Barnett, *Fact-Finding Hearings and the Implementation of the President's Practice Direction: Residence and Contact Orders: Domestic Violence and Harm, A Report to the Family Justice Council* (Family Justice Council Domestic Abuse Committee, 2013) 5.

Consequently, the 2009 case of *S v S (Interim Contact)*[127] is a clear example of how decisions might now be reasoned in courts: lack of resources has led to long delays and these delays are bad for children because they are delaying the start of contact and so delays should not be allowed to hinder contact and so the weight to be given in the balancing exercise to the (potential) good of contact now outweighs the risk of harm. Such ideas filter down to legal advisers and mediators.

The issues that have arisen regarding the use of courts are not confirmed to the intended 'scarcity' of split hearings, or the high standard of proof that may be required to assert abuse and become an exception in the new legal aid rules. The strong assumptions about the overriding good of contact and 'dual' parenting are of concern in relation to the courts as well as mediation. Rhoades found, for example, that the 'friendly parent' principle introduced in Australian law 'had created a disincentive to disclosure of family violence' and that legal services had complained that 'its presence had discouraged vulnerable parents from raising safety concerns in court out of fear of appearing "unfriendly"'.[128]

The judiciary is also at pains to convey ideas about what counts as parental responsibility which reflect those of mediators and recent policy papers. For example, in a recent judgment Lord Justice McFarlane provided a 'postscript' in which he said,

> Where all are agreed, as in the present case, that it is in the best interests of a child to have a meaningful relationship with both parents, the courts are entitled to look to each parent to use their best endeavours to deliver what their child needs, hard or burdensome or downright tough that may be. The statute places the primary responsibility for delivering a good outcome for a child upon each of his or her parents, rather than upon the courts or some other agency.[129]

In this postscript can also be found an instance of 'equalising' parenting burdens in a way similar to a mediator strategy: 'It is not easy, indeed it is tough, to be a single parent with the care of a child. Equally, it is tough to be the parent of a child for whom you no longer have the day to day care and with whom you no longer enjoy the ordinary stuff of everyday life.'[130]

Further, there are also instances of judgments that appear to justify a differential approach to the caregiving of the father and the mother. For example, in *Re L (A Child) (Shared Residence Order)* (2009), the court noted that Wilson LJ had described the day-to-day care provided earlier by the father as 'most unusual and

---

127 [2009] EWHC 1575 (Fam).
128 Rhoades 'Legislating to Promote Children's Welfare' 167, referring to Richard Chisholm, *Family Courts Violence Review* (Attorney-General's Department, 2009); Family Law Council, *Improving Responses to Family Violence in the Family Law System: An Advice on the Intersection of Family Violence and Family Law Issues* (Family Law Council, 2009).
129 *Re W (Children)* [2012] EWCA Civ 999 [76].
130 Ibid [75].

highly significant'.[131] Where fathers have experience of caring for their child that practical contribution may, therefore, be seen as exceptional so that relative short periods of caring are treated as more weighty than longer periods of caring by the mother. Judges have also granted residence to the father or shared residence with the main residence with the father in circumstances where the child has been most of his or her life with the mother.[132] At a more recent appeal from that county court, also involving a transfer of residence to the father the case was sent back for rehearing.[133] However, the evidence presented at the appeal suggested that the education of at least one of the boys (with a disorder on the autistic spectrum) had been compromised by a sudden change of school and that the availability of the father's partner to care for the boys (the father being a police officer) 'may now be compromised to a degree'.[134] There being no approved version of the judgment at first instance the merits of the decision cannot be assessed but insufficient weight appears to have been given, *inter alia*, to the father's lack of availability to care for the boys.

There are of course other problematic outcomes if a parent is assessed as unsuitable for mediation and Baroness Hale has recently posed a series of questions which focus on those problems:

(1) What will happen to those cases which the assessors think unsuitable for mediation but which do not qualify for legal aid?

(2) Will there be a huge temptation to assess the case as suitable even when it would not have been thought suitable previously? Domestic abuse is not the only reason why bullying may be a risk or mediation a non-starter.

(3) What if the non-legally aided party refuses to play ball? Will there be any more pressure placed upon him (it is more often him) to take part? How can the system work if he does not? Will at least an exploratory and information meeting have to become mandatory?

(4) Will it be necessary to develop new models of mediation to cater for a different sort of case – shuttle diplomacy rather than face to face meetings, for example.

(5) How should practice develop to take account of the fact that one or both parties may not have access to their own lawyer to check the agreement?

(6) What will happen to the issues which are not resolved in mediation? Although often successful in resolving some issues, mediation often does not resolve them all.

(7) Will many more mediations fail?

---

131 *Re L (A Child) (Shared Residence Order)* [2009] EWCA Civ 20, [2009] 1 FLR 1157; also known as *Re L (a child) (internal relocation: shared residence order)* [46].

132 See, for example, *Re R (A Child) (Residence Order: Treatment of Child's Wishes)* [2009] EWCA Civ 445 and *In the matter of F (A Child)* [2009] EWCA Civ 313, discussed in Piper, 'Investing in a Child's Future' 15–17.

133 *Re F (children) (residence order: appeal against change in residence)* [2012] EWCA Civ 1793.

134 Ibid [10] (Lord McFarlane).

(8)   Above all, perhaps, what will be the future of regulation? Can it be left to the Family Mediation Council? What, as a minimum, should NFM and FMA, as the major players in the field, insist upon? Will the government have to step in?[135]

Conclusion

To those of us operating in academia in the 1980s and 1990s all this is very familiar. The same sorts of arguments are being made by politicians and practitioners about the benefits of mediation, the 'evils' of the courts and lawyers, the overriding good of parental responsibility, and what counts as the child's best interests as were made then and with the same kinds of financial and ideological motivations but the context is different. The coalition government is very committed to 'encouraging' the use of mediation, privatise child support and family conflict, and drastically to reduce the legal aid bill. The recession is providing an incentive and a justification. However, the drastic policy changes also fit in with the coalition government's ideological commitment to a 'strong family' and the 'Big Society':

> Strong families are where children learn to become responsible people.
> When you grow up in a strong family, you learn how to behave, you learn about give and take.
> You learn about responsibility and how to live in harmony with others.
> Strong families are the foundation of a bigger, stronger society.
> This isn't some romanticised fiction.
> It's a fact.
>
> (David Cameron, Prime Minister, speech 23 May 2011)[136]

There is now, I would argue, a more determined effort to turn the clock back regarding the re-privatisation of the personal and the removal of the sphere of the family from the realm of law. Yet at the same time, current policy and, increasingly, practice – ignoring the messages from the 'battles' some of us thought had been won – are being presented as 'new'. The worrying result, as Diduck foresaw a decade ago, is that 'The principles and practice of mediation are ideal for the normative twenty-first century family'[137] and that 'confining familial matters within the welfarist discourse reinforces the idea that family disputes are not the stuff of "real" law'.[138] Those campaigning over the years for more protection and rights for women and, in particular, mothers, have had an uneasy relationship

135 Hale, '30 years of National Family Mediation' 1342–3.
136 David Cameron MP, 'Speech on the Big Society' (Cabinet Office and Prime Minister's Office, London, 23 May 2011) (www.number10.gov.uk/news/speeches-and-transcripts/2011/05/speech-on-the-big-society-64052, accessed 26 May 2013).
137 Diduck, *Law's Families* 103.
138 Ibid, 120.

with law as a strategy. However, it must be of concern that the current combination of (non-)access to justice policies and the dominant welfarist discourse returns women to the vulnerable position they once had in relation their children on parental separation. Law may no longer be depriving mothers automatically of control and care of children but great care needs to be taken in the coming months and years to ensure that they do not become very vulnerable in other ways.

Chapter 8

Child protection and the modernised family justice system

*Felicity Kaganas**

Introduction

The family justice system,[1] together with the regulation of social work practice in relation to public law cases, is undergoing comprehensive reform. Significant changes are in prospect,[2] not least the creation of a unified family court[3] and of a family justice service. Courts will be reorganised, judicial case management stressed and a better IT system introduced. This chapter, however, focuses on the changes that will affect the courts and child welfare professionals engaged in dealing with the safeguarding and protection of one of the most vulnerable groups in society: children. It will focus on the Family Justice Review, the Munro Review, the government response to these and the proposals for a 'modernised family justice system'. It will seek to examine the implications of the impending changes for the child protection system and it will suggest that these changes will not necessarily lead to better decision-making in relation to vulnerable children and their families. In addition, the changes will leave social workers and perhaps even judges more vulnerable than ever to criticism.

The background

The practice of social work and the way social work is regulated have changed frequently over the years, often in response to perceived crises or child abuse scandals. In particular, *Working Together*, first published in 1999 and revised a number of times since,[4] has set out ever tighter guidance governing what procedures social workers

---

* My thanks to Christine Piper for her comments on an earlier draft.

1 In relation to both public and private law.

2 Mr Justice Holman, *The Family Justice Modernisation Programme. Implementation Update Number One* (Judiciary of England and Wales, 2012).

3 Crime and Courts Act 2013 which amends the Matrimonial and Family Proceedings Act 1984. See also Holman *Family Justice Modernisation Programme* 3; David Norgrove, *Family Justice Review. Final Report* (Ministry of Justice, 2011) 'Executive Summary' para 36.

4 While the notion of 'safeguarding', present in the 2010 and the new, 2013, versions of Working Together require a broader approach to securing children's well-being, child protection remains a

should follow. The guidelines provided were intended to prevent the recurrence of the 'mistakes' made by professionals that were identified in successive inquiries. However the emphasis on procedure has been criticised as having led to the over-bureaucratisation of social work. In addition, the guidance has not, it seems, solved the problems besetting the child protection system which is still seen to be deficient. In particular, the Peter Connelly (Baby Peter) case brought child protection centre stage again and highlighted the shortcomings of social workers.[5]

Contemporary concerns about social work in the context of child protection emerged in the wake of the Maria Colwell inquiry in 1974. Often cited as the event that led to the modern-day construction of child abuse as a social problem, this inquiry turned the spotlight on the risks posed by families to the children within them. According to the inquiry report, those risks should have been identi-fied; social work had the knowledge base needed to decide when and how to intervene to protect children. However, it said, the social workers involved were incompetent and had failed to do what was required.[6] And criticisms of this nature have persisted ever since.

Parton records that there were twenty-nine inquiries during the decade that followed. He observes:

> There was a remarkable similarity between the findings … Most identified: a lack of interdisciplinary communication; a lack of properly trained and experienced frontline workers; inadequate supervision; and too little focus on the needs of the children as distinct from those of their parents and families as a whole. The overriding concern was the lack of coordination between the various agencies.[7]

The Jasmine Beckford case, he says, portrayed social workers as essentially '"naïve", "gullible", "incompetent (and negligent)", "barely trained …"' as well as "powerful, heartless bureaucrats"'.[8] The Tyra Henry and Kimberley Carlile inquiries concluded that social workers did too little too late.[9] The Colwell and the Laming reports,[10] separated by nearly thirty years, both criticised the abilities of the individuals and pointed to faults in the systems in place at the relevant

major concern. See Department for Education, *Working Together to Safeguard Children: A Guide to Inter-Agency Working to Safeguard and Promote the Welfare of Children* (Stationery Office, 2010); Department for Education, *Working Together to Safeguard Children: A Guide to Inter-Agency Working to Safeguard and Promote the Welfare of Children* (Stationery Office, 2013).

5 Nigel Parton, 'Child Protection and Safeguarding in England: Changing and Competing Conceptions of Risk and their Implications for Social Work' (2011) *Brit J of Soc Work* 854, 867.

6 Nigel Parton, *Safeguarding Childhood: Early Intervention and Surveillance in a Late Modern Society* (Palgrave Macmillan, 2006) 4, 6.

7 Ibid, 32.

8 Parton, *Safeguarding Childhood* 33.

9 Ibid.

10 Lord Laming, *The Victoria Climbié Inquiry: Report of an Inquiry by Lord Laming* (Home Office, Cm 5730, 2003).

times. There was 'confusion and failure to communicate'; 'poor ... recording' of information; 'a general failure to use the case file in a productive and professional way'; 'a failure to engage and communicate directly with the children themselves'; and 'a severe lack of consistent and rigorous supervision'.[11] The Cleveland Report was also critical of social workers but, in that case, the problem was seen as over-zealous interference within the families concerned; state intervention in the family was viewed as being potentially abusive.[12] Each inquiry led to calls for better communication and coordination between the various organisations involved in child protection and for better knowledge of 'the signs and symptoms of child abuse so that it could be spotted in day-to-day practice'.[13]

The social work profession, the legal system and governments have all struggled to find ways of responding to these criticisms and of protecting children while preserving the privacy of the family. It came to be seen as important, in order to achieve this balance, to identify 'high risk' families.[14] Policies, practices and the law have gone through successive changes, in pursuit of 'better' ways of identifying risk, preventing abuse and supporting families. As noted above, measures were also introduced to tighten up social work practice and to ensure that social workers act within set time limits, record decisions and follow the correct procedures.[15] Increasingly, the proceduralisation of social work has come to be seen as a way of managing risk and, more recently, the provision of universal and targeted services has come to be seen as a way of averting risk.

So, concerns about the child protection system are not new. And the responses to concerns have differed depending, at least to some extent, on the political climate and on the nature of the criticisms directed at social work. The Maria Colwell case led to a downgrading of the blood tie while research[16] showing that children in care were allowed to 'drift' contributed to a move in favour of permanency. In contrast, the Cleveland inquiry, with its emphasis on parents' rights, helped to shape the Children Act 1989 so that the legislation and guidance stress the need for restraint when it comes to coercive intervention.[17] Now it seems there is strong political support, backed up by research, for a move back to prioritising permanency and away from postponing the removal of children in order to try to effect the change that might keep the family together.

The impetus for the current re-evaluation of the child protection system came initially from political, economic and professional concerns first, about the way courts have been dealing with cases and, second, about the pressures on social

11 Parton, *Safeguarding Childhood* 48 (http://dera.ioe.ac.uk/6086/2/climbiereport.pdf, accessed 25 May 2013).
12 Ibid, 35.
13 Ibid, 34.
14 Parton, *Safeguarding Childhood* 854, 858.
15 See for example, Department for Education, *Working Together* (2010).
16 Jane Rowe and Lydia Lambert, *Children Who Wait: A Study of Children Needing Substitute Families* (Association of British Adoption Agencies, 1973).
17 See Alison Diduck and Felicity Kaganas, *Family Law, Gender and the State* (Hart, 2012) 622–3, 636–8.

workers. The main problem motivating change in the way care cases are dealt with in court was, and still is, the perception that inordinate delays within the family justice system when proceedings are initiated are having a harmful impact on children. Allied to this have been concerns that the proliferation of experts within the family courts has been compounding delay and ramping up costs. Concerns about social work practice have centred on the perception that it has become bureaucratised to the point where procedures, rather than 'real' social work, are dominating practice. As a result, the government commissioned the Family Justice Review under the chairmanship of David Norgrove, as well as the Munro Review of Child Protection, headed by Eileen Munro. Following these reports, the Family Justice Modernisation Programme was entrusted to Mr Justice Ryder. The Family Justice Review focuses on the progress of cases when they get to court and the Munro Review focuses on social work.

The terms of reference[18] of the Family Justice Review stipulated a number of 'guiding principles' intended to provide a 'framework' for the review. The first of these reiterated the paramountcy principle and added: 'delays in determining the outcome of court applications should be kept to a minimum'.[19] The only other guideline relating to public law was that courts should protect the vulnerable and 'avoid intervening in family life except where there is clear benefit to children ... in doing so'.[20] The document does, however, go on to give a general instruction that, 'The review should take account of value for money issues and resource considerations in making any recommendations'.[21]

The terms of reference of the Munro Review are contained in a letter to Professor Munro from Michael Gove MP.[22] He stated:

> My first principle is always to ask what helps professionals make the best judgment they can to protect a vulnerable child?

> I firmly believe we need reform to frontline social work practice. I want to strengthen the profession so social workers are in a better position to make well-informed judgments, based on up to date evidence, in the best interests of children free from unnecessary bureaucracy and regulation.[23]

> Three principles will underpin the Government's approach to reform of child protection: early intervention; trusting professionals and removing bureaucracy so they can spend more of their time on the frontline.[24]

18 Ministry of Justice, *Family Justice Review*, Terms of Reference (2010) in David Norgrove, *Family Justice Review. Interim Report* (Ministry of Justice, 2011) Annex A.
19 Ibid, 190.
20 Ibid.
21 Ibid, 191.
22 Letter from Michael Gove to Professor Munro (10 June 2010) (www.education.gov.uk/childrenandyoungpeople/safeguardingchildren/protection/b00219296/munro, accessed 25 May 2013).
23 Ibid, 1.
24 Ibid, 2.

He went on to pose the question: 'How can risk be managed so that agencies do not develop a blame culture and their focus remains on protecting children?'[25]

The terms of reference, of course, set out the government's concerns and priorities and construct the problems to be addressed. The reports, accordingly, focus on these issues. It is not surprising, therefore, that the focus of the Family Justice Review is on delay and cost while the focus of the Munro Review is on bureaucracy.

The Family Justice Review and the modernised court system

Constructing the problem

The main problem bedevilling court hearings was constructed both by the government and the Family Justice Review as that of delay. The Parliamentary Under Secretary for Children and Families at the time, Tim Loughton, made it clear that the government's priority was to address this: 'Reducing delay is our main purpose in reforming public family law.'[26] Norgrove,[27] in turn, identified delay as the principal focus of the Family Justice Review. The Interim Report did concede that, 'Not all cases can be resolved quickly'. But, it continued, 'these should be the exception and deliberate, not the norm and happenstance'.[28] Throughout the Interim Report, delay is constructed as being harmful to children in most cases and the solution posited is that decisions should be made more quickly:

> 60. Our starting point is that delay harms children. Long proceedings mean children are likely to spend longer in temporary care, are more likely to suffer placement disruption, and may miss opportunities for permanency. The longer they spend in temporary care, particularly at a young age, the more difficult it becomes to secure them a permanent and stable home. Long proceedings may mean children are subject to unsatisfactory arrangements for contact with their families. They may also delay the implementation of therapeutic and other support intended to address the harm they have suffered.[29]

And the Final Report maintained this focus:

> Cases take far too long. With care and supervision cases now taking on average 56 weeks (61 weeks in care centres) the life chances of already damaged

---

25 Ibid, 3.
26 Tim Loughton, 'Law Society Family Justice Review Summit' (Department for Education, 2012) (www.gov.uk/government/speeches/tim-loughton-speaks-at-the-law-society-family-justice-review-summit, accessed 25 May 2013). Tim Loughton was Parliamentary Under Secretary for Children & Families.
27 Norgrove, *Family Justice Review* 'Foreword'.
28 Ibid, para 61.
29 Ibid, 'Executive Summary'; ibid, 'Foreword' para 14.

children are further undermined by the very system that is supposed to protect them.[30]

The cost both to the taxpayer and often the individual is high.[31]

The delays, the Interim Report said, can be attributed not only to rising case loads[32] but also to a dysfunctional system where distrust among professionals leads to duplication of work as well as the appointment of too many experts.[33] Judges, in their quest for certainty, and because of their distrust of the assessments presented to them by social services, order too many expert reports.[34] In addition, Norgrove suggested, judges appear to hope that the combination of the lapse of time and the submission of expert reports might 'reconcile parents to accept a decision or at least to go along with it'. [35] The court's scrutiny of care plans, which is further evidence of distrust of the judgement of local authority staff, leads to further delays[36] and discourages local authority staff from preparing cases thoroughly.[37] The result of all these delays, according to Norgrove, is that children, who need stable attachments, are damaged.[38] Moreover, the cost of cases is spiralling.[39]

Solutions to the problem

The solutions put forward to address the problems identified within the family justice system included measures to streamline the organisation of courts.[40] So, for example, the Report recommended judicial continuity[41] as a way of achieving better case management[42] as well as greater speed and efficiency.[43] However, the main recommendation to address the problem of delay was far more direct. A

30 See also Norgrove, *Final Report* 'Executive Summary' para 5; ibid, para 56
31 Ibid, 'Executive Summary' 5; see also House of Lords, *Draft Legislation on Family Justice. Draft Bill Provisions about Family Justice* (Department for Education, Cm 8437, September 2012) para 42.
32 There was a significant increase in the number of applications after the 'Baby Peter case' in 2008, see Norgrove, *Family Justice Review* para 2.33.
33 Ibid, 'Executive Summary' paras 10, 63.
34 Ibid, para 2.52.
35 Ibid, 'Executive Summary' para 64.
36 Ibid, para 66; ibid, para 4.70.
37 Ibid, para 4.70ff.
38 Ibid, paras 8–9; ibid, para 4.58ff; Norgrove, *Final Report* paras 2.9–10.
39 Norgrove, *Family Justice Review* 'Executive Summary' para 12; ibid, para 2.37; Norgrove, *Final Report* para 2.12.
40 Norgrove, *Final Report* 'Executive Summary' para 6; ibid, para 2.23.
41 Ibid, 'Executive Summary', para 32; ibid, paras 2.119ff; see also President's Guidance: Listing and hearing care cases (bulletin number 3, 2011) and President's Guidance: Allocation and continuity of case managers in the Family Proceedings Courts (bulletin number 4, 2011).
42 Norgrove, *Family Justice Review* 'Executive Summary', para 31.
43 Ibid, 'Executive Summary', para 29; ibid, para 3.60.

six-month time limit, which could be extended only in exceptional cases, would be imposed for the completion of care cases.[44]

The Report also proposed measures that would require a change not only in the way that courts function, but also in the attitudes as well as the practices of judges. The thrust of these proposals is that judges should be more ready to remove children from parents and be less concerned to oversee the work of social workers. So, the Report said, judges should not allow parents' rights to prevail at the expense of their children's best interests.[45] They should stop trying to police the content of care plans; the limitations of the law need to be recognised and courts should stop trying to predict the future in their scrutiny of such plans.[46] And they should not require or allow so many expert reports.[47]

The Interim Report suggested that the courts appear to be motivated by doubts concerning the ability of local authorities to deliver 'high quality care plans'.[48] But, it said, it is not the proper function of the courts to 'inspect the work of a local authority'.[49] Although satisfactory social work practice is 'sometimes missing' this is a problem that will somehow have to be dealt with.[50] The Final Report too makes it clear that faster decision-making is constructed as better for children and that courts are expected to set aside their misgivings about removing children and about the reliability of local authorities.

> Prejudice against care as an option for children and distrust of local authorities are fuelling delays in the system ... Courts need to recognise the limits of their ability to foresee and manage what will happen to a child in the future. They must also learn to trust local authorities more.[51]

Quicker decisions by the courts

The Family Justice Review recommendations have been applauded as an important antidote to delay; 'robust' case management is regarded as crucial.[52] However, it has also been pointed out by commentators that delay is unavoidable in some cases and that some delays are not caused by the courts. There are parents who are unable to face their circumstances and so do not instruct

---

44 Ibid, 'Executive Summary' paras 80–1; Norgrove, *Final Report* 'Executive Summary' paras 70–4.
45 Norgrove, *Family Justice Review* 'Executive Summary' para 71; Norgrove, *Final Report* para 57.
46 Norgrove, *Final Report* 'Executive Summary' para 62; see also Norgrove, *Family Justice Review* 'Executive Summary', paras 72–3, para 77ff, paras 4.115–17.
47 Norgrove, *Family Justice Review* 'Executive Summary', paras 89ff.
48 Ibid, para 4.153
49 Ibid, para 4.167.
50 Ibid, para 4.167.
51 Norgrove, *Final Report* 'Foreword'; and ibid, 4.
52 See for example, 'Law Society Supports Family Justice Modernisation Plans', *Family Law Week* (September 2012) 1–2 (www.familylawweek.co.uk/site.aspx?i=ed99504, accessed 25 May 2013).

solicitors.[53] Delay is also caused by parents' chaotic lifestyles and failure to attend assessments. Delays can also be attributed to local authorities. They sometimes do not have assessments completed in time. They fail to hold family group conferences in time. In addition, potential family carers are not identified until late in the proceedings.[54]

Apart from these problems, and the Interim Report of the Family Justice Review acknowledged this, attempts to improve case management in the past through the Judicial Protocol and then the Public Law Outline have been unsuccessful.[55] Those 'at the coalface' thought that most of the cases they dealt with were too complex to fit the required structure.[56] This may be an indication that the new time limit may not be strictly implemented; it may be treated as inappropriate in many cases because of the complexity of cases.[57]

Certainly, the Norgrove recommendations have not found universal favour within the legal profession. Judge Crichton has indicated that he disagrees that cases can be concluded in six months and he has denied that courts spend an inordinate amount of time scrutinising care plans.[58] The Association of Lawyers for Children has 'consistently' opposed the time limit and the curtailment of the court's ability to scrutinise care plans.[59] Representatives of the Association contend that when cases come to court, the information available to the judge is often of poor quality and is not up to date, there is no attempt or plan to effect change in the family and there is no adequate assessment of problems like substance abuse. The Association's representatives conclude:

> The judges cannot be asked to abandon the paramountcy of the child's welfare in order to meet a 6 month time limit nor to turn a blind eye if the local authority's plans for the child are not in his best interests.[60]

Nevertheless the Children and Families Bill 2013 embodies both a restriction on the scrutiny of care plans and a time limit. The court must examine the care plan when deciding whether to make a care order but it is only required to consider the 'permanence provisions' specifying the long-term arrangements for the child's care such as parental care or adoption.[61]

53 Catherine Baksi, 'Cautious Welcome for Children and Families Bill', *Law Society Gazette*, 10 May 2012 (www.lawgazette.co.uk/news/cautious-welcome-children-and-families-bill, accessed 25 May 2013).
54 Jonathan Guy, *Three Weeks in November … Three Years on … Cafcass Care Application Study* (Cafcass, 2012) (www.chimat.org.uk/resource/item.aspx?RID=128631, accessed 25 May 2013).
55 Julia Pearce, Judith Masson and Kay Bader, *Just Following Instructions? The Representation of Parents in Care Proceedings* (University of Bristol, 2011) cited in Norgrove, *Family Justice Review* para 4.89.
56 Pearce et al, *Just Following Instructions?* cited in Norgrove, *Family Justice Review* para 4.90.
57 However, exceptions are going to be rare, according to the judge in *Devon CC* v *EB & Ors* [2013] EWHC 968 (Fam).
58 Judge Nicholas Crichton, 'Comment. The Family Justice Review' (2012) *Family Law* 3.
59 Martha Cover and Alan Bean, 'Comment: The Government and the FJR' (2012) *Family Law* 381.
60 Ibid.
61 Clause 15.

A time limit of twenty-six weeks is imposed for the completion of court proceedings.[62] This period can be extended only if the court considers this step 'necessary to resolve the proceedings justly'.[63] Extensions are for up to eight weeks at a time and are 'not to be granted routinely' and require 'specific justification'.[64]

Mr Justice Ryder suggests that the twenty-six-week pathway will probably apply where the 'threshold is agreed or is plain at the end of the first contested interim care order hearing by reason of the decision made at that hearing'.[65] However, even in 'planned and purposeful' delay cases, he said, courts will be encouraged to decide whether the parent can resume care within the child's timetable.[66] Courts will have to be mindful that:

> It is not a parent's right inherent in Articles 6 and 8[67] to have their parenting improved by the state in care proceedings in every case and certainly not at the expense of the child.[68]

Expert evidence: restricting the use of 'old' experts and the making of new ones

One of the most frequently cited reasons for delay (and expense) is the proliferation of expert evidence. The solution, therefore, is to curb the use of experts. Both the Norgrove Report[69] and Mr Justice Ryder[70] saw this as one of the ways to facilitate the streamlining of court proceedings. The emphasis now is on timeliness.[71] Judges will be expected to adopt a 'rigorous approach to case management' which will promote fairness and which will entail balancing the rights of the parents against the prospect of harm to the child caused by an adjournment and the lapse of time.[72] The commissioning and instructing of experts will be an important part of the judge's case management duties.

62 Clause 14(2). The time limits restricting the duration of interim orders are to be removed.
63 Clause 14, introducing a new s 32(5) to the Children Act 1989.
64 Draft s 32(7) Children Act 1989, Children and Families Bill 2013, clause 14.
65 Mr Justice Ryder, *The Family Justice Modernisation Programme. Fourth Update from Mr Justice Ryder* (March 2012) 3 (http://www.judiciary.gov.uk/publications-and-reports/reports/family/the-family-justice-modernisation-programme/family-newsletter-april-2012, accessed 25 May 2013).
66 Ibid.
67 Of the European Convention on Human Rights.
68 Mr Justice Ryder, 'Keynote Address' (Association of Lawyers for Children Annual Conference, 16 November 2012) 12 (www.alc.org.uk/news_and_press/news_items/annual_conference_2012_keynote_speech/, accessed 25 May 2013); see also Re *G (Interim Care Order: Residential Assessment)* [2005] UKHL 68 [2006] 1 FLR 601 [24].
69 Norgrove, *Final Report* 'Executive Summary' paras 89–92.
70 Mr Justice Ryder, *Judicial Proposals for the Modernisation of Family Justice* (Judiciary of England and Wales, July 2012) (www.judiciary.gov.uk/Resources/JCO/Documents/Reports/ryderj_recommendations_final.pdf, accessed 25 May 2013).
71 Ibid, para 40.
72 Ibid, para 39; ibid, para 6.

The Family Justice Review cited research[73] revealing the use of multiple experts in a large proportion of cases[74] and observed that there was a correlation between duration and the use of experts. Although the study referred to suggested that duration might also be related to the greater complexity of the cases concerned,[75] the Review focused on criticisms of the use of experts and, in particular, the use of independent social workers. In its Interim Report, it considered the argument that independent social workers merely replicated what local authority social workers did,[76] and it went on in its Final Report to say that judges should rely on local authority social workers instead:

> Expert evidence is often necessary to a fair and complete court process. But growth in the use of experts is now a major contributor to unacceptable delay. … [J]udges must order only those reports strictly needed for determination of the case …
>
> **The court should seek material from an expert witness only when that information is not available, and cannot properly be made available, from parties already involved in proceedings. Independent social workers should be employed only exceptionally** as, when instructed, they are the *third* trained social worker to provide their input to the court.[77]

Mr Justice Ryder in turn said that experts are 'misused and over used' and maintained that in each case, the judge should ask whether the expert evidence a party seeks to introduce is not within the expertise of the court or existing witnesses.[78]

There is indeed some evidence that reliance on experts may be a waste of time and money. In her study, Ireland found that one-fifth of the psychologists surveyed were not qualified to provide a psychological opinion and that 'nearly all' of the experts were not in clinical practice but had become full time 'professional' expert witnesses. They were out of date and were using assessments that were defunct or which had no validity.[79] The Chair of the Experts Committee of the

---

73 Judith Masson, Julia Pearce, Kay Bader, Olivia Joyner, Jillian Marsden and David Westlake, *Care Profiling Study* (Ministry of Justice Research Series 4/08, Ministry of Justice, 2008).
74 Norgrove, *Family Justice Review* para 4.106.
75 Ibid, para 4.107.
76 Ibid, para 4.111.
77 Norgrove, *Final Report* 'Executive Summary' paras 86–7 (bold in original).
78 The use of experts should not be limited 'arbitrarily' but they should not be called to provide a report on 'common place research' (Mr Justice Ryder, 'The Modernisation of Family Justice: An Interview with Mr Justice Ryder' (*Family Law Week Update*, 3 December 2012).
79 Jane Ireland, *Evaluating Expert Witness Psychological Reports: Exploring Quality* (University of Central Lancashire, 2012) 30 (http://netk.net.au/Psychology/ExpertReports.pdf, accessed 25 May 2013).

Family Justice Council has also commented that there is a need for better quality control in relation to expert reports.[80]

However, Ireland cautioned that her research was preliminary and not generalisable.[81] And the research of Brophy et al[82] into the work of independent social workers (ISWs) concludes that, far from duplicating the work of the local authority social worker, ISWs perform a valuable role. The study found that they were not used, as suggested by the Family Justice Review,[83] as a 'second opinion' by parents to support claims based on human rights. Instructions were usually joint and the independent social worker acted as an independent expert witness for the court.[84] Forty per cent of care cases come to court without a core assessment, and there was therefore no duplication in such cases.[85] Where the ISW was asked to assess a person when it appeared that a local authority assessment had already taken place, this was because the earlier assessment had not included that person or because circumstances had changed.[86] The assessments therefore added new information. ISWs were also able to engage and assess parents who were in conflict with local authority social workers. Reports were of a high quality and generally filed in time.[87] Rather than being a cause of unnecessary delay, ISW reports may help to reduce the likelihood of a contested hearing and make it easier to adhere to timetables.[88] Significantly, Brophy et al conclude:

> Findings ... indicate that in certain circumstances courts may be severely hampered in the absence of access to the skills and expertise provided by ISWs – not least in case managing to meet the six month 'standard' for completion of care cases recommended by the FJR and accepted by Government ...

> The FJR did not seek hard information on the use of ISWs. Moving forward on policy change in the absence of evidence runs a high risk not simply of failing children through poor outcomes – but of increasing delay.[89]

80 Dr Heather Payne, quoted in 'Research evaluates expert witnesses and quality of court reports in the family courts' (*Family Law Week*, April 2012) 10 (www.familylawweek.co.uk/site.aspx?i=dl97193, accessed 25 May 2013).

81 It seems the research has not been peer reviewed. See National Centre for Applied Psychology, 'Psychologists as Expert Witnesses – The Facts' (*Psychology Direct*, 2012) (www.psychologydirect.co.uk/psychologists-as-expert-witnesses-the-facts/, accessed 25 May 2013).

82 Dr Julia Brophy, Charlie Owen, Judith Sidaway and Dr Jagbir Jhutti Johal, *The Contribution of Experts in Care Proceedings. Evaluation of independent social work reports in care proceedings* (CISWA-UK, 2012) (www.ciswa-uk.org/2012/04/the-contribution-of-experts-in-care-proceedings-evaluation-of-the-work-of-independent-social-work-assessments, accessed 27 February 2013).

83 Norgrove, *Final Report* para 3.133.

84 Brophy et al, *Contribution of Experts in Care Proceedings* 'Executive Summary' iv.

85 Ibid, vi.

86 Ibid, v.

87 Ibid, vii.

88 Ibid, vii.

89 Ibid, viii.

Nevertheless, the Children and Families Bill 2013[90] imposes constraints on the use of experts. It provides that expert evidence from an independent expert cannot be presented unless the court has authorised the instruction of the expert or unless it consents to the evidence being admitted.[91] And the court may give permission only if it is 'of the opinion that the expert evidence is necessary to assist the court to resolve the proceedings justly'.[92] Factors to be taken into account when making this evaluation include delay, the availability of other sources of the relevant information and cost.[93]

The use of 'unnecessary' expert evidence, then, is seen as an 'inappropriate' 'multi-layered alternative to judicial decision-making'.[94] Judges will be expected to rely more on the abilities of local authority social workers and Cafcass. They will have to assess what specialist knowledge is needed to do justice in each case and they will be required to reach swift and confident decisions. This means that the single Family Court,[95] when it comes into operation, will face a paradox; while being expected to act more quickly and more decisively in cases involving vulnerable children, the information available to judges on which to base their decisions will be limited. The answer to this problem, it seems, is to seek to ensure that judges develop their own knowledge base.

Judges who decide family cases are to be encouraged to become specialists not only in family law[96] but also, to some extent, in child welfare. In making their decisions, judges are supposed to be efficient case managers and to be knowledgeable about children as well,[97] particularly as far as the effects of time on children are concerned:[98]

> 4.213 Case management is a skill but it also needs a change of culture, so that the judge ceases to be solely an arbiter … The case management function in public law cases is complex. It involves traditional judicial skills of forensic analysis of evidence and interpretation of the law, inquisitorial skills used to reach conclusions about what might happen, an ability to measure

90 See also *Draft Legislation on Family Justice* (n 31).
91 Clause 13(1) and (2) read with cl 13(8).
92 Clause 13(6); see also cl 13(11). This has been criticised as likely to generate litigation: The Law Society, 'Family Justice Review Draft Legislation. Law Society Submission' (Law Society, October 2012) 4 (www.lawsociety.org.uk/representation/policy-discussion/family-justice-review-draft-legislation, accessed 28 May 2013).
93 Clause 13(7). It has been suggested by two practitioners that the better experts are in demand and so are more expensive and take longer to report. Within the context of a twenty-six-week limit, they warn, 'a crisis potentially looms' (Jo Delahunty and Kate Purkiss, 'What Price Justice? Experts or Treating Clinicians? *LB Islington* v *Al Alas and Wray*' (2012) *Fam Law* 832, 835).
94 Ibid, para 41.
95 Matrimonial and Family Proceedings Act 1984, s 31A. See also Norgrove, *Final Report* paras 2.158ff.
96 Ibid, paras 2.109, 2.133ff.
97 Ibid, paras 2.32, 2.215.2.221, 2.227.
98 Ibid, 'Executive Summary' para 68.

and balance relative risks and benefits to children, an understanding of child development and social work practice and an ability to manage time, resources and people.[99]

Judges are expected to be prescient risk assessors, evaluating risk and achieving a balance between perceived risks and protections against it.[100] Now, to help them do this, instead of calling upon expert witnesses, they themselves will be expected to find out what they need to know; they will be required to consult a framework of good practice. The materials provided, which will be contained in a virtual Family Court Guide, will signpost the 'good practice which should be used to improve outcomes for children'.[101] In addition, '[p]eer-reviewed research materials which are accepted by a reasonable body of professional opinion will be made available to judges and practitioners'.[102]

Everyone involved, then, is supposed to become conversant with child welfare knowledge. And judges in particular must have a 'good' knowledge about child development, including the impact of abuse, neglect and delay. They must know about recent research. They must also have knowledge about safeguarding issues as well as domestic violence and have an awareness of risk assessment and management.[103] Judges, in effect, will be the new 'experts'.

Judicial expertise

The first overview of research materials has now been published.[104] It provides an account of research showing the detrimental impact of neglect and abuse on children's development and how the effects of maltreatment resound throughout the child's or young person's life. It refers to research identifying delays within the child protection process. It blames the use of experts and in particular the use of repeated assessments and the use of assessments of groups of relatives. It maintains that professionals focus too much on the interests of the parents, rather than on those of the children.[105] It argues that there is a need for quicker decisions.

The culture of the professionals, which is fostered by the philosophy of the Children Act, is that it is best for children to be brought up in their families, This,

99 Norgrove, *Final Report*; also ibid, 'Executive Summary' paras 47, 50.
100 Ryder, *Judicial Proposals for the Modernisation of Family Justice* para 42.
101 Ibid, para 44.
102 Ibid, para 51.
103 Norgrove, *Final Report* para 2.194, Fig 1.
104 Rebecca Brown and Harriet Ward, *Decision Making within a Child's Timeframe. An Overview of Current Research Evidence for Family Justice Professionals Concerning Child Development and the Impact of Maltreatment* (Childhood Wellbeing Research Centre, Working Paper 16, 2012) (www.education. gov.uk/publications/standard/publicationDetail/Page1/CWRC-00117-2012, accessed 25 May 2013).
105 Ibid, 'Summary' ch 5, paras 5.18 and 5.20.

say the authors of the overview, is causing too much hesitation in the form of excessive deliberation.[106] There is a short period within which action can be taken to safeguard children and delay limits the opportunity to do so.[107] Where parents cannot overcome their problems, it is better for children to be in the care of the local authority and adoption for very young children is best.[108]

The authors draw attention to a study showing that 93 per cent of the parents in that study who could change did so within the first six months of the child's birth. The authors concede that the study involved a very small number of children and a small sample. Nevertheless they conclude, somewhat surprisingly, that it has 'obvious implications for timescales for decision-making and for intensive interventions'.[109] Indeed, they state that the evidence of the impact of child neglect and abuse provides 'a compelling case for taking early decisive action'.[110]

Part of the reason for making overviews of current research such as this available appears to be to enable courts to dispense with the services of expert witnesses in respect of the matters considered.[111] However, as one barrister has pointed out, the reason courts use experts is not because lawyers are incapable of looking up basic principles in different disciplines. It is because they are not best placed to apply those principles in individual cases.[112] A judge may well have no difficulty understanding that early decisive action is preferable in most cases. However, the question is whether it is what is needed in the case before him or her.

One possible effect of requiring judges to rely on their own research might be to exacerbate the tendency of the law, identified by King and Piper,[113] to be selective when it is expected to take account of the available research and also to oversimplify the research chosen. Judges faced with research showing the benefits of contact in the private law arena have translated this into a presumption or 'assumption' that contact is good for children and should be ordered unless the assumption is 'offset'.[114] Given a research overview that unequivocally states that swift and decisive action should be taken to remove children from parents who are found wanting, judges may well devise a new assumption to that effect. There is the danger that 'expert' judges will prioritise speed over other important considerations.

---

106 Ibid, paras 5.6 and 5.11.
107 Ibid, 'Summary' ch 5.
108 Ibid, paras 5.2; 5.6
109 Ibid, para 5.7.
110 Ibid, para 4.58.
111 See Ryder, *Family Justice Modernisation Programme* 4.
112 Leanne Buckley-Thomson, 'Expertly done? A look at the use of experts in family proceedings and changes proposed by Mr Justice Ryder prior to the announcement of his final proposals' (*Family Law Week*, 23 July 2012) (www.familylawweek.co.uk/site.aspx?i=ed99194, accessed 25 May 2013).
113 Michael King and Christine Piper, *How the Law Thinks about Children* (2nd edn, Arena, 1995) 50–2.
114 *Re L (Contact: Domestic Violence)*; *Re V (Contact: Domestic Violence*; *Re M (Contact: Domestic Violence)*; *Re H (Domestic Violence)* [2000] 2 FLR 334, [364], [370].

The Munro Review and the reform of social work

Within the family justice system, then, expert evidence is to be limited. It will be rendered unnecessary because judges will be able to rely on their own enhanced expertise. In addition, they are to be expected to rely more on the skill and knowledge of social workers. Social work expertise too is to be upgraded and, it is said, social workers will be given the freedom to allow it to be used to best advantage. Alongside the review of and changes to the legal system, there has been a review and there have been changes to social work. Munro set out the aims of the review:

> 1   ... This final report sets out proposals for reform which, taken together, are intended to create the conditions that enable professionals to make the best judgments about the help to give to children, young people and families. This involves moving from a system that has become over-bureaucratised and focused on compliance to one that values and develops professional expertise and is focused on the safety and welfare of children and young people.[115]

For Munro the principal impediment to sound social work is what she considers to be the excessive regulation of social work practice. In her view, targets and performance indicators became goals in themselves, obscuring what should be the focal point of social work: the welfare of the children. The time limits specified in *Working Together* also became ends in themselves. According to Munro, practitioners and their managers saw targets and local rules as limiting their ability to stay child centred and as reducing their capacity to work directly with children and families. Also, the standardisation of the child protection process meant that social workers could not tailor their responses to the needs of each child and family.[116]

> 2   ... The review's first report ... described the child protection system in recent times as one that has been shaped by four key driving forces:
> - the importance of the safety and welfare of children and young people and the understandable strong reaction when a child is killed or seriously harmed;
> - a commonly held belief that the complexity and associated uncertainty of child protection work can be eradicated;
> - a readiness, in high profile public inquiries into the death of a child, to focus on professional error without looking deeply enough into its causes; and

115 Professor Eileen Munro, *The Munro Review of Child Protection. Final Report – A Child-Centred System* (Department for Education, Cm 8062, 2011) 'Executive Summary' (www.education.gov.uk/publications/standard/publicationDetail/Page1/CM%208062, accessed 25 May 2013).
116 Ibid, 'Executive Summary' para 5.

- the undue importance given to performance indicators and targets …
which have skewed attention to process over the quality and effectiveness of help given.

3   These forces have come together to create a defensive system that puts so
much emphasis on procedures and recording that insufficient attention is
given to developing and supporting the expertise to work effectively with
children, young people and families.

6   The review is recommending that the Government revise statutory,
multi-agency guidance to remove unnecessary or unhelpful prescription
and focus only on essential rules for effective multi-agency working and
on the principles that underpin good practice.

The government had previously identified bureaucracy as the problem in its terms
of reference for the Munro Review, so it is not surprising that, in its response to
the Review, the government endorsed Munro's characterisation of the problems
besetting social work and her proposed solutions:

2   … Together, we want to build a child protection system where the focus
is … on the experience of the child or young person's journey from
needing to receiving help. That means reducing central prescription and
interference and placing greater trust in local leaders and skilled frontline
professionals … It means a system characterised by:
- children and young people's wishes, feelings and experiences placed
at the centre;
- a relentless focus on the timeliness, quality and effectiveness of help …
- recognising that risk and uncertainty are features of the system where
risk can never be eliminated but it can be managed smarter;
- trusting professionals and giving them the scope to exercise their professional judgment in deciding how to help children, young people
and their families;
- the development of professional expertise to work effectively with
children, young people and their families.[117]

The new, stripped-down version of *Working Together*[118] has implemented the main
recommendations made by Munro to remove time limits and to eliminate the
distinction between initial and core assessments. However it is, in substance, not
very different from the earlier version of *Working Together* when it comes to the
investigation and assessment of possible significant harm. The document makes

---

117 Department for Education, *A Child-Centred System: The Government's Response to the Munro Review of Child Protection* (2011) (www.education.gov.uk/publications/standard/publicationDetail/Page1/ DFE-00064-2011, accessed 25 May 2013).
118 Department for Education, *Working Together* (2013).

provision for the development of local protocols for assessment[119] but stipulates that a 'good assessment'[120] should investigate the three domains making up the triangular *Assessment Framework*,[121] which effectively reproduces its predecessor.[122] It also requires that work with children and families be conducted in accordance with specified principles.[123] These include involving children and families, being child centred and being informed by evidence. These are not new. In addition, the guidance given is similar to that in the earlier version of *Working Together* and the same sort of flowcharts are provided to help professionals decide what steps to take depending on the outcome of each stage of an assessment. The same processes, such as the setting up of a child protection conference and the drafting of a child protection plan are specified.

The document does also include what might be thought to be aspirational goals such as 'high quality' assessments,[124] reaching a judgement about the nature and level of needs and risks,[125] understanding children's needs and the impact on them of parental behaviour,[126] timeliness[127] and rigour in assessing and monitoring children to 'ensure they are adequately safeguarded'.[128] The way in which these aims are described is vague. In this respect it echoes the Munro Review and the government response to it; notions of 'timeliness', 'quality' and 'effectiveness' are mentioned as aims without any indication of how these aims are to be achieved. The main concrete policy initiatives that emerge from these documents are that measures should be taken to improve social work training and that the bureaucratisation of social work should be dismantled; social work expertise and local practices should be the basis upon which decisions are to be made.

Munro has been criticised[129] for producing '[t]hree manuals of rhetoric, which, infuriatingly, tell us where we are in great detail but do not offer the path to a better child protection system'. She has failed to give any guidance on where thresholds for intervention should be set and her insistence on localism, say her critics, means there could be a 'postcode lottery', with different thresholds being adopted in different areas. It has been pointed out that she does not explain what measures work with uncooperative parents; the examples she gives of programmes which

---

119 Ibid, para 62.
120 Ibid, para 33.
121 Ibid, para 34.
122 Department of Health, Department for Education and Employment, and Home Office, *Framework for the Assessment of Children in Need and their Families* (Stationary Office, 2000).
123 Department for Education, *Working Together* (2013) para 32.
124 Ibid.
125 Ibid, para 34.
126 Ibid, para 37.
127 Ibid, para 54.
128 Ibid, para 30.
129 Perdeep Gill and Julie Sheppard, 'Munro Debate: A critical take on the review and Professor Munro's reply' (*Community Care*, 13 June 2011) (www.communitycare.co.uk/articles/13/06/2011/117002/munro-debate-a-critical-take-on-the-review-and-professor-munros-reply.htm, accessed 25 May 2013).

she says offer effective intervention rely on parental cooperation. In addition, the long-term impact of the types of interventions to which she refers is unproven.

Social work's 'impossible' task

It is perhaps unrealistic to expect the detailed guidance which Munro's critics say is lacking. The vagueness of the Munro Review and the new *Working Together* masks the unpalatable fact that there is often no way of knowing what the right decision is in the context of child protection. Michael King[130] has argued that the task of social workers is 'impossible' except in cases, for example, where children's lives or health are clearly in danger. The task is impossible because social workers are expected to predict the future and to anticipate the likely consequences for children of future events.[131] What is more, their understanding of the situations they deal with, as well as their decisions, rely on available conceptual frameworks and values that may change in the future; different types of harm to children are always being 'discovered'. In addition, not only is it not possible to accurately identify or predict abuse, it is not always apparent what 'works' in terms of intervention. 'In the final analysis', says King, 'subsequent events, the effects on the child's development of the social work and legal intervention, are probably the only way of knowing whether the decision was right or wrong.'[132]

So failures are inevitable. As a Department of Health publication, *Child Abuse: A Study of Inquiry Reports 1980–1989*, acknowledged:

> It is not possible confidently to predict who will be an abuser, for the potential for abuse is widespread and often triggered by the particular conjunction of circumstances which is unpredictable. Almost anyone with whom the professionals work could be an abuser, and when an incident 'breaks' it is also easy to look back with the confidence of hindsight and to see cues that were missed, small mistakes and tell tale signs.[133]

An examination of forty serious case reviews involving cases where children died or were seriously injured came to similar conclusions. Of the cases studied, only one was classified as 'highly predictable' and three were 'highly preventable'.[134] The authors observed that the predictive value of known indicators of abuse is limited.[135] The likelihood of abuse depends on an 'interplay of a range of

---

130 Michael King, 'Law's Healing of Children's Hearings: The Paradox Moves North' (1995) 24(3) *J of Social Policy* 315.
131 Ibid, 319.
132 Ibid, 319–20.
133 Department of Health, *Child Abuse: A Study of Inquiry Reports 1980–1989* (Stationery Office, 1991) 63; Lynn Davis, 'Invisible Gorillas and Child Protection' (2012) 42 *Fam Law* 686.
134 Ruth Sinclair and Roger Bullock, *Learning form Past Experience. A Review of Serious Case Reviews* (Department of Health, 2002) 46, 96.
135 Ibid, 17–18.

factors' and it is not possible to determine the significance of particular features or characteristics.[136]

Another study, conducted by Masson et al and based on data derived from court files from 2004, bears testimony to the difficulty of predicting sudden deteriorations in children's conditions. Forty-two per cent of cases were 'unplanned crisis interventions'.[137] In the majority of cases the families were known to social services and there had been some social services involvement in the past. Nevertheless social workers had not been able to foresee the events that occurred.

Yet despite what we know about the imponderables that beset child protection work, social work holds itself out, and must continue to hold itself out, as a profession that is able to protect children. As a result, it cannot abdicate from the task it has taken on and which society assumes it can, and should, carry out effectively. It is expected that social workers have the knowledge to assess risks. Child abuse is assumed to be identifiable and preventable.

In Luhmann's[138] terms, the damage or loss caused by child abuse is a foreseeable risk rather than an unforeseeable danger. Risks, he says, are losses that social processes attribute to decisions, while 'dangers are defined as those losses which are seen as occurring independently of decisions'.[139] The process of the 'production of risk' is the process by which the factors that are seen as contributing to future loss become knowable, and once known, as controllable through decisions.[140]

The difficulty is that, because the social work profession is perceived to have, and presents itself as having, the knowledge necessary to avoid the loss or damage caused by abuse, when a child known to social workers dies or is harmed, that event is attributed to bad decision-making or 'error'.[141] As the many child abuse enquiries have shown, the loss is seen as the fault of the social workers concerned. However, neither the social work profession nor the law can countenance the possibility that the knowledge base upon which child protection rests is not sound. At the very least, it is assumed that the knowledge base can be made sound.

Law relies on the 'science' of social work to validate its decisions while at the same time, by relying on it, law reinforces the perception that there is a reliable body of knowledge which can serve as the basis for good decision-making. The law gives the impression that the right decision is always possible: 'Even if the particular expert is unsound, reliable expertise is nevertheless believed to exist.'[142]

---

136 Ibid, 18.
137 Masson et al, *Care Profiling Study* 25.
138 Niklas Luhmann, *Risk: A Sociological Theory* (de Gruyter, 1993), cited in Michael King and Felicity Kaganas, 'The Risks and Dangers of Experts in Court' in Michael Freeman (ed.), *Current Legal Issues 1998: Volume 1* (Oxford University Press, 1998) 221, 238.
139 Ibid.
140 Ibid.
141 See for example David Howitt, *Child Abuse Errors: When Good Intentions Go Wrong* (Rutgers University Press, 1993).
142 Ibid, 239.

As Ashenden[143] suggests, to acknowledge that there is a deficit in the social work knowledge base would be to call into question the legitimacy of intervention in the family by child protection agencies. So, where social workers or experts are found wanting, this generally does not lead to questions about whether it is possible to identify and predict risk. Instead, the consequence is that there are calls for more research and for the development of better predictive techniques. In the case of inquiries, 'better' experts have been summoned to evaluate the expertise and professionalism of the experts and professionals who were deemed to have failed. The fact that there are 'better' experts can be seen as offering the promise of more 'reliable' expertise. In this way, says Ashenden, the legitimacy of the system is preserved.

King observes:

> The paradox for social work's self-image as the preventer of child abuse, there-fore, stems on the one side from the impossibility of performing this task in any reliable 'scientific' manner, given these inherent problems of harm identifica-tion and prediction. On the other side lies the inconceivability of admitting the task is indeed impossible, for to do so would threaten the very existence of this social identity and be likely to cause immeasurable damage to general social morale (to say nothing of the morale of social workers), such are the collective anxieties in our society produced by the prospect of children being damaged and corrupted by those adults charged with their care and welfare.[144]

Public education as a way of lowering expectations

It is notable that the Munro Reports do indeed highlight the problems of assessing risk and of applying the knowledge that social workers have:

1.43   Professionals can make two types of error: they can over-estimate or underestimate the dangers facing a child or young person. Error cannot be eradicated and this review is conscious of how trying to reduce one type of error increases the other.

1.46   All of these areas of uncertainty make decisions about children and young people's safety and well-being very challenging. A well thought out decision may conclude that the probability of significant harm in the birth family is low. However low probability events happen … Public understanding that the death of a child may follow even when the quality of professional practice is high is therefore very important.[145]

---

143 Samantha Ashenden, *Governing Child Sexual Abuse: Negotiating the Boundaries of Public and Private, Law and Science* (Routledge, 2004) 164.

144 King (n 131) 315, 320.

145 Professor Eileen Munro, *The Munro Review of Child Protection, First Report – Child Protection: A Systems Analysis* (Department for Education 2010) (www.education.gov.uk/publications/

8.25   ... It is a major challenge to all involved in child protection to make the system less 'risk averse' and more 'risk sensible'.[146]

One fundamental change that is needed is for all to have realistic expectations of how well professionals can protect children and young people. The work involves uncertainty ... Too often, expectations have become unrealistic, demanding that professionals 'ensure' children's safety, strengthening the belief that if something bad happens 'some professional is to blame'.[147]

The Munro Reports, then, acknowledge the inherent fallibility of social work and concede that unpredictable harm to children is inevitable. Munro does not claim that social work is perfectible. Instead she calls for public education to help people understand the uncertainty that surrounds child protection, so that there are lower expectations of social work and so that there will be less blame when things go wrong. However, she is certainly not saying that social work lacks a reliable knowledge base or that the task of child protection is 'impossible'; to do so would render social work devoid of content and social workers' decisions no better than common sense. It would make the outcome of efforts at child protection no more predictable than a lottery.

What Munro is saying is that good practice will not necessarily avert disaster. Although the outcome may be a bad one, the decision might have been the 'right' one in the context of what could be known about the family. In addition, there is throughout the Reports an insistence that social work practice can improve,[148] that better research will help and that children can be better protected. So even if the decision was the wrong one, there is the possibility of avoiding such wrong decisions in the future. 'Social work', says Munro, can and should be a 'highly skilled job' and social workers can be capable of helping families to overcome their problems.[149]

Bureaucracy as an impediment to protecting children

In Munro's view, the main impediment to 'better' social work is the bureaucracy that has grown up within the system. As long as social workers have the time to get

---

standard/publicationDetail/Page1/DFE-00548-2010, accessed 25 May 2013); see also ibid, para 1.42.

146 King, 'Law's Healing of Children's Hearings'.

147 Professor Eileen Munro, *The Munro Review of Child Protection. Progress Report: Moving towards a Child Centred System* (Department for Education, 2012) 'Executive Summary' 3 (www.education. gov.uk/publications/standard/publicationDetail/Page1/DFE-00063-2012, accessed 25 May 2013).

148 See for example, Professor Eileen Munro *The Munro Review of Child Protection – Interim Report: The Child's Journey* (Department for Education 2011) para 4.13 (www.education.gov.uk/publications/ standard/publicationDetail/Page1/DFE-00010-2011, accessed 25 May 2013).

149 Munro (n 147) para 4.27

to know and form relationships[150] with families and as long as they can exercise their 'creativity', they will be able to make better decisions. And as long as they have adequate training, professional development[151] and supervision, they will be 'right' more often.[152]

There is, however, no evidence that this is the case. It can probably be assumed that social workers will be able to understand families better if they know the families concerned well, and they may be able to identify some types of harm more easily if they spend time with the child and family. The feedback from pilot studies reported by Tim Loughton, the then Under-Secretary of State for Children and Families, was that flexibility was leading to better assessments.[153] But time and space to relate and reflect are not panaceas; there is still the chance in any individual case that the 'wrong' decision, at least in the sense that the outcome is a bad one, will be made. There is also still the chance that social workers will be deceived by the family,[154] that they will fail to make accurate predictions[155] or that they will fail to identify abuse.[156] Many of the problems highlighted in past inquiries can be repeated yet again: over-identification with parents, gullibility, and failure to communicate and coordinate with other agencies.[157] And it is not an excess of bureaucracy that creates these problems.

King maintains that criticisms of 'managerialism',[158] such as those that lament the eclipse of old-style compassion, are somewhat misplaced. Social work, he argues, has always been shaped by its environment. He concedes that the modern day managerial drive towards efficiency and the focus on procedure might lead social workers to believe that the 'space for "helping" and "doing good" has disappeared', that social work has ceased to attach sufficient importance to the values of altruism and caring that were considered to lie at its heart.[159] However, he says:

---

150 See for example Munro (n 148) para 3.29

151 Ibid, para 4.13.

152 See Munro, *Munro Review of Child Protection* (2012) para 4. 2. A College of Social Work has been established. See ibid, para 4.10; Department for Education, 'Tim Loughton Addresses Community Care Live' (Department for Education, 16 May 2012) (www.education.gov.uk/inthenews/speeches/a00209139/community-care-live, accessed 25 May 2013).

153 Ibid.

154 See for example Munro, *Munro Review of Child Protection* (2012) para 1.41.

155 See for example Munro, *Munro Review of Child Protection* (2011) para 1.13

156 See for example ibid, para 1.12

157 Marian Brandon, Peter Sidebotham, Sue Bailey, Pippa Belderson, Carol Hawley, Catherine Ellis and Matthew Megson, *New Learning from Serious Case Reviews: A Two Year Report for 2009–2011* (Department for Education, 2012). Professionals were found to be too ready to accept unreasonable explanations for bruises. There was a sense of disconnection from the children and professionals did not pay attention to children's emotional development or get to know the children (Executive Summary 7)

158 And what Munro calls bureaucracy. See, for references to the use of the term 'managerialism', Michael King, 'Doing Good for Children – Mission Impossible?' in Michael King, *A Better World for Children: Explorations in Morality and Authority* (Routledge, 1997) 96, 98

159 Ibid, 105.

[I]t would be an illusion to suggest that a golden age of social work existed in earlier decades this [twentieth] century when helping intervention *really helped*, when therapeutic practices *really made people's lives better*.[160]

It is not the case that removing some of the managerial constraints will free up social workers to apply some 'pure', lost form of social work. Social work has always been influenced by factors such as politics. And there is no suggestion that social work was 'better' in the past. Munro herself admits that there was no 'golden age'; every reform of social work has been in response to perceived deficiencies.[161] She also concedes that, 'Freeing up social workers from bureaucracy is necessary but not sufficient to produce high quality practice'.[162] Indeed, things may remain largely the same in some areas: defensive rule-bound practices might continue at a local level.[163] And Munro does not dispute that it is 'highly improbable that the relaxation of assessment timescales alone will significantly improve the quality of assessing and planning'.[164]

Indeed while there will be a relaxation of some of the strictures created by managerialism, there may be new pressures to come for the social work profession. The Norgrove Interim Report criticised local authority workers for their inadequate preparation of cases which leads to 'duplication and delay'.[165] The government has accordingly promised to work to 'to ensure that court preparation and presentation skills become an integral part of initial and continuing social work training'. In addition, the government wants 'high quality' work with families and children to ensure that, when cases come to court, 'they are supported by robust evidence and systematic work with the family'.[166]

Social workers, then, will have to become more proficient at preparation for court. This will entail collecting information and evidence for the court. This in turn may lead to renewed protests that the relationship between client and social worker is being neglected in favour of surveillance and evidence collection, that there is a focus on behaviour rather than its cause, that flexibility and creativity are again being limited. All this brings to mind the complaints of Nigel Parton in earlier years that collecting information for the purposes of judging risk meant that social work practice became superficial: 'Depth explanations drawing on psychological and sociological theories were superseded by surface considerations', leaving little room for understanding.[167]

---

160   Ibid, 106 (emphasis in original).
161   See for example Munro, *Munro Review of Child Protection, First Report* (2010) 9.
162   Munro, *Munro Review of Child Protection* (2012) para 4. 2.
163   Ibid, paras 6.2, 6.8.
164   Ibid, para 2.26.
165   Norgrove, *Family Justice Review* para 4.217.
166   Ministry of Justice and Department for Education, *The Government Response to the Family Justice Review: A System with Children and Families at its Heart* (Cm 8273, 2012) paras 45, 47.
167   Nigel Parton, 'Changes in the Form of Knowledge in Social Work: From the "Social" to the "Informational"?' (2008) 38(2) *Brit J of Social Work* 253, 259–60.

So the removal of bureaucratic rules will not necessarily make for better decisions. And what is more it will make social workers more vulnerable to criticism.[168] The bureaucratic framework decried by Munro was constructed in order to guide social workers so that they were less likely to make 'mistakes', to ensure that full records were kept of events and also to provide evidence of their adherence to approved practice. The procedural constraints have probably provided some protection for social workers whose cases go badly: at least a decision can be defensible, even if wrong, provided the correct procedures are followed.[169] Once stripped of the cover provided by procedure, social workers' failures to make the 'right' decisions will be laid bare and attributed to their shortcomings.

Assessing the changes

Will the changes give rise to a leaner, more efficient court process and freer, more innovative and effective social work practice? Will both become better at protecting children and securing their welfare? Possibly.

The courts

As far as the courts are concerned, the changes will lead to greater speed and less information. Whether this will benefit vulnerable children is not self-evident. The Family Justice Review, while confidently arguing that delay harms children and that speedy decisions best serve their interests, also concluded: 'Quicker decisions may well be no worse than slower decisions and they have the great merit of having taken less time.'[170] While it is undoubtedly true that quicker decisions take less time, it is notable that the panel did not profess to have any clear evidence that quicker decisions 'may be no worse'.[171]

It is also open to question whether the courts will accept this view in many cases. While it is possible that courts will follow the new policy of swift intervention and may do so too rigidly, there is also the possibility that they may well declare complex cases to be exceptions to the twenty-six-week rule on the grounds that they need more evidence, more assessments, more information and more certainty. The assertions of the Family Justice Review that many children fare well

---

168 See, for practitioners' perceptions of themselves as being vulnerable to criticism, Sonya N. Stanford, 'Constructing Moral Reponses to Risk: A Framework for Hopeful Social Work Practice' (2011) 8 *Brit J of Social Work* 1514, 1518.

169 Nigel Parton, 'Child Protection and Family Support: Current Debates and Future Prospects' in Nigel Parton (ed.), *Child Protection and Family Support. Tensions, Contradictions and Possibilities (The State of Welfare)* (Routledge, 1997).

170 Norgrove, *Family Justice Review* para 4.145.

171 The possibility of making feedback available on their decisions is being mooted, however (Norgrove, *Final Report* para 2.205). See, for a critique of the time limit, the College of Social Work and Family Rights Group, *Children and Families Bill. Joint Briefing on Clauses 1 and 14 by the College of Social Work and Family Rights Group* (accessed through Family Law Week, 28 May 2013) (www.familylawweek.co.uk/site.aspx?i=ed113827).

in care may not persuade the court in any particular case that it should not delay sending a child there.

Courts may also find it difficult to rely on local authority social workers whom they do not trust, rather than authorise or consent to independent experts; it appears that such experts do indeed often provide fresh information. Judges run risks if they do not seek expert opinion; future loss to the child as a result of being removed inappropriately or left with an abusive family could be attributed to the judge's failure to make the right decision.[172] Courts are undoubtedly aware that they could be vulnerable to criticism. Once the possibility of expert knowledge has been recognised, one cannot turn the clock back. Once risks are thought to be identifiable and preventable, 'it is extremely difficult, if not impossible, to reverse the process and declare that what was previously believed to be a decision-avoidable loss should now be seen as a matter of chance or the result of totally uncontrollable events'.[173]

Social work

It is worth pointing out that the changes in relation to social work practice do not appear to be as radical as they are claimed to be. Also, Munro admits that, 'The recommendations in this report will not solve all the complex problems inherent to child protection'.[174] Yet she does argue that all her recommendations taken together will make things better. And she expresses the hope that the media and the public will become more ready to accept that child abuse and even child deaths are inevitable in the face of the complexity and uncertainty that surrounds child protection.

This is already beginning to seem optimistic. In particular, social work practice and individual social workers are vulnerable to the ebb and flow of politics. In the past, child protection practice has had to respond in different ways to outrage in politics and the media following child abuse scandals. Sometimes the blood tie has been downgraded. Sometimes it has been prioritised. Now, within politics, there has emerged a growing consensus that local authority children's services are not acting decisively or quickly enough to remove children from abusive or neglectful parents. There appears to be a clear shift in favour of coercive intervention and permanency. And this shift is beginning to shape what is perceived to be the 'right' way of protecting children. Social workers who do not heed this will be vulnerable.

In recent months there have been numerous statements criticising social work practice and it is incompetence, rather than uncertainty and complexity, that is identified as the problem; social workers are simply not making the 'right' decisions.

172 King and Kaganas, 'Risks and Dangers of Experts in Court' 221, 240–1.
173 Ibid, 241.
174 Munro, *Munro Review of Child Protection. Final Report* (2011) 1.29.

For Michael Gove, Secretary of State for Education, there is little doubt as to what would be the 'right' way to deal with child protection cases. He has lost no time in lambasting social workers, claiming that they put parents' interests before those of children, that they leave children in homes blighted by neglect, and that they expose children to 'criminal mistreatment'. He says that when there is a decision to intervene, it comes too late, that children are returned home to be 'exposed to danger' again, that it takes too long for children to be placed, and that prospective adopters are badly treated. Social workers are misguided because of the 'optimism bias'; they believe wrongly that families can change if they are given support and they are desensitised to squalor. They should see as a danger sign a 'sequence of males in a relationship with vulnerable women' and they should remove children from substance-abusing parents. In short, he contends that children should be removed faster and in more cases:

> Too many local authorities are failing to meet acceptable standards for child safeguarding …

> I firmly believe more children should be taken into care more quickly, and that too many children are allowed to stay too long with parents whose behaviour is unacceptable.[175]

> I want social workers to be more assertive with dysfunctional parents, courts to be less indulgent of poor parents, and the care system to expand to deal with the consequences.

> I know there are passionate voices on the other side of the debate.

> They express sincere concerns about children being separated from loving parents in stable and secure families and heart-breaking battles to bring those children home.

> I don't deny that such cases exist. But there is no evidence that they are anything other than a truly tiny number.

> Whereas there is mounting evidence that all too many children are left at risk and in squalor – physical and moral – for far too long.[176]

---

175 See also Lord Carlile of Berriew, *The Edlington Case: A Review by Lord Carlile of Berriew CBE QC* (Department for Education, 2012) (www.education.gov.uk/publications/standard/publication-Detail/Page1/DFE-00124-2012, accessed 25 May 2013). Lord Carlile refers to the disquiet evoked by the 'lengths to which the system acts' to uphold the principle that children are best raised by their parents. He suggests that in some circumstances the burden should be on the parents to convince the court that their child should not be removed (para 53). See also paras 69 and 129.

176 Michael Gove, 'The Failure of Child Protection and the Need for a Fresh Start' (Department for Education, 2012) (www.education.gov.uk/inthenews/speeches/a00217075/gove-speech-on-child-protection-, accessed 25 May 2013).

The Education Committee has clearly come out in favour of coercive intervention and permanency.[177] The Committee recommends that Ministers should raise public awareness of the benefits of being taken into care.[178] It also supports the government's policy to speed up adoption and increase the numbers of children adopted.[179] The Committee states that care should be considered as a viable option at an earlier stage for many children;[180] the evidence before the Committee indicated that social workers are delaying because they are too optimistic about parents' capacity to change.[181] The Committee states that 'earlier protection and the safeguarding of the long-term needs of the child' are necessary; children are left in neglectful situations too long.[182] If necessary, government must act to ensure that local authorities respond quickly enough to problems of neglect.[183]

There has been little sympathy for social workers who have been found wanting in the past. For example, Lord Laming,[184] in his report after the death of Peter Connelly (then known only as Baby P) said:

> It would be unreasonable to expect that the sudden and unpredictable outburst by an adult towards a child can be prevented. But that is entirely different from the failure to protect a child or young person already identified as being in danger of deliberate harm. The death of a child in these circumstances is a reproach to us all.

There seems little reason to believe there will be sympathy in the future. Michael Gove argues that to better protect children, we need to recruit 'high quality' social workers whose judgement can be trusted. And, he says, there should be greater transparency in holding those who fail responsible:[185] 'Where there is clear evidence of failure or incompetence, individuals and organisations need to be held to account.'[186]

It is clear that neither understanding of uncertainly nor tolerance of 'failure' is likely to be forthcoming if social workers do not act quickly to remove children from their families. And it is probably not only politicians who will criticise social

---

177 House of Commons – Education Committee, *Children First: The Child Protection System in England* (Stationary Office, HC 137, Fourth Report of Session 2012–13, 2012) para 207.
178 Ibid, 'Conclusions and Recommendations' para 38.
179 Ibid, para 39.
180 Ibid, para 208.
181 Ibid, para 207.
182 Ibid, para 66.
183 Ibid, para 67.
184 Lord Laming, *The Protection of Children in England: A Progress Report* (Stationery Office, HC 330, 2009) 3.
185 Michael Gove MP, 'The Failure of Child Protection'.
186 Michael Gove MP, 'Letter from the Education Secretary on the Publication of the Edlington SCR' (Department for Education, 2012) (www.education.gov.uk/in%20the%20news/a00205952, accessed 25 May 2013).

workers for making the 'wrong' decision. The public and media will be likely to react much as they have done in the past to child deaths.

Conclusion

The government, in its quest to reduce costs and as part of its effort to be seen to be 'doing something' about child abuse, has led the way in reconstructing notions of welfare in the context of child protection. Government policy, the Family Justice Review, the Children and Families Bill, and the research for the use of professionals have all focused on delay as the primary obstacle to better decisions for vulnerable children. However, while it seems likely that decisions might be made differently, more cheaply and faster, there is no evidence that they will necessarily be 'better'. Indeed, the construction of delay as the main impediment to better protection may mean that the courts will focus on this at the expense of other factors affecting children's welfare.[187] There is also the possibility that judges will call in aid 'assumptions' about the benefit of speed to help them make decisions.

And it is not only children but also the professionals who may be adversely affected by the changes. The drive to speed up decisions and to limit the independent expertise available to the courts will most likely increase judges' dependence on local authority social work expertise as well as their own. Social work expertise is meant to develop and become more reliable once freed from the shackles of bureaucracy. However the uncertainties and imponderables that are inherent in child protection are not and cannot be affected by the proposed changes. What will change is that social workers will be stripped of the some of the protective layers provided by procedural rules that were created specifically to guide them and on which they could rely to defend their decision-making processes. Instead of being met with more understanding when things turn out badly, they may find themselves more exposed to criticism. In addition, social workers, although they will have been freed from some constraints, will be affected by others, including resources, workload and the expectation that they will be more proficient at court craft. It is not certain that they will have significantly more time to spend with families and nor is it certain that more time will lead to significantly better decisions.

There will always be cases where children are harmed despite the best efforts of the social workers concerned. And while Munro and the government say that instances of harm should be accepted as inevitable, this is not the way politicians like Michael Gove seem to be thinking. It is assumed that there is the knowledge

187 See, for a discussion of a first instance decision based partly on considerations of time, *Re W (Children: Domestic Violence)* [2012] EWCA Civ 528; see, for a critique of the twenty-six-week limit, '26 week time-limit for care proceedings is "impracticable", Justice Committee told' (*Family Law Week*, December 2012). Cf 'London pilot shows early success in speeding up care proceedings' (*Family Law Week*, December 2012).

base within social work that makes it possible to protect children. So, if things go wrong, someone must be held to account. What is almost inevitable is that the next child death will be blamed on local authority deficiencies or individual social workers' incompetence. Conversely, it is also possible, given a Cleveland-type event and a consequent change in the political climate, that local authorities, social workers and courts will be criticised for making the wrong decisions and for being too ready to place children in care. It is not only children who are vulnerable if the 'wrong' decisions are made. It is also the courts and the professionals who are.

Chapter 9

Child support, child contact and social class

Stephen McKay

Introduction

In Britain the systems of child support and the opportunities for separated parents to see their children are strongly demarcated by social class, with the greater opportunities available to the less vulnerable. This is rarely investigated, with analyses of both child support and child contact arrangements generally focusing on marital status or the quality of the relationship between parents. Social divisions within child maintenance and child contact may be exacerbated by the current direction of policy. Continued moves towards voluntarism in child support and more private ordering, and similarly an emphasis on agreement in contact disputes, seem unlikely to challenge this basic pattern, and indeed may put pressure on those least confident in dealing with such issues without independent and professional guidance.

As societies evolve and there are more complex family ties, questions are increasingly raised about the sorts of responsibilities that are, or should, be entailed by different forms of private relationships. Moreover, what should be the role of the state in governing family life? In most countries there is a legal duty to ensure that biological children are provided for by both parents. This generally applies irrespective of the marital (and indeed civil partner) status of the parents, or whether they have previously lived together as a couple.[1] Policy towards child support aims to protect the material living standards of children after parents have separated and to help reduce the chances that they will face poverty when their parents separate.[2]

Naturally the ways in which child support is secured vary between countries. Different mechanisms include courts or specific agencies responsible for child support; amounts may be set using discretion or a prescriptive set of rules; payment of child support may be guaranteed (or advanced) or instead dependent on the liable person making payments of child support. The effects of different systems on

---

1 Nick Wikeley, 'Child Support and Parental Responsibility' in Ian Curry-Sumner and Christine Skinner (eds), *Persistent Problems, Finding Solutions: Child Maintenance in the Netherlands and the United Kingdom* (Wolf Legal Publishers, 2010).

2 Jonathan Bradshaw, 'Child Support and Child Poverty' (2006) 14(3) *Benefits* 199–208.

rates of poverty are therefore also relatively diverse.[3] In most countries, however, children in lone-parent families are at increased risk of experiencing poverty, with the proportion of lone parents below 60 per cent of median income in the EU-27 reaching 33.5 per cent in 2011, compared with an overall poverty rate of 16.8 per cent.[4] In some cases the children of lone-parent families may also have reduced contact with one of their biological parents, with an apparent connection between child contact and the receipt of child support (as discussed below).

The financial links maintained between parents (where met or enforced) may also have consequences for the other ways in which parents interact with their children. While the issue of causation, and the direction of causation, is perhaps controversial, parents paying child support are more likely to be seeing their children on a regular basis,[5] and to be doing so more frequently.[6] This association between child support and child contact, and hence presumably with positive outcomes for the children involved,[7] may be seen to represent an opportunity for public policy to improve the well-being of children involved in parental separation by working on their continuing financial links. However, UK policy seems to be proceeding on the optimistic premise that the positive association between contact and financial support can be 'rolled out' as a matter of policy to a wider group of families. Little account seems to have been taken of the idea that the cause and effect are in the other direction (contact helping maintenance, not the reverse). Or that there are a number of potential confounding influences (such as the quality of the ongoing relationship between parents and their other resources, such as disposable income) that may in fact be influencing both contact arrangements and the payment of appropriate levels of child support. The statistical association between contact and child support therefore cannot be relied upon as a basis for policy, as there are likely to be a complex range of factors affecting each. Policies aimed at other parts of the process, such as the relationship quality, may have benefits for the key financial and non-financial outcomes.

UK child support

The history of child support in the UK has been quite troubling in recent times. Since 1993 in particular, policy has frequently responded to seemingly intractable

---

3 Mia Hakovirta, 'Child Maintenance and Child Poverty: A Comparative Analysis' (2011) 19(3) *Journal of Poverty and Social Justice* 249–62.

4 For details, see the Eurostat indicators website, available at http://epp.eurostat.ec.europa.eu/portal/page/portal/statistics/themes, accessed 25 May 2013 (and under population and social conditions). Data is derived from the EU Survey on Income and Living Conditions (EU-SILC), which measures material deprivation in addition to monetary poverty.

5 Paul Amato and Joan Gilbreth, 'Non-Resident Fathers and Children's Well-Being: A Meta-Analysis' (1999) 61(3) *Journal of Marriage and the Family* 557–73.

6 Jonathan Bradshaw, Carol Stimson, Christine Skinner and Julie Williams, *Absent Fathers?* (Routledge, 1999).

7 Jan Pryor and Bryan Rodgers, *Children in Changing Families: Life after Parental Separation* (Blackwell, 2001).

failings of administration, and to changes in the policy focus and the key underlying objectives (both declared and implicit). The Child Support Agency (CSA) was introduced in 1993, with a major aim of reducing public expenditure on benefits for low-income families, and in particular lone-parent households. It soon ran into a mixture of difficulties, experiencing computer-based problems and being perceived as imposing new retrospective obligations on existing payers to a greater extent than tracking down the non-payers who had been widely seen as the targets of the reform.[8]

Minor reforms to the formula used to calculate child support in 1995 did little to improve the parlous administrative failings of the CSA. Major reform came by way of the Child Support, Pensions and Social Security Act 2000 (enacted from 2003, but only for new cases at first).[9] One of the clearest changes was the abandonment of a complex child support formula, in favour of a simplified formula based on 15 per cent/20 per cent/25 per cent of net income (for one, two, or three or more children). Child support would also depend on overnight stays (and at a lower threshold than before, 52 nights a year rather than 104) and the non-resident parent (NRP) having other children in their household.

Other parts of the reform tended to place greater emphasis on the anti-poverty perspective, rather than on the financial savings to government. Hence suitable regulations introduced a £10 a week disregard on child maintenance for those receiving Income Support,[10] while those on the new in-work benefit run by HMRC, Working Families Tax Credit (and subsequent tax credits), were to retain all the child maintenance being paid. However, despite these changes, and the considerable simplification of the calculation of child support, the 2000 Act was largely ineffective at changing the accurate public perception of a failing agency, beset by administrative problems, and continuing to target the 'wrong' people.

The system of 2013 is largely based on the Child Maintenance and Other Payments Act 2008. The Act removed the compulsion for parents with care on income-based benefits (Income Support or Jobseeker's Allowance (Income Based)) to pursue a claim for child support through the Agency. Moreover, existing recipients of CSA maintenance may opt to cease their claims. This had a fairly immediate effect on the number of cases being received for assessment and collection of child support. In the period from June 2003 until September 2008, an average of around 75,000 applications were received each month. From December 2008 until June 2012, the monthly average was only 27,000. A side effect of the reform and the much reduced throughput of cases is that very few cases are now outstanding, where no child support decision has been made – this applied to around 16,000 cases in June 2012, compared with a peak outstanding number of uncleared cases of 317,500 cases in December 2004. Around 88 per

---

8   Alison Garnham and Emma Knights, *Putting the Treasury First: The Truth about Child Support* (Child Poverty Action Group, 1994).

9   Nick Wikeley, *Child Support: Law and Policy* (Hart, 2006).

10   Home Office, *Supporting Families* (Stationery Office, 1998).

cent of applications are now cleared within 12 weeks, compared with around 30 per cent in December 2004. It is perhaps worth a reminder that the 1990 White Paper *Children Come First* that led to the CSA criticised the *seven*-week average decision time of the courts as evidence of the then system's failure. Such levels of failure now appear unattainable.

The reduction in the numbers of claims being handled by the CSA is likely to lead to improvements in reported compliance, if those parents with the lowest expectations of receiving support decide (or are persuaded) not to progress an application for child support. Even where a claim is taken forward, there is a long lead time between application and maintenance successfully starting to flow. Since relationship break-up is often associated with significant changes in family finances, this may be a loss of potential income at a particularly crucial juncture.

The key aim of this reform was to largely shift child maintenance obligations back into the hands of parents. They are now to be expected to reach their own voluntary agreements. The CSA was abolished and its functions taken over by a new non-executive agency of the Department for Work and Pensions (DWP), the Child Maintenance and Enforcement Commission (CMEC). The clawback of maintenance paid, in terms of lowered benefit payments for those receiving means-tested benefits (Income Support, typically) was ended from 2010, there having been some increase in disregarded amounts in the run-up to the reform.[11]

The new coalition government went on to issue a new Green Paper suggesting the future path of reform.[12] This set the stage for further change, albeit perhaps more concerning matters of detail and process than radical changes to the infrastructure of child support. It was felt that use of the statutory system remained too common, acting as a default option for parents, many of whom might be capable of making their own arrangements, and to better effect. Instead, parents were to be incentivised away from CMEC and its successor system, which would charge percentage fees to both parties. The ability to levy fees was already available to CMEC, and indeed was part of the original 1991 legislation and were originally levied by the CSA – but this was not enacted from 2008, and indeed was rapidly abandoned after 1993 in response to parlous levels of service.

This was followed in July 2012 by a consultation that concerned transforming the child maintenance system, repeating the emphasis on supporting families to come to their own arrangements.[13] This mainly set out a plan for charging parents for using the statutory service, now to be known as the Child Maintenance Service, which was opened to a 'pathfinder' group of new applicants in October 2012. There is also an important shift from basing assessments on net income to

---

11 The reduction of benefits in line with child support received was seen as largely cost-ineffective, with the Department for Work and Pensions recovering £105 million in benefits against the CSA's running costs in 2007/08 of £563 million – July 2012 consultation.

12 Department for Work and Pensions, *Strengthening Families, Promoting Parental Responsibility: The Future of Child Maintenance* (Cm 7990, 2011).

13 Department for Work and Pensions, *Supporting Separated Families: Securing Children's Futures* (Cm 8399, 2012).

those based on gross income, which should enable data used for HMRC tax collection purposes to be used – though at present (mid-2013) only a small group of new applicants with large families have been incorporated into that approach.[14]

The idea that child support policy should aspire to reduce child poverty has, along with the idea of clawing back public spending on social security benefits, largely been abandoned. Secretary of State Duncan Smith argued that child support essentially had no effect on levels of child poverty.[15] In any case, while payment might help to increase incomes and reduce poverty among lone-parent families, it also has the potential to reduce incomes and raise poverty among non-resident parents)[16] with the latter effect tending to be less commonly measured (because it is often much more difficult to measure accurately).

Overall the direction of policy reform is away from the state playing a role, and towards parents coming to their own agreements, with a fees-based state scheme as a kind of back-up. Overall it seems likely that the outcome will be less state involvement in child maintenance arrangements than at any point since the creation of the CSA in 1993. The 2012 consultation paper argues that the role of the state needs to become residualised, 'providing a safety net where needed'.[17] Research suggests that parents who do not use the CSA are less likely to arrange effective maintenance in line with the statutory formula.[18] Successful private arrangements are not random, but are associated with a number of important parental and relationship characteristics. These include: an amicable parental relationship, the father's continuing engagement with the children, and higher parental incomes – so that low-income mothers and those who do not have a good relationship with the father are therefore especially unlikely to succeed.[19] Yet those same mothers will have the most difficulty paying the contemplated charge for using the CSA. Faced with a fee for starting the process, and with both parents paying ongoing percentage fees for collection, there are strong incentives to avoid using this system. The likely result is that fewer fathers will pay maintenance at the level prescribed by statute, or even at all. Child poverty levels may thus increase with a corresponding impoverishment in child outcomes. If these effects arise, child maintenance policy may again be high on the political agenda, from where politicians have long been keen to remove it in favour of privatising and individualising responsibility for it. Perhaps only if there are tangible effects on

14 Rhian Jervis, 'CSA: A Basic Guide for Practitioners' (2013) 43(1) *Fam Law* 61.

15 Letter from Duncan Smith to Anne Begg (January 2011) 'Child maintenance and enforcement commission' (chair of the Work and Pensions Select Committee) online at www. publications. parliament.uk/pa/cm201011/cmselect/cmworpen/writev/cmec/sos2.pdf, accessed 27 May 2013.

16 Bradshaw, 'Child Support and Child Poverty' 199–208.

17 Department for Work and Pensions, *Supporting Separated Families* 13.

18 Nick Wikeley, Eleanor Ireland, Caroline Bryson and Ruth Smith, *Relationship Separation and Child Support* (Department of Work and Pensions, Research report, No 503, 2008).

19 See Adele Atkinson and Stephen McKay, *Investigating the Compliance of Child Support Agency* (Department of Work and Pensions, Research Report, No 285, 2005), and especially ch 5 for quantitative evidence.

child poverty, as a result of lower flows of child maintenance, will there again be an appetite for tackling the difficult issue of child support in the UK.

Contact with children after separation

The key legislation for England and Wales remains the Children Act (England and Wales) 1989. This sets out the paramount consideration in determining the care of children to be the welfare of that child. Each case is considered on its own merits, without any presumptions about appropriate slices of time that might be spent with parents. Most cases do not appear before courts, and even within the courts the guiding principle is that an order should only be made if it is in the child's interest to do so. Parents are expected to reach their own agreements, with the courts reserved for those unable to do so.

This picture is emphasised in recent policy analyses and reviews. What is common to the Family Justice Review,[20] the review of legal aid in this field,[21] and the above discussion about child maintenance is a focus on enabling and empowering parents to reach their own agreements, post-separation. Critics would tend to suggest that the emphasis has perhaps been more on leaving parents to reach such agreements, rather than putting in place a system of support that would provide equal or equitable access to relevant resources. See Diduck and Wallbank this volume (Chapters 6 and 5 respectively).

Fehlberg et al[22] set out the current situation with respect to children maintaining contact with birth parents. They also cite the evidence, some of it based on experience in Australia, and express a view against introducing a presumption in favour of shared care, which was then shared in the final report of the Family Justice Review,[23] stating that: 'no legislation should be introduced that creates or risks creating the perception that there is a parental right to substantially shared or equal time for both parents', in paragraph 109 of the Executive Summary. However the coalition government was not swayed by this view,[24] and continues to seek to amend legislation to promote greater shared parenting.[25]

20 David Norgrove, *Family Justice Review. Final Report* (Ministry of Justice 2011).
21 Ministry of Justice (2010) *Proposals for the Reform of Legal Aid in England and Wales* (Stationery Office).
22 Belinda Fehlberg, Bruce Smyth, Mavis Maclean and Ceridwen Roberts, 'Caring for Children after Parental Separation: Would Legislation for Shared Parenting Time Help Children?' (Department of Social Policy and Intervention, Family Policy Briefing Paper No 7, 2011); Liz Trinder, 'Shared Residence: A Review of Recent Research Evidence' (2010) 22(4) *CFLQ* 475–98; Sonia Harris-Short, 'Resisting the March towards 50/50 Shared Residence: Rights, Welfare and Equality in Post-Separation Families' (2010) 32(3) *Journal of Social Welfare and Family Law* 257–74.
23 Norgrove, *Family Justice Review*.
24 Matthew O'Grady, 'Shared Parenting: Keeping Welfare Paramount by Learning from Mistakes' *Family Law*, April 2013.
25 Department for Education and Ministry of Justice, *Co-operative Parenting following Family Separation: Proposed Legislation on the Involvement of Both Parents in a Child's Life* (Stationery Office, 2012).

Key research questions

The aim in this section is to consider the association between social class, and the payment of maintenance and also the extent of continuing contact with children after parental separation. The policy reforms in child support and in legal aid put the onus on parents to reach successful settlements. The extent to which the current pattern of 'success' in these areas is shared equally, or instead more restricted to the upper social classes, is examined.

Data and methods

The following is based on analysis of two different datasets, each with different strengths given the objectives of this research. First, the *Family Resources Survey* (FRS),[26] and second the new *Understanding Society*[27] survey. The FRS is the main survey used each year to measure incomes and benefits, in particular to produce statistics on the incidence of poverty and the shape of the income distribution. It is also used to looking at benefit take-up and at how the incomes of pensioners have changed over time. *Understanding Society* is a new, very large household panel survey, starting in 2009. Households are reinterviewed each year, although each 'wave' of interviews is spread over two years. In some ways it may be regarded as a successor to the British Household Panel Survey (BHPS), the main UK household panel dataset that ran from 1991 onwards. It collects data on all our key variables of interest. The first wave of data collected from 2009–10 from almost 51,000 individuals aged 16 or older is used.

Social class in the UK

There are a number of different class schema in use in the UK. For the purposes of this analysis the National Statistics Socio-economic Classification system (NS-SEC)[28] is examined. Social class schemes (eg Goldthorpe's class schema and the Registrar General Social Class) tend to have similar systems of rankings: they start with service class occupations, then intermediate class occupations and end with working-class occupations, with varying granularity of classification. For ease or presentation, the three-group version of NS-SEC, plus a further group of

26 Department for Work and Pensions, National Centre for Social Research and Office for National Statistics, Social and Vital Statistics Division, *Family Resources Survey, 2009–2010* (computer file, 2nd edn, UK Data Archive October 2012) SN:6886 (http://dx.doi.org/10.5255/UKDA-SN-6886-2, accessed 25 May 2013).

27 University of Essex, Institute for Social and Economic Research and National Centre for Social Research, *Understanding Society: Waves 1–2, 2009–2011* (computer file, 4th edn, UK Data Archive January 2013) SN:6614 (http://dx.doi.org/10.5255/UKDA-SN-6614-4, accessed 25 May 2013).

28 David Rose, David J Pevalin and Karen O'Reilly, *The National Statistics Socio-economic Classification: Origins, Development and Use* (Palgrave Macmillan, 2005).

those outside of classification owing to a limited relationship to the labour market is used.

Results

In this section a number of different outcomes is considered, linked to the focus on child support and contact with children after parents have separated.

Payment and receipt of child support

It is surprisingly difficult to find consistent figures over time on the payment and receipt of maintenance. Perhaps the best information comes from the survey the FRS, but there have been a number of changes to the more detailed questions that have been asked over time. The most consistent information is on whether child maintenance is declared as either being paid by NRPs, or received by parents with care (PWC). As in some other sources, the accounts given by non-resident parents and by parents with care certainly differ in this respect. This is despite a very open attempt to measure the receipt of child support. Respondents are asked:

> Are you receiving any formal or informal money payments from a previous partner for your [child/children]? Please include payments you receive regularly and those you receive only now and again. It doesn't matter whether payments are received directly, passed on by a court, the CSA or DWP.[29]

Charting the proportion of *eligible* parents who receive child support presents rather more difficulties, as there are few surveys that measure in a meaningful way those who might be eligible. This is not limited to lone parents (e.g. step-parents will often be eligible), and among lone parents some will be widowed (and thus generally not eligible, unless there are multiple partners). However, the following figures from a range of different historical periods seem to be relatively representative:

*   In a 1982/3 study of lone mothers with experience of Supplementary Benefit, 41 per cent said they received maintenance.[30]
*   In a 1989 study of lone parents,[31] 29 per cent of lone mothers were receiving maintenance. This included only 22 per cent of those who were receiving Income Support (then the majority of lone parents), but 44 per cent of other lone parents.

29 Question MntRec in Department for Work and Pensions and National Centre for Social Research and Office for National Statistics, Social and Vital Statistics Division, *Family Resources Survey, 2009–2010* (2011) 374.
30 Albert Weale (ed.) et al, *Lone Mothers Paid Work and Social Security: A Study of the Tapered Earnings Disregard* (Bedford Square Press, 1984).
31 Jonathan Bradshaw and Jane Millar, *Lone Parent Families in the UK* (HMSO, 1991).

- In a 1991 study of lone parents,[32] 30 per cent of lone mothers were receiving maintenance. Again there was a split by circumstances, with 24 per cent of those receiving Income Support in receipt of maintenance, compared with 42 per cent of other lone mothers.
- In a 2002 study of families with children (FACS4), 32 per cent of lone mothers had received some maintenance (just lone mothers with a living ex-partner) (16 per cent for those working fewer than 16 hours, but 47 per cent for those working 16 or more hours a week).
- 2009/10 FRS. 37 per cent of lone parents receiving maintenance.

There is overall *something* of a trend towards defending the proportion of lone parents who receive child maintenance. In more recent years that trend may have been turned around towards a slight increase. However, the admittedly limited evidence base provides no firm guidance to whether more lone parents received maintenance in 2010 than did in the early 1980s, well before the introduction of the Child Support Agency and the increased state involvement in this area.

Arrangements for child support

Where child support is being received, for most cases this is through a voluntary agreement. The breakdown of maintenance being *received* by the type of arrangement in place was as follows (from FRS 2009/10):

- Child Support Agency (CSA) or CMEC 33 per cent.
- A court order: 7 per cent.
- A voluntary agreement: 55 per cent.
- Other arrangement: 4 per cent.

Voluntary agreements represent the majority of ways in which child maintenance is actually being paid. The formal agency (CSA, CMEC) has now reached the point where about one-third of maintenance, where actually paid, is the responsibility of the agency.[33] Court orders now represent around 7 per cent of ongoing child maintenance being paid. The statutory system, originally planned to be the main route to child maintenance payment, may have led to the decline (though not elimination) of court-based settlements but has done little or nothing to affect the high number of voluntary agreements. Indeed it is the seeming success of voluntary agreements that has caught the eye of reform, seeking to extend this approach to all families, without having to meet the cost of a statutory system to assess, collect and distribute child maintenance.

---

32 Alan Marsh and Stephen McKay, *Families, Work and Benefits* (Policy Studies Institute, 1993).
33 These are often low-income cases with small and zero assessments. Hence the volume of maintenance being delivered by the statutory system may well be rather less as a proportion.

The type of child maintenance arrangement in place appears to vary somewhat with the social class of the recipient (as shown in Table 1). The use of the statutory agencies is most common for non-working and lower social class recipients. The middle class are rather more likely to still have court orders (over one in ten of the higher two social classes), or to be using voluntary agreements (around six recipients in every ten).

In other words, the key means of assessing and paying child support that the government is trying to promote, voluntary agreements, are least common for the poorest families. The statutory system from which the policy is moving away is most common for lower income families, who thus appear to be the more vulnerable to any negative effects from the current programme of child support reform.

Table 1 Type of maintenance arrangement, where money being paid

Type	Management/professional	Intermediate	Routine	Others
CSA/CMEC	23	26	36	50
Court order	11	13	2	3
Voluntary agreement	61	59	57	43
Other	3	4	4	3
Sample size	226	144	230	224

Source: Family Resources Survey 2009/10.

Social class groupings tend to be less reliable for women than for men. Given that child maintenance is mostly intended to reach lone-parent families, many of whom are female-headed, an analysis of social class may not be entirely reliable. An alternative approach, which is shown as Table 2, instead looks at the qualifications of the recipient of child support. This supports the picture of Table 1: graduates tended to be the least likely to be using the agencies, and the most likely to have a court order. The extent of voluntary agreements did not tend to show any kind of systematic pattern.

Table 2 Type of maintenance arrangement, where money being paid

Type	University graduates	O level C +	Others
CSA/CMEC	23	35	28
Court Order	14	7	4
Voluntary agreement	56	55	63
Other	6	3	3
Sample size	226	144	230

Source: Family Resources Survey 2009/10.

The proportion of non-resident parents who (say that they) *pay* any child support rises quite sharply with income. Results are shown in Figure 1. They vary from fewer than three in ten paying anything at the low end, to around nine in ten for those on the highest incomes. This strongly implies that rates of payment will also vary with social class, and using a three-class version of the NS-SEC and analysis confirmed a strong gradient of this class, with rates of payment declared as being around eight in ten among those working in a professional or managerial occupation, and less than half that proportion among those with the weakest connection to the labour market. As argued above, for many middle-class families the reforms to child support are largely irrelevant. They have reliable child support agreements in place. It is those more vulnerable families who are the more likely to use the statutory system, and hence have more to lose from policy that shifts to greater individual responsibility, and where the residual state backup is likely to be costly.

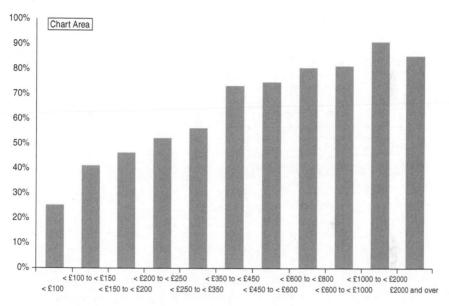

Figure 1 Paying maintenance, by NRP income

Contact with children

This section considers the association between social class measures and the extent of contact between non-resident parents and their children. In *Understanding Society*, non-resident parents were asked:

> Can you tell me how often you visit, see or contact your child(ren) under 16 living outside the household.[34]

34 This is variable Seekid; see page 202 of questionnaire documented in: University of Essex. Institute for Social and Economic Research and National Centre for Social Research, *Understanding Society: Waves 1–2, 2009–2011* [computer file], 4th edn. Colchester, Essex: UK Data Archive [distributor], January 2013.

Among the absent parents identified in the first wave of *Understanding Society* N = 1,351, there was a strong association between class status and the frequency of contact with children (see Table 3). Those in the highest NS-SEC group, professional and managerial workers, were the least likely to be having no contact (14 per cent), compared with close to one-third (31 per cent) among those not in work, and with proportions within this range for intermediate and routine social class parents. However, there was rather less of a difference in the proportions with the most frequent contact, either daily or said to be '50/50' arrangements,[35] which applied to around one in six of all absent parents.

Table 3 Status of non-resident parent and contact with children

Frequency	Managerial/professional	Intermediate	Routine	Others
Never, few times a year	14	20	28	31
Monthly	22	17	17	15
Weekly	49	49	40	34
Daily or 50/50	15	14	15	20
Sample size	282	174	386	495

Source: *Understanding Society*, wave 1, 2009/10. chi-sq(9) = 48.1***.

This theme is continued by looking at how often children had overnight contact with their absent parent. Where the absent parent saw or had some contact with their children (ie excluding those with no contact) they were asked:

Do they stay with you for weekends or school holidays on a regular basis, an irregular basis, or not at all? [variable Wekid]

Table 4 shows that there was a statistically significant association between class status and the extent of overnight contact with children among absent parents. Over two-thirds of the professional group (with any contact) had regular overnight contact with their children, compared with just over half of the NS-SEC class 3, and 39 per cent of the unclassified group. Even among the professional group, in one-fifth (19 per cent) of cases there was no overnight contact. All these figures exclude those without any kind of contact.

35 A total of 31 absent parents said that they had 50/50 care arrangements, which equated to 2.6 per cent of contact arrangements. This updates the figure in Fehlbert et al 2011 which was based on only part (half, broadly speaking) of the first wave of this dataset. Moreover, three of those 31 did not have the child(ren) to stay on a regular basis, which sounds at odds with the idea of 50/50 care. The question wording is also consistent with a 'LAT' arrangement, where a committed couple do not happen to live in the same dwelling.

Table 4 How often children stay with their absent parent

Frequency	Managerial/ professional	Intermediate	Routine	Others
Regular basis	68	58	55	39
Irregular basis	13	14	15	20
Not at all	19	28	29	42
Sample size	264	158	330	403

Source: *Understanding Society*, wave 1, 2009/10. chi-sq(6) = 61.1***.

Perhaps unsurprisingly, those from the managerial/professional group often lived closer to their children than those from other groups. Over two in five (41 per cent) lived 'less than 15 minutes' away, slightly higher than the overall proportion of 37 per cent. This may be reflecting an ability to select housing that is close to the original family, rather than living somewhat further apart. There was also an association between the social class of the non-resident parent and the perceived relationship with the children that were not living with them. Some two-thirds (67 per cent) described a relationship that was 'very close' with a further 22 per cent saying it was 'quite close'.

Previous research suggests caution about determining the extent of payment of maintenance from self-reported data, as such accounts often conflict quite sharply with the accounts of resident parents.[36] Nevertheless, the social class gradient found in contact with children also applied with respect to the reported payment of any child maintenance. This was being paid by 60 per cent of the absent parents in *Understanding Society*, but by some 81 per cent of those from the professional group, 76 per cent for the intermediate group, 67 per cent for those working in routine occupations, and only one-third (34 per cent) of the unclassified group.[37]

Overall, the better-off fathers reported closer relationships with their children, which may have been borne of their closer geographical proximity. They were rather more likely to be seeing their children, and were more likely to be having these children stay with them on a regular basis. They were also more likely to report that they were paying child support to the resident parent. The lower the social class, the less the degree of contact and number of overnight stays, with something of a tendency to report a less close relationship.

Conclusion

Current policy towards child support emphasises the ability of parents to reach their own agreements, largely independent of statutory bodies. It is assumed that the advantages enjoyed by those who have such cooperative relationships will

36 Bradshaw et al, *Absent Fathers?* ch 8.
37 Again, recognising appropriate cautions about this self-reported data, the professional group claimed to be paying a *median* of £62 per week, compared with £40 for the intermediate group and £35 for routine workers. This was as low as £11 for the unclassified occupational group.

then extend to newly separating parents who might otherwise have used the services of either the CSA or CMEC. Policy in this area has seen a full-scale retreat from state involvement. No one is obliged to seek child maintenance; any money paid in maintenance is not included in the calculation of income for benefits. It has become a largely private matter, albeit with the availability of a child maintenance service as a last resort for those unable to reach agreement, with punitive charges levied on the amounts of child maintenance being collected (and likely an upfront fee).

Those using the statutory system at present tend to be drawn from more vulnerable groups. The formal agencies do not seem to be used (at least not to the same extent) by more middle-class families. This latter group are able to access court-based settlements, arguably a form of voluntary agreement, and to set up their own successful arrangements. In these more middle-class families there also seems to be greater contact between non-resident parents and children, they live closer together, and there seem to be better relationships between the children and the non-resident parent. It is, of course, a noble thing to try to extend the benefits of voluntarism and cooperation to groups that do not currently enjoy them, but there seems to be little consideration of the causal pathway by which such families ended up with their particular solutions. A resort to the courts or a child maintenance collection agency may often be the result of an inability to reach an amicable and mutually agreed settlement. It is a long-established conclusion that the better-off tend to make best use of whatever systems present themselves,[38] and available resources tend to be superior in richer areas.[39]

It is too soon to be able to demonstrate the effects of current policies. The extent of change needed to establish successful child support remains great, and the experience of those who are currently successful may not be a good guide to how a policy may be enacted for all families. At present it seems that policy is being delivered on the assumption that what works well in well-functioning families can be extended to families with fewer resources and greater vulnerability. We have already seen massive falls in new CSA/CMEC cases, resulting from removing the requirement to cooperate for Income Support cases. Unless there is some unexpected upsurge in voluntary agreements, there is likely to be less child support flowing between families. The direction of reform is moving further towards the state as a residual player. The complete disregard of child maintenance within benefits is unusual internationally, and forms part of a system where child maintenance is only a private matter. In the case of child contact, the coalition government has only recently ended a consultation on legislating for shared parenting, and seems determined to proceed against the views of its family law review. Again a system that may work well for better-off families with committed parental roles is unlikely to be a good model for other families.

---

38 Julian Le Grand, *The Strategy of Equality: Redistribution and the Social Services* (Allen & Unwin, 1982).
39 Julian Tudor Hart, 'The Inverse Care Law' (1971) 297(7696) *The Lancet* 405–12.

Chapter 10

Labour law, family law and care: a plea for convergence

Nicole Busby

Introduction

The overlapping demands of family life and paid work can often cause or contribute to a specific problem or dilemma. In such circumstances, the principles and policies underpinning labour law and family law might have dual relevance to the issues under review. For example in deciding on a fair division of assets based on the parties' needs following a separation the court might usefully take account of their working lives, including the performance of unpaid care, and future prospects. When considering a claim that a workplace policy has indirectly discriminated against a lone mother with sole responsibility for a dependent child, the employment tribunal might be guided by an assessment of that child's best interests in formulating its judgment regarding his parent's circumstances. However, although such examples show how the conventions of both legal areas might assist the parties involved in making sense of their particular dilemmas, their exclusive operation makes any joined-up decision-making impossible.

The respective legal and policy frameworks in which labour and family law are situated are separate and distinct: they come from different traditions, are subject to different influences and are increasingly based on different – often conflicting – assumptions about work and family life within contemporary society by both policy-makers and those charged with interpreting and enforcing the law. Nevertheless, by transforming theoretical concepts into laws and policies both regimes constitute normative frameworks which shape and reflect individuals' lives and provide the means by which specific disputes are resolved. Where the individuals affected suffer discrimination or social exclusion as a result of a specific personal characteristic, or because the particular circumstances in which they find themselves leave them unprotected and susceptible to exploitation, such differences can serve to accentuate and in some cases increase existing inequalities.

In this chapter I explore how labour law's effectiveness in responding to the issues raised by attempts to combine paid work with unpaid care is currently limited due to the boundaries created by its internal demarcation.[1] This analysis

---

1 Although the focus is on paid employment, I do not assert that this is an ideal for all of those who provide care. Of course similar arguments relating to the exclusionary effect of law's institutions

will focus on the classifications surrounding work such as the distinctions between paid and unpaid work and the 'private' and 'public' contexts within which it takes place and also within the legal system itself. The manifestation of such internal division is clearly illustrated by the lack of convergence between the relevant provisions of family law and labour law (and particularly the subcategory known as 'employment' law)[2] which, despite their overlapping relevance to an individual's particular circumstances at any given time, remain distinct and remote from each other. In my analysis, I use Fineman's definition of vulnerability as 'universal and constant, inherent in the human condition'[3] to argue that such compartmentalisation produces institutional barriers which can make it difficult for those who combine paid work and the provision of unpaid care to gain access to specific rights arising from their employment status and also in relation to the fair distribution of goods and services. This can leave worker/carers and those for whom they care particularly susceptible to the vagaries of the labour market.

In the first part of the chapter the concept of vulnerability will be considered and I will advocate the use of Fineman's assertion that we are all inherently vulnerable so that it is the institutional threats or risks to our vulnerability that should provide the central focus for law's response to inequality in well-being, be it of an economic, social, physical or psychological nature. This is of particular relevance in the current context as it provides for the development of an inclusive framework capable of incorporating the needs both of carers and all of those for whom they care – potentially a wider group than those catered for under the current legal and policy regime. Regardless of the nature of the care relationship, one feature that does persist is the gendering of care so that it is overwhelmingly women who provide it regardless of who is being cared for.[4] For this reason, the individual costs of care and, in particular, its effects on women's labour market participation will be considered. This analysis will highlight the specific threats to our vulnerability in this context and the shortcomings of the current legal provisions in dealing adequately with the economic hardship and social and psychological impacts which can result from the lack of recognition of carers' needs. The historical development of labour law will be used to illustrate how the compartmentalisation of law and policy can create barriers to effective solutions in both individual cases and in the development of a more cohesive law and policy framework. I will argue that, given law's normative effect, greater convergence between labour and family

can be made in relation to those who cannot or choose not to perform paid work alongside unpaid care and related areas such as social security law.

2 The term 'labour law' is commonly used to refer to the legal regulation of work by individual and collective means through the application of contract law, statutory provisions and collective bargaining. Employment law, in contrast, is restricted to those who work under contracts of employment and, thus, excludes other 'non-standard' working arrangements from its scope.

3 Martha Fineman, 'The Vulnerable Subject: Anchoring Equality in the Human Condition' (2008) 20(1) *Yale Journal of Law & Feminism* 1–23.

4 See Lisa Buckner, Sue Yeandle et al, *Who Cares Wins: The Social and Business Benefits of Supporting Working Carers – Evidence from the 2001 Census* (Carers UK, 2006).

law would do much to increase policy support, improve access to justice and thus assist in overcoming the inequality experienced by those who seek, through choice or necessity, to combine paid work with unpaid care. The chapter concludes with a call for the need to redraw the boundaries between law's internal jurisdictions – a long-term project for those with an interest in the development of labour and family law from both theoretical and practical perspectives.

Care and vulnerability

Laws and policies which are intended to overcome the difficulties of combining unpaid care alongside paid work are often targeted specifically at those with responsibility for young children. The task of encouraging or compelling mothers of pre-school and primary school age children to become and/or remain active in the labour market was seen as a priority of the previous New Labour government and continues to provide a central plank of the current coalition government's social policy.[5] However, the term 'informal care' increasingly incorporates a wide range of different arrangements beyond those based on the relationship between (female) parent and dependent child. Demographic factors such as falling birth rates and increased life expectancy have resulted in 'an aging population' which, alongside other social changes including patterns of migration, increased labour market participation among women and the cultural impact of a more ethnically diverse society, have all contributed to the emergence of a changing landscape for care provision.[6]

In recent years such changes have resulted in an increase in the provision of informal care by those classified as economically active for a wider range of recipients including elders and those with disabilities and chronic illness with the care relationship not always based on familial ties.[7] In this chapter the term 'care relationship' is used to denote a mutually supportive arrangement whereby the recipient depends on the care provided in order to manage his or her day-to-day activities so that it is the nature and quality of the relationship that is relevant to its classification, not its form or the ties on which it is based. This includes the provision of assistance and/or support whether physical, practical, psychological or emotional (but typically incorporating all these aspects) for children, elders and other adults with a range of needs and varying levels of dependency. This is wider than the parameters within which the current legal and policy framework operates which, in the employment sphere, tends to be focused on a narrow range of relationships such as that between child and parent (typically mother)[8] and even

---

5 See New Labour's pursuance of its 'welfare to work' agenda which included initiatives such as the Lone Parents New Deal which has been continued through the coalition government's 'Work Programme' and policies relating to welfare reform.

6 See Buckner et al, *Who Cares Wins*.

7 Ibid.

8 See, for example, the regulatory regime relating to maternity and paternity leave and pay and unpaid parental leave provided under the Employment Rights Act 1996 (ERA) and the Maternity and Parental Leave etc Regulations 1999, which focuses on the needs of working parents.

where such traditional boundaries are traversed, associated rights are extremely limited.[9] Such restriction is unhelpful on two related grounds: first, it simply fails to take account of the complexity of relationships which characterise contemporary life and which, if we recognise the importance of interdependence, ought to be supported and encouraged; and, second, it reinforces existing gendered roles and related inequalities rather than facilitating gender-free care. By adopting a broader view of the care relationship in the following analysis, it is possible to identify existing restrictions which may serve to exclude both the providers and recipients of care from the scope of protection and related social policy.

Alongside the relevant definition of care, it is also necessary to identify the specific conception of vulnerability that is used in the chapter. Rather than the negative notion of 'vulnerable person' as the undesirable opposite of the autonomous individual promoted by liberalism's ideal,[10] vulnerability should be accepted as an inevitable state, central to our humanity. Fineman's proposition that 'Vulnerability is – and should be – understood to be universal and constant, inherent in the human condition' provides the starting point so that emphasis is placed on the role played by the 'structures our society has and will establish to manage our common vulnerabilities'[11] rather than on the personal characteristics of individuals which, due to structural deficiencies, may leave them susceptible to disadvantage.[12] This distinction is particularly important in the context of the care relationship which has interdependence at its core. As Kittay argues, our motivation for providing care arises from our own intrinsic need for a codependent relationship.[13] This cycle of care, within which an individual may be at once giver and recipient, is the source of deep and satisfying bonds which 'count among those we most cherish'.[14]

At its most basic level, care is crucial for perpetuation of the species through the nurturing that takes place during infancy and beyond and the provision of support to those who are or become dependent in the years between birth and death is the most fundamental expression of a decent and civilised society. As with the

---

9 For example, the right to request flexible working under ERA, ss 80F–80I which includes the carers of adults as well as parents. However, the right is merely to make a request to change working arrangements to accommodate caring responsibilities, which the employer can refuse on a number of specified grounds relating to the needs of the business. The right to take time off for emergencies under ss 57 and 57A ERA incorporates a wider range of dependants including someone living in the same household and any person who reasonably depends on an employee for care. However, the entitlement is only to a 'reasonable' amount of time off to deal with an emergency and/or unforeseen circumstances (ie a day or two) and there is no associated right for the time off to be paid.

10 Martha Fineman, *The Autonomy Myth: A Theory of Dependency* (The New Press, 2004).

11 See Fineman, 'Vulnerable Subject' 1.

12 Furthermore, it can be argued that the 'non-vulnerable' are only classified as such because they benefit from a range of structural arrangements giving them advantages that mask their vulnerability.

13 Eva Feder Kittay, *Love's Labor: Essays on Women, Equality and Dependency* (Routledge, 1999); Eva Feder Kittay, 'A Feminist Public Ethic of Care Meets the New Communitarian Family Policy' (2001) 111(3) *Ethics* 523.

14 Ibid, 527.

term 'vulnerability', the liberal ideals of autonomy and personal choice impose a pejorative meaning on the term 'dependency' which requires a contextual reassessment. Rather than an undesirable consequence of poor personal decision-making or extraordinary misfortune, dependency is a fundamental component of the human condition: it is the natural response to the vulnerability that we all experience and is, thus, a positive force as relationships of care are imperative for the individual well-being of both recipient and carer and, in the collective sense, for the achievement and maintenance of a just society.

This reconsideration of vulnerability and dependency as natural states enables the following analysis of law and policy to take account of both the carer and those for whom she cares. This wider view is not generally possible within the current labour law framework which, due to the focus on the contractual nexus, only takes account of the carer in her role as worker and does not concern itself with the needs of the recipient(s) of her care.[15] On this basis, application of the relevant provisions of equality law is determined by a worker's personal characteristic[16] on the grounds of which her treatment is generally compared with that received by another worker who does not possess the relevant characteristic[17] in order to determine whether unfavourable treatment has occurred. Even where such comparison is deemed inappropriate, such as in the case of pregnancy, determination of whether the treatment received by a woman who has recently given birth on her return to work is 'unfavourable' because of her pregnancy[18] will require a consideration of her circumstances within a relatively narrow time frame and will take no account of the relative needs of her baby or other dependent children (or adults) requiring her care.[19] By restricting the application of the equality principle in this way, the law not only denies the existence of the other party to the care relationship but actually impedes a thorough consideration of the worker's own circumstances which, through the mutual ties of vulnerability and dependency, are inexorably bound to those for whom she cares.

---

15 However, although the concept of associative discrimination is not specifically defined in the Equality Act 2010 (hereafter EqA), the definition of direct discrimination in s 13 which arises from less favourable treatment 'because of a protected characteristic' is wide enough to ensure that the victim of discrimination does not personally have to have the protected characteristic herself. See further Case C-303/06 *Coleman v Attridge Law* [2008] ECR I-5603.

16 EqA, s 4 specifically provides for protection against discrimination on grounds of the following 'personal characteristics': age, disability, gender reassignment, marriage and civil partnership, pregnancy and maternity, race, religion or belief, sex and sexual orientation.

17 The Act does not only apply to employment, but also to the provision of goods and services and education.

18 EqA, s 17 (2).

19 The appropriate time limit beyond which the 'special protection' afforded to pregnant workers or those who have recently given birth is the end of the maternity leave period which is currently subject to a maximum of twelve months (see C-394/96 *Brown v Rentokil Ltd* (1998) IRLR 445, ECJ). This takes no account of individual circumstances which might have a direct impact on the child's well-being such as the continuance of breast feeding following the mother's return to work or issues connected with the child's health.

To move beyond the reliance on personal identity as a means of highlighting and responding to inequality is not to deny the importance of the 'personal characteristic' approach in responding to direct and indirect discrimination, but rather to recognise its severe limitations as the sole means by which the causes and effects of inequality can be diagnosed and addressed.[20] By acknowledging this, the central inquiry is opened up to the inclusion of a whole range of potentially relevant circumstances in which individuals find themselves, not solely on the basis of identity arising from specific personal characteristics, but due to certain institutional factors that serve to privilege some and exclude others. This includes the legal system itself as law's failure to respond adequately to inequalities in women's and men's labour market experiences which arise largely through the low value accorded to caregiving can be attributed to its established and often unyielding conventions. Central to this critique is the use of almost exclusionary reliance on the equal treatment model.

Equal treatment and institutional inequality

Although adequate as a means of dealing with discrimination related to a single personal characteristic, the equal treatment model cannot satisfactorily capture and respond to the disadvantage that emerges as a by-product of certain social processes. Inequity in family incomes and resulting manifestations such as child poverty may well be attributable to a range of interrelated factors rather than one personal characteristic (PC).[21] Indeed social class may be a better indicator of an individual's life chances than the existing range of PCs but increased social mobility and the use of occupation as a key indicator renders its mere classification unreliable and fraught with difficulty with respect those who do not participate in paid employment.

The equal treatment model's use of identity presents one further problem: attributing the causes and effects of inequality to an individual's identity places responsibility for the resulting disadvantage and/or discrimination on the individual herself so that she is required to seek redress for her own inability (or failure) to conform to a preordained standard. In some cases this redress may take the

20 Inequality can, of course, be the result of a combination of personal characteristics referred to as intersectionality. In legal parlance, the terms multiple discrimination and intersectional discrimination are used interchangeably but, as Hepple notes, these terms can be distinguished as intersectional discrimination is a wider concept incorporating not only the type of treatment which arises as a result of the combination of dual (or multiple) facets of an individual's identity but also 'cases where there is less favourable treatment on more than one occasion, each on a separate ground' (Bob Hepple, *Equality: The New legal Framework* (Hart, 2011), 61); see further, Nicole Busby, 'Carers and the Equality Act 2010: Protected Characteristics and Identity' (2012) 11(2) *Contemp Issues L* 71.
21 When the Equality Act was drafted, dual discrimination claims (but not multiple claims) were to be permitted under s 14. However, in his 2011 Budget Statement, Chancellor George Osborne announced that this provision would not now be enacted; see HC Deb 23 Mar 2011 col 955. See ⟨www.publications.parliament.uk/pa/cm201011/cmhansrd/cm110323/debtext/110323-0001.htm#11032368000001, accessed 7 May 2013⟩.

form of financial compensation for loss or to reimburse a specific cost incurred, or by the application of legitimate 'special' treatment aimed at levelling the playing field so that the complainant can continue to participate in the game regardless of her pregnancy or disability. This does nothing to address the root causes of the inequality and neither does it contribute to the normalisation of the personal characteristic that led to the disadvantage in the first place. Instead law's intervention in such circumstances is conditional on the individual's ability to identify and to draw attention to their difference. This conceptualisation of vulnerability as an indication of individual weakness which requires remedial action in order to enable conformance further emphasises the (erroneous) liberal assumption that we are all autonomous beings, free to exercise choice and capable of taking responsibility for our own destinies.

The assumptions underpinning this notion of autonomy as a natural or normal human state are highly contested.[22] The exclusion of those who are denied legal capacity due to mental illness, criminality and nonage renders many of those who are the recipients of care unable to conform to law's ideal of the autonomous being placing responsibility for the disadvantage suffered by the members of certain societal groups and those who provide their care beyond law's reach. This reinforces the particular standard against which all others must be judged in order that their differences can be identified and anchors law's institutions to this standard so that equality law can be seen to contribute to the very mischief that it was intended to address. Rather than attributing responsibility for disadvantage to the inability of an individual to conform to what is, in any event, an idealised standard, a more useful approach would engender the identification of the particular institutions and their specific functions that present barriers to individual achievement by privileging some and excluding others.[23] The focus on institutional factors avoids the singling out of certain individuals or social groups enabling an inclusive approach so that consideration can be given to both carers and those for whom they care regardless of such factors as age or mental (in)capacity.

In summation, my adoption of Fineman's concept of vulnerability with its emphasis on the institutional causes of inequality is not intended to preclude explorations of personal identity which are in themselves crucial indicators of the structural and systemic causes of disadvantage and which, as such, have an undeniably valuable role to play as the foci of targeted legal intervention designed to overcome discrimination. What I contend is that such intervention is incapable of further evolution without the parallel development of state action targeted at the institutional causes of disadvantage and the means by which it is perpetuated. In the next section, the personal costs incurred by those who provide care will be considered.

22 See Fineman, 'Vulnerable Subject'; Kittay, 'Feminist Public Ethic of Care'.
23 The 'reasonable adjustment' requirement in relation to disability is based on this approach – see s 32 EqA – but it could be extended.

The costs of care

The detrimental effects of the need to balance caring responsibilities alongside paid work on women's employment experience has been well documented elsewhere[24] and the cumulative effects of this dual burden can be measured by gendered pay gaps and occupational segregation with women clustering in low-paid, part-time jobs. The effects of caregiving on an individual's economic and social well-being are not confined to time spent in the labour market as exclusion from occupational pension schemes and comparatively disadvantageous benefits available to part-time workers can leave many women in poverty beyond retirement.[25]

The personal costs of care can be significant for both providers and recipients as, alongside the obvious negative impacts on earnings and related benefits, individual carers are likely to suffer other hidden but substantial costs in terms of their own health and well-being and the unquantifiable impacts of social exclusion. The authors of a statistical analysis of the 2001 Census found that the combined effects of high levels of care commitment and labour market participation left many carers vulnerable to ill health and excluded from opportunities to improve their employment prospects.[26] Working carers were found to pay a considerable penalty in terms of their own health, were more likely to be unqualified and less likely to likely to hold university degrees than other people in employment and carers of both sexes were more likely to be clustered in lower-level jobs than other workers and had less access to higher level positions. For the individual carer, the combination of financial hardship, opportunity costs and social exclusion is likely to result in the non-achievement of personal goals and aspirations, low self-esteem and, ultimately, the denial of self-actualisation.

As I have argued elsewhere,[27] what is required is a fundamental reassessment of the value of care which should take place in the wider socio-economic context alongside recognition that the burden of care for another – be it a dependent child, disabled or infirm adult or elder – imposes obligations on the whole of society which can only be discharged through a community ethos to provide care for the carer. The undervaluing of care and the lack of recognition of the often substantial personal costs that it extracts arise from society's failure to accord carers a specific status worthy of protection. The preoccupation with the marketisation of human endeavour has assigned care a lowly status due to its perceived lack of market value so that it is often performed silently and without recognition of its substantial contribution to all aspects of capitalism. This is undeniably linked to women's performance of care, which, since the post-war rise of women's paid

24 Nicole Busby, *A Right to Care: Unpaid Care Work in European Employment Law* (Oxford University Press, 2011); Nicole Busby, 'Unpaid Care-giving and Paid Work within a Rights Framework: Towards Reconciliation?' in Nicole Busby and Grace James (eds), *Families, Care-giving and Paid Work: Challenging Labour Law in the 21st Century* (Edward Elgar, 2011).
25 See Nicole Busby, 'Only a Matter of Time' (2001) 64(3) *MLR* 489.
26 Buckner et al, *Who Cares Wins*.
27 (n 24).

employment, has increasingly taken place alongside paid work. This is not to say that women have not been both vocal and visible in their attempts to claim specific rights arising from their contemporary role as worker/carers, or that policy-makers have failed to respond to such calls.

There is now a substantial body of law and associated policy aimed at equalising pay and other conditions between men and women at work[28] regardless of working time[29] as well as a range of specific rights intended to enable mothers and others with care commitments to balance these with paid employment.[30] However, the resulting legal framework, as well as suffering from the limitations of the equal treatment approach, regards unpaid care as an ancillary activity rather than as the main focus of such state intervention.[31] In other words, law's response to the unpaid care–paid work conflict has been focused on the means by which care can be accommodated within the largely unyielding arrangements surrounding paid work rather than on a reconsideration of those arrangements.[32] It is the labour market which provides the centrifugal force around which all related aspects are organised so that only contributions which are measurable in financial terms, and thus commodifiable, are valued. This is perhaps unsurprising given the placement of the relevant body of law within the confines of what is known as 'labour law'. Despite its origins as a response to the exploitation associated with the commodification of labour, the relevant legal framework in its contemporary neo-liberal incarnation appears to have little space within which to situate relationships of care. As the following analysis demonstrates, the demarcation between paid work and unpaid care goes beyond the ideological distinctions between different forms of work and arises from the very classification of law itself.

Classifications of law: coexistence or conflict?

In both of its forms as a practice-based occupation and an academic discipline, the law is full of divisions. These divisions arise from the ways in which law is carved up into jurisdictions or specialisms so that policy-makers, practitioners, the judiciary and even those concerned with esoteric considerations of what law is are, from a relatively early stage, shunted into specific lines along preordained tracks. Even where broader knowledge of the law's whole is deemed desirable,

28 See EqA 2010.
29 Part-time Workers (Prevention of Less Favourable Treatment) Regulations 2000.
30 Provisions covering maternity and paternity leave and pay, parental leave and the right to request flexible work are contained in the: Employment Rights Act 1996; Employment Relations Act 1999; Employment Act 2002; Maternity and Parental Leave Regulations 1999, SI 1999/3312), as amended in 2001, 2002 and 2006; Work and Families Act 2006; Additional Paternity Leave Regulations 2010, SI 2010/1055.
31 The terminology used in the policy defines care as a minority occupation: phrases such as 'family friendly policy' and 'work/family balance' presuppose that mere concessions should be made to care and that it is not work but an exception to the norm rather than a part of most people's everyday lives.
32 See Sandra Fredman, *Women and the Law* (Oxford University Press, 1997).

such as within the early years of legal education, these lines are drawn around and between our understanding of the law and its practical application. Law's divisions are reflected within its institutions so that specialist court and tribunals deal with specific legal areas often in isolation from each other. Until relatively recently the epistemology of law was also restricted to the doctrinal study of distinct areas which were, by implication, presumed to be self-standing and autonomous. The introduction of law and society courses to the undergraduate LLB syllabus[33] and the growing body of theoretical and empirical studies collectively categorised as 'socio-legal' have contributed to a growing awareness of the limitations imposed by the construction of the discipline's own internal barriers. However, law's self-analysis, which takes place both in practice-based considerations of specific legal problems and through more abstract academic discourse is still largely confined to subject-specific ruminations of the 'black letter' variety which are led and supported by law's internal system of demarcation.

In common law jurisdictions this begins with the binary distinction between public and private law by which actions will be deemed to fall into either the administrative sphere involving settlements between the state and other legal actors under the classification of public law, or will consist of some form of dispute resolution between two private individuals. This assumes that the serious challenges which people encounter in their everyday lives will fit neatly into one or other area. In reality, many casual and indeed more formal interactions with the law fall at the intersections of the private and public spheres. This can make disputes difficult to resolve as, in the case of conflict between paid work and unpaid caregiving, the organisation of law simply does not facilitate resolution in a coherent and cohesive way.[34] Furthermore the use of 'public' and 'private' categorisations reinforces a particularly unhelpful connotation in the current context. The public–private dichotomy provides a binary separation by which paid work performed on the labour market is perceived as part of the public life of an individual and thus regulated by state intervention, whereas unpaid care work, which occurs within the confines of the family, is seen as a private activity which takes place behind closed doors away from the prying eyes and interference of the state.[35]

This separation of – and distinction between – the different forms of work, which endorses and supports divisions in other forms of participation in public

33 Which arguably still suffers from an over-abundance of commercial law courses in favour of those concerned with broader considerations of the meaning and philosophy of law and/or other areas of legal practice.
34 Research on legal clusters is helpful in this context as it reiterates the point that everyday problems do not necessarily fall neatly into law's classifications. However, findings are necessarily based on overlap between separate legal problems as defined using existing classifications. See for example, Richard Moorhead and Margaret Robinson, *A Trouble Shared: Legal Problems Clusters in Solicitors' and Advice Agencies* (Department of Constitutional Affairs, 2006).
35 See Susan Moller Okin, *Justice, Gender and the Family* (Basic Books, 1989); Carole Pateman, *The Sexual Contract* (Polity, 1988); and Fredman, *Women and the Law*.

life including the political realm, has been attributed as the cause and effect of woman's subjugation and man's dominance.[36] While such distinctions are not reflective of the organisation of contemporary society in which many individuals are likely to engage at some stage during the life cycle in both paid work and unpaid care either simultaneously or separately, the gendering of this binary divide and its lasting effects are pernicious and pervasive. This is partly because the very institutions that are intended to facilitate law's evolution in line with societal change are themselves steeped in traditional notions of social construction and are thus susceptible to gender (and other forms of) blindness.

Beyond the courts and associated institutions, law's demarcation is also reflected in the very provisions of social policy and labour and family law as well as in the operation of the labour market itself. The binary distinction between public and private perceptions of work has itself contributed to the current division between regulated and unregulated forms of work. Due to its occurrence within the family and its association with reproduction, unpaid care continues to be viewed as a private matter inferring that it has no market value in contrast with its public counterpart. Underpinning this categorisation is the assumption that labour is a commodity which, alongside other goods and services, can be bought and sold freely.[37] The provision of unpaid care exposes the inaccuracy of this view as the ethic of care, which determines why and how such work takes place, is not based on financial considerations dictated by individual autonomy, but rather by the recognition that interactions such as reciprocity and interdependence are natural expressions of the human condition.[38] Furthermore, the assumption that market value is only measurable on the basis of financial calculation overlooks the invaluable contribution of care's affective dimension which undoubtedly makes a significant contribution to market integration as the means by which successive generations of labour market participants are nurtured and supported.

The effects of care's negative conceptualisation are not confined to direct economic calculations of labour market activity but are all pervasive. Its undervaluation has an impact on the types of paid work performed alongside, and thus associated with, unpaid care. The 'women's work' that keeps the service sector afloat, much of which has an explicit 'care component', and jobs performed on a part-time basis to facilitate care obligations are often low paid and precarious so that the vulnerability of those who do such work is an easy target for exploitation. Disputes, where they arise in such inequitable circumstances, are increasingly privatised as they are either non-actionable in law, or dealt with by non-judicial means (thus preserving confidentiality between the parties) or as single action claims under the jurisdiction of private civil law. This circumvents collation of the issues raised and law's cumulative responses, thus disenabling the important

---

36 Pateman, *Sexual Contract.*
37 See Judy Fudge, 'Labour as a "Fictive Commodity": Radically Reconceptualizing Labour Law' in Guy Davidov and Brian Langille (eds), *The Idea of Labour Law* (Oxford University Press, 2011).
38 See Fineman, 'Vulnerable Subject'; Jonathan Herring (Chapter 3 in this volume).

translation of private disputes into matters of public concern and detracting from labour law's democratic function[39] which, from its origins, was seen as an essential component of work's regulatory framework.

Labour law and vulnerability

In the early days of law's engagement with the employment relationship, labour law's primary role was seen as being to manage the power relations between the parties. As Kahn-Freund[40] saw it, the principal purpose of labour law was 'to regulate, to support and to restrain the power of management and the power of organised labour'.[41] State intervention in industrial relations was minimal with a tradition of legal abstentionism so that relations were largely regulated by a system of voluntarism consisting of agreements between the parties. Nevertheless, the law operated as a series of checks and balances aimed at providing the means by which disputes, where they arose, could be resolved. This was deemed necessary in the early days of capitalism following the industrial revolution as trade unions provided a means of harnessing the collective voices of workers otherwise susceptible to exploitation in response to the demands of evermore powerful employing organisations. The employment protection legislation introduced in the late 1960s and 1970s recognised the movement away from collective forms of engagement. The new rights afforded to employees were aimed at redressing the imbalance in power between individual workers and employing organisations, which in many cases continued to expand in size, influence and geographical dispersal characterised by the growth of the multinational corporation.

Alongside the changes taking place within the labour market, the composition of the workforce itself was also changing as increasing numbers of women combined paid work with unpaid caring responsibilities and UK society's transformation from mono- to multicultural was reflected in greater numbers of migrant workers. Changes in family structures such as the growth of the lone-parent family also impacted on the ways in which individuals interacted with paid work so that assumptions regarding (male) 'bread winners' and (female) 'home makers' were no longer reflective of individuals' labour market behaviour, if indeed they ever had been.[42]

Despite changes to the nature and organisation of labour law and the predominating structures within which it operates, labour law's justification has always been political[43] as it is the relative bargaining power of the parties between whom the exchange of work and pay takes place that determines the outcomes of disputes. As Hepple acknowledges, '[t]he labour legislation of the future, like

---

39 Keith Ewing, 'Democratic Socialism and Labour Law' (1995) 24(2) *ILJ* 103–32.

40 The architect of labour law as an academic discipline.

41 Paul Davies and Mark Freedland, *Kahn-Freund's Labour and the Law* (3rd edn, Stevens & Sons, 1983) 15.

42 Rosemary Crompton, *Employment and the Family: The Reconfiguration of Work and Family Life in Contemporary Societies* (Cambridge University Press, 2006).

43 Ewing, 'Democratic Socialism and Labour Law' 119.

that of the past, will be the outcome of processes of conflict between different social groups and competing ideologies'.[44] In the current context, such conflict arises from the demands of paid work and the obligations of unpaid care, which are currently out of sync with each other. This contributes towards the economic disadvantage suffered by carers in the labour market leaving those for whom they care with reduced levels of support. What is required in order to respond effectively to such conflict is a repositioning of law's boundaries to incorporate the whole range of activities with which an individual engages in his or her endeavour to live a (re)productive life. The resulting changes to the nature and organisation of work that have occurred over the past fifty years have led to a general call for labour law's boundaries to be reconsidered and redrawn and it is this long-term project with which the remainder of this chapter will concern itself.

Redrawing labour law's boundaries

The need to reposition labour law through its incarnations both as an academic pursuit and as an area of legal practice has been recognised over the last decade by those generally concerned with the restrictive (and narrowing) scope of employment law as well as by feminist legal scholars seeking to ensure that women's experiences of work – both paid and unpaid – are incorporated into any future reconstruction of the discipline's boundaries. Supiot's study of the future of labour law in Europe identified the need to move 'beyond employment' and identified the concept of social citizenship as the foundation for a more useful participative regulatory framework within which the ultimate subjects of substantive and procedural guarantees would be involved in the framing and realisation of their rights.[45] Hepple has also called for a reimagined framework based on participation within which labour law's scope would be broadened to provide 'an adequate floor of rights for non-standard workers' alongside a new integrative function incorporating innovative welfare measures aimed at combating social exclusion making it easier to combine paid work and care responsibilities.[46] The whole system would be underpinned by an ideology capable of legitimising and reinforcing this vision with the overriding value of equality replacing 'misleading claims' of legal abstention and state neutrality and reasserting that labour is not a commodity.[47] In addition, Hepple counsels against the assumption that social rights will emerge as a natural consequence of citizenship, instead suggesting that they should be recognised as fundamental human rights – 'those moral rights which one has simply because one is a human being'.[48]

---

44 Bob Hepple, 'The Future of Labour Law' (1995) 24 *ILJ* 303, 305.
45 Alain Supiot, 'The Transformation of Work and the Future of Labour Law in Europe: A Multidisciplinary Perspective' (1999) 138(1) *International Labour Review* 31–46; Alain Supiot, *Beyond Employment: Changes in Work and the Future of Labour Law in Europe* (Oxford University Press, 2001).
46 Hepple, 'Future of Labour Law'.
47 Ibid.
48 Ibid, 317.

In calling for the need to incorporate a wider range of personal experiences than the current labour law framework encompasses, Conaghan has suggested the deployment of 'multiple standpoints'[49] to 'illustrate how a focus on work and family can contribute to a better understanding of labour law by reassessing it from the standpoint of those who engage in large amounts of unpaid, care-giving work'.[50] This perspective reveals the power deficit between those who combine paid work with unpaid care and employing organisations which has resulted from the traditional separation of 'work' and 'family' which has informed the development and provision of labour law. The relationship between productive and reproductive work has always existed but it is the law's failure to take account of this which has caused and perpetuated the current conflict between paid work and unpaid care. The resulting distinction between the 'official narrative' and the 'hidden reality' which conceals the gendering of unpaid care–paid work can only be remedied by recognition of paid work's place within its wider socio-economic environment.

In her analysis of the development of feminist labour law scholarship, Fudge asserts that women's experiences of paid work and care, rather than being confined to the identification and development of relevant legal intervention, should inform our understanding of labour markets more generally:

> Feminists have long claimed that women's location in the labour market should be addressed as a moral matter of substantive inequality; now we are also arguing that it is a conceptual necessity to attend to the specificity of women's paid and unpaid work in order to understand how labour markets operate.[51]

Fudge's vision for a feminist reconceptualisation of labour law requires recognition of the fact that the relations of social reproduction are as important as employment relations in enabling development of both the individual and viable and sustainable societies.[52]

What emerges from these observations and from the preceding discussion is the need to rethink the current classifications surrounding 'work' so that the diversity of working relationships, including those based on the provision and receipt of care, can be incorporated in a regulatory framework fit for the post-industrial age. The need to take account of caregiving as a natural human response to our universal vulnerability and inherent dependency emphasises the importance of rights in this respect which, as well as improving the experiences of worker-carers and

---

49 Joanne Conaghan, 'Work, Family, and the Discipline of Labour Law' in Joanne Conaghan and Kerry Rittich (eds), *Labour Law, Work and Family* (Oxford University Press, 2005) 25.

50 Ibid.

51 Judy Fudge, 'From Women and Labour Law to Putting Gender and Law to Work' in Margaret Davies and Vanessa Munro (eds), *The Ashgate Research Companion to Feminist Legal Theory* (Ashgate, 2013) 14.

52 Ibid.

consequentially those for whom they care, can also serve as a levelling tool as the enhanced status associated with protection could facilitate and encourage gender-free care.[53] This necessitates recognition of the narrow confines within which employment law currently operates relative to its wider labour law reification as only the latter is capable of incorporating unpaid work and non-standard forms of paid work alongside the more conventional – and increasingly outdated – notions of 'standard' work which are predicated on the (mis)conception that all workers are autonomous beings capable of entering into employment contracts freely and independently. A more widely drawn regulatory model would also reinvigorate labour law's democratic function enabling private disputes, once again, to be reformulated as matters of public concern.

In seeking to secure synergy between individual disputes and the development of public policy responses, it is also necessary to reconsider the means by which disputes are dealt with. Employment law's exclusive reliance on a rights-based approach contributes to the personalisation of claims so that their resolution takes place within a narrow and, all too often, closed environment with the publication of outcomes thwarted by the confidentiality clauses of compromise agreements. As well as contributing further to the 'privatisation' of employment disputes as con-tractual matters and, consequently, to the related loss of collective notions of soli-darity and public scrutiny, this raises questions surrounding the guarantee of legal certainty and legitimate expectation for 'end-users' as divergence in standards, norms and procedure may go unchecked giving rise to conflict and contradiction. This matters for the individuals affected whose access to justice may be restricted by the options available for resolution[54] but also has wider-reaching implications such as its influence on the operation of law's normative effect by which it is capa-ble of establishing behavioural norms, setting the agenda for reform and drawing the parameters for the values by which we live. Reconsideration of the ways in which disputes are resolved requires a shift away from an activity-based preoc-cupation with marketised work towards a more people-centred approach based on the performance of human activity which places relational bonds[55] rather than commercial exchange at its heart and it is to family law that we now turn for some useful guidance in this respect.

Family law and labour law – an argument for cross-fertilisation?

Family law suffers from many of the shortcomings associated with employment law: it too is a 'private law' area and thus is susceptible to a closed approach to disputes which can have a restrictive effect on their individual resolution as well as

---

53 See Busby (n 27).
54 Which will, in turn, depend on personal resources including financial, emotional and time.
55 See Jonathan Herring 'Relational Autonomy and Family Law' in Julie Wallbank, Shazia Choudhry and Jonathan Herring (eds), *Rights, Gender and Family Law* (Routledge, 2010) in which the author cautions against the growing import of individual autonomy as a fundamental value in family law.

preventing the collation of seemingly distinct issues so that the delivery of access to justice can be assessed and deficiencies identified. In fact, the need to preserve privacy is subject to even more emphasis than in employment law as a failure to do so risks exposing the intimate relationships, and more specifically the breaking-down of those relationships with which this area of law is concerned. In seeking to enable individuals to utilise law effectively in dealing with the complex problems with which we are all, from time to time confronted as well as deploying law's social justice function, new ways of conceptualising and resolving such disputes will have to be devised.

In articulating a case for the extension of family law to incorporate a rights-based approach alongside its more traditional welfare-based approach, Diduck has observed that 'the intimate relationship between public and private respon-sibility for individual and social well-being' is also relevant to the operation of family law so that the values associated with family life 'that give meaning to fairness include also values that animate public and political life'.[56] The recogni-tion of rights and obligations in the context of family relationships in place of the unquestioning acceptance of 'family values' is undoubtedly a necessary step in the development of a feminist family law. By this approach, human rights standards such as equality and non-discrimination can be imbibed into the regu-latory framework by legislative means alongside the judicial interpretation that, if unchecked, is susceptible to patriarchal influence. However, what a rights-based framework does not encourage is the extension of those rights to parties outside of the relevant relationship so that one obvious advantage that family law has over its employment law counterpart is its ability to focus attention on the relational ties which lie at the heart of its provisions. This arises from its application of the welfare approach and, just as family law might benefit from the application of clearly defined legal rights, labour law could learn much from this wider juridical nexus.

James and Callus have mooted that Article 3 of the UN Convention on the Rights of the Child (UNCROC)[57] could be interpreted as providing a basis on which tribunals and courts should consider the interests of children when decid-ing on questions relating to the employment rights of their parents.[58] Although centred on the needs of the child, the application of this provision is balanced by Article 3(2), which expressly acknowledges that account must nevertheless be taken of the rights and duties of parents. This 'ultimate balancing' or 'parallel

---

56   See Alison Diduck, 'Public Norms and Private Lives: Rights, Fairness and Family Law' in Wallbank et al, *Rights, Gender and Family Law* 205, in which the author provides examples of a rights-based approach in family law from the Canadian and South African jurisdictions.

57   Which provides, 'in all actions concerning children, whether undertaken by public or private social welfare institutions, courts of law … the best interests of the child shall be a primary consideration'.

58   Grace James and Thérèse Callus, 'Child Welfare and Work–Family Reconciliation Policies: Lessons from Family Law?' in Busby and James (eds), *Families, Care-giving and Paid Work* 185.

rights' test[59] enables the interests of all relevant individuals to be taken into account when selecting the solution which is least detrimental for the children involved. Accepted as relevant by the Supreme Court in the context of immigration law, this approach takes account of the welfare of the family unit as a whole. As Baroness Hale has opined, the 'central point about family life … is that the whole is greater than the sum of its individual parts'.[60] Of course this analysis is subjective and would always require contextualisation as 'For some of course, the family unit might be the cause of welfare concerns – it depends on a person's "family"' and "life"'.[61] Subject to the necessary safeguards, this approach provides an interesting contrast with the restrictive contractual nexus relating to employment rights that might be of value in developing a broader conceptual basis on which to build a more inclusive labour law framework. Of course UNCROC is limited as an instrument specifically directed at providing basic rights for children, but could this approach be adopted in further conceptually similar provisions which encompass the interests and welfare of *all* recipients of care? Such innovation would not be intended to replace but rather to complement the hard-won and undoubtedly crucial employment-based rights which should be extended to all working relationships beyond those which are dependent on the existence of a contract of employment.

Conclusions

Over the past two decades, the employment rights framework has been inordinately stretched to incorporate maternity, paternity, and parental responsibilities and the provision of flexible working arrangements aimed at enabling workers to manage their family lives and employment obligations. The current provisions are based on a system of rights, incorporating both the 'negative' right not to suffer discrimination alongside positive rights, such as the right to paid maternity leave. The application of these rights often depends on the existence of a contract of employment alongside other qualifying conditions. As well as overemphasising commercial considerations, this approach is not able to deal effectively with many of the issues related to its operation. An employee who provides unpaid care may find that the way in which she is able to perform her paid work is directly affected by the needs of those for whom she cares with such needs subject to wide variations from one care relationship to another. However, within the current regulatory framework, those recipients are both invisible and silent and yet, in discharging the obligations inherent in the provision of such rights for individual workers, employers *do* implicitly take account of the needs of those for whom they

---

59 Shazia Choudhry and Helen Fenwick, 'Taking the Rights of Parents and Children Seriously: Confronting the Welfare Principle under the Human Rights Act' (2005) 25(3) *Oxford J Legal Studies* 453.

60 *Beoku-Betts v Secretary of State for the Home Department* [2008] UKHL 39, para 4.

61 James and Callus, 'Child Welfare and Work–Family Reconciliation Policies' 186.

care. That they are required to do so without explicit guidance regarding how far they should consider the circumstances of the other parties to such arrangements is unhelpful, denies both our vulnerability and dependency, and halts progress in the reconciliation of the paid work–unpaid care conflict. Fineman's definition of vulnerability as universal and her emphasis on the structural causes of inequality brings all of those affected, including the recipients of care, into the framework and exposes the role of law and its institutions in constructing and perpetuating the myth of individual autonomy on which the rights-based approach is largely based.

In looking to family law for suitable alternatives, I do not wish to suggest a wholesale replacement for the hard-won rights aimed at enabling unpaid care to be combined with paid employment. As I have argued elsewhere, pursuance of a more clearly articulated and widely available system of rights is critical in this context.[62] Furthermore, as Fudge has asserted, where paid employment is valued as the primary path to citizenship, treating unpaid care work as a matter of social or family law rather than labour law 'reinforces the idea that such work is not only a woman's natural role, but also that in the social hierarchy it is of lower value than paid employment'.[63] What I am suggesting is that the objective of those with an interest in the development of improved legal responses to the paid work and unpaid care conflict should be to find ways in which labour and family law can move closer together, through the integration of common concepts and shared approaches aimed at providing better means by which resulting dilemmas can be addressed. This is a long-term project but undoubtedly a worthwhile one.

---

62 Busby, *A Right to Care.*
63 Fudge, 'Labour as a "Fictive Commodity"' 136.

Chapter 11

Relational vulnerability, care and dependency

Jo Bridgeman

Introduction

A challenge to the dominant view of the autonomous, rational, legal and economic actor and a different perspective from which to develop responses to social and legal problems is offered by an emphasis upon vulnerabilities.[1] Advocating for a vulnerabilities approach, Martha Fineman has argued that:

> Vulnerability is inherent in the human condition. It comes partly from our materiality – our embodiment – and, as such, it is both universal and constant. Our bodily vulnerability is apparent at the beginning of life when we are totally dependent on others for our survival. Vulnerability in this sense accompanies us continually throughout life, as we age, become ill, disabled or need care from others and, finally, die.
>
> But vulnerability extends beyond the body with its interior weaknesses and fallibilities. Even fully realized and functioning adults remain vulnerable: to external 'natural' forces, such as the environment or climate or to the machinations of human institutions, which are themselves often vulnerable to corruption, capture or decline. Much of our vulnerability whether of a bodily, natural, or societal form is beyond our control as individuals; some vulnerabilities we cannot even anticipate, let alone protect ourselves against.[2]

In this chapter, I consider and develop three aspects of the vulnerabilities approach identified here by Martha Fineman: the nature of our inherent vulnerabilities; unanticipated vulnerabilities; and the relationship between the institution of the law and our vulnerabilities.

---

1 Susan Dodds, 'Depending on Care: Recognition of Vulnerability and the Social Contribution of Care Provision' (2007) 21(9) *Bioethics* 500–10, 500.
2 Martha Fineman, 'Responsibility, Family and the Limits of Equality: An American Perspective' in Craig Lind, Heather Keating, and Jo Bridgeman (eds), *Taking Responsibility, Law and the Changing Family* (Ashgate, 2011) 37–49, 46.

The nature of our inherent vulnerabilities

Martha Fineman argues that a vulnerabilities approach disrupts assumptions about the nature of the individual which shapes current understandings of social and legal problems and their solutions:

> Understanding the significance, universality, and constancy of vulnerability mandates that politics, ethics, and law be fashioned around a complete, comprehensive vision of human experience if they are to meet the needs of real-life subjects. Currently, dominant political and legal theories are built around a universal subject defined in the liberal tradition.[3]

In contrast to the legal subject of the liberal tradition, as Martha Fineman observes in the quotation above, appreciation of vulnerabilities is closely linked to recognition of the effects of dependencies upon others for care. Dependency, dependency work and derivative dependencies[4] have been highlighted in academic analysis across a range of disciplines, by critics of social policy and in journalistic writings. But, as Fineman suggests, while feminists have highlighted care work, relationships and dependency, this has done little to disrupt the understanding of the legal subject: where dependency upon care is acknowledged, it is viewed as an episodic disruption to ordinary life, arising from bodily infirmity, and part of life's cycle in which care is briefly given and, in turn, taken. However, while bringing a focus to dependency, a vulnerabilities approach also needs to emphasise our connectedness; whether those connections arise from blood ties such as between parent and child, commitments of marriage, partnership, or friendship, or from caring relationships. The account given above of vulnerabilities risks repeating the construction of the subject as an atomistic individual who may require care in instances of bodily frailty but receives it intermittently and, on other occasions, provides it in reciprocal arrangements. It is important also to highlight vulnerabilities which arise from attachments, emotional connections and the affective nature of the self: not only the 'embodied' and 'socially embedded' but also the 'relationally constituted'.[5] In this chapter I consider just one aspect of our relational vulnerabilities – vulnerabilities which arise from reliance upon others to whom we entrust the care of someone we care about.[6]

Unanticipated vulnerability

Martha Fineman suggests that vulnerability can be understood as a 'state of constant possibility of harm', a 'persistent susceptibility to misfortune and

---

3   Martha Fineman, 'The Vulnerable Subject: Anchoring Equality in the Human Condition' (2008) 20(1) *Yale Journal of Law & Feminism* 1–23, 10.

4   Ibid; Eva Feder Kittay, *Love's Labor: Essays on Women, Equality and Dependency* (Routledge, 1999).

5   Dodds, 'Depending on Care' 501.

6   There is scope here to consider only one aspect of relational vulnerability which remains yet to be fully conceptualised.

catastrophe'.[7] Fineman, strategically, focuses upon those vulnerabilities which are unarguably universal: those arising from our physical embodiment; our defencelessness against the excesses of mother nature; or exposure to corrupt institutions of modern society. The concept of vulnerability may be used inconsistently in different disciplines[8] but however it is defined it is grounded in our susceptibility to damage, injury or harm. That is implicit in Martha Fineman's definition above and explicit in the definition offered by Doris Schroeder and Eugenijus Gefenas: 'To be vulnerable means to face a significant probability of incurring an identifiable harm while substantially lacking ability and/or means to protect oneself.'[9] But we must not be confined by established ways of understanding harm. We are at risk of developing sickness; disease; infirmity in old age; of broken limbs; mental illness; stress; the negative consequences of unhealthy lifestyles and other embodied harms. We may also be vulnerable to earthquakes; flooding; damage by hurricanes; fire; and other natural dangers. We risk being harmed by the deliberate actions of terrorists; fraud in the food supply; collapse of financial institutions; neglect of safety systems or equipment; institutional cover-up; we can suffer injuries or losses due to the momentary carelessness of those around us or other institutional or systemic human-made hazards. But we need also to acknowledge the extent to which our connectedness to others makes us vulnerable, exposing us to the risk of damage, injury or harm. Humans are vulnerable also because we care, love, are intimately connected to others. We worry about the health, safety, well-being of those we care *for*. As Jonathan Herring observes, to harm the cared for is to harm the carer.[10] In this respect too our relational vulnerabilities may be unanticipated; on those occasions when we are let down by individuals or institutions to whom we entrusted the care of one we care about.

Limited legal recognition of vulnerability

Martha Fineman argues that replacing the ideal of the autonomous individual subject with the vulnerable subject would not only be 'more representative of actual lived experience and the human condition'[11] but would result in a more responsive state. Institutions, such as the law, can respond to – recognise, redress, remedy, adjust, compensate – our vulnerabilities or ignore, reinforce and increase our vulnerabilities. However, until our relational vulnerabilities are recognised we

---

7 Fineman, 'The Vulnerable Subject' 11–12.
8 Jonathan Herring, 'Vulnerability, Children and the Law' in Michael Freeman (ed.), *Law and Childhood Studies: Current Legal Issues Volume 14* (Oxford University Press, 2012) 243–63, 244.
9 Doris Schroeder and Eugenijus Gefenas, 'Vulnerability: Two Vague and Two Broad' (2009) 18(02) *Cambridge Quarterly of Healthcare Ethics* 113 quoted in Herring, 'Vulnerability, Children and the Law' 243–63, 245.
10 Jonathan Herring, 'Where Are the Carers in Healthcare Law and Ethics?' (2007) 27(1) *Legal Studies* 51–73, 66.
11 Fineman, 'Vulnerable Subject' 1–23, 2.

cannot ask the further question of what, if any, should be the response of the law.[12] First, I offer examples of relational vulnerabilities arising from dependency upon others to provide care. Then, I examine the extent to which the law does currently recognise relational harm. My purpose is the simple one of presenting the argument for recognition of our vulnerabilities arising from our relatedness which the laws of a 'more responsive state' will recognise, minimise and, in appropriate cases, remedy.

Entrusting care to others

The primary responsibility for the provision of care rests with family members; parents, or mothers, of children; spouses and adult children of older people. Family members also have to rely upon others to provide care. We trust nursery nurses, nannies, child-minders to tend to, nurture and entertain our children, we entrust their education and well-being to teachers, we rely upon the expertise of sports coaches, lifeguards and others to ensure their safety as they learn sport and engage in supervised activities. We may need the assistance of community health workers, respite carers or care home workers in the care of children with chronic illnesses, special needs or disabilities or to provide compassionate care to older people. We depend upon doctors for diagnosis, advice, treatment and the provision of care to sick relatives. We also depend upon the police, fire officers, ambulance crews to protect and rescue and upon public services provided by local authorities. Although the primary responsibility to care for dependants rests with family members, they cannot be solely responsible for care but will need to entrust those they care about to the care of others with expertise, special skills or responsibilities. Vulnerability arises from dependency upon those entrusted to provide care to fulfil their obligations to take proper care.

Parents who gave evidence to the Bristol Royal Infirmary Inquiry[13] into the quality of care provided to children undergoing complex heart surgery gave expression to this dependency and vulnerability when they spoke of having to live with the feeling that as parents they had failed in their duty to their child because they had entrusted their child to the care of another who had failed to take care of them. The parents knew their children were seriously ill, that heart surgery was delicate and complex, and there was a risk that it would not be successful, that complications could arise or that their child may not survive. In their statements, many expressed how the small comfort they were able to take after the death of, or severe injury to, their child from the belief that they had secured the best possible

---

12 Robin West, *Caring for Justice* (New York University Press, 1997) 176.
13 Department of Health, *The Report of the Public Inquiry into Children's Heart Surgery at the Bristol Royal Infirmary 1984–1995: Learning from Bristol* (CM, 5207(I), July 2001) (www.bristol-inquiry.org.uk accessed, 24 May 2013). This was established to determine whether the care provided to children undergoing cardiac surgery at the Bristol Royal Infirmary between 1984 and 1995 was adequate and, in the light of that conclusion, to make recommendations to improve the quality of care provided by the NHS in the future.

care for them had been swept away by revelations about the quality of care provided.[14] Some of the parents who discovered that the care provided to their child undergoing complex heart surgery had been 'less than adequate'[15] expressed feelings of regret, that they had let their child down, self-doubt, stupidity for believing what they had been told, or of guilt for trusting the care of a seriously ill child to professionals who failed to take care of them.[16] As Lesley Smith, whose daughter Katherine died after surgery, said:

> When you place your child in the hands of surgeons you want to know that these are the best. We have had that taken away and now have to live with the idea that we are to blame for her death as we did not do the best for her.[17]

Similar feelings were expressed in relation to the care of their child after the child's death by parents giving evidence to both the Bristol Inquiry[18] and the Alder Hey Inquiry[19] into the retention of organs following post-mortem. These included feelings of guilt for letting their child down, for failing to protect their child as was their responsibility, for trusting others who failed to treat their child with dignity:

> They feel that they protected their child in life but in death when he needed their protection even more than ever, they feel guilty that they let him down in allowing or permitting organ retention.[20]

> Their child lost his dignity and was treated like a piece of meat in a butcher's shop ... They feel guilty that they did not protect their child in death.[21]

> [A]s a parent ... she would have done anything and everything in her power to protect her child. That was what she was there to do even more so in death

---

14 Written statements from parents were published, along with all the evidence considered by the Inquiry, on the Inquiry website, www.bristol-inquiry.org.uk, accessed 24 May 2013. The Inquiry received 145 written statements from mothers, 46 from fathers, three joint statements and six which were written by one parent but which were expressly stated to be the recollection of both. They included accounts from parents whose child had been treated successfully, who survived surgery but sustained mental or physical disability as a consequence, and who died during or shortly after surgery. Discussed in Jo Bridgeman, 'After Bristol: The Healthcare of Young Children and the Law' (2003) 23(2) *Legal Studies* 229–50.

15 Department of Health (n 13) s 1, 'Conclusions', para 6.

16 Bridgeman, 'After Bristol' 247.

17 From statement of Lesley Smith (WIT 0286) to the Bristol Inquiry.

18 Prof Ian Kennedy et al, *The Inquiry into the management of care of children receiving complex heart surgery at the Bristol Royal Infirmary Interim Report,Removal and retention of human material* (Bristol Royal Infirmary Inquiry May, 2000).

19 Michael Redfern, Dr Jean Keeling and Elizabeth Powell, *The Royal Liverpool Children's Inquiry: Report* (January 2001) (www.officialdocuments.gov.uk/document/hc0001/hc00/0012/0012_ii.pdf, accessed 24 May 2013).

20 Sam died following surgery at the age of 18 months (ibid, 425).

21 Jordan, stillborn (ibid, 416).

because it was the only thing she could do for her child at that stage. She had put her trust in the doctors, the midwives, the pathologists that they would respect her child and that they would deal with her in the way one would wish to deal with a dead person. They did not, they desecrated her. She feels let down. There was only one thing she could do and that was to protect her in death and she did not do it and she has to live with that.[22]

More recently, the serious case review into the abuse, neglect, torment, humiliation, bullying and assault of adults with learning difficulties at Winterbourne View Hospital by those entrusted with their care described the 'private trauma, self-blame and regret' of families that they had accepted the failure to respond to their complaints and dismissal of their concerns leaving their relatives 'isolated, disenfranchised and exposed to continuing violence'.[23] Families reflected upon failures to assess, get to know, seek to understand the behaviour and needs of, or help their relative to fulfil their potential.[24] Personal relationships were not valued and the expertise which family members had gained of their relative's needs and interests or ways of dealing with difficult behaviour were simply ignored. The parents of Terry Rooney described their devastation at the knowledge that their son had been abused at Winterbourne View Hospital by those they had trusted to look after him and feelings of responsibility for what he had gone through. His mother explained in a newspaper interview, 'I carry a lot of guilt. We should have never asked social services to help. We should have managed and kept going – we thought we were helping him and thought that people would be getting involved who would make his life better, not worse.'[25] Steve Sollars, whose son Sam has Down's syndrome and autism and was regularly restrained by staff at the hospital in the two years he lived there, explained, 'As a father, I want to look after my son but everything that has happened makes me feel I have let him down.'[26] Family members observed, following the convictions of 11 care workers, that the adults involved were left with physical and mental scars and they were left with 'unbearable guilt at failing to protect' 'exacerbated by fears for their future' and the inability to trust those they have to rely upon to care for their relative.[27]

Entrusting a loved one to the care of doctors, surgeons or care workers provide obvious examples of dependence on others, those with professional expertise and

---

22 Alexandra, stillborn (ibid, 408).
23 Margaret Flynn, *South Gloucestershire Safeguarding Adults Board, Winterbourne View Hospital: A Serious Case Review* (2012) 4.1.1. Concerns by family members were ignored by managers, police and the Care Quality Commission until shown on BBC *Panorama*. See Michael Chapman (director), *Undercover Care: The Abuse Exposed* (BBC, 2011).
24 Flynn, *South Gloucestershire* 4.1.2.
25 Quoted in 'Parents fear son suffered abuse at Panorama care home' *Western Morning News* (24 June 2011) 18–19.
26 Ian Onions, 'The abuse brings up so much anger in me' *Western Daily Press* (10 August 2012) 12–13.
27 Geoff Bennett, '"Corrupt, debased and monstrous" culture of abuse at home' *Bristol Evening Post* (29 October 2012) 4–5.

specialist skills which family members lack, to meet the particular needs of the one cared for. However, the same trust was expressed by Margaret Aspinall, chair of the Hillsborough Family Support Group, whose 18-year-old son James was killed in the disaster at the Sheffield Wednesday football ground in April 1989. She had entrusted the care of her son to the police, who failed to take care of him:

> We sent our children and loved ones to a football match. We entrusted their lives to the care of those policemen ... The deaths of our loved ones, then the cover-up and failure of anybody to accept responsibility for the disaster, has been torture for us – 23 years of torture. Now we are hoping for some truth, and accountability.[28]

It is notable that when the truth about the events of that day was finally revealed by the Hillsborough Independent Panel in September 2012, the response was a call for truth to be followed by justice. Despite a judicial inquiry, civil litigation, criminal and disciplinary investigations, inquests, judicial review, judicial scrutiny of new evidence and private prosecutions of senior police officers,[29] justice had not yet been done. Where it is necessary to rely upon others, possessed of special skills or expertise, to provide care, we are vulnerable to unanticipated relational harm arising from their failure whether due to carelessness, thoughtlessness or deliberate actions. As did parents whose children were failed by the quality of care provided at Bristol, who discovered that organs had been retained from their children at post-mortem, relatives of those killed in the Hillsborough disaster and of adults harmed by care workers at Winterbourne View Hospital, we may look to the law for recognition of the wrong.

Recognising relational harm

The law recognises harm sustained by the autonomous, rational, legal subject, limiting interference with, and infringement of, the boundaries of the separate individual through rules of reciprocal autonomy.[30] The law has yet fully to recognise relational harms to connections and interdependencies of humans in their communities, work and families. The leading case on relational harm is, of course, the House of Lords in *Alcock*[31] concerning claims brought by relatives of those killed or injured at the Hillsborough Stadium disaster. The requirements of a successful claim established by their Lordships in that case being that the claimant can establish they suffer from a recognised psychiatric illness, that psychiatric

---

28 Quoted in David Conn, 'From Orgreave to Hillsborough: one police force, two disgraces' *Guardian* (13 April 2012) 17 (www.guardian.co.uk/football/2012/apr/12/hillsborough-battle-orgreave, accessed 24 May 2013).

29 *Hillsborough: The Report of the Hillsborough Independent Panel* (Stationery Office, HC 581, 2012) 3–4.

30 Carol Gilligan, *In a Different Voice: Psychological Theory and Women's Development* (repr., Harvard University Press, 1993) 37–8.

31 *Alcock and Others and Chief Constable of South Yorkshire Police* [1992] 1 AC 310.

harm was reasonably foreseeable, proximity in time and space to the event which caused physical injury and perception of the harm in a sudden shocking event appreciated with their own senses: an arbitrary set of criteria which permits recovery by an individual who witnesses the horrific scene, or immediate aftermath, of a traumatic event which causes death, injury or endangerment of a loved one but not harm to relational integrity.[32] The principles do not amount to recognition of the harm arising from damage, violation or loss of relationship or connection in which harm to the other is harm to the self and to the relationship. But rather 'consequential' injury to the feelings of a third party considered 'legal on-lookers … unconnected with the event':[33]

> In those cases in which, as in the instant appeals, the injury complained of is attributable to the grief and distress of witnessing the misfortune of another person in an event by which the plaintiff is not personally threatened or in which he is not directly involved as an actor, the analysis becomes more complex. The infliction of injury on an individual, whether through carelessness or deliberation, necessarily produces consequences beyond those to the immediate victim. Inevitably, the impact of the event and its aftermath, whether immediate or prolonged, is going to be felt in greater or lesser degree by those with whom the victim is connected whether by ties of affection, of blood relationship, of duty or simply of business. In many cases those persons may suffer not only injured feelings or inconvenience but adverse financial consequences as, for instance, by the need to care for the victim or the interruption or non-performance of his contractual obligations to third parties … [T]he common law has, in general, declined to entertain claims for such consequential injuries from third parties.[34]

While the common law may, in general, decline such claims, that there are losses which the law should recognise has been acknowledged through the creative application of principles by lower courts, in powerful dissenting opinions and in recognition of violated rights.

Judicial creativity

In *Kralj and another v McGrath and another*,[35] Woolf J held that damages awarded for the pain and suffering arising from the personal injuries to the mother sustained as a result of 'horrific treatment' during her labour[36] could take into account that

---

32 Joanne Conaghan, 'Tort Law and Feminist Critique' in Michael Freeman (ed.), *Current Legal Problems 2003. Volume 56* (Oxford University Press, 2004) 175–209, 192; Robin West, 'Jurisprudence and Gender' (1988) 55(1) *U Chi L Rev* 1–72, 20–1.

33 *Merthyr Tydfil County Borough Council v C* [2010] EWHC 62 [31].

34 *Alcock* (n 31) 408–9 (Lord Oliver).

35 *Kralj and another v McGrath and another* [1986] 1 All ER 54.

36 Ibid, 59.

her injuries may have been worsened by her grief at the death of her child shortly after his birth from injuries he sustained as a result of negligence.[37] Damages were also awarded to her for the shock of witnessing the injuries of her child in the period prior to his death.[38] Locating the harm as consequential upon her physical injuries and as harm arising from witnessing injuries of another because, as Woolf J explained, the legal principles did not permit the award of damages for the 'natural' grief resulting from the death of a child. Even though, as Joanne Conaghan has argued, grief must surely be 'crucially expressive of the loss of connection sustained' and for many 'infinitely greater than any imaginable violation of their physical autonomy' and far more enduring than any physical injuries.[39] The court also sought to recognise the loss occasioned by negligence causing the death of a child by those entrusted with their care, hinged upon the personal injury to the mother, in *Briody v St Helen's & Knowsley HA*.[40] Ebsworth J awarded damages for grief and 'deep sadness' with which she would continue to live due to bereavement and infertility, sustained when as a result of medical negligence the claimant's baby was stillborn and an emergency hysterectomy performed denying her the chance of future children. The judge awarded damages for the physical injuries she had sustained and the consequential 'desperate loss and grieving following the loss of a second baby and of her fertility' leaving her with a 'sense of loss and isolation' and unbearably lonely.[41]

Post-*Alcock* we have witnessed some creative interpretation and application of the principles in attempts to give some measure to the loss occasioned by those entrusted to care as can be demonstrated by *Farrell*.[42] The claimant sought damages for depression following negligence during the birth of her son, Karol, which left him severely brain-damaged and for which the hospital admitted liability. Damages were awarded for the physical injuries which she sustained due to poor ante-natal care, emergency caesarean performed without pre-medication and the failure to administer antibiotics with the result that she developed an infection. Fitting the claim within the principles established in *Alcock*, Steel J considered her to be a primary victim 'personally and directly owed a duty by the defendant' whose harm was a direct result of the 'trauma of the birth' which extended from the point of induction through to being told of his severe disabilities over 24 hours later. As noted above, it was necessary to identify the cause of her depression as the trauma of the events of the birth rather than the 'strain of continual care for

---

37 Ibid, 62.
38 Ibid.
39 Conaghan, 'Tort Law and Feminist Critique' 192.
40 *Briody v St Helen's & Knowsley HA* [2000] 2 FCR 13.
41 Ibid [7]; her claim for the costs of a surrogacy arrangement were denied – the CA held that the award would be for loss of amenity arising from the 'grievous injury' of the deprivation of fertility and it was then a matter of choice as to how she spent damages awarded under this head (*Briody v St Helen's & Knowsley HA* [2001] EWCA Civ 1010 [34]).
42 *Farrell v Merton, Sutton and Wandsworth Health Authority*, 31 July 2000, Official Transcript, HQ9900094.

Karol',[43] her inability to share his care with others, mistrust in the ability of doctors to care for her son and an all-encompassing focus upon meeting the needs of her child. Furthermore, Steele J awarded compensation to recognise that failure to take care to ensure the safe delivery of her son resulted in his severe disabilities, which also:

> resulted in both injury to the Claimant, physical and psychological, and a complete change of lifestyle. Partly for financial and partly for emotional reasons, she has committed herself to the care of her child making this an overriding priority and changing her life. It was put on her behalf that her life had been ruined.
>
> It is not a question of economic loss but a loss of private life far beyond the normal constraint imposed by bringing up a healthy child who can be left for short periods in the care of family or baby-sitter and where this way of life will continue well beyond the time most children have a degree of independence.[44]

Steel J thus applied the existing principles as best she could and in doing so recognised aspects of the harm caused, the physical injuries to the child, the mother's physical injuries, the psychiatric harm sustained – albeit from the shock of events surrounding his birth rather than the responsibility she felt towards him when she had been so fundamentally let down by those who should have cared for him – and the 'loss of private life'. An attempt, given existing principles, to account comprehensively for the harms caused to both mother and child without being able to recognise the relationship lost with the child she no longer had.

Likewise, in *Walters*, the Court of Appeal demonstrated a willingness to apply the principles of law in such a way as to allow recovery by a mother for pathological grief reaction caused by the failure of the doctors she had consulted to diagnose that her ten-month-old son was suffering from acute hepatitis.[45] She was entitled to recover as a 'passive and unwilling witness' to a 'succession of blows'[46] characterised as 'a seamless tale with an obvious beginning and an equally obvious end,'[47] from being woken early one morning in the hospital room by the sound of her son fitting, assured he was unlikely to have been harmed, agreeing to his transfer for a liver transplant operation only to be told upon arrival that he would not survive with any quality of life and asked to agree that his life support should be switched off. Classifying her as a passive witness of harm to another rather than someone directly involved and locating the harm in the individual

---

43 Ibid.
44 Referring to the 'conventional sum' for loss of reproductive autonomy introduced by Lord Millett in *McFarlane v Tayside HA* [1993] 3 WLR 1301.
45 *North Glamorgan NHS Trust v Walters* [2002] EWCA Civ 1792.
46 Ibid [40].
47 Ibid [34].

rather than in the relationship violated[48] by those to whom she had entrusted the care of her son.

Likewise, while the High Court determination of the claims brought by parents who had discovered years later that organs had been retained from the bodies of their children after removal during post-mortem was a careful application of the principles of the civil law of tort, the parents were forced to formulate their claims in terms which did not accord to their experience of harm.[49] Parents quoted above identify the professional failure to respect the relationship between parent and child and betrayal of the trust the parents had extended to the professionals. The conclusion that the parents were primary victims of the healthcare professionals' negligence was a pragmatic conclusion necessary to avoid application of the limitations developed in *Alcock* as applicable to relational claimants but one which amounts to a failure to grasp the reality of the harm. Gage J held that the question of duty turned on whether a doctor–patient relationship existed between the clinician and parent at the point when consent to the post-mortem was sought,[50] and foreseeability of psychiatric harm depended upon whether the clinician viewed the bereaved parent as 'robust' and 'unlikely to collapse under the strain'[51] or 'emotionally fragile',[52] being forced to approach the claim in individual rather than relational terms. Gage J recognised that the necessity of presenting the alternative in the tort of wrongful interference with the child's body and hence in terms of possessory rights and ownership was particularly inappropriate to a claim based upon failure to treat the child with dignity and respect.[53] Parents spoke of the harm caused by those to whom they had entrusted their child by a failure to treat the child with dignity and respect and through failure to respect the relationship of responsibility and care which they had with their child.[54]

While the principles of law required the lower courts to strike out the application by the parents and Lord Slynn admitted that the parents would face difficulties in establishing a duty given the existing principles of law, his Lordship considered the case of *W v Essex* should be permitted go to trial.[55] The parents

---

48 Conaghan, 'Tort Law and Feminist Critique' 192.
49 Jo Bridgeman, 'When Systems Fail: Parents, Children and the Quality of Healthcare' in Jane Holder and Colm O'Cinneide (eds), *Current Legal Problems 2005. Volume 58* (Oxford University Press, 2006) 183–213.
50 *AB and Others v Leeds Teaching Hospital NHS Trust; Cardiff Vale NHS Trust* [2004] EWHC 644, [200] (Gage J) considering 3 lead cases representing 2,140 claims on the Nationwide Organ Group Litigation register.
51 Ibid [253] which was the conclusion in respect of Mrs Harris whose daughter Rosina's brain, heart, lungs and spinal cord were retained following post-mortem after her death at the age of 3 days old.
52 Ibid [268] which was the conclusion in respect of Mrs Shorter whose brain was retained from her daughter Laura who had been stillborn.
53 Ibid [134].
54 Bridgeman, 'When Systems Fail' 183–213, 209.
55 *W v Essex* [2000] 2 WLR 601. Although the case was settled, presumably to avoid the creation of a precedent rather than due to the certainty of success of the parents' claim.

had been approved by the local authority as specialist foster carers and, as they had four young children of their own, expressly told the council that they were not willing to accept placement with them of any child who was known or suspected to have committed sexual offences. The social worker placed with them a boy known to have been cautioned by police for an indecent assault on his sister and under investigation for alleged rape. In addition to the claims brought in relation to the children themselves, the parents brought proceedings against the council for psychiatric harm they sustained, and devastating consequences including the breakdown of their relationship, when it was alleged that the child placed with them had committed acts of sexual abuse against their children. In entertaining the possibility of a claim, Lord Slynn identified the harm sustained by the parents in terms of their sense of responsibility for bringing the abuser into contact with their children rather than in terms of the failure of the council to fulfil the trust placed in them, by the parents, to respect their specific request directed at ensuring the safety of their children. Following this authority, Hickinbottom J refused to strike out a claim by a mother for damages in respect of the failure of the local authority to act upon reports from her that her children had been sexually abused by a neighbour's child. Expert evidence from a consultant psychiatrist identified the harm she had sustained as 'irrational guilt feelings that she has been unable to protect her children' and 'tormented by uncertainty about how she could protect them in the future'.[56] Whereas her concern and uncertainty could be entirely rational given that she had taken all the steps she herself could take to protect her children but depended upon the local authority which had failed to fulfil its responsibility to investigate reports concerning the protection of children.

Dissenting voice?

While appreciating how devastating the situation had been for the parents, the majority of their Lordships concluded that it was not possible for the law to recognise the particular vulnerability of the parents arising from their dependence upon professionals to treat both their child with care and recognise the parental interest in their child's well-being in the case of *JD v East Berkshire Community Health NHS Trust and Others*.[57] The House of Lords considered an application to strike out claims by parents in three families who had sustained psychiatric harm as a consequence of careless investigation by professionals of concerns that they were responsible for the deliberate abuse of their children. In all three of the cases it was reasonable to suspect abuse, but the professionals whom the parents had consulted about their concerns regarding their child's health were negligent in their failure to undertake further investigations to rule out other potential causes of injury or illness during

---

56 *Merthyr Tydfil County Borough Council v C* [2010] EWHC 62 [5].
57 *JD v East Berkshire Community Health NHS Trust and Others* [2005] UKHL 23. The reasoning survives the Human Rights Act 1998 which enables parents to seek a remedy under s 7 for breach of article 8, *Lawrence v Pembrokeshire CC* [2007] EWCA Civ 446.

which time the condition remained untreated. For example, in the East Berkshire case, the mother of a child who suffered from severe allergies suffered acute anxiety and depression after a paediatrician negligently (beyond his expertise and without proper examination) suspected her of fabricating her son's condition as a result of which he was placed on the 'at risk' register.[58] Approaching the parents and children as isolated individuals and the children as particularly vulnerable, the majority of their Lordships concluded that the doctors could not owe a duty to the parents to investigate carefully suspicions of abuse or harm to their child because that would be inconsistent with their obligations to the child which had to take priority.[59] Lord Brown 'readily acknowledging' the 'legitimate grievances' of the parents considered that the law could not recognise them while safeguarding the welfare of children.[60] Lord Nicholls appreciated that being suspected of deliberately harming their child was a 'nightmare' for the parents[61] but found the conflict of interests argument most compelling; professionals were not to be distracted from 'single-minded' protection of the welfare of the child nor their judgement 'clouded' by congruent duties.[62] Lord Rodger focused upon the reluctance of the law to extend remedies to third parties for the consequences of injuries to others. As Michael Jones observed: 'Most parents would probably be astonished to be informed that so far as the law is concerned, they are "third parties" when it comes to the interests of their children.'[63] As Michael Jones explained, the duty to parent and child is the same – to take reasonable care in taking the history, making a diagnosis, providing treatment and where abuse is suspected referring to the relevant authorities – and both parent and child have an interest in reasonable care being taken to identify the cause of the child's injury or illness and if that arises from abuse to identify the fact and the identity of the abuser.[64] Dissenting, Lord Bingham recognised that parent and child share an interest in the diagnosis of child abuse and in protection from the 'separation or disruption' of the family which results from careless misdiagnosis.[65] His Lordship's review of the authorities led him to the conclusion that 'far from presuming a conflict between the interests of child and parent the law generally presumes that they are consonant with each other' and that professionals should have 'close regard to the interests of parents as people with, in the ordinary

---

58 The other two cases went on to be considered by the ECHR and are discussed further below: the Dewsbury case, *MAK and RK v United Kingdom* [2010] 2 FLR 451; and the Oldham case, *RK and AK v United Kingdom* [2009] 1 FLR 274.

59 *JD v East Berkshire* (n 57), 'counterveiling interests' [71] (Lord Nicholls); 'inconsistent obligations' [113] (Lord Rodger), understood as the protection of children from abuse by their parents, against the protection of parents from unnecessary intervention in family life.

60 Ibid [138] (Lord Brown).

61 Ibid [52] (Lord Nicholls).

62 *JD v East Berkshire* (n 57) [85]–[6].

63 Michael Jones, 'Child Abuse: When the Professionals Get It Wrong' (2006) 14(2) *Med L R* 264–76, 275.

64 Ibid, 271.

65 *JD v East Berkshire* (n 57) [37] (Lord Bingham); Paula Case, 'The Accused Strikes Back: The Negligence Action and Erroneous Allegations of Child Abuse' (2005) 21 *Prof Neg* 214–32.

way, the closest concern for the welfare of their children'.[66] His Lordship continued to observe that 'it is hard to think of a relationship very much more proximate than that between parent and doctor when the parent, concerned about the medical condition of the child', and in fulfilment of parental responsibility, seeks the professional advice of a doctor.[67] In the majority of cases in which parents seek medical attention for their child they will not have harmed them but depend upon the expertise of the professionals whom they consult. The role of the law should be to foster this relationship and support professionals to work together with parents and this means professionals having responsibilities to parents as well as to children. The relational vulnerabilities of parents and children are ignored when they are seen as separate individuals with conflicting interests and the resultant harms of separation, loss and disruption to valued relationships not recognised.[68]

Relational rights?

As Lord Bingham observed, the failure of the law of tort has left 'difficult and, in human terms, very important problems to be swept up'[69] by the Convention with the article 8 right to respect for private and family life providing scope for acknowledging the harm caused to relationships by failures on the part of those entrusted to care.[70] The House of Lords, in *M (a minor) and another v Newham LBC*,[71] held that a duty was owed to neither mother nor child in respect of carelessness in the investigation of suspicions of the abuse of a four-year-old child resulting in their separation for a year; had the mother seen the transcript of the interview she would have been able to explain that the child referred not to the mother's boyfriend but to her cousin who had lived with them in the past. Joanne Conaghan has observed that domestic law 'lacks the vocabulary to express the nature of the harm'[72] arising from wrongful separation which was recognised by the ECtHR as breach of their article 8 rights.[73] Parent and child should not be separated

---

66 Ibid [44] (Lord Bingham).

67 Ibid.

68 Neither, we should note, are the harms sustained by the children as individuals being recognised. Separation of babies from their parents is viewed as causing no lasting damage or recognisable injury; for example, whilst it was accepted that removal from parents into foster care would cause some 'degree of trauma' there was no 'identifiable' psychological harm of a nature giving rise to damages in removal from parents for four months when one year old (*D v Bury Metropolitan BC; H v Bury Metropolitan BC* [2006] All ER (d) 68 [82]). And while the House of Lords accepted that a duty was owed by both the local authority and health authority to nine-year-old RK, she was in practice unable to pursue a claim given the withdrawal of her legal aid certificate on the grounds that the 'likely costs were disproportionate to the value of the claim' (*MAK and RK* (n 57) [20]).

69 *JD v East Berkshire* (n 57) [50] (Lord Bingham).

70 Shazia Choudhry and Jonathan Herring, *European Human Rights and Family Law* (Hart, 2010) 319.

71 *X and others (minors) v Bedfordshire CC; M (a minor) and another v Newham LBC and others; E (a minor) v Dorset County Council and other appeals* [1995] 3 All ER 353.

72 Conaghan, 'Tort Law and Feminist Critique' 193.

73 Joanna Miles, '*Z and Others v United Kingdom; TP and KM v United Kingdom:* Human Rights and Child Protection' (2001) 13 *CFLQ* 431–54.

for longer than is necessary for protection of the child's interests; parents have an interest in being provided with information regarding allegations of abuse to enable them to respond to concerns about their ability to protect the child or come to terms 'with traumatic events effecting the family as a whole'.[74] In the view of the ECtHR, the mother had not been adequately involved in the decision-making process concerning the care and protection of her daughter and this amounted to a failure to respect *their* family life. The 'loss of opportunity' to have reduced the length of their separation caused distress, anxiety and, to the mother, feelings of frustration and injustice for which damages were awarded.[75]

Investigation of suspicions that a parent has abused their child interferes with the right to family life while pursuing the legitimate aim of protection of the child but carelessness in the investigation which extends the interference may amount to a violation of the rights of both parent and child. Thus rights to respect for family life were violated by the failure of a paediatrician to secure an immediate consultation with a dermatologist when bruising on a child's legs placed the father under suspicion of abuse,[76] and 'fundamental errors' in the conduct of an investigation of suspicions of deliberately inflicted injury and in assessment of a family caused a disproportionate extension and exacerbation of the interference with the right to respect for family life.[77] Whereas the court concluded that removal of a baby from the care of her parents due to suspicions of deliberately inflicted injury did not breach their right to respect for family life. The baby was placed with her aunt, her parents were allowed supervised access and she was returned to her parents following a further injury and diagnosis of brittle bone disease. The 'genuine and reasonably held concerns' were misguided but not incompatible with article 8 despite communication problems in the absence of an interpreter, and the failure of the hospital to take an accurate history or to pursue any other investigations. There was, as in all the cases discussed, a violation of article 13 as there should have been available an effective means within domestic law for claiming violation of their Convention rights and securing appropriate relief.[78] However, that hardly amounted to recognition of the substance of their complaint that their relationship with their daughter in the first year of her life and with her grandmother – given the erroneous record that the child had been 'yanked' when picked up by her – were severely disrupted as a consequence of failures on the part of those they had sought help from and failure to diagnose the child's condition by those they had entrusted to care for her.[79] And the development of an effective remedy requires an understanding

---

74 *TP and another v United Kingdom* [2001] ECHR 28945/95 [78–9]. Iain Steele has argued that a focus upon rights opens the way for identification of relevant interests ('Public Law Liability – A Common Law Solution?' (2005) 64(03) *CLJ* 543–6).

75 Ibid [115].

76 *MAK and RK* (n 58) [74].

77 *AD and OD v UK* [2010] 2 FLR 1 [88]–[90].

78 *TP and another* (n 74); *MAK and RK* (n 57) [88]; *AD and OD* (n 76) [103].

79 *RK and AK* (n 58) 274.

not only of minimum guarantees but also how responsibilities to care are best met, professional as well as parental. Starting from a position, not of individual conflict, but which appreciates the vulnerabilities arising from dependency upon those entrusted to care.

Relational vulnerability, care and dependency

As Susan Dodds has argued, 'we are all vulnerable to the exigencies of our embodied, social and relational existence and, in recognising this inherent human vulnerability, we can see the ways in which a range of social institutions and structures protect us against some vulnerabilities, while others expose us to risk'.[80] Appreciating vulnerabilities in relation to families requires recognition of relational vulnerabilities which arise from dependency upon those who care. We need to identify and articulate the ways in which we are vulnerable, including those which arise out of relationships, and the ways in which we can be harmed as a consequence if we are to work out whether and if so, how, the law should respond.[81] In many cases the ways in which to respect relational vulnerability and to avoid causing relational harm are very simple instances of recognition, respect and care for the relationship: respecting the expertise which carers have of those they care for pertinent to decisions about their care, appreciating the concern they have about the well-being of the one whose care they entrust to another, understanding the interest they have in receiving information about their loved one. In other words, an understanding of connections and caring relationships and the vulnerability of carers dependent upon those with particular expertise, special skills or responsibilities. As Peter Cane has observed, the law is 'at least as concerned with telling us what our responsibilities are, and with encouraging us to act responsibly, as with holding us accountable and sanctioning us in case we do not fulfil our responsibilities'.[82] Unless our relational vulnerabilities are articulated, we cannot identify ways in which the law can foster and support those partnered with family members in the provision of care to respect their caring relationship. Or the ways in which causing relational harm may be remedied. Monetary compensation may be necessary to redress physical or psychological injuries but relational harms may not so appropriately be addressed in financial terms.[83] For example, the settlement agreed in respect of organ retention at the Alder Hey Children's Hospital included a sum of £5,000 in respect of each child, a letter of apology, a donation to a charity chosen by the parents, a plaque to

---

80 Dodds, 'Depending on Care' 507.
81 West, *Caring for Justice* 176.
82 Peter Cane, *Responsibility in Law and Morality* (Hart, 2002) 30.
83 Michael Jones has observed that the sum of damages awarded to the successful claimant in *AB and Others* of £2,500 plus special damages may have amounted to 'an apparent trivialisation of what was undoubtedly a tragic and emotionally damaging situation' resulting from a 'failure to exercise some basic humanity' ('Retained Organs: The Legal Fallout' (2004) 20 *Prof Neg* 182–91, 191, 190).

commemorate the children, a contribution to a memorial and a commitment to push the government to reform the law in relation to the removal and retention of tissue.[84] Changing the law in response to 'actual real lived experience' to recognise what it is that we value in life[85] is about as much as we can ask of a responsive state.

84 Victoria MacCallum, 'Alder Hey apologises to parents after mediation' (*Law Society Gazette*, 6 March 2003) (www.lawgazette.co.uk/news/alder-hey-apologises-parents-after-mediation, accessed 24 May 2013).

85 Nancy Levit, 'Ethereal Torts' (1992–3) 61 *Geo Wash L Rev* 136–92, 190.

Chapter 12

Safeguarding and the elusive, inclusive vulnerable adult

Alison Brammer

Introduction

> Vulnerable people are of course not an homogeneous group and arriving at a definition of vulnerability which is neither under- nor over-inclusive presents some difficulties.[1]

The opening statement was made by the Law Commission in 1993 in their consideration of public law protection for mentally incapacitated and other vulnerable adults. Nearly twenty years on, despite apparent advances in knowledge and understanding, developments in law, policy and practice, it remains an insightful reflection.

The construction of the vulnerable adult in law policy and practice has been influenced by recognition that adults may be abused. It is inextricably linked with growing awareness of the prevalence and impact on adults of such abuse and calls for action to prevent and/or respond to such abuse as part of a policy of safeguarding. This chapter will begin by setting out some of what is known about adult abuse, its recognition, terminology, forms, prevalence, victims and perpetrators.

Examination of the concept of vulnerability is at the heart of this collection. It is arguable that all adults are vulnerable at some point in their lives. Such vulnerability has been explained as relating to characteristics of the individual and situations (inherent/situational).[2] Both elements feature in attempts to arrive at a definition which can be applied in safeguarding practice, with the most recent formulations focusing more on risk. For the purposes of this chapter the focus is on adults for whom there are safeguarding concerns within family settings. At the outset it is recognised that this provides an incomplete analysis as a

---

1 Law Commission, *Mentally Incapacitated and Other Vulnerable Adults: Public Law Protection* (Law Com No 130, 1993).

2 M. Dunn, I. Clare and J. Holland, 'To Empower or to Protect? Constructing the "Vulnerable Adult" in English Law and Public Policy' (2008) 28 *Legal Studies* 234.

significant number of adults suffer abuse in residential settings. Indeed the irony exists that for some adults, removal from an abusive family may lead to an abusive residential placement.

In tracing development of law and practice concerning the vulnerable adult within safeguarding a number of themes emerge. Courts appear increasingly willing to extend their involvement in adult safeguarding. In case law prior to the introduction of the Mental Capacity Act 2005 (MCA) this was evident in *Re F*[3] where Dame Butler-Sloss indicated a willingness of the court to intervene on a case-by-case basis in the absence of legislation.[4] The MCA now deals with cases where individuals lack capacity, but the courts have continued to use the inherent jurisdiction in cases where the vulnerable adult has capacity and so falls outside the remit of the legislation. Examination of the case of *DL v A Local Authority*[5] captures the latest consideration of the broad remit of the inherent jurisdiction by the Court of Appeal. This contrasts with the approach of government which in providing a framework for safeguarding is characterised by limitation both of the ambit of the term vulnerable adult, and the types of abuse to which safeguarding activities should be directed. Resulting gaps have been partially filled by the courts through the inherent jurisdiction, but this may not be a satisfactory longer-term approach. One response has been to call for specialist adult protection legislation, though there is an apparent reluctance on the part of the government (in England) to introduce statutory powers beyond a duty to make enquiries and formal governance through statutory Safeguarding Adults Boards. This chapter will trace the development of safeguarding policy through consultations which focus on the vulnerable adult and case law. This will be used as a base from which to consider development of future practice, explored further in Chapter 13 of this volume.

Recognition of the abuse of adults – what do we know about abuse?

Knowledge and understanding of the abuse of adults, and the consequent need for some form of safeguarding framework, continues to grow, and is attracting increasing policy and media attention.[6] A triangle of interrelated questions arise – what is abuse, who is abused and who abuses? – and continue to be debated. Early accounts of abuse focused on older people, adopting terminology which referred to elder abuse, mistreatment, miscare and even 'granny bashing',[7] and drew heavily on US literature. Other accounts of the abuse of adults with learning

---

3 [2000] 3 WLR 1740.

4 Re F [2000] 3 WLR 1740 [1752 b].

5 [2012] EWCA Civ 253.

6 For example, the *Panorama* television documentary *Undercover Care: The Abuse Exposed*, aired on 3 June 2011, into abuse of adults with learning disabilities at Winterbourne View Care Home, Bristol.

7 A Baker, 'Granny bashing' (1975) 5(8) *Modern Geriatrics* 20.

disabilities also emerged.[8] Local authority polices developed in a fairly haphazard way but from initial focus on distinct groups, eg elder abuse policies, took a generic approach to 'vulnerable' adults. The first practice guidelines were issued in 1993[9] and focused on abuse in domestic settings, although there was simultaneously greater recognition of the existence of abuse in residential settings.[10] Policy thus took a limited focus drawn on a limited knowledge base.

Definition of 'abuse' of adults has proved controversial.[11] Action on Elder Abuse were commissioned by the Department of Health to produce a definition, which was included in many agency policies and read: 'Elder abuse is a single or repeated act or lack of appropriate action occurring within any relationship where there is an expectation of trust, which causes harm or distress to an older person.'[12] While not confining abuse to domestic settings, this definition does restrict abuse to existing relationships and excludes targeted abuse by strangers. In 2000, *No Secrets* was issued as formal guidance[13] and contains the definition in current use. A different conceptual emphasis is apparent, no doubt influenced by the Human Rights Act 1998: 'Abuse is a violation of an individual's human and civil rights by any other person or persons.' Beyond this broad statement, *No Secrets* elaborates with further detail: 'Abuse may consist of a single act or repeated acts. It may be physical, verbal or psychological. It may be an act of neglect or an omission to act or it may occur when a vulnerable person is persuaded into a financial or sexual transaction to which he or she has no consented or cannot consent. Abuse can occur in any relationship and may result in significant harm to, or exploitation of, the person subjected to it.'[14]

No Secrets marked a change in direction away from the earlier separate focus on adults with particular characteristics which was evidenced by policies for example on elder abuse. There is an argument that the introduction of policy which sees vulnerable adults as one single category is too overarching and risks losing sight of the complexities surrounding the abuse of an adult who is elderly and neglected or the abuse of an adult with a learning disability who is sexually abused. Undoubtedly there are differing factors which may be associated with the circumstances of abuse and the range of possible responses to it. Ageism may

8 H. Brown, J. Stein and V. Turk, 'The Sexual Abuse of Adults with Learning Disabilities: Report of a Second Two-Year Incidence Study' (1995) 8(1) *Mental Handicap Research* 3.

9 Department of Health *No Longer Afraid: The Safeguard of Older People in Domestic Settings* (HMSO, 1993).

10 F. Glendenning and P. Kingston (eds) *Elder Abuse and Neglect in Residential Settings: Different National Backgrounds and Similar Responses* (Haworth Press, 1999).

11 See analysis in A. Brammer and S. Biggs, 'Defining Elder Abuse' (1998) 20(3) *Journal of Social Welfare and Family Law* 285.

12 Action on Elder Abuse, Newsletter (Age Concern, 1994); adopted by the World Health Organization in *Toronto Declaration on the Prevention of Elder Abuse* (WHO, 2002).

13 Guidance in similar terms was introduced in Wales. National Assembly for Wales *In Safe Hands: Implementing Adult Protection in Wales* (National Assembly for Wales, 2000).

14 Department of Health, *No Secrets: Guidance on Developing and Implementing Multi-Agency Policies and Procedures to Protect Vulnerable Adults from Abuse* (Department of Health, 2000), para 2.6.

impact on both the abuse of an older person and the response to it.[15] Disability discrimination may impact on the harassment of a disabled adult and perceptions of whether that person might provide cogent evidence in court should a criminal prosecution proceed. A counter-argument to differentiation may be that of course individuals do not necessarily exhibit single characteristics as elderly or disabled. That has been recognised recently in the Equality Act 2010 which allows individuals to bring claims for dual discrimination in respect of one or more protected characteristics, supporting the case for a definition based on vulnerability. A further argument may be suggested that a dangerous hierarchy of abuse of different types of vulnerable adult could emerge, with the potential for greater attention and resources to be focused on one 'more deserving' group at the expense of and consequential marginalisation of others.

Attempts have been made to measure abuse, no doubt partly driven by the desire for legitimisation of a social problem, thereby requiring a response. In part due to the lack of consensus over definitions it has been difficult to arrive at reliable prevalence rates. It is also likely that with increasing awareness of the phenomena, actual prevalence may remain steady while reporting rates may suggest an increase. Despite major methodological challenges studies have produced broadly consistent results. An early study by Ogg and Bennett in 1992[16] surveyed 2,000 older people in the community and found rates of 5 per cent for psychological abuse and 2 per cent for physical and financial abuse. This study has acknowledged limitations; it did not include people in residential accommodation and was unlikely to include the very frail older person as it was conducted by OPCS interviews. It did, however, replicate prevalence figures from a study in Boston conducted by Pillemer and Finkelhor.[17]

In the 2003/4 parliamentary session, the House of Commons Health Committee heard evidence on elder abuse. Action on Elder Abuse presented evidence of calls to its national telephone helpline between 1997 and 1999 which suggested that psychological abuse was the most prevalent form of abuse followed by physical and financial abuse.[18] This operated as a genuine helpline and produced valuable insight into individual experiences; however, caution must be exercised in any attempt to extrapolate prevalence rates from this data. It did nevertheless contribute to the decision of the Committee to recommend the need for a national prevalence study. Such a study was co-funded by the charity Comic Relief with the Department of Health and reported in 2007.[19] The study comprised a survey of 2,100 people throughout the UK, aged 66 and over in

---

15 See eg Herring, *Older People in Law and Society* (Oxford University Press, 2011) ch 5.

16 J. Ogg and G. Bennett, 'Elder Abuse in Britain' (1992) 305 *British Medical Journal* 998.

17 K. Pillemer and D. Finkelhor, 'The Prevalence of Elder Abuse: A Random Sample Survey' (1998) 28(1) *Gerontologist* 51.

18 G. C. J. Bennett, G. Jenkins and Z. Asif, 'Listening Is Not Enough: An Analysis of Calls to the Elder Abuse Response Helpline' (2000) 2(1) *Journal of Adult Protection* 6.

19 M. O'Keeffe, A. Hills, M. Doyle et al, *UK Study of Abuse and Neglect of Older People: Prevalence Survey Report* (National Centre for Social Research, 2007).

private households (ie people in residential and nursing accommodation were not included). Utilising the term 'mistreatment' to include all forms of abuse and neglect, the survey found that 4 per cent of people had experienced mistreatment involving a family member, close friend, care worker, neighbour or acquaintance. In this survey, neglect was the most common form of mistreatment, followed by financial abuse. The full report provides a breakdown by country, age and sex (and other categories); considers the characteristics of perpetrators and the impact of mistreatment. The highest prevalence was found in the older age group (85 and over) and people in this age range were significantly more likely to have experienced neglect than those younger than 85. Women were more likely to have experienced mistreatment than men. Perpetrators lived in the same household as the respondent in 53 per cent of cases and overall included spouses/partners (51 per cent), other family members (49 per cent), care workers (13 per cent) and close friends (5 per cent). The authors conclude that its estimate is likely to be conservative, noting that, 'Judging the reliability and validity of the measurement of mistreatment is a complicated issue,'[20] particularly when based on self-reports.

The studies mentioned are necessarily limited by their own terms, for example to older people in domestic settings, excluding adults with severe dementia, and have adopted differing definitions. There has been no research attempt to ascertain the prevalence of abuse to all adults who might come to the attention of safeguarding teams. It may not be realistic to attempt such a study. What is becoming increasingly valuable as a supplement to the research-based prevalence studies, however, are records of referrals to safeguarding teams and progress towards a national data collection system. Such records are reflected in the recently published 'experimental statistics' from the Information Centre for Health and Social Care.[21] The statistics[22] cover the period from 1 April 2010 to 31 March 2011 and are drawn from a return from the 152 councils with adult social services responsibilities. Data is included as to: who is being abused; what type of abuse (following the *No Secrets* classification, and therefore excluding self-neglect); where abuse takes place; and the relationship between alleged victim and perpetrator. Key findings included that over the year there were 92,865 alerts about safeguarding (not all councils recorded the initial alert stage and this information is based on the return of 101 councils). The total number of referrals from 152 councils, ie those cases which met local safeguarding thresholds, reached 95,065, of which 41 per cent were wholly or partly substantiated. Analysis of the detail of those referrals found that 62 per cent of referrals were for women and 61 per cent were for adults

20 Ibid, 17.
21 NHS Information Centre, Social Care Team, *Abuse of Vulnerable Adults in England 2010–11: Experimental Statistics: Final Report* (Health and Social Care Information Centre, 2012).
22 The document explains that 'Experimental statistics are defined in the UK Statistics Authority Code of Practice for Official Statistics as new official statistics undergoing evaluation. They are published in order to involve users and stakeholders in their development and as a means to build in quality at an early stage' (6).

aged over 65. Referrals were more likely to be made by health and social care staff (63 per cent) than family members (8 per cent).The breakdown into categories of abuse identified allegations of physical abuse at 30 per cent, neglect at 23 per cent, financial abuse 20 per cent, emotional or psychological abuse at 16 per cent, sexual abuse at 6 per cent, institutional abuse at 3 per cent and 1 per cent discriminatory abuse. The most likely setting for abuse was the person's own home, 41 per cent of cases, followed by 34 per cent of cases in care homes. Perpetrators were recorded in cases as family members (25 per cent), social care staff (25 per cent), other vulnerable adults (13 per cent), friends, neighbours, volunteers, other professionals or strangers, (12 per cent) healthcare workers (3 per cent) and other or unknown (22 per cent). Outcomes data is also included in this report and ranged from no further action (31 per cent), increased monitoring (26 per cent) other (13 per cent), to community care assessment and services (10 per cent). Predictably there are some limitations to the statistics. It is unclear, for example, why the classification of perpetrators would group strangers with friends and other professionals. Not all councils were able to submit a complete return, which suggests inconsistency in data collection. Nevertheless there is a level of detail in this report which gives a real indication of safeguarding activity in England. The studies give a valuable indication of the characteristics of victims of abuse, which, it is suggested, any definition of the vulnerable adult for safeguarding purposes needs to capture.

The complexity of the concept of vulnerability is readily apparent from the attempts to arrive at a definition in the context of adult safeguarding. Definitions and descriptions have emerged in policy and guidance, legislation and case law, and range between narrow and focused to over-inclusive approaches.

Vulnerable adult

The current definition of a vulnerable adult in *No Secrets* refers to a person, over 18, 'who is or may be in need of community care services by reason of mental or other disability, age or illness; And who is or may be unable to take care of him or herself, or unable to protect him or herself against significant harm or exploitation.'[23] Two elements are comprised in this definition: first, a link to individual characteristics and eligibility for community care services; second, an element of risk via a real or perceived inability on the part of the individual to prevent the abuse.

A review of *No Secrets*, including key terminology, was announced in 2007 by Ivan Lewis, then Minister for Care Services, stating:

> Seven years on, and in the light of several serious incidences of adult abuse, it is timely to review this guidance and to consult with other government departments that have an interest in this field. New guidance is necessary to reflect the evidence in today's report and respond to the new demographic

23 Department of Health, *No Secrets*, para 2.3.

realities which are affecting our society. We will also consider the case for legislation as part of the review process.[24]

The report referred to is the UK prevalence report.[25] This indication of rising government priority for adult abuse prompted a national consultation exercise, held through 2008/9. It was led by minsters from four government departments: the Department of Health; Ministry of Justice; Solicitor General; and the Home Office.[26]

Respondents to the *No Secrets* review were critical of the term 'vulnerable adult' and its link to community care services.[27] It is true that some people eligible for community care services may also be vulnerable to abuse: risk factors identified in the national prevalence study included being in receipt of, or in touch with, services. However, there will also be adults who do not qualify for services but are vulnerable to abuse. This reference in relation to community care perpetuates a 'welfarist approach to abuse'.[28] Respondents echoed a view expressed by the ADSS, advocating safeguarding adults as the preferred term to adult protection. Their view was that vulnerable adult is a contentious term is explained: 'One reason is that the label can be misunderstood, because it seems to locate the cause of the abuse with the victim, rather than placing responsibility with the actions or omissions of others.'[29] The preferred term to emerge from the *No Secrets* consultation was 'adult at risk'.

Alongside the *No Secrets* consultation, a review of adult social care law undertaken by the Law Commission commenced in 2008. Initially a scoping report[30] was published, followed by a consultation paper in 2010,[31] an analysis of the consultation responses in 2011[32] and a final report with recommendations for the reform of adult social care,[33] also in 2011.

Central to safeguarding practice, the Committee recommended the introduction of a duty on social services authorities to investigate, or cause an investigation

---

24 This statement is included at page 2 of the review.
25 M. O'Keefe et al, *UK Study of Abuse and Neglect of Older People: Prevalence Survey Report* (National Centre for Social Research, 2007).
26 Department of Health, *Safeguarding Adults: A Consultation on the Review of the 'No Secrets' Guidance* (Department of Health, 2008).
27 Department of Health, *Safeguarding Adults: Report on the Consultation on the Review of 'No Secrets'* (Department of Health, 2009) para 8.28.
28 J. Williams, 'State Responsibility and the Abuse of Vulnerable Older People: Is there a Case for a Public Law to Protect Vulnerable Older People from Abuse?' in J. Bridgeman, H. Keating and C. Lind, *Responsibility, Law and the Family* (Ashgate, 2008).
29 ADSS, *Safeguarding Adults: A National Framework of Standards for Good Practice and Outcomes in Adult Protection Work* (ADSS, 2005) 4.
30 Law Commission, *Adult Social Care: Scoping Report* (Law Commission, 2008).
31 Law Commission, *Adult Social Care: A Consultation Paper* (Law Commission No 192, 2010).
32 Law Commission, *Adult Social Care Consultation: Analysis* (Law Commission 2011).
33 Law Commission, *Adult Social Care* (Law Commission No 326, 2011).

to take place in individual cases concerning an 'adult at risk',[34] as an alternative to the *No Secrets* vulnerable adult. Many consultees criticised the term 'vulnerable adult' as 'stigmatising, dated, negative and disempowering'.[35]

The *No Secrets* review process made reference to the existence of the Adult Support and Protection (Scotland) Act 2007 (and the need to monitor its implementation).[36] The term 'adult at risk' also features here and is defined in section 1 as adults who:

(a) Are unable to safeguard their own well-being, property, rights or other interests,
(b) Are at risk of harm, and
(c) Because they are affected by disability, mental disorder, illness or physical or mental infirmity, are more vulnerable to being harmed than adults who are not so affected.

In section 2 the Act further defines an adult as at risk of harm (as in s 1(b)), where:

(a) Another person's conduct is causing (or is likely to cause) the adult to be harmed, or
(b) The adult is engaging (or is likely to engage) in conduct which causes (or is likely to cause) self-harm.

This is significantly broader in scope than the *No Secrets* definition as it encompasses self-harm and is not linked to provision of services. The Code of Practice accompanying the Act states further that, 'No category of harm is excluded simply because it is not explicitly listed … Also what constitutes serious harm will be different for different persons.'[37]

Statutory definition of the vulnerable adult

Use of 'vulnerable adult' also carries potential for confusion as it already features in two existing pieces of legislation directly relevant to adult safeguarding, bearing a different definition in each. The Care Standards Act 2000, with its emphasis on regulation of service provision (including residential accommodation), defines a vulnerable adult in section 80 as:

(a) An adult to whom accommodation and nursing or personal care are provided in a care home,

34 Spencer-lane, T., 'Reforming the legal framework for adult safeguarding: the Law Commission's final recommendations on adult social care' (2011) 13(5) *Journal of Adult Protection* 275.
35 Law Commission, Adult Social Care (Law Com No 326, 2011).
36 See K. Mackay, C. McLaughlan et al, *Exploring How Practitioners Support and Protect Adults at Risk of Harm in the Light of the Adult Support and Protection (Scotland) Act 2007* (University of Stirling, 2011).
37 Scottish Government, Adult Support and Protection (Scotland) Act 2007: Code of Practice (Scottish Government, 2009) 13.

(b) An adult to whom personal care is provided in their own home under arrangements made by a domiciliary care agency, or

(c) An adult to whom prescribed services are provided by an independent hospital, independent clinic, independent medical agency or National Health Service body.

A different emphasis is evident in the Domestic Violence Crime and Victims Act 2004 where a vulnerable adult is defined in section 5(6) as:

> a person aged 16 or over whose ability to protect himself from violence, abuse or neglect is significantly impaired through physical or mental disability, through old age or otherwise.

The phrasing of that definition fits with the objective of that legislation in providing a strengthened scheme of provision of remedies against domestic violence and introduction of the offence of 'causing or allowing the death of a child or vulnerable adult'.[38] The former focuses on setting and eligibility for services, whereas the latter links to individual characteristics and risk.

The vulnerable adult and the inherent jurisdiction

Identifying the characteristics of a vulnerable adult has also featured in a line of case law of which *Re SA (Vulnerable Adult with Capacity: Marriage)*[39] is described as a 'high point'.[40] Munby LJ delivered the following influential statement:

> the inherent jurisdiction can be exercised in relation to a vulnerable adult who, even if not incapacitated by mental disorder or mental illness, is, or is reasonably believed to be, either (i) under constraint or (ii) subject to coercion or undue influence or (iii) for some other reason deprived of the capacity to make the relevant decision, or disabled from making a free choice, or incapacitated or disabled from giving a real and genuine consent.[41]

And further:

> I would treat as a vulnerable adult someone who, whether or not mentally incapacitated, and whether or not suffering from any mental illness or mental disorder, is or may be unable to take care of himself, or unable to protect himself against significant harm or exploitation, or who is deaf, blind or dumb,

---

38 The Domestic Violence, Crimes and Victims (Amendment) Act 2012 has extended the ambit of this offence to include 'serious injury'.
39 [2005] EWHC 2942 (Fam).
40 McFarlane, LJ in *DL v A Local Authority & Others* [2012] EWCA Civ 253 [11].
41 Ibid [77].

or substantially handicapped by illness, injury or congenital deformity. This is not, and is not intended to be a definition. It is descriptive, not definitive; indicative rather than prescriptive.[42]

While expressly excluding definition, this final passage does describe elements and characteristics of an individual's circumstances which justified the High Court intervention in a case with safeguarding elements even though the adult concerned was considered to have capacity. The case was decided prior to implementation of the Mental Capacity Act 2005, and its application would now be limited to those cases where the adult has capacity and MCA does not apply.

The case concerned an 18-year-old woman who was profoundly deaf and partially sighted and whose only means of communication was British sign language which her Punjabi-speaking family did not use. The court had to consider whether it could continue the protection offered in her minority to protect her from the risk of an unsuitable arranged marriage. It was accepted that she did not lack the capacity to marry and understood the concept of marriage, but would have difficulty understanding a specific marriage contract to a specific individual which would involve moving to Pakistan.

Munby J referred to SA as, 'plainly a vulnerable adult. She is substantially handicapped by her disabilities. And, particularly because she is deaf and dumb, she may well be unable to take care of herself and protect herself against significant harm or exploitation if placed in unfamiliar surroundings or deprived of access to those able to communicate with and for her in British sign language.'[43] Orders were made to prohibit her from entering into a marriage without her consent and from removal to Pakistan.

The case was decided prior to the implementation of the MCA. Other decisions following *Re SA* have endorsed the Munby notion of a vulnerable adult (sometimes referred to as 'Munby vulnerable') and confirmed the survival of the inherent jurisdiction.

Re A and C (Equality and Human Rights Commission Intervening)[44] was a case relating to an adult and a child, both of whom suffer from Smith–Magenis syndrome. Perhaps not surprisingly, Munby J confirmed, 'The High Court has an inherent jurisdiction in relation not merely to adults who lack capacity but also to vulnerable adults.'[45] In *Re A (Capacity: Refusal of Contraception)*,[46] Bodey J found that Mrs A was incapacitated (regarding decisions relating to contraception) in the *Re SA* sense of being subject to coercion or undue influence. The particular case was dealt with under the MCA. However, *obiter* comments suggested that the inherent jurisdiction should be limited to the extent that its purpose, 'is to create a situation

---

42 Ibid [82].
43 [120].
44 [2010] EWHC 978 (Fam).
45 *Re A and C (Equality and Human Rights Commission Intervening)* [2010] EWHC 978 (Fam) [68].
46 [2010] EWHC 1549 (Fam).

where he or she can receive outside help free of coercion, to enable him to or her to weigh things up and decide freely what he or she wishes to do'.[47]

This approach was followed in *LBL v RYJ and VJ*.[48] In relation to a young woman judged by the Court of Protection to have capacity to decide where she wished to live, the local authority requested the exercise of inherent jurisdiction to overrule her mother's views on the matter. The Official Solicitor argued that to use the inherent jurisdiction to give the local authority powers over where the woman should live would subvert the constitutional scheme of the Mental Capacity Act 2005. Here Macur, J stated that, 'relevant case law establishes the ability of the court, via its inherent jurisdiction, to facilitate the process of unencumbered decision-making by those they have determined have capacity free of external pressure or physical restraint in making those decisions'.[49] The latter cases suggest a narrowing of the powers of the court in relation to the very wide notion of the vulnerable adult.

Perhaps the most significant safeguarding case before the High Court since *Re F* [2000] 3 WLR 1740 came next. In *A LA v DL*[50] the court responded to a local authority's application for a non-molestation order to prevent aggressive and violent behaviour towards an older couple by their adult son. While awaiting a full hearing, the court made a series of ex parte interim injunctions requiring the son not to behave unlawfully.[51]

At the full hearing in the Family Division, the opening paragraph of the judgment of Theis J captures the significance of the case:

> This case raises important questions about the extent of the court's inherent jurisdiction in relation to vulnerable adults following the implementation of the Mental Capacity Act 2005.[52]

Further, 'to what extent, the court's inherent jurisdiction is available to make declarations and, if necessary, put protective measures in place in relation to vulnerable adults'.[53] In the subsequent Court of Appeal judgment McFarlane LJ expresses the question as to whether a 'jurisdictional hinterland exists outside its borders to deal with cases of "vulnerable adults" who fall outside that Act and which are determined under the inherent jurisdiction'.[54]

---

47 *Re A and C* (n 45) [79].
48 [2010] EWHC 2665 (COP).
49 *LBL v RYJ and VJ* [2010] EWHC 2665 (COP) [62].
50 [2011] EWHC 1022 Fam.
51 The court also concluded that in addition to its inherent jurisdiction, it had alternative authority under s 222 Local Government Act 1972 to make an injunction that would prevent the son from continuing to impede the local authority in fulfilling its statutory function of providing community care services.
52 (n 40) [1].
53 Ibid [7].
54 Ibid [1].

The assumed facts, which are denied by the son DL are set out in the judgment and are worth recounting as they give a clear indication of a range of allegations of behaviour which fits models of elder abuse and demonstrate why the local authority were prompted to act.

The case concerns an elderly married couple, Mr and Mrs L who live with their son DL who is in his fifties. Mrs L is disabled and receives direct payments and community care support. At the time the proceedings were commenced it was accepted that Mr and Mrs L had capacity to manage their affairs and decide whether their son should live with them and what their relationship would be. By the time the matter came before Theis J in the High Court Mr L had moved into a care home and was assessed not to have capacity to make his own decisions. Concerns over the son's alleged aggressive behaviour towards his parents prompted the local authority application to obtain protection for them from him. It is clear that the local authority had been involved with the family for some time:

> The local authority has documented incidents going back to 2005 which, it says, chronicle DL's behaviour and which include physical assaults, verbal threats, controlling where and when his parents may move in the house, preventing them from leaving the house, and controlling who may visit them, and the terms upon which they may visit them, including health and social care professionals providing care and support for Mrs L. There have also been consistent reports that DL is seeking to coerce Mr L into transferring the ownership of the house into DL's name and that he has also placed considerable pressure on both his parents to have Mrs L moved into a care home against her wishes.[55]

An Independent Social Work Expert produced a written report for the full hearing in which he concluded that GRL and ML had capacity to decide on residence and contact for the purposes of the MCA. However, he considered that, 'both GRL and ML are unduly influenced by DL to an extent that their capacity (in the SA sense) to make balanced and considered decisions is compromised or prevented'.[56]

The local authority case relies on the existence of the inherent jurisdiction in relation to vulnerable adults in the Re SA sense. On behalf of DL it was argued that the inherent jurisdiction no longer exists for adults who did not fall within the MCA jurisdiction, or if it did, only to the extent to enable the person to make decisions.

Theis J details the arguments in *Re SA* and subsequent case law (discussed above) as to the continued existence of the inherent jurisdiction based on the *Re SA* vulnerable adult. She concludes that the jurisdiction does exist and that, 'its

55 Ibid [6].
56 Ibid [6].

primary purpose is to create a situation where the person concerned can receive outside help free of coercion to enable him or her to weigh things up and decide freely what he or she wishes to do'.[57]

DL progressed to the Court of Appeal[58] whose judgment confirmed that the inherent jurisdiction continues to exist in addition to the Mental Capacity Act 2005, and its existence is compatible with article 8 of the European Convention.

In the leading judgment of McFarlane LJ several strands emerge. First he emphasises the argument that the common law provides a safety net filling necessary gaps in the law. The view advanced that the MCA introduced a statutory code which thereby excluded the continuation of the inherent jurisdiction was rejected. He notes that the 'MCA 2005 makes no express provision limiting or extinguishing the use of the inherent jurisdiction'[59] and observes the contrast to the stance adopted in both the Children Act 1989 and the Family Law Act 1996 Part 4A. The former specifically limits the High Court's inherent jurisdiction in relation to children; the latter confirms that its introduction does not affect the inherent jurisdiction in relation to forced marriage. Where the MCA applies, the inherent jurisdiction would have no role, but it remains for those cases where the MCA does not apply. More importantly he recognises a broader justification for the continuation of the jurisdiction demonstrating insight into the motivation behind local authority recourse to the jurisdiction:

> There is in my view, a sound and strong public policy justification for this to be so. The existence of 'elder abuse' … is sadly all too easy to contemplate. Indeed the use of the term 'elder' in that label may inadvertently limit it to a particular age group whereas, as the cases demonstrate, the will of a vulnerable adult may, in certain circumstances, be overborne. Where the facts justify it, such individuals require and deserve the protection of the authorities and the law so that they may regain the very autonomy that the appellant rightly prizes.[60]

It is clear that in McFarlane's view the victim of elder abuse may be a vulnerable adult who would potentially benefit from the inherent jurisdiction. Beyond this example he recognises the range of individuals who may suffer abuse:

> I, like Munby J before me in *Re SA*, am determined not to offer a definition so as to limit or constrict the group of 'vulnerable adults' for whose benefit this jurisdiction may be deployed.[61]

57 Ibid [26].
58 (n 40).
59 Ibid [51].
60 Ibid [63].
61 Ibid [53].

Second he rejects the argument that *Re SA* is a standalone unsupported case, reciting at length from the *Re SA* judgment the sections referring to those cases 'where a person's ability to make decisions may be overborne by the undue influence of another, rather than lost as a result of mental incapacity'.[62]

Finally, he clarifies the extent of the jurisdiction. In the early part of her judgment, Theis J refers to the protective measures that the inherent jurisdiction may provide. Her concluding remarks suggest she views the jurisdiction as constricted to measures necessary to regain capacity to make a decision and unlikely to extend to longer term protective measures. Such limitation was also evident in *LBL v RYJ and VJ*, but can no longer be considered correct following the Court of Appeal decision in *DL*.

McFarlane LJ resists any limitation on the scope of the court's exercise of the jurisdiction:

> it must follow from my unreserved endorsement of the full jurisdiction described by Munby J in *Re SA* and applied subsequently in a number of cases at first instance that I reject the idea that, if it exists, the exercise of the inherent jurisdiction in these cases is limited to providing interim relief designed to permit the vulnerable individual the 'space' to make decisions for themselves, removed from any alleged source of undue influence. Whilst such interim provision may be of benefit in any given case, it does not represent the totality of the High Court's inherent powers.[63]

It is arguable that the first priority of the court in exercising the inherent jurisdiction for vulnerable adults will be to take steps which would facilitate unencumbered decision-making of the adult in question. Such an approach is enabling and proportionate. It is clear, however, that where necessary and proportionate the court will not be so limited and will make appropriate orders of longer-term effect if necessary. Future decisions may illuminate the extent of such orders: whether, for example, in a *DL* situation the court would authorise removal of those who require protection, rather than seeking to limit and thereby provide relief from the actions of the person perpetrating abuse.

The current position can be summarised thus: the vulnerable adult as described in *Re SA* in the broadest terms can benefit from the widest powers of the inherent jurisdiction, on a case-by-case basis, filling the gap of redress unavailable to such adults under the MCA or other avenues. It is then appropriate to consider the extent of the gap and whether any other avenues exist which would reduce the need for this safety net.

---

62 Ibid [21].
63 Ibid [68].

Filling the gap

In practice, local authorities may warmly welcome the decision in *DL v A Local Authority* when faced with difficult cases where there are safeguarding concerns and no apparent protective legal remedy. Authorities will also be aware that the inherent jurisdiction has limitations, including the cost associated with applications. While local authorities may be unlikely to consider it on a routine basis when faced with growing numbers of safeguarding cases, it must be seen as an option in the context of their positive obligations to act to protect vulnerable adults as clearly established in *Opuz v Turkey*.[64]

In *DL* itself, it is clear that in their attempt to meet their safeguarding obligations the local authority explored the gap and found no applicable law to secure protection for the vulnerable adults. The case includes an account of other legal avenues considered by the authority prior to commencing the proceedings:

> It has considered (and rejected) using the criminal law. It has considered (and rejected) an application to the Court of Protection under the Mental Capacity Act 2005 ... It has considered (and rejected) an application for an ASBO ... under the Crime and Disorder Act 1998. It has considered (and rejected) an application under s 153A of the Housing Act 1996.[65]

In its application to the High Court, the local authority sought as a third party to obtain injunctions on behalf of vulnerable adults. Such a scenario was envisaged by Parliament in s 60 of the Family Law Act 1996 but has not been implemented.

The state of the law relating to adult safeguarding had been extensively criticised. For example, LJ Munby has commented, 'There is the remarkable fact that the formal safeguarding agenda in relation to vulnerable adults rests entirely upon Ministerial guidance and otherwise lacks any statutory basis – a state of affairs that, unsurprisingly, can leave local authorities uncertain as to their function and responsibilities in this vital area.'[66]

To an extent the use of the inherent jurisdiction in this way reinforces such criticism and gives weight to calls for new laws which specifically address adult safeguarding. Support for legislation from respondents to the *No Secrets* consultation was described as 'widespread and vociferous'.[67] The wider potential impact of legislation on practice is noted by McKeough:

> There remains an urgent need for legislation that puts adult protection on a similar footing to the statutory model of child protection and puts out the

---

64 [2009] ECHR 33401/02.
65 *A LA v DL* [2011] EWHC 1022 Fam [6].
66 Munby LJ 'Dignity Happiness and Human Rights' (2011) 1(1) *Elder Law Journal* 32, 34.
67 Department of Health, *Safeguarding Adults: A Consultation on the Review of 'No Secrets' Guidance* (DH, 2008) 91.

signal that the abuse of an adult is as serious as the abuse of a child. Such an approach will help increase the status of adult protection work within health and social care organisations.[68]

Clarity of definition and consistency in approaches to safeguarding are important: for local authorities in framing their role and responsibilities and of course for those who may experience abuse. Definitions are crucial as the starting point and have generated much debate but are only important in the context of the possible outcomes arising from inclusion within the definition. Currently *No Secrets* emphasises a preventative approach and does not include any specific powers of intervention. In contrast the exercise of the inherent jurisdiction depends on whether the proposed intervention is necessary and proportionate.

A further argument for clarity draws on human rights and in particular the positive obligations on the state under articles 3 and 8. Indeed Herring suggests that this 'obligation on the state to protect victims and ensure there are legal remedies available' actually requires a public law of protection.[69] Article 3 states that no one 'shall be subjected to torture or to inhuman or degrading treatment or punishment'. Where an adult suffers abuse which amounts to an infringement of article 3 as an absolute right without exceptions then intervention to prevent continuation of that abuse may not only be justified, it may in fact be required. A concern may follow as to the form of such intervention and the potential for further violation of individual rights, if for example an adult is removed against their wishes from the family home. Here, the article 8 rights provide a balance and it is reassuring to note that in existing case law this has prompted very careful consideration of the level of risk to an adult remaining in the family home. The much publicised *Neary*[70] decision relating to deprivation of liberty is a clear example, with their enforced separation viewed as an infringement of both father (as carer) and son's article 8 rights. Again, Munby J provides a steer to local authorities with his recognition that

> We have to be conscious of the limited ability for public authorities to improve on nature. We need to be careful not to embark upon 'social engineering'. And we should not lightly interfere with family life. If the State – typically, as here, in the guise of a local authority – is to say that it is the more appropriate person to look after a mentally handicapped adult than her own partner or family, it assumes, as it seems to me, the burden – not the legal burden but the practical and evidential burden – of establishing that this is indeed so.[71]

68 C. McKeough, 'Reflections and Learning from Adult Protection Policy in Kent and Medway' (2009) 11(1) *Journal of Adult Protection* 9
69 J. Herring, *Older People in Law and Society* (Oxford University Press, 2009) 196.
70 *Hillingdon London Borough Council v Neary* [2011] EWHC 1377 (COP).
71 *Local Authority v MM* [2007] EWHC 2003 [116].

For the purposes of article 8 protection, 'family' for vulnerable adults has been interpreted to include carers. The removal of a vulnerable adult from his foster carer without involvement of the carer in the decision-making process and the prevention of contact for several months was a serious breach of article 8 rights in *G v E*.[72] Baker J noted that:

> Article 8 gives the families of such adults (and by 'families' I include relationships between such adults and long-term foster carers) not only substantive protection against any inappropriate interference with their family life but also procedural safeguards including the involvement of the carers in the decision-making process, seen as a whole, to a degree sufficient to provide them with the requisite protection of the families interests. If they have not, there will have been a failure to respect the family life of the incapacitated adult (and, of course, the carer).[73]

If human rights arguments strengthen the case for the introduction of legislation to offer a clear framework for the protection of vulnerable adults, could such legislation incorporate the Munby vulnerable adult? Here it is interesting to consider the scheme provided by the Adult Support and Protection (Scotland) Act 2007 (a third tier of legislation in addition to the Adults with Incapacity (Scotland) Act 2000 and the Mental Health (Care and Treatment) (Scotland) Act 2003). The protection orders provided by the Act should not normally be granted without consent of the adult. However, refusal to consent can be ignored where it is believed the adult has been unduly pressurised to refuse consent and no other steps could reasonably be taken with the adult's consent, to offer protection from the harm which the order or action is intended to prevent. The guiding principles act as a balance for such action; however, it remains a potentially controversial element of the legislation providing powers to override the perceived wishes of the individual concerned. The Act provides an example of a situation in which 'undue pressure' is present. It states that an adult at risk can be considered to be under undue pressure if the person causing the harm that the order, or action, is intended to prevent is someone in whom the adult at risk has confidence and trust, and the adult at risk would consent to the order or action if he or she did not have confidence and trust in that person. This is primarily intended to cover situations where the adult refuses to consent to action because someone else (a family member, partner, spouse, friend or anyone else with a close person relationship to the adult), is pressuring him or her. This sounds very close to the arguments in *Re T (Adult: Refusal of Treatment)*,[74] and *Re G* as rehearsed in *Re SA* which referred to situations where, 'a person's ability to make decisions may be overborne by the undue influence of another'.[75]

---

72 [2010] EWHC 621 (Fam).
73 *G v E* [2010] EWHC 621 (Fam) [88].
74 [1993] Fam 95.
75 *DL* at [21].

Conclusion

A survey of the development of the concept of the vulnerable adult at the centre of safeguarding policy reveals a tension between policy efforts to confine the scope of safeguarding practice and the judicial position, most recently expressed by McFarlane LJ, to keep the door of the inherent jurisdiction wide open with scope to exercise a full range of powers in relation to a broadly interpreted vulnerable adult.

For local authorities frustrated by limited options to protect vulnerable adults the judicial approach is welcome in principle, though in practice the inherent jurisdiction may be an expensive route reserved only for selected cases. It may be as Singer J stated in *Re SK (Proposed Plaintiff) (An Adult by way of her Litigation Friend)*,[76] 'a sufficiently flexible remedy to evolve in accordance with social needs and social values'. As a flexible remedy, cases within the inherent jurisdiction 'safety net' are not decided within a framework of clearly articulated principles, in contrast to cases decided by the Court of Protection under the Mental Capacity Act 2005. In some instances this has led to an unfortunate analogy of vulnerable adults requiring protection in the same way as children. It is perhaps not surprising that alternative ways to fill or reduce the gap might be sought, including the possibility that a statutory framework offering clarity of definition for all safeguarding adults cases might be more accessible. In assessing such a route, however, the words of Action on Elder Abuse are perceptive, acknowledging that:

> Legislation on its own is not the panacea that can guarantee safeguarding in each and every situation. It can only be one option among a range that must include the education of society to alter their perceptions and responses to vulnerability.[77]

76 [2005] 2 FLR 230 para 8.
77 AEA (2007).

Chapter 13

When are adult safeguarding interventions justified?

Michael Dunn

Introduction

The last decade has seen significant developments in how legal and political institutions have identified, and acted upon, their obligations to safeguard adults from other individuals within society.[1] These developments have been broad and multifaceted. At one level, the concern of law- and policy-makers has been to articulate a systematic framework for governing the safeguarding process within public authorities; at another level, the concern has been to identify the practical steps – those powers of intervention[2] – that can be instigated to safeguard a person. What powers of intervention are justified has been an important focal point: can it, for example, ever be justified to forcibly remove a person from her private home if she is identified as being at risk of abuse, has been judged to have the capacity to refuse support, and is exercising that refusal?

The ways in which powers of intervention have been identified and put into practice connect to key questions concerning the appropriate relationship between the state and the citizen, and about the limits of state involvement in adults' private lives. Perhaps unsurprisingly, therefore, these legal and policy developments have

1 'Adult safeguarding' is often commonly referred to as 'adult protection'. The term 'safeguarding' is preferred here as 'protection' implies certain kinds of normative presuppositions about harm-based considerations that will be critically examined in the latter sections of the chapter.
2 Commonly, powers of intervention are referred to those active and invasive steps taken to intervene in the private affairs of an adult. Within an adult safeguarding service, such powers are likely to include powers of entry, powers to enquire into an adult's affairs (including conducting medical examinations), powers of removal from a private home, and powers of relocation to alternative accommodation. It should be noted, however, that other less-invasive safeguarding practices will more commonly by deployed to safeguard adults effectively; the focus on intervention powers here is not to presume that such powers are the only weapon in the adult safeguarding armoury. One significant area of safeguarding practice will involve the pre-emptive detection and prevention of abuse. Another area of safeguarding practice will focus on collecting and collating evidence about abuse once an initial report has been received. Yet another area of safeguarding practice will be to respond to situations when abuse (or heightened risk of abuse) has been established. In such cases, it will commonly by appropriate to make use of non-invasive practices such as the provision of information, child support, and family therapeutic interventions.

sparked extensive analysis from a number of disciplinary perspectives. The majority of the work conducted thus far has sought to examine the concepts that have been used to justify interventions, and these analyses have had both a theoretical and empirical dimension. Legal analysis has documented how a new legal subject – the 'vulnerable adult' – has been invoked in English law to justify protective interventions for an adult who does not meet the criteria for substitute decision-making under the Mental Capacity Act 2005.[3] Practical ethicists have drawn upon philosophical methods of conceptual analysis to differentiate vulnerability from harm, exploitation and personal autonomy as a way of determining the practical duties that arise in the contexts of medical research, healthcare practice and social welfare services.[4] Empirical social scientific analysis has revealed how those working in safeguarding services conflate harm and abuse in order to act in ways that enable them to meet their perceived obligations to help the people they are tasked to support.[5] This conceptual work has been important in drawing attention to some of the problems with, and inconsistencies in, the recent changes that have taken place in the UK. Equally significantly, these analyses have functioned to raise 'vulnerability' to the forefront of legal, philosophical and social scientific inquiry, with this book itself being evidence of this trend within the field of family law.

Increasingly, however, analyses of adult safeguarding law and policy have become explicitly normative rather than conceptual in nature. Herring, for example, has argued for a rights-based approach to determine when it would be justified to intervene to safeguard an adult, claiming that older adults have a positive right to be protected from abuse.[6] In contrast, Hough argues that recent developments in adult safeguarding law and policy constitute a move away from the contemporary values of personalisation, control and citizenship endorsed within public services to embrace a paternalistic impetus that will impact negatively on the private affairs of people with learning difficulties.[7] As the chapter develops, I

3 Michael Dunn, Isabel C. H. Clare and Anthony J. Holland, 'To Empower or to Protect? Constructing the "Vulnerable Adult" in English Law and Public Policy' (2008) 28(2) *Legal Studies* 234–53; Jonathan Herring, 'Protecting Vulnerable Adults: A Critical Review of Recent Case Law' (2009) 21 *CFLQ* 498.

4 Robert Goodin, *Protecting the Vulnerable: A Reanalysis of Our Social Responsibilities* (University of Chicago Press, 1985); Daniel Callahan, 'The Vulnerability of the Human Condition' in Peter Kemp et al (eds), *Bioethics and Biolaw. Volume 2* (Rhodos, 2000); Michael H. Kottow, 'Vulnerability: What Kind of Principle Is It?' (2004) 7 *Medicine, Health Care and Philosophy* 281–7; Mary C. Ruof, 'Vulnerability, Vulnerable Populations and Policy' (2004) 14(4) *Kennedy Institute of Ethics Journal* 411–25; Samia A. Hurst, 'Vulnerability in Research and Health Care: Describing the Elephant in the Room?' (2008) 22(4) *Bioethics* 191–202; C. Mackenzie, C. Rogers, W. and S. Dodds (eds), *Vulnerability: New Essays in Ethics and Feminist Philosophy* (Oxford University Press, in press).

5 Fiona Sherwood-Johnson, 'Problems with the Term and Concept of "Abuse": Critical Reflections on the Scottish Adult Support and Protection Study' (2012) 42(5) *British Journal of Social Work* 833–50.

6 Jonathan Herring, 'Elder Abuse: A Human Rights Agenda for the Future', in Israel Doran and Ann Soden (eds), *Beyond Elder Law* (Springer, 2012).

7 Rebecca Emily Hough, 'Adult Protection and 'Intimate Citizenship' for People with Learning Difficulties: Empowering and Protecting in Light of the *No Secrets* Review' (2012) 27(1) *Disability and Society* 131–44.

will take issue with both of these arguments, and put forward what I believe is a more nuanced ethical approach to understanding why, and when, safeguarding interventions are justified.

It should, of course, be noted that these normative and conceptual projects will be connected. A conceptual analysis of vulnerability could espouse an account of a particular duty in relation to those who fall within the boundaries of the concept, and this duty might be articulated such that it is able to effectively guide practitioners' action in a particular safeguarding setting.[8] Alternatively, this conceptual analysis might contend that vulnerability is a concept that lacks specific evaluative content, and functions as nothing more than a placeholder to direct ethical attention towards examining the ways in which a person might be wronged in any given context.[9] I am persuaded by the arguments made by scholars advocating this latter approach, and believe that a convincing normative analysis of adult safeguarding intervention powers can be conducted independently of a substantive conceptual account of vulnerability.[10] In this chapter, I undertake such an analysis. In so doing, I hope to show that nothing of ethical significance hinges on a claim about vulnerability, or the status of a person as being identified as vulnerable.

I begin by documenting how safeguarding intervention powers *have been justified* in legal and policy settings by drawing briefly upon a recent judgment in the Court of Appeal, and the government's proposals for adult safeguarding reform under the Care Bill. I go on to examine whether safeguarding interventions *can be justified* in the ways that judges and policy-makers have claimed. First, I scrutinise the role of an adult safeguarding service in its entirety; how ought such a service function, and what ought it to be safeguarding adults from? Having identified 'abuse' (once properly conceptualised) as the problem that determines the scope of adult safeguarding work, I examine what role, if any, intervention powers ought to play in safeguarding adults from abuse. I consider a range of arguments that connect claims about personal autonomy and freedom to the everyday lives of adults situated within interpersonal relationships that are characterised by asymmetric power dynamics. I move on to argue that safeguarding a person's substantive freedoms can provide us with the right kind of reason for using interventions powers to respond to certain rare and specific situations in which a person is being abused. I conclude by outlining the practical implications of my arguments for those working in health and social care services, and argue for the need to reconfigure the current legal and political approaches to justifying adult safeguarding interventions on these grounds.

---

8 Goodin's analysis of vulnerability would be an example of this approach (*Protecting the Vulnerable*).

9 Hurst's analysis of vulnerability would be an example of this approach ('Vulnerability in Research and Health Care). I would like to thank Anthony Wrigley for clarifying my understanding of this way of thinking about the concept of vulnerability.

10 This is a shift away from the approach I have adopted in previous work, where I attempted to delineate competing conceptual accounts of vulnerability in order to diagnose normative problems in the development of law in this area (see Dunn et al, 'To Empower or to Protect?').

The current legal and policy landscape of adult safeguarding interventions

A good starting point for this normative project is to review the arguments under-pinning the current legal and policy landscape. In Chapter 12 (this volume), Alison Brammer provides a detailed account of how English law and public policy has evolved to authorise adult safeguarding interventions for 'vulnerable adults'. In brief summary, the current legal position is affirmed in the Court of Appeal's judgment in *DL v A Local Authority*.[11] Here, safeguarding interventions for an older adult were authorised on the grounds that a person being subjected to abuse might be stripped of the capacity to make a valid autonomous decision by reasons other than an impairment of, or disturbance in the functioning of, the mind or brain.[12] McFarlane LJ concluded that an adult (1) under constraint, (2) subject to coercion or undue influence, or (3) otherwise disabled from making a free choice falls within the protective authority of the High Court's inherent jurisdiction. As he put it, '[w]here the facts justify it, such individuals require and deserve the protection of the authorities and the law so that they may regain the very autonomy that the appellant rightly prizes'.[13] In other words, the justification for a protective intervention is dependent on determining whether a person is deprived of the ability to make free and autono-mous decisions by reason of the maligned influence of another person, and whether an intervention can restore the person's ability to make such decisions.

A couple of further observations about this line of argument are useful. First, the conflation between freedoms and autonomy in McFarlane LJ's reasoning here is not unproblematic,[14] as I will explore at greater length in the fourth section of this chapter. Indeed, this approach reflects a broader problem concerning the failure to distinguish appropriately and precisely between liberty and autonomy in practi-cal decision-making in the courtroom.[15] Second, it is striking that McFarlane LJ does not connect his autonomy/freedoms-oriented reasoning to considerations of harm. Following *DL*, the law would now appear to permit interventions into an adult's life under the inherent jurisdiction in situations where the exercise of free action and autonomous decision-making is undermined by coercion, constraint or undue influence, but the adult is not identified as being subject to (or at risk of) harm as standardly defined.[16]

---

11 *DL v A Local Authority and Others* [2012] EWCA Civ 253.
12 If the reason that the person was unable to make a decision was because they lacked mental capac-ity under s 2 Mental Capacity Act 2005, there would have been legal recourse to act in the person's 'best interests' under s 4 of that Act.
13 *DL v A Local Authority and Others* (n 11) [63].
14 One can see how his discussion here fluctuates between considering how a person might be 'disa-bled from making a free choice' to 'enhancing or liberating the autonomy of a vulnerable adult' (see ibid [54]).
15 John Coggon and José Miola, 'Autonomy, Liberty and Medical Decision-making' (2011) 70(3) *CLJ* 523.
16 Department of Health, *No Secrets: Guidance on Developing and Implementing Multi-Agency Policies and Procedures to Protect Vulnerable Adults from Abuse* (Home Office, 2000) paras 2.5–2.7 (www.dignity

Alongside these shifts in the common law, the Department of Health is now completing an extensive review of the current policy, *No Secrets*,[17] outlining how public authorities ought to take the necessary steps to safeguard adults from abuse, and how the relevant sections of the Care Bill will function to modify the exercise of the inherent jurisdiction as outlined in *DL*. In relation to powers of intervention specifically, the direction of change is now clear. The government has recognised the need to attend carefully to unwanted intrusions in people's private lives, and has recently finished conducting a public consultation to guide its decision-making about introducing powers of intervention within adult safeguarding. The only specific proposal put forward in the consultation was a new power of entry into a person's home that could be implemented when (1) the person has been identified as being at risk of abuse, (2) is judged to have the mental capacity to refuse support and (3) is exercising her refusal to allow local authority staff to enter her property. The justification offered here was laid out in terms of ensuring that the person's refusal is a true expression of her wishes and feelings given the harm that she faces, and that this decision has been made without undue pressure or coercion.[18] The outcome of this consultation was a significant divide between those supporting and not supporting this new power, with 49 per cent of respondents in favour, 40 per cent against, and 11 per cent undecided.[19] In response to the consultation, the government has clarified that it has no intention to introduce a new power of entry, and this power does not form part of the Care Bill.

The English government's decision not to introduce new powers of intervention differs markedly with the approach adopted recently in Scotland. The Adult Support and Protection (Scotland) Act 2007 (ASPA) introduces 'investigation orders', 'assessment orders', 'removal orders' and 'banning orders'[20] that can be made use of without the consent of a person with the mental capacity to give consent, if (1) the interventions are judged likely to benefit the person 'at risk', and place the least restrictions on the person's freedom,[21] and (2) if it is apparent that the person 'at risk' has been unduly pressured to refuse the intervention, or that

---

incare.org.uk/_library/Resources/Dignity/OtherOrganisation/No_Secrets.pdf,   accessed   28 May 2013).

17 Ibid.

18 Department of Health, *Consultation on a New Safeguarding Power* (Stationery Office, 2012) (www. gov.uk/government/consultations/consultation-on-a-new-adult-safeguarding-power, accessed 28 May 2013).

19 Department of Health, *Government Response to the Safeguarding Power of Entry Consultation* (Stationery Office, 2013) (www.gov.uk/government/uploads/system/uploads/attachment_data/file/197739/Gov_Response_to_PoE.pdf, accessed 28 May 2013). The difference between opinions becomes even more stark once the responses are broken down by the source of the respondents. Of the responses from health care settings, 90 per cent were in favour of the new power, with 0 per cent against, 72 per cent in favour and 12 per cent against from the local authority setting, and only 18 per cent in favour and 77 per cent against from service user, carer, and other non-professional settings.

20 Adult Support and Protection (Scotland) Act 2007, ss 7–20.

21 Ibid, s 1.

there are no other steps that could be taken with her consent that would prevent them from being harmed.[22]

Placing the legal and policy positions side by side, it can be seen that the English government's proposals will significantly limit the scope of the work of adult safeguarding services in ways that would be permitted under the law following *DL*. While the government clarified in its consultation on a new adult safeguarding power that it did not intend to rely on the common law to guide general policy on safeguarding interventions, it is unclear how the inherent jurisdiction might continue to develop once the new legislation is introduced without any recourse to intervention powers by those working in adult safeguarding services.

Interestingly, nothing within current law and policy hinges on the adult in question being judged to be vulnerable. Within the policy domain, the term 'vulnerable' disappears entirely, and, in the legal domain, the reasons offered in defence of the exercise of the inherent jurisdiction focus on safeguarding DL's personal autonomy, rather than responding to her vulnerability. The aim of this chapter is to subject the competing justificatory accounts presented in the legal and policy domains to ethical scrutiny. I hope to show that the reasons relating to harm and personal autonomy that are espoused in both legal and policy contexts to draw very different conclusions fail to convince in devising a general policy, or shaping the outcomes of specific cases. Before exposing the arguments about intervention powers to analytic scrutiny, it is important to take a step back and consider how adult safeguarding work itself can be justified.

Justifying adult safeguarding services

One immediate concern in articulating a justification for adult safeguarding is to clear exactly what adult safeguarding services are *for*. The contemporary development of community-based care services are characterised by a value base that emphasises concepts such as 'choice', 'control' and 'personalisation'. These concepts do not sit easily alongside notions of 'protection' or 'safeguarding', and therefore the justification of safeguarding work, and how its boundaries ought to be drawn, have been poorly articulated. In line with other commentators, I have argued that a safeguarding service should be established to protect an adult from the actions of another individual when these actions are appropriately conceptualised as 'abuse'. Abuse, as it ought to be understood in relation to safeguarding work, is a concept that captures those wrongful behaviours instigated within interpersonal relationships that cause harm,[23] and it is quite possible that an adult

---

22 Ibid s 35(3). The only exception here is the power to conduct a medical examination. This power cannot be instigated without the explicit consent of the person, even if the criteria outlined in s 1 and s 35(3) are met.

23 Michael Dunn, 'Rehabilitating the Concept of Abuse in Adult Safeguarding Policy and Practice' (in press 2013) *Journal of Care Services Management*.

will be identified as having been abused, or identified as being at heightened risk of abuse.

Wrongful actions within interpersonal relationships can be accounted for in a number of ways, and are likely to present themselves differently depending on the particular power dynamics that are prevalent in all relationships between individuals. Such wrongs are likely to include the kinds of actions that McFarlane LJ identifies in his analysis: the imposition of constraints on a person's actions, subjecting a person to coercion or undue influence, or otherwise disabling an adult from making a free choice. When interpersonal relationships are characterised by the presence of particular duties (as will be the case in professional care relationships), the failure to by the duty-holder to act in line with her duties will also fall within this category of wrongful behaviour.

Importantly, however, these wrongful actions are only rightly termed abusive if they also cause harm to the adult who is subject to them. It is quite possible that a person has their choices limited, or are coerced into agreeing to certain courses of actions, within relationships in ways that do not lead that adult to be harmed (even on a broad account of harm that includes psychological distress). Without establishing the causal connection between certain kinds of wrongful behaviours that occur within interpersonal relationships, many such relationships are likely to be termed abusive, and thus requiring the response of an adult safeguarding service when this would appear to be entirely counter-intuitive.

Equally, it is also possible that a person could be exposed to significant harm within an interpersonal relationship without that harm having resulted from any wrongful behaviour. Acts undertaken within sadomasochistic relationships are the obvious example here. In this sense, harm is a necessary but not sufficient criterion for abuse. An action cannot be termed abusive if the action does not cause harm, but not all harmful actions are abusive. The justification for the involvement of an adult safeguarding service cannot therefore be determined by harm-related considerations alone, and harm is connected appropriately to abuse by attending to the wrongful behaviours that can occur within interpersonal relationships between individuals.[24]

Once adult safeguarding services are justified in terms of an obligation to protect adults from abuse, and it is recognised that abuse should be understood here as wrongful behaviours within interpersonal relationships that cause harm, the nature and scope of adult safeguarding services can be determined. First, the relationships between different protective services within social welfare departments can be clarified. Adult safeguarding services designed for those in need of social care on the grounds of age or disability are underpinned by exactly the same justification as those services that seek to protect those experiencing, or identified as being at risk of experiencing, domestic violence or forced marriage. There are good reasons for bringing these disparate services together as one unified safeguarding service. Equally, the relationship between safeguarding services and

24 Ibid, 6.

the police becomes clearer. Some types of harm that are identified in safeguarding contexts will constitute criminal offences, and others will not. It is quite possible that a person who has been abused will have been subject to harm of a nature and degree that requires joint enquiries to be undertaken by the police and the safeguarding service. There will also be situations where there is no evidence of a criminal offence having been undertaken, but abuse will have been identified (or an adult has been identified as being at heightened risk of abuse) justifying action by a safeguarding service alone.

Second, self-harm and self-neglect are distinct from cases of abuse as abuse can only occur within interpersonal relationships, and the same justification for responding to self-harm or self-neglect cannot be provided. This is not to deny there might be some situations where an adult engages in self-harming behaviour as an additional response to the harms that she experiences as a result of the wrongful behaviour that takes place within an interpersonal relationship. In these situations, it would be appropriate to see self-harm as a matter for an adult safeguarding service. There may also be good practical reasons for extending safeguarding services to adults identified at risk of self-harm or self-neglect. In so doing, however, it would be very important to recognise that a very different kind of justification would need to underpin any responses made by the service in light of evidence of self-harming or self-neglecting behaviours.[25] For its work in safeguarding adults from abuse, the focus ought to be on the dynamics of interpersonal relationships, and the harm that is caused by any wrongful behaviour that is directed towards that adult within these relationships.

Once the justification of adult safeguarding services is clarified, it is important to return to the question of what powers safeguarding services ought to be equipped with in order to discharge its responsibilities to protect adults from abuse appropriately. As outlined in the introduction, an adult safeguarding service is likely to have a range of roles to fulfil. One role will be to take active and preemptive steps to prevent abuse from occurring within communities. Another role will be to collect and collate evidence on reports of abuse, or reports of adults at risk of harm within community settings. Yet another role will be to respond to situations in which it has been shown that abuse is taking place, or that an adult is at heightened risk of abuse. In those circumstances when the adult is refusing assistance from the service, one way of responding would be for practitioners to make use of those powers of intervention into a person's private affairs. It is to the justification of these powers that I now return.

---

25 It is likely that such reasons would concern a requirement to act in the best interests of an adult who is engaging in self-harm or self-neglect when that adult is judged to lack the capacity to make a decision for herself (under the Mental Capacity Act 2005), or a requirement to protect the adult from the harm she poses to herself if she is diagnosed with a mental disorder that justifies assessment or treatment in a mental health care environment (under the Mental Health Act 1983).

Justifying adult safeguarding intervention powers

As a starting point for approaching the justification of intervention powers, one might think that the nature and degree of harm that an adult experiencing abuse (or judged to be at risk of abuse) is exposed to is of moral significance. Harm-based considerations might be formulated in the following initial claim:

> Claim 1: *Intervention powers are justified when an adult is identified as being subject to abuse, and is being exposed to (or at risk of) serious harm*

The idea here is that, within an adult safeguarding service, the responses that practitioners make to instances of abuse ought to be calibrated to the degree of harm that the adult is being exposed to. Moreover, there will be a threshold of harm over and above which intervention powers can be implemented, potentially against the will of the adult for whom they will be used. This 'seriousness threshold' is likely to be defined by particular kinds of harm (those involving inflicting physical, emotional and/or sexual violence of a particular degree, for example), and will also likely be sensitive to the duration and severity of this harm.

A common and immediate rebuttal to attending to harm in discussions about adult safeguarding is that adults should be allowed to make their own decisions even if these decisions are judged by others to be unwise on the grounds that they are harmful. Imposing intrusive and personal interventions into these adults' lives without their explicit consent is – so that argument goes – a clear infringement of the ethical principle of respecting those adults' autonomy.[26]

While this rebuttal provides a clear reason for not acting to intervene to safeguard a person from harm, there might remain a residual intuition that things are different when a person is being subject to abuse, rather than just harm. However, as soon as the concept of abuse is deployed to qualify the harm-based claim, it is no longer simply the harm that provides the justification for using safeguarding powers. As was outlined in above, abuse is not equivalent to harm, with the concept of abuse connecting harm to wrongful behaviours that take place within relationships between individuals. The notion that there will be reasons to justify intervening in situations of abuse, rather than simply in cases where a person agrees to have harm inflicted upon her by another person, shifts our attention away from harm and on to those wrongful actions taking place within relationships.

One common way of connecting the relational dynamics in play in situations of abuse and the justification to use intervention powers is by attending to the ability of the adult to make decisions to accept or refuse assistance. This account of ability is typically captured by considering the person's mental capacity, and would require the initial claim to be modified in the following way:

---

26 This is a central element of the argument put forward by Hough, 'Adult Protection'.

Claim 2: *Intervention powers are justified when an adult is identified as being subject to abuse, and that adult lacks the capacity to make a decision to refuse support*

Such a claim has widespread support,[27] with capacity being interpreted as a key threshold concept for limiting interventions into adults' lives against their wishes. Thus, while the decision to refuse support from a safeguarding service ought to be respected, however unwise that decision is judged by others, such a decision does not need to be respected if it is not made by a person with the ability to make it. This position is adopted as a core principle of the Mental Capacity Act 2005, where in common with other legal jurisdictions and the dominant ethical arguments, decision-making capacity is understood in terms of a person's cognitive and communicative abilities.

There are two practical ways in which considerations of mental capacity might arise in the contexts of adult safeguarding work. First, there may be a direct connection between the wrongful behaviours that an adult is exposed to within relationships and that adult's ability to understand, retain and weigh up information in the process of making a decision. It is possible to imagine situations when a person is threatened, manipulated, coerced and harmed in ways that cause her to lack the capacity to make decisions in her life. This is likely to be the case in situations where the behaviours of another person instil such fear in her that these external pressures impact directly on her ability to make decisions about whether to accept assistance from a safeguarding service, or to decide about where she lives or who she has contact with. Second, there may be no direct connection between the abuse and the person's decision-making capacity. It is known that abuse is commonly directed towards people with particular impairments, those with dementia or intellectual disabilities, for example. Because of these impairments, these people may lack the capacity to make decisions about their living circumstances or the support they receive. Here, the inability to make decisions about assistance from an adult safeguarding service is entirely independent from the abuse that triggers the initial involvement of that service.

Notwithstanding these two kinds of situations, mental capacity should be thought of as largely a red herring in debates about the ethics of adult safeguarding. Active protective steps can be taken to support a person who lacks the capacity to decide about such support, if the determination of that person's best interests point towards such interventions.[28] However, the problem cases arise in situations when there is little doubt that a person is able to refuse assistance, but where there are alternative arguments that justify the provision of assistance over and above the person's capacity to give or withhold consent. A case can help to clarify this kind of issue.

---

27 Department of Health, *Safeguarding Adults: Report on the Consultation on the Review of 'No Secrets'* (Stationery Office, 2009).

28 The justification for intervention in such situations would be the same as that in those situations of self-neglect or self-harm where a person is judged to lack the capacity to decide to refuse assistance.

Case 1: Mrs A[29]

Mrs A is a woman in her eighties. Her son, Mr B, has recently moved into his mother's house. There is evidence that Mr B is subjecting Mrs A to physical and psychological abuse. Mr B forces his mother to write 'lines' if she does not act in the way that he prescribes. When Mrs A leaves the chair in the living room, Mr B will drag her physically across the floor and back to this chair. Mrs A is physically impaired, but does not lack the capacity to make decisions about whether she receives support from the local authority. She is refusing to allow the local authority to intervene in her life in order to provide her with additional supports.

An inquiry is undertaken and Mrs A acknowledges that her son has been pressuring her to refuse help from 'any outsiders who want to poke their nose into our business', threatening to lock her in the house all day if she agrees to support. However, she also emphasises that she enjoys living with her son. While she recognises that she is not able to take part in her hobbies, or to see her friends, because of the way her son behaves, she says that she would not have it any other way. She acknowledges that her son is harming her, but she argues that he does so out of a misguided sense of love for her. She makes it clear that she wishes to continue to reside with Mr B, and accepts that this means that he will continue to harm her. Mrs A adds that this abuse is a small price to pay for keeping her only son close to her in her last few years of life.

Mrs A is engaging with the safeguarding inquiry and is giving an entirely considered, reflective endorsement of the actions of her son. She is demonstrating a clear understanding of her current living circumstances, the ways in which her liberty is being restricted, and the harm that she recognises that her son is inflicting upon her. Any justification for intervening in a case like this cannot, therefore, hinge upon a claim about Mrs A's mental capacity. Aside from harm-based reasons, what other grounds are there for questioning the validity of a person's decision in cases like Mrs A?

The reasoning of McFarlane LJ in *DL* can be instructive here. Endorsing a more general position in practical ethics, he focuses on the interpersonal dynamics of abusive relationships and argues that there are ways in which a person's consent can be undermined by factors other than that person's mental capacity. Reflecting the first case in which the inherent jurisdiction was extended to apply to protect those adults judged to be 'vulnerable' as opposed to incapacitated,[30] McFarlane LJ emphasises the need to consider whether the person's decisions (including the decision to refuse support) are voluntary, or whether they have been made in ways

29 This case is a heavily modified version of *DL* designed to tease out the central ethical issue in adult safeguarding in its purest form.

30 *Re SA (Vulnerable adult with capacity: Marriage)* [2006] 1 *FLR* 867.

that have been subject to undue influence, coercion or constraint.[31] This line of reasoning leads to the articulation of a third claim:

> Claim 3: *Intervention powers are justified when an adult is identified as being subject to abuse, and that adult is exposed to external pressures that influence her decision to refuse support*

For McFarlane LJ in *DL* (and the broader development of the 'vulnerable adult' jurisdiction in the last five years), these external pressures can be exercised on an adult's decision-making in ways that mitigate that adult's refusal to consent to support from social welfare services. More generally, McFarlane LJ articulates an autonomy-based justification for intervening in such circumstances that requires the necessary steps to be taken to remove these external pressures in ways that enable the adult in question to make decisions for herself such that she is able to pursue a life that is in accordance with her own values.

A more extensive analysis of Case 1 above can reveal why this line of argument is problematic. Here, it is quite clear that Mrs A is being subject to pressure from Mr B to refuse support from the safeguarding service. Her son is placing conditions on her choice to accept support, and threatening to restrict his mother's freedom to leave the house if she chooses not to refuse help from the safeguarding service. However, Mrs A remains able to choose between the (conditional) options that she is presented with by her son. The very fact that a person changes her mind in the face of an external pressure does not imply that this choice is not valid, and this is the case regardless of the degree of pressure applied.[32] Moreover, Mrs A is also clearly able to articulate to the service why the decision that she has been pressured into making is the right decision for her. She gives an account of what she values, and why the decision she has been pressured into making is in accordance with the values that she holds. Importantly, it is precisely when a person's choices are manipulated in this way that the person is forced to evaluate her values and commitments in life – such an evaluation that is seen on most accounts to be entirely consistent with the exercise of personal autonomy.[33]

---

31 Further analysis is required here to differentiate between these three concepts, and to explain how different kinds of pressure can be morally problematic in ways that are significant for determining when interventions would be justified. Prior to undertaking this analysis, I shall group these concepts under the term 'external pressures' to differentiate them from those 'internal' factors that might be associated with a person's beliefs or desires.

32 This is not to deny that the imposition of such pressures may be wrong for reasons other than the voluntariness of the choice made by the person subject to such pressures. Further ethical analysis would need to tease out whether imposing such pressures was wrong, and whether the nature of this wrongful behavior means that the choice made by the person subject to such pressure ought not to be respected. This argument is introduced in Michael Dunn, Daniel Maughan, Tony Hope et al, 'Threats and Offers in Community Mental Health Care' (2012) 38(4) *Journal of Medical Ethics* 204–9; and further developed in Mark Sheehan and Michael Dunn (in preparation) 'Voluntariness Is Not a Component of Valid Consent'.

33 This line of argument implies that if the threats made by Mrs A's son are indeed wrong, the wrongfulness of these threats cannot be explicated by reference to the impact on Mrs A's personal autonomy.

Accepting this counter-argument to Claim 3 means accepting the position that there is no sense in which external pressures can impact on a person's ability to make a voluntary choice. Thus, any justification for intervening to prevent the person from making that choice must lay in factors other than features of her choice-making. Before turning away from choice-making entirely, a slight modification of this claim would be to focus on the content of the decision made, rather than on the process of making that decision. Should, for example, the same weight be accorded to a person's decision when the content of that person's decision is underpinned by values that ought not to be held by people who are subject to abuse? It might be argued that it is wrong for people to hold the values that Mrs X holds, given the harms and pressures that she is exposed to (or, more generally, that no right-minded or rational person would ever endorse such values when facing such circumstances). This kind of claim would be articulated as follows:

Claim 4: *Intervention powers are justified when an adult is identified as being subject to abuse, and that adult is making the wrong decision to refuse support*

Claim 4 involves making an evaluative judgement about whether a person should ever be allowed to endorse values that cause her to continue to experience abuse. In relation to the case above, the service would be justified to intervene to safeguard Mrs A because Mrs A is acting in light of personal values that ought not to be respected when a person is being abused. This argument is unconvincing in a society that endorses value pluralism in the formulation of its laws and public policies. If we are to allow people to expose themselves to significant harms within personal relationships that are not characterised by wrongful behaviours – in the case of the sadomasochists, for example – we have no good reason not to extend the same freedoms to abusive situations like those facing Mrs A.

A second, more compelling way of expressing the idea that there might be something wrong with the content of Mrs A's decision is to argue the values that Mrs A holds, as clearly elucidated as they are, ought not to be respected because such values are, in some sense, derived from the problematic relationship she has with her son, rather than being genuinely her own. This argument might be fleshed out in terms of authenticity: the values that Mrs A holds do not reflect the 'real' Mrs A, and she would not have endorsed these values if her relationship with her son were not characterised by his abusive behaviours towards her. The following claim encapsulates this position:

Claim 5: *Intervention powers are justified when an adult is identified as being subject to abuse, and that adult is not making an authentic decision to refuse support*

This claim connects to important philosophical questions about the nature of the self, personal identity, and the value of personal autonomy. While intuitive, this claim also fails to convince when scrutinised in more detail. The argument underpinning this claim would necessarily dissociate the person from the social context in which that person makes sense of who she is, in which she forges her identity, and in which she develops an account of what is important to her. It would require Mrs A to be seen as passive in the course of events that have led her relationship with Mr B to develop, and that she is unable to step back from that relationship to evaluate her priorities in light of the relational context in which she finds herself. Given that Mrs A is undertaking exactly this kind of detached evaluation of her relationship with Mr B – and that she is endorsing that she wants to continue that relationship in its current form on the basis of that evaluation – this argument fails to convince.[34] Indeed, following such an argument to its logical conclusion would have significant ramifications for judgements about each and every person's ability to make their 'own' decisions in light of the relational and social contexts in which they live their lives. And, I would contend, any attempt to distinguish Mrs A's situation from each and every other decision made by people situated within interpersonal relationships would likely hinge on a problematic judgement about Mrs A's values being wrong (as outlined in Claim 4 above), rather than in terms of these values not reflecting the 'real' Mrs A.

If neither the form nor content of a person's decision can be undermined by the external pressures imposed within interpersonal relationships that are characteristic of abuse, it follows that any justification for intervention powers must have regard to ethical considerations other than the validity of the decisions made by those who are refusing assistance. A very different way in which such a justification might be provided is to attend to considerations about the adult's liberty.

By way of starting to think about how considerations of an adult's freedoms might be relevant here, a claim about the extent to which the adult *feels free* to act in line with her interests and values when subject to abuse can be outlined:

Claim 6: *Intervention powers are justified when an adult is identified as being subject to abuse, and that adult feels that her liberty is constrained such that she cannot pursue a life of value to her*

A different kind of case can illustrate how the argument underpinning this claim might operate.

Case 2: Ms X
Ms X is a first-year undergraduate student who has just moved from a village in rural Surrey to halls of residence in central Manchester. She presents herself at the offices of the City of Manchester Adult Safeguarding

---

34 Mrs A's autonomous choices look to meet the high standards imposed by dominant 'coherentist' accounts of autonomous decision-making that define personal autonomy (or, more accurately, free will) in terms of a person's second-order identification with her first-order desires. See, for example, Harry Frankfurt, 'Freedom of the Will and the Concept of the Person' in Harry Frankfurt (ed.), *The Importance of What We Care About*: Philosophical Essays (Cambridge University Press, 1988).

Team and says that she needs their assistance in being provided with alternative accommodation. Ms X reports that she feels very afraid in her current living environment, that she has seen people being attacked in the street outside, and she is being taunted by her fellow students for spending most of her time in her room. She makes it clear that that she does not feel that she is free to leave her accommodation. Ms X adds that this is not the kind of life she wanted to pursue as a student: she is unable to attend her lectures, take part in all the university's social events, and is missing out on all the activities that she identified as being important to her before she began her studies.

Here, Ms X does not feel free, in her given social circumstances, to act in line with her own values and interests, and active interventions by the service could serve both to safeguard her from abuse and enable her to feel that she is free to act in line with her values. When applied to the case of Mrs A above, we would be required to draw a different conclusion. While providing Mrs A with alternative accommodation could act to prevent her from being abused, the enquiry undertaken by the safeguarding service has established that Mrs A feels entirely free to be able to act in line with her own interests. Her interests revolve around having her son close to her at the end of her life, and the restrictions that her son places on her freedom do not prevent her from feeling she that she is unable to act in line with these interests.

This sixth formulation of the justification for adult safeguarding interventions is also problematic, however. Regardless of how she feels, Ms X in fact retains the liberty to act in line with her idea of student life, and enjoys the freedom to pursue and explore her interests as a student as she wishes. There is no sense in which the social and relational pressures she outlines impose insurmountable obstacles on her freedom to act in line with these interests. A comparison with the justification for human rights protections can be useful here. The simple fact that a person feels that her rights are being violated is not taken to be sufficient to show that a violation of those rights have taken place. Rather, rights-based protections are articulated in terms of the protection of substantive freedoms – understood in impersonal, objective terms.

Can a better connection between the wrongful behaviours within interpersonal relationships and the effect of these behaviours on a person's freedom to act be established? Following on from the reference to the justification for human rights protections above, it is possible to articulate an account of the obligation to safeguard a person's substantive freedoms in the context of abuse. Consider the following, final claim:

Claim 7: *Intervention powers are justified when an adult is identified as being subject to abuse, and that adult's substantive freedoms are constrained such that she cannot pursue a life of value to her*

For this claim to be convincing, there must be (1) a clear distinction between actions that constrain a person's freedoms and those actions that constrain a person's substantive freedoms, and (2) adult safeguarding interventions are only justified in response to those actions that constrain a person's substantive freedoms.

What is meant by the qualifier 'substantive' here? The following case can help us to make progress on differentiating substantive freedoms from mere freedoms.

Case 3: Miss M

Miss M is a young woman who decides to join a religious cult and relocates to live with the cult members on a remote farm in the Lake District. She cuts all contact with her family, shares her money with the other members of the cult, works on the farm, and conducts all her social activities within the farm environment. After 12 months with the cult, Miss M happily signs a new Code of Conduct instigated by the cult leader. This Code involves the leader of the cult locking all members into their farm cottages at night, and indicates that any members of the cult who attempt to leave the farm will be prevented from doing so, and will be punished for violating the Code.

Miss M's choice to join the cult has clearly impacted on the range of freedoms she is able to enjoy in her life. However, in the first 12 months of her time with the cult, she remains substantively free to act otherwise. She is able to leave the cult, to pursue a different life course, to embark on a new career, and to reconnect with the family and friends that she has chosen to move away from. In this sense, the concept of substantive freedoms cannot simply be concerned with the range or number of freedoms that a person is able to enjoy. In contrast, the actions of the cult-leader 12 months later should be interpreted differently. While Miss M still chooses to act in line with her current interests as she perceives them by signing the Code of Conduct, this choice (and the consequences of the choice) means that she is not able to leave the cult should her values change, or to explore and modify other interests that she might acquire as she continues to develop as a person in the future.

In this sense, the justification for intervening to safeguard a person's substantive freedoms emerges out of the ethical requirement to safeguard the foundations upon which an adult can pursue a life of meaning and value to her. Here, an important distinction must be drawn between (1) respecting the person's current interests (which would point against intervening to safeguard the person) and (2) safeguarding the person's ability to enjoy the freedoms that are necessary for that person to modify these interests as her values shift and are refined over time. The ability to continually modify and act differently on the basis of one's values and interests is fundamental to the project of self-development, and the obligation to respect a person's self-determination requires that those freedoms that support self-development are not undermined. Moreover, because substantive freedoms underpin the very conditions that make autonomous agency possible, such freedoms ought to be safeguarded even when the intervention judged necessary goes against a decision that reflects the person's current values and interests.

Personal liberty understood in this substantive sense can be objectively determined, but its identification (and the role it plays in practical decision-making) will depend on specific details about a person's living environment. As being free in the substantive sense focuses on the foundations required for a person to be able to pursue a life of meaning and value to her, objective markers of being substantively free can be established without importing an evaluative judgement about what constitutes the good life.

In practical settings, a judgement about whether a person is substantively free needs to attend to the nature, quality and degree of freedoms that a person is able to enjoy. In some cases (for example, those involving the decision to sell oneself into slavery or agreeing to a life of solitary confinement) it will be clear that a person's substantive freedoms will be constrained as a result of her action. In other cases (for example, those involving the decision to join a religious order or to donate one's money to charity and to move to a low-income country), it will be clear that the person's freedoms will be constrained by this course of action, but not in the substantive sense. In yet other cases (for example, the decision to write a Ulysses Contract (or advanced directive for mental healthcare) that authorises detention in a psychiatric institution upon the onset of mental illness), the judgement about whether the person's substantive freedoms will be constrained is less clear-cut.

These points can be illustrated and connected back directly to adult safeguarding situations by revisiting the case of Mrs A above. Here, a convincing case could be made that the restrictions that Mrs A has agreed to her son placing on her life constrain her substantive freedoms such that adult safeguarding interventions are justified, despite her autonomous endorsement of such restrictions. If Mr B acts to prevent his mother leaving the house, her freedoms to pursue a different kind of life are curtailed dramatically. She would be unable to enjoy the degree of freedoms necessary to explore other interests, such as engaging in a range of social activities or continuing her friendships, for example, and therefore unable to modify her current values in light of the range of experiences that she is being denied.

Were the circumstances of Mrs A's life different, however, the judgement about the justification of safeguarding interventions might also be different. For example, we know that Mrs A is physically impaired. If her impairments were such that she was physically unable to leave the house, the restrictions imposed by her son are unlikely to impact upon her substantive freedoms in the same kind of way. Mr B is restricting Mrs A from leaving the house but, given the limited range of her physical abilities, these restrictions do not impact on the range of options that she would otherwise be able to pursue. Substantive freedoms for a housebound Mrs A are more limited than they would be for the Mrs A who is able to leave the house, were it not for the actions of her son. One might further contend that the judgement about whether Mrs A's substantive freedoms were constrained in such circumstances would be different were a housebound Mrs A prevented by her son from entering one or more rooms in the house, rather than prevented from leaving the house entirely.

When properly specified, this argument offers a better connection to how wrongful behaviours within interpersonal relationships can, in rare cases, constrain adults' freedoms such that those adults are unable to pursue a life of value to them. Adult safeguarding intervention powers would be justified in such cases to safeguard adults' substantive freedoms, and not by having regard to whether the decisions made by such adults in light of these relationships are valid and autonomous decisions that reflect these adults' current values. This is because considerations of liberty – understood in this substantive sense – should trump any residual concerns about respecting autonomous decision-making; maintaining such freedoms provides the necessary foundations for the exercise of personal autonomy. Within the context of safeguarding work, this liberty-based argument places the emphasis on practitioners to ascertain whether a person remains substantively free to forge, refine and pursue a life of meaning and value, and it focuses their attention down on to the ways in which certain relationships or social contexts might constrain such freedoms in ways that are specific to the life-world of the person.

Implications for law, policy and practice

While adult safeguarding interventions can be justified in the face of a refusal of support made by a person with mental capacity to exercise that refusal through recourse to a claim about personal freedoms, this justification is only likely to be applicable infrequently. It is intuitive to hypothesise that the impact of an abusive relationship on an adult's life will not involve the imposition of constraints on that adult's substantive freedom in the majority of safeguarding situations. There would need to be evidence of the adult being confined to a particular place for long duration of times, or of that adult having extensive limitations placed upon her freedom of movement or action.

For practitioners working in adult safeguarding services, a detailed inquiry into an adult's living circumstances would need to be conducted carefully in order to justify any further interventions into that person's life. Social workers (or other professionals) will need to enable the adult to share her personal experiences in considerable depth if correct judgements are going to be made about whether that person's freedoms are restricted in the substantive sense. The adult's voice and experiences will be central to making correct judgements. Such judgements cannot be made simply by having regard to objective facts about the person's life obtained through consulting medical records, or evidence from neighbours or friends. Any justification for taking further steps to (1) remove a person from her living environment, (2) to provide her with alternative supported accommodation, (3) and/or to impose restrictions on who is allowed to have contact with her will be ascertained by the quality of the relationship that the practitioner forges with the adult in question.

It is also possible that, in some cases, the powers used to safeguard the person's substantive freedoms might impose their own restrictions on that person's liberty. If removing an adult from her home and providing her with alternative accommodation against her will does not enable her to be free in the sense that she is now able to pursue a life of value to her, the justification for making use of such powers would be undermined. Making professional judgements about when and how intervention powers should be used will be a challenging task, but one that is vitally important if adults' freedoms are to be safeguarding appropriately.

More broadly, the arguments articulated in this chapter have significant implications for legal reasoning and the new policy framework for adult safeguarding in England. In the legal domain, the focus on autonomy and freedom-related considerations, rather than harm-related considerations, is to be commended. However, it is important that reasoning in the courtroom attends to the important differences between the values of autonomy and liberty, and that the implications of this for making judgements about the exercise of the inherent jurisdiction are clarified.[35] The application of the High Court's inherent jurisdiction in adult safeguarding cases must shift away from considering how an adult's decisions can be undermined by the pressures imposed upon that adult within an abusive relationship. There is no sense in which the form or content of the decisions made by an adult can be rendered invalid by such external pressures, and therefore allowing protective interventions on the basis of respecting an adult's ability to make her own choices cannot be justified.

In the policy domain, the power to enable local authorities to enter a person's private home in order to conduct investigations about the person's life would certainly be necessary, despite the English government's recent decision not to introduce such a power. This is because there is an obligation to determine whether an adult's substantive freedoms are being subject to constraint in abusive situations, regardless of any decision made by that adult to refuse access to practitioners from the safeguarding team. One immediate concern that might be raised here is that powers of entry and investigation look to be justified in every single instance when abuse/risk of abuse has been identified. All of the information necessary for accurate judgements about the support that ought to be put in place is likely to be impossible to obtain without entering into a person's home, and sitting down with that person to talk in detail with her in a protected environment. A further implication for policy is that additional intervention powers will, in some cases, be necessary to safeguard a person's substantive freedoms. It is quite possible that invoking powers of removal, providing alternative accommodation, and imposing banning or restriction orders will be justified in order to safeguard an adult's substantive freedoms appropriately. If no further powers are made available,

---

35 Again, this is a point made by Coggon and Miola, 'Autonomy, Liberty and Medical Decision-making'.

practitioners will be paralysed; duty-bound to act to safeguard the person, but lacking the practical means to do anything to fulfil that duty.

Concluding remarks

Adult safeguarding is an area of social welfare practice in which a significant ethical issue arises, and in which the legal and policy framework to govern this issue remains in flux. Adult safeguarding work is justified by recourse to the need to protect people in situations where they have been identified as being subject to abuse or at heightened risk of abuse. Adult safeguarding intervention powers are justified in the rare situations in which it is judged necessary to act to safeguard an adult's substantive freedoms, and such powers can be deployed even if that adult makes a valid decision to refuse assistance.

These normative arguments have been articulated without relying on a conceptual claim about adults' vulnerability. However, there is a sense in which vulnerability could be reintroduced here to connect abuse, safeguarding and liberty, and the concept of the 'vulnerable adult' could be deployed to differentiate a freedom-related justification for intervening in an adult's private life from the standard mental capacity-based justification. However, this approach should be resisted on the grounds that it muddies, rather than clarifies, the relevant moral considerations that need to be weighed up in making practical decisions within adult safeguarding contexts. The appropriate development of law, policy and practice in adult safeguarding requires articulating a clear moral justification for intervening into adults' private lives against their wishes, and the recent decision to advance such a justification by abandoning the concept of vulnerability in legal judgements and policy papers is to be applauded.

Index